Monumental Tombs of the Hellenistic Age

Most of the grandiose and often ostentatious Hellenistic monumental tombs were powerfully expressive and symbolic structures built to glorify and display the wealth and power of kings, queens, nobles, and other persons of influence. They served as shrines for the worship of the heroized dead and were inventive in design and form, created to demonstrate the achievements of the dead in a public architecture of permanence and durability.

This well-illustrated monograph brings together previously scattered information about Hellenistic funerary monuments and the author's own research on the exterior architecture of these impressive structures in the Mediterranean region. The study first establishes a typology of main tomb forms and then considers some of the predecessors of the Hellenistic tombs. Attention is given to the variations of form that resulted from differences in climate, building materials, and social and religious customs. Adherence to strong local traditional practice in building is visible in each region, but new ideas and novel funerary architecture were welcomed everywhere in the Hellenistic world. Fedak's wide-ranging approach makes the work of interest not only to specialists in Greek architecture and archaeologists, but also to students of classical studies and historians of art and religion.

JANOS FEDAK is assistant professor in the Department of Fine Arts, University of Prince Edward Island.

PHOENIX

Journal of the Classical Association of Canada
Revue de la Société canadienne des études classiques
Supplementary Volume XXVII
Tome supplémentaire XXVII

JANOS FEDAK

Monumental Tombs of the Hellenistic Age:
A Study of Selected Tombs from the Pre-Classical to the Early Imperial Era

UNIVERSITY OF TORONTO PRESS
Toronto Buffalo London

© University of Toronto Press 1990
Toronto Buffalo London
Printed in Canada
ISBN 0-8020-2694-X

Printed on acid-free paper

Canadian Cataloguing in Publication Data

Fedak, Janos, 1946–
Monumental tombs of the Hellenistic age

(Phoenix, Supplementary volume ; 27 = Phoenix.
Tome supplémentaire, ISSN 0079-1784 ; 27)
Includes bibliographical references.
ISBN 0-8020-2694-X

1. Tombs - Mediterranean Region.   2. Architecture,
Hellenistic –Mediterranean Region.   3. Mediterranean
Region – Antiquities.   I. Title.   II. Series: Phoenix.
Supplementary volume (Toronto, Ont.) ; 27.

NA6139.F42 1990   726'.80'91822   C90-093318-6

This book has been published with
the help of a grant from
the Canadian Federation for the Humanities,
using funds provided by the Social Sciences and
Humanities Research Council of Canada.

TO THE MEMORY OF MY PARENTS, ANNA AND JÁNOS

CONTENTS

Appendix 2: The Relationship of Monumental Sarcophagi, Tholoi, and Other Buildings to Monumental Tombs 173

PREFACE

This book's primary concern is the exterior architecture of Hellenistic monumental tombs in the Mediterranean region. Most of the grandiose and often ostentatious funerary monuments were constructed for kings, nobles, and other persons of wealth. These tombs are powerfully expressive and frequently symbolic structures; the idea underlying them was to glorify the deceased person(s) and to reserve for the dead the immortality of gods. In the planning of many of the Hellenistic 'prestige tombs' the symbolic component dominated the design. Architecturally, besides temples, various other structures provided the inspiration for these tombs. With a few exceptions, imperishable materials were used for durability and permanence.

The study first establishes a typology of the main tomb forms and then looks at some of the possible predecessors of the different Hellenistic funerary monuments. Dates used to the end of the second centruy are BC when not in figures.

The earliest known monumental tomb, which strongly influenced the composition of subsequent Hellenistic structures, is the Nereid Monument in the Lycian city of Xanthos. The Nereid Monument presents a new combination of known architectural features, partly derived from Greek temple architecture and partly from eastern and local sources. All tombs discussed following the Nereid Monument have some Greek architectural influence in their design. (The illustrations at the back of the book, including plans, are not uniform in scale. Where no source is given, the photographs are my own. Every effort has been made to trace the owners of other material illustrated in this volume and to secure permission; any errors or omissions are deeply regretted.)

In the later development of Hellenistic monumental tombs through the centuries there were, naturally, variations of form in the several regions resulting from differences of climate, available material, and social and religious characteristics. Adherence to strong local traditional practice is often visible in a given region but, none the less, the process of assimilating new ideas and thus creating an expressive and novel funerary architecture was welcomed everywhere.

No synopsis of Hellenistic or Greek and Roman monumental funerary architecture exists. Publications devoted to individual tombs, or groups of them, appear in a multitude of periodicals and scattered excavation reports. In writing this book I tried to synthesize the currently available information and the results of my own research.

This material is not only for specialists in Greek architecture. I hope that the work will be of interest also to students of classical studies, historians of art, and to some degree the public in general as a resource book. Students are provided with a general framework into which they can easily fit the knowledge that they may acquire from new discoveries, subsequent readings, or observations.

In preparation of the study I was helped by a number of individuals and institutions. It is my pleasant task to thank above all Professor F.E. Winter and Professor E. Rosenbaum-Alföldi for making valuable suggestions that either have been incorporated into the text or have led to its modifications.

I should like also to express my thanks to the American School of Classical Studies in Athens, to the German Archaeological Institute in Berlin and Rome, and to the various archaeological services in the Mediterranean countries for giving me the opportunity to exchange information and ideas with experts and for providing access to the numerous sites that I visited during my field research.

Janos Fedak
June 1989

Monumental Tombs of the Hellenistic Age

Introduction

Monumental tombs occupy a special place in the history of Greek architecture because they show more freedom of design, and greater variety of form, than other types of building; in fact there are no two large tombs that are exactly alike. The classification of the tombs, both individually and as groups showing typological affinities, poses a number of problems. Many of the monuments have been previously described in publications, but often not accurately enough or not in detail. Others have been noted only briefly, or not at all, whether on account of their poor state of preservation or for some other reason. The investigation of tombs unrecorded in publications and the re-examination of monuments only partly excavated is an enormous task, requiring large numbers of workers and technical specialists. Such an enterprise would also require both sound financial backing and excavation permits for the various sites. Thus, a study undertaken by a single person has its limits, especially if such a project is further restricted by limited resources.

Many practical problems are encountered in studying large, elaborate tombs. Most of the monuments – whether built tombs, rock-cut tombs, or tumuli – were outside the limits of cities, many of them in isolated areas; access to them is physically rather difficult. For instance, many rock-cut façade-tombs can be reached only with the help of ropes and mountain-climbing equipment. In other cases, the risk of falling material may prevent detailed investigation of the structures. Again, ancient sites may now be overgrown or covered with soil, which makes it impossible to study moulded blocks without extensive excavations. In still other examples, though the blocks are free of any natural obstructions, they are too heavy for even two or three people to turn over, let alone to lift. For these reasons the accurate measuring of many tombs is often impossible.

As a result of the difficulties involved, it seemed best to restrict the present study to those tombs that are either well documented in literary sources or have already been excavated and have had information about them published in some detail. Even with this limitation there are still problems. It is becoming increasingly clear that early investigators, especially in the last century, often relied on their imagination rather than on observable facts; and when factual, their work may have been superficial, or simply incomplete, leaving many questions unanswered. Consequently, at a number of major tomb sites new excavations have been undertaken and some of these are still in progress. For example, one of the largest and most famous tomb sites – that of the Mausoleum at Halikarnassos – is still being investigated, and no final account has been published yet, apart from some preliminary reports. Thus, in the present study, discussion of structures still in the process of investigation and their relationship to other monuments is necessarily somewhat tentative.

Two examples may serve to illustrate the problem involved in dealing with tombs about which the available information is very sketchy or still unpublished. In both cases the remains suggest that the tomb resembled the 'temple tomb' on a podium (i.e., the so-called mausoleum-type) arrangement.[1] One of the tombs, discovered in 1919 at ancient Alyzia in Akarnania and tentatively dated to the second or first century BC, recalls 'certains constructions orientales, le mausolée d'Halicarnasse, ou le monument des Néréides de Xanthos (Lycie).'[2] The other tomb, previously unmentioned by scholars in the field, is located in the Elmali region on the eastern border of Lycia, near the village of Islamlar. The site is known to the locals as Eskişehir. Judging from the architectural fragments lying around the tomb, the structure must have resembled the Nereid Monument. However, in the absence of positive data, further speculation about these and other little-known monumental tombs would be futile.

The first serious investigations of tomb architecture per se date from the nineteenth century. One of the earliest general studies of the subject is Baron von Stackelberg's *Die Gräber der Hellenen* published in Berlin in 1837. Subsequent investigations added greatly to the number and variety of tombs available for study. Nevertheless, no attempt has yet been made to synthesize the results of regional studies, identifying similarities and differences between one region and another. F. Matz's article, and the chapters in handbooks, such as those of Fyfe, Lawrence, and Kurtz and Boardman, are far from adequate.[3] Furthermore, the particular circumstances that led to the great tomb-building activity of the fourth century have still to be examined in detail. Of course, the collecting of all relevant information on these topics is an enormous task, and one that could scarcely be expected in publications such as those mentioned above; even the present study can hardly claim to be more than a beginning. This attempt to show the origins and development of the tombs of western Asia Minor, both within and outside their local context, will in general be limited to a relatively small selection of the better-known funerary monuments. Only when such a framework exists, and additional information becomes available about some of the key monuments, can a more comprehensive work be undertaken.

The tombs discussed below were not typical or everyday types of burial. Rather they were peculiar to royal or oligarchic societies, which alone had the concentration of resources needed to finance such undertakings. Even so, many of the tombs remained unfinished after the initiator's death. The purpose served by these tombs, other than as places of interment, will be noted from time to time; but at the outset we may note that the desire for heroization, or self-glorification, was a major factor in the erection of overwhelmingly large funerary monuments. A good example is a certain Artemidoros of Perge, a wealthy but half-educated veteran of the army of Ptolemy IV (late third century). Artemidoros spent a large sum of money to lay out a temenos that contained elaborate funerary arrangements; Rostovzeff aptly notes that 'for his merits and piety Artemidoros was sure – so he was told by Delphi – of living as a theios heros even after his death.'[4] As a result of over-elaboration, many of the monumental tombs acquired other than funerary connotations and displayed a strongly stated symbolism both in architectural design and in decorative details. In certain instances they may also have served a practical purpose, as landmarks for sailors and overland travellers.

The magnificent exteriors of many of these tombs might lead us to expect a corresponding degree of adornment within, and such interior decoration was, in fact, provided, except for rock-cut, and especially façade-, tombs, where the interior chambers were small and roughly executed. Sometimes the tombs could be used to show implements, tools, or military equipment descriptive of the career of the deceased person. Such a custom may have originated in the practice of dedicating the instruments of one's craft to the gods after retirement from active life; this practice is already known in the *Odyssey* (3.26). Armour (especially shields) and weapons may also have been thought to provide a symbolic protection for the deceased in his 'last fight.'[5] Besides ornaments, in certain instances tombs also carried epitaphs and/or inscriptions revealing the identity of the deceased person. For example, in a number of tomb monuments of the Nabataeans at Hegra the inscription begins in the following way: 'This is the tomb made by ... or belonging to ... '[6]

The factors governing the spread of certain types of tomb design from one region to another can be identified only in part. Because architecture is firmly fixed in a particular location (and cannot be transported from one place to another, as can works of sculpture or the minor arts), any discernible cross-influences were doubtless in large measure the result of people who travelled back and forth between different regions and were impressed by the large and magnificently executed tombs that they encountered. However, ideas may sometimes have been transferred in the form of drawings of plans and elevations; there are no extant examples of such drawings of Hellenistic date, but it is likely that some Hellenistic technical manuals were in fact illustrated.[7]

The 'lifetime' of large grave monuments varied. Except for some tumuli, none of them has survived intact to our own time. They were damaged or destroyed either by natural causes (earthquakes) or by people. After the interment, tombs could usually be protected against damage as long as some sort of orderly administration existed in a given community. One might think that the largest tombs would fare best, but such is not the case. Of the Mausoleum at Halikarnassos, nothing remains in situ except some of the foundation courses; of the magnificent funerary complex of the Ptolemies, which included the final burial-place of Alexander the Great, not a single trace has been identified, and even its site cannot be determined with certainty from the descriptions of ancient authors. Only a few of the large tombs explored in modern times were found intact. In many cases stone-robbers subsequently demolished the empty tombs so completely that it is difficult to determine their original appearance.

In the ancient Greek world there were no special areas consecrated as cemeteries, such as existed later in Rome or are in use today; tombs could be built almost anywhere outside inhabited areas. They were most often found along the roads leading out from major gateways, though the burial-places of important persons were carefully chosen and were frequently within the city walls.

In selecting the monumental tombs to be discussed in the following pages, certain chronological and geographic limits have been observed. The main emphasis will be on Hellenistic developments, from the fourth century down to the Julio-Claudian era of the Roman Empire. In examining the origins of the Hellenistic grave monuments, we shall have to go back to the archaic age, or even earlier, and to consider structures other than tombs. Eventually Hellenistic monumental tomb-types spread throughout the Mediterranean world, and some of their descendants continued in use well into Roman imperial times.

Geographically, Hellenistic monumental tomb architecture did not have any strictly defined limits: the influence of the tombs of western Asia Minor was felt wherever Hellenistic ideas penetrated.

MAPS

Map 1
Greece, Asia Minor,
and the Near East

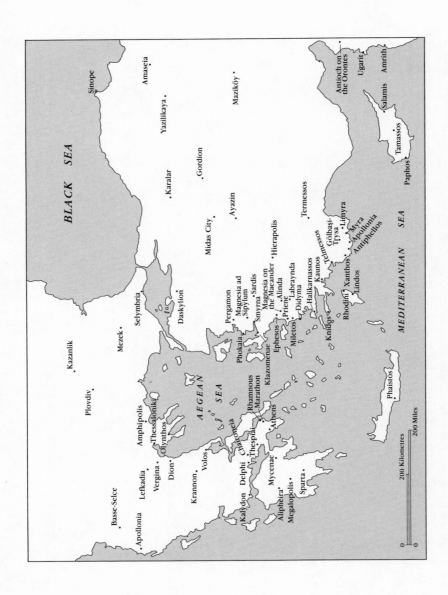

Map 1a Detail, Greece and Asia Minor

BLACK SEA

MEDITERRANEAN SEA

AEGEAN SEA

Sinope
Amaseia
Yazilikaya
Karalar
Gordion
Mazıköy
Midas City
Ayazin
Selymbria
Mezek
Daskylion
Kazanlik
Plovdiv
Pergamon
Magnesia ad Sipylum
Smyrna
Sardis
Hierapolis
Phokaia
Magnesia on the Maeander
Ephesos
Priene
Alinda
Labraynda
Miletos
Didyma
Klazomenae
Halikarnassos
Kaunos
Knidos
Termessos
Telmessos
Gölbasi-Trysa
Xanthos
Rhodini
Lindos
Myra
Limyra
Apollonia
Antiphellos
Antioch on the Orontes
Ugarit
Amrith
Salamis
Tamassos
Paphos

Basse-Selce
Apollonia
Lefkadia
Amphipolis
Vergina
Thessaloniki
Olynthos
Dion
Volos
Chaironeia
Rhamnous
Marathon
Krannon
Delphi
Athens
Thespiai
Kalydon
Mycenae
Alipheira
Megalopolis
Sparta
Phaistos

200 Kilometres
200 Miles
0
0

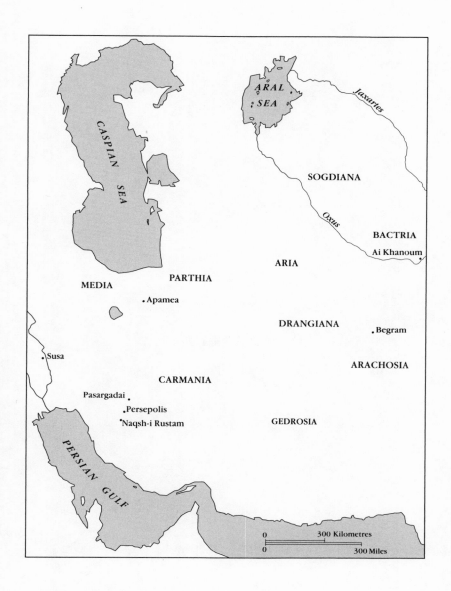

Map 2 The Middle East

GALLI

Glanu

Mass

HISPANIA

MEDITER

Iol Tipasa

•Siga

MAURETANIA   NUMIDI

0   200 Kilometres

0   200 Miles

Map 3 Italy and North Africa

1

Types of Monumental Tombs and Terminology

The number of recorded monumental tombs in the Mediterranean basin for any given period in the first mellennium BC down to Roman imperial times is substantial.

When political stability and economic prosperity coincided, this type of building activity usually increased. Dynasts and persons of authority were eager to erect large-scale tombs as permanent memorials to their own glory; and these tombs display a greater variety of form than is found in any other clearly definable category of building. Other types of building (e.g. of fountain houses, theatres, and bouleuteria) all tend to follow a single general pattern of design and construction that was satisfactory to their particular function. As is still true today, after an early experimental period the most practical designs are also the most widespread and popular. For instance, ancient gateways, granaries, and gymnasia had above all to be functional in order to serve their particular purpose as well as possible. The same cannot be said of tombs, where individuality and uniqueness were often the main considerations in planning an impressive building or complex.

The arrangement of monumental tombs according to types has been attempted ever since the nineteenth century, when larger groups and necropoleis were first documented by scholars. However, existing classifications, which are generally the result of research more or less limited to a particular region, have only a limited value. The most common method has been, and still is, to set up systems of classification according to geographical regions.

The principles of classification also vary. Often divisions are made on the basis of construction, as opposed to stylistic considerations. To date, no study of tomb architecture has attempted an overall introductory classification; rather, the classification emerges, as it were, from discussion of the monuments of the particular region or site. Detailed descriptions are obviously of great value, especially when they point out the peculiarities and common trends of the buildings under discussion; indeed, the preparation of a workable system must be based on such descriptions. However, so many classifications have been formulated for particular buildings or sites that monuments at different sites, though structurally and typologically identical, or at least closely related, may be grouped under different (and frequently misleading) headings.

No system of classification should employ primary divisions that are based on a mixture of structural, formal, and stylistic considerations. Clear separation of the main criteria for division is, in fact, an essential preliminary step toward a unified system, applicable, at least in its main outlines, to many geographically distinct regions and groups of monuments. If such a 'synoptic' classification should prove possible, tombs that are structurally, formally, and stylistically similar could then all be placed under headings appropriate to each group. The first task, then, must be to decide whether the number of examples is large enough to permit establishment of a new and more integrated classification system. From the point of view of construction, an integrated system seems quite feasible; if based on considerations of form and style, such a system becomes more difficult to apply consistently.

Some of the earlier proposals for a broadly applicable classification go back to the nineteenth century. With respect to the formation of the 'Greek types' of monumental tomb of the fifth and fourth centuries (especially of the so-called mausoleum type), research carried out in Lycia provides the most relevant results. Moreover, Lycia is also the region where, to the best of our knowledge, the first full-fledged ancestor of the Hellenistic monumental tomb is to be found: the Nereid Monument at Xanthos.[1] In addition to the Nereid Monument, this region, together with neighbouring Karia, also provides us with a great variety of other types of funerary monument. Thus, the tombs of these two districts of southwestern Asia Minor are a starting point for a broad, general classification of monumental tombs.

An early proposal for the arrangement of tomb-types, based on the unity of form and construction observable in certain groups of Lycian tombs, was that of C. Fellows. In his account of discoveries in Lycia, Fellows notes: 'The annexed sketch will show the varieties of rock-architecture, and the one following, those in the built tombs seen in Lycia.'[2] In the accompanying drawings (fig. 1) there are shown sixteen different forms of Lycian rock-cut tombs and nine of built tombs. In his subsequent discussion of the possible origins of the different shapes, Fellows uses terms such as 'temple-like forms,' 'portico in antis,' 'various cottages,' and 'box-like barns'[3] as designations for the different types of structures. He is, of course, correct in indicating that typologically similar buildings can still differ technically.[4]

Another attempt at setting up a classification system was made by Benndorf and Niemann in the late nineteenth century.[5] They divided the Lycian tombs into four main groups: (1) rock-cut tombs, (2) sarcophagi, (3) obelisks or pillar tombs, and (4) 'Hellenized' monuments. The primary principle followed in these four divisions is chronological. The oldest are the simple rock-cut tombs, which with the passage of time acquired architecturally recognizable forms. The subgroups in the first main entry include (A) two-sided, (B) three-sided, and (C) four-sided house tombs, the last being completely freed from the surrounding rock formation, i.e., rock-cut but free-standing. At a later point in the architectural history of Lycia, the sarcophagi appeared (Benndorf's and Niemann's group no. 2); the authors noted some 2000 examples in the region. No clearly distinguishable subgroups are indicated here; however, it is implied that the shape of the roofs could serve as a basis for further subdivision. The tombs of group no. 3, 'Obelisken oder Pfeilergräber,' are a unique type of burial, probably of eastern origin. The fourth main class includes tombs for which the model is Greek, or that were influenced by Greek art. The subdivision of the group is based on a theory of development in which the earliest examples have only some Greek-derived decoration, while those at the other end of the line are the completely Greek type of monuments, whether free-standing or façade-tombs. For a possible fifth main class, the authors propose the Roman tomb monuments.[6]

In connection with the tombs of Lycia, other valuable suggestions have been put forward by Dinsmoor, Akurgal, and more recently French and Danish scholars.[7] However, up to the present time, the most comprehensive attempt to achieve a unified system for the funerary monuments in Lycia is that of J. Borchhardt.[8] He distinguishes two primary categories, (A) free-standing monuments and (B) rock-cut monuments. The subdivisions within each of the two main groups are: I, pillar tombs; II, house tombs; III, temple tombs; IV, sarcophagi; V, double tombs. Each of these subgroups contains its own series of subheadings, which may then be broken into still smaller subsections.

A substantial number of the major tomb-types found in Lycia also appear, with some local variations, in other regions of the Mediterranean. Consequently, they can be designated under the same main heading but with appropriate subdivisions whenever needed. Necropoleis with a great concentration and variety of tombs around one city (e.g., Cyrene, Jerusalem,

Petra), or groups of monuments extending over a whole region (e.g., Macedonia, Numidia, Galatia) but typologically more or less analogous in character, are of the greatest value for establishing a broadly applicable system. Apart from methods of construction, tombs of unusual form can only be described individually and grouped in a special 'residual' category ('others').

The approach to a uniform classification at this stage must necessarily be gradual and experimental because no comprehensive study of monumental tombs now exists. The chapters that handbooks devote to such monuments are far from adequate with respect to classification. The collection and organization of the thousands of known large-scale burials, and their typological and formal arrangement, is an enormous task that would require years of field and library research, perhaps assisted by a computer to process the data. Therefore, the 'classifications' proposed here are definitions, limited to an attempt to establish groups representing the most common types, whether in Asia Minor or in some other part of the Mediterranean. The definitions of tomb-types will provide an introductory glossary of terms for the study to follow.

When dealing with a large and varied corpus of tombs the easiest and most obvious distinctions to be made are those based on materials and methods of construction used. Few tombs of monumental dimensions consisted exclusively of perishable materials such as timber;[9] either they were built of stone or they were rock-cut – or they were a combination of the two.

Tumuli are a special group and will be classified accordingly (on the basis of exterior construction and the execution of the ceiling of the tomb chamber). In the case of built tombs the first series of subdivisions is made, as far as possible, on the basis of the exterior form of the buildings. With rock-cut tombs the primary division has been made on the basis of the extent to which the tombs were freed from the surrounding rock, and thus imitated free-standing buildings. Each category is then subdivided on the basis of exterior form. Although the built tombs are almost without exception free-standing, rock-cut tombs are rarely so. When there is a combination of built and rock-cut techniques, it is convenient to set the tombs apart as 'mixed constructions,' without changing the subdivisions. As far as additional subclasses are concerned, formal and stylistic considerations may change from group to group, depending on the usefulness of each criterion. Interior arrangements, except in the case of tumulus tombs, will have no bearing on this initial classification.

The four main groups are the following:

19 Types of Tombs and Terminology

I BUILT TOMBS

II ROCK-CUT TOMBS

III TOMBS OF MIXED CONSTRUCTION (partly built and partly rock-cut tombs)

IV TUMULI

These are subdivided into the following groups and subgroups:

I *Built Tombs*

A Altar tombs

B Column tombs

C Courtyard complexes (within walled enclosures, and including a variety of architectural units)

D House tombs (with or without podia). Further classification is possible according to the shape of the roofs: e.g., house tombs with flat, hipped, or gabled roofs.

E Mastaba tombs

F Pharos tombs (in the form of a lighthouse)

G Pillar tombs (with or without decoration)

H Portico tombs (with real or false/engaged columns on a single-tiered or two-tiered façade)

I Pyramidal tombs (of smooth or stepped sides)

J Sarcophagi (whether or not elevated, and with or without architectural and/or sculputural decoration)

K Temple tombs (with or without podia and with hipped, gabled, or pyramidal roof)
   1 in antis
   2 prostyle
   3 amphiprostyle
   4 peripteral
   5 pseudoperipteral

L Tholos and cylindrical tombs (with or without free-standing or engaged columns)

M Tower/pinnacle tombs (usually of multi-storey arrangement). Further classification is possible according to the disposition of the tomb chambers or loculi.

N Others (need specific descriptions)

II *Rock-cut Tombs*

A Free-standing

B Engaged (at least one side still attached to rock surface behind)

B_1 Façade in niche

B_2 Sunken façade

B_3 Flush façade

B_4 Projecting, or relief façade

Groups and subgroups A and/or B
  1 Aedicula tombs
  2 Chamber tombs (without elaborate architectural façades)
  3 Courtyard tombs (partly or entirely cut below ground level and with or without a columnar arrangement)
    (a) oikos type (rooms along a central axis)
    (b) peristyle type (rooms around a central courtyard)
  4 Cube tombs (with or without decoration)
  5 House tombs (with or without elevation). Further classification is possible according to the shape of the roofs: e.g., house tombs with flat, hipped, or gable roofs.
  6 Portico tombs (with real or false/engaged columns in a single- or double-storey arrangement; these façades sometimes imitate a proskenion or scaenae frons)
  7 Pylon and 'Hegra' tombs (with pylon, stepped, crenellated, or gabled roofs)
  8 Sarcophagi (with or without a hyposorion and with or without carved decoration)
  9 Temple tombs (with or without podia and with hipped, gabled, or pyramidal roof)
    (a) in antis
    (b) prostyle
    (c) based on peripteral design
  10 Theatre tombs (with elements recalling the cavea and orchestra of a theatre)
  11 Others (need specific descriptions)

III *Mixed Constructions*
A Free-standing and/or
B Engaged
with any of the appropriate subentries from Built (I) and Rock-cut (II) groups.

IV *Tumuli*
A Earth mounds (layered)
B Earth mounds (layered) with enclosing stone rings
C Built mounds of cut-stone construction
D Mixed construction (partly rock-cut, partly built)

Subdivisions for (IV) A, B, C, and D:
  1 Built barrel-vaulted chambers (a) without architectural façade, (b) with architectural façade (so-called Macedonian tombs). Further subdivisions are possible according to the applied architectural decoration on the façades.
  2 Built corbel-vaulted chambers (with corbel domes or corbel vaults)
    (a) square or rectangular on plan with corner pendentives
    (b) circular plan

3 Built 'diagonal' (also called 'lantern') roofing
4 Built hipped roofing
5 Built flat roofing (slabs)
6 Multi-chamber arrangements with different roofing techniques ('apartment' type)
7 Rock-cut chamber(s) – can be any of the above plus 'fan-shaped' roof
8 Timber chambers
9 Simple or basic burial arrangements
  (a) sarcophagus (beneath the mound)
  (b) cist grave(s) (beneath the mound)
10 Others (need specific descriptions)

Built tombs include all masonry structures: they may be built of a single type of stone or of a combination of different types, and they may exhibit one or several styles of masonry. Their location in general is not predetermined by local geological conditions.[10]

Rock-cut tombs developed only at places where workable rock formations existed, whether a single projecting cliff or a series of such formations. Rock-cut tombs were not bound by the conventional principles of thrust and support. Therefore modules, measurements, and proportions show great flexibility and a lack of consistency not found in built tombs, which in other respects they frequently imitate. Rock-cut tombs could also be more easily expanded to receive additional burials than could their built counterparts.

The most widespread form of rock-cut funerary monument is the engaged tomb with a conspicuous architectural façade. These façade-tombs are two-dimensional units, and often appear in groups constituting independent necropoleis. They could be arranged in rows, or irregularly placed where the vertical rock surfaces seemed to be the most suitable. On the basis of cutting the fronts (the three other 'sides' were often part of the rock), four main forms can be distinguished, even though some examples may overlap from one group to another. The façade in niche (e.g., fig. 120) basically indicates that the façade of the tomb is set back inside a recess cut into the face of the cliff. The sunken façade (e.g., fig. 42) designates a rock-cut tomb where the design of the façade is set back from the natural cliff face, but not placed in a specially cut recess or niche. In the flush façade (e.g., fig. 45), the façade is in the same plane as the surrounding rock. In the projecting or relief façade (e.g., fig. 41), the carved decoration on the front stands slightly free of the surrounding rock or projects from it in relief.

The so-called mixed-construction group refers to tombs that are partly rock-cut and partly built. It is highly unlikely that for large built tombs, directly exposed to the effects of the weather, perishable materials could have been used. However, there are a few known rock-cut tombs in present-day Albania (ancient Illyria), in which the 'pronaos' consisted of a wooden construction (fig. 148).[11] In tumuli, especially in Phrygia, wooden beams appeared quite often as building material for the tomb chamber (fig. 50). The most common forms of mixed construction are tombs with rock-cut lower and built upper portions, and built façades in front of a rock-cut chamber.

Although tumuli may belong structurally to built tombs, rock-cut tombs, or mixed constructions, their peculiar form makes them a separate group. Often, but not exclusively, tumuli are circular in plan. They are usually low and wide mounds with a conical top; the width exceeds the height.[12] On the exterior, usually at the summit, there may be grave markers (cippus, phallus, mushroom, stele, and so forth); these markers emphasize the fact that tumuli were meant to be noticed. The exterior gives no hint of the form of the interior construction. Many tumuli have a dromos, but this feature is not essential. The nucleus, the tomb chamber, is frequently off-centre within the mound, and may be square, rectangular, circular, or (if multi-roomed) any or all of these. The technical execution of the visible exterior mound provides the basis for distinguishing the primary subclasses. It should be added here that classes iva and ivb often consist, for stability and safety of 'earth' mounds, of different layers of pebbles, clay, and other broken filling materials, and are not simply piled-up earth. The execution of the interior ceiling seems to provide the best basis for further subdivision of tumulus tombs.

The subclasses within the other three primary divisions (i, ii, and iii) include tomb forms of recognizable derivation, i.e., imitating private houses, palaces, utilitarian buildings, temples, and other familiar types of structure; the suggested terminology should make such tombs easy to recognize. More difficult, perhaps, are the designations mastaba and 'Hegra' tombs. Although these terms, like 'temple' and 'pyramid,' refer to certain forms of funerary monuments without describing them in detail, they should become self-explanatory within the overall framework of ancient Near Eastern tomb architecture (see pages 127 and 150).

Large or spectacular tombs often have names of their own; e.g., the Nereid Monument at Xanthos, the Archokrateion at Lindos on Rhodes, and the Corinthian Tomb at Petra. Yet in the proposed typology, these tombs also fit easily under the appropriate headings (e.g., Nereid Monument iK4), even though it is useful to include the standard names found in the literature. 'Regional' designations can sometimes be applied to entire groups of monuments such as the 'Macedonian tombs' (IVA1b), which have in common certain characteristic features that distinguish them from other types of tumuli. However, in other instances geographical distinctions can be misleading; for example, 'Alexandrian tombs' would include monuments belonging to entirely different categories.

Difficulties also arise from the widespread use of the words 'mausoleum' and 'heroon': these terms have become quite comprehensive and do not necessarily refer to a single type of monument. 'Mausoleum,' of course, was originally the name of the monumental tomb of Mausolos, dynast of Karia from 377 to 353 BC. Later, in both Roman and modern usage, the term has been widely applied to large-scale, but often typologically different, tombs. We find references to 'small-scale,' 'tumulus-like,' 'commemorative,' 'tower,' 'rock-cut,' and other mausolea. In other words, the name is easily attached to tombs of varied origin and size. Their common characteristics, if the original fourth-century structure is used as a touchstone, ought to be extremely decorative appearance and large scale. On this basis, the monuments belonging to the group of temple tombs are closest to the ideal 'mausoleum type'; they often consist of a high and massive podium with a lighter superstructure above. Structures of this sort were especially popular in Asia Minor.

The term 'heroon' ($\dot{\eta}\rho\tilde{\omega}ov$) is even more widely applicable than mausoleum; it designates a funerary monument at which the cult of the hero was perpetuated. A heroon can be a single edifice or a sumptuous funerary ensemble. The cult places of the dead assumed impressive architectural forms in Asia Minor. By the fourth century and especially after Alexander, hero cults, housed in sizeable structures, sprang up in numerous localities.[13] Yet the earliest literary references to heroa all post-date Alexander the Great. From the island of Thera comes one of the most important epigraphic testimonials relating to private hero cults. The author of this inscription from Thera is a certain Epicteta.[14] The document, of the late third or early second century, explicitly describes the dead as heroes and their resting places as $\dot{\eta}\rho\tilde{\omega}\iota\alpha$. A mouseion was to be set up containing the statues of Epicteta herself and the other deceased (the same idea is found in the fourth-century Philippeion at Olympia); the mouseion in turn was an integral part of the temenos that housed the actual memorial edifices, the $\dot{\eta}\rho\tilde{\omega}\iota\alpha$ of the persons buried there.

A good example of an earlier heroon-temenos complex still exists at Gölbaşi-Trysa in Lycia.[15] Within the walls of the enclosure there were provisions for funerary banquets and for other cultic functions. A larger and truly impressive creation must have been the heroon-temenos of Antigonos Gonatas, containing, besides funerary buildings, a stadium, a round portico, and baths.[16] The heroon at Kalydon is a more compact late Hellenistic example (ca 100 BC) of the type; the courtyard was once entirely surrounded by roofed-over structures, the outer walls of which provided complete privacy (fig. 2).[17] The plan finds its closest parallels in gymnasia and basilicas.

Architecturally, the simple heroon buildings can perhaps be best described as a combination of a tomb and a modified temple structure. The most common form, especially in Asia Minor and the islands, is a burial chamber in a high basement with a 'naos' section above it. Examples include a fourth-century heroon at Limyra (fig. 69), the Charmyleion on Kos (fig. 103), and the Ta Marmara heroon (fig. 110) near Didyma. In fact, the tomb of Mausolos at Halikarnassos can also be noted here, as a monumental heroon-mausoleum. In general, the term heroon, from the architectural point of view, is not a useful criterion for classification because it refers to the purpose or function of a building rather than to its form. In those instances where the heroon comprises several separate units, the individual buildings could be assigned to the appropriate headings. Because the term is attached to a number of well-known tombs, it will be used to identify these structures by their names known from earlier literature and only in a limited sense to describe tombs as types.

Cenotaphs are sepulchral monuments erected in honour of a person whose body has been lost or buried elsewhere. Such 'empty tombs' are known to have existed ever since the time of Homer.[18] They were given the same honour and respect as real burials. Legendary heroes and military personnel are the people who were most frequently honoured by these monuments. In a number of instances the dedication is uncertain, as in the late fourth-century cenotaph-heroon within the city walls at Paestum. Like mausolea, cenotaphs may take different forms. For example, the cenotaph of King Nikokreon at Salamis on Cyprus was in the form of a tumulus of burned material (from the funeral pyre?) raised over a mud-brick platform.[19] Statues of the deceased (recalling once again the Philippeion and Epicteta heroon on Thera) occupied the circumference of this mound. The monument is datable to the end of the fourth century. Much later is the large, relatively well-preserved and adequately documented cenotaph of Gaius Caesar at Limyra in Lycia.[20] He died AD 4 (21 February) at Limyra, and his body was transported to Rome to be buried there in Augustus's own mausoleum. The commemorative cenotaph in Lycia must have been erected shortly afterward.

Unfortunately, because of the present ruinous condition of many of these edifices and because the contents have been removed, it is frequently hard to distinguish cenotaphs from real tombs. Such is the case with the Lion Tomb at Amphipolis,[21] which may be either a real burial or a cenotaph. Among large scale and unique buildings the so-called Throne at Amyklai near Sparta, the Karyatid Porch of the Erechtheion, and the Tholos at Epidauros can all be regarded as cenotaphs.[22]

Communal tombs are usually mass burials as opposed to family burials; most of them do not adhere to any particular form or shape. Frequently they are simple constructions without much architectural elaboration, like the earth mound raised over the fallen Plataeans and slaves at Marathon, or the Lion Tomb at Chaeronea, erected after 338 BC.[23] However, the communal Lion Tomb at Knidos (fig. 85) is one of the more remarkable creations of Hellenistic architecture.

The peribolos tomb, a common form of Athenian and other Attic burial grounds, is related to monumental tombs, but strictly speaking not part of the group. A peribolos tomb consists of a rectangular area enclosing a number of graves. The best examples are found in the Kerameikos cemetery at Athens and at Rhamnous.[24]

Kline tombs: Heuzey and Daumet introduced the use of this term for burials where the body was laid out on a stone or on a wooden or metal 'couch,' the kline.[25] K.G. Vollmoeller surveyed various regions of the Mediterranean world where interments took place on klinai.[26] Unfortunately in both publications there appears the notion of the kline as a distinct tomb form.[27] It is true that there are certain tomb groups and periods in which klinai dominated the interior furnishing. Nevertheless, from the architectural point of view, the kline cannot be a valid criterion for purposes of classification because burials on klinai took place in tombs of many different types.

Loculus burials differ to some extent from the klinai. Loculi are rectangular niches, either built or hewn out of the rock, for the interment of bodies. In tomb architecture their role was simply to facilitate multiple burials. From the early Hellenistic period, when loculi were first employed, until the appearance of catacomb complexes, one can speak only of burials with loculus arrangements. Naturally the process was gradual; the change from single kline burials to loculi is especially well documented in the Sidi Gaber cemetery at Alexandria.[28] The design of catacombs in time became entirely determined by the various methods of cutting and arranging the loculi.

To avoid possible ambiguity, altar tombs need to be briefly clarified. Altar tombs, properly so called, are simply grave monuments that imitate the form of altars. In contrast, when altars appear in the vicinity of tombs (e.g., in the Archokrateion at Lindos) they indicate the heroization of the deceased (fig. 107). Tombs in altar form are rare in the Hellenistic age but became somewhat more numerous in the Roman era.

The best examples of oikos and peristyle types of tombs come from Alexandria. They are rock-hewn complexes, partly or entirely underground, dating to the third and second centuries. Oikos, from Homer on, is used to describe not only a house but also a single room or chamber in a private or sacred building. However, in our context the meaning is slightly expanded to suit the tomb-type. The main court is there, but the rest of the units are disposed along a central axis.[29]

The peristyle type of tomb complex can be similarly defined. In Dinsmoor's terminology it is 'a covered colonnade which surrounds a building' or 'an inner court lined with a colonnade.'[30] As can be seen in the well-known peristyle tombs in Alexandria (the most complete is Mustafa Pasha Tomb no. 1, fig. 174) and in Cyprus (the Palaeokastro tomb complex near Nea Paphos, fig. 3), these tombs are dominated by an inner court surrounded by covered colonnades and rooms opening off from it.

Other terms and descriptive names, which occasionally arise in connection with monumental tombs, have only an auxiliary value; for the purpose of this study a short list of these will be sufficient. Some terms refer to sections of tomb buildings, while others have a more general meaning. Where several interpretations are possible, only those relevant to funerary architecture are mentioned.

bomos (βωμός) – a sub-basement, a large raised platform, or an altar with its supporting base; especially common in Asia Minor.

ensorion (ἐνσόριον) – a place for a sarcophagus; also another name for *loculus*.

hyposorion (ὑποσόριον) / *hypogeion* (ὑπόγειον) – underground chamber, place for interment, usually in the podium section of monumental tombs, including (elevated) sarcophagi. Hyposorion can also refer to a vault under the σορος (see page 27):

kamara (καμάρα) – in tomb architecture indicates a vaulted ceiling.[31]

koimeterion (κοιμητήριον) – a sleeping room, or 'sleeping area' for the sleep of death; in funerary context designates and area used for burials (a cemetery).

k(o)urgan – the word is of Tartar origin; it refers to a burial mound, a tumulus, or barrow found in the Black Sea region.

loculus (a 'niche') – usually a narrow chamber for the placement of a body or receptacle (i.e., coffin, urn, etc.).

mnema (μνῆμα), *mnemeion* (μνημεῖον), *mnemorion* (μνημόριον) – all have a broad range of meaning referring to a memorial, monument, tomb mound, or building in honour of the dead.[32]

nefesh (nafs, nefshâ, wagr) – in Semitic languages can have a number of different meanings: soul, life, person, etc. In tomb architecture the nefesh is an important element of Semitic tombs, usually in the form of an elongated pyramid on top of a monumental tomb. It symbolizes the soul of the deceased person.

orthostasis or *orthostates* (ὀρθοστάτης) – a rarely used term, designating a 'funeral monument with pillars.'[33] However, Kubinska prefers to interpret it as 'quelque sorte de soubassement.'[34] In architectural terminology an *orthostate* is an upright shaft, pillar, or building stone – the last constituting a visible 'horizontal' base of a wall.

platas (πλάτας) – a platform on which tombs were placed.

polyandrion (πολῦανδρειον) – indicates a communal burial place.

sarcophagus (σαρκοφάγος) – literally the meaning of the word is 'flesh-devouring.' Originally it referred to a type of limestone quarried at Assos in Troas. According to legend, such a limestone sarcophagus could consume or eat away the dead flesh and bones. A sarcophagus, depending on its size, could be used for single or multiple burials.

sekos (σηκός) – besides being a sacred enclosure, precinct, cella of a temple, it can also signify a burial place, sepulchre,

sema (σῆμα) – in general, a token, mark, but also a 'sign' by which a grave is known, whether it is a mound, cairn, or even a rock-cut tomb. A sixth-century inscription from the base of an Attic kouros monument gives only a suggestion of what was meant by sema: 'Stand and mourn at the sema of dead Kroisos ...'[35]

soros (σορός) – a vessel, urn, or sarcophagus for holding human remains.

syngonion (συγγώνιον) – in connection with tombs indicates a monument incorporating a portrait gallery of the deceased person's ancestors. It was usually created to glorify the members of a ruling family.

taphos (τάφος) – used of various forms of sepulchre.

theke (θήκη) – a receptacle, chest, coffin, burial vault, grave, tomb; in function similar to loculi but often smaller in size (e.g., a box to contain the ashes of the deceased).

thema (θέμα) – can mean either a common burial place or a private graveyard.

thorakeion (θωρακεῖον) – used in connection with large supports, usually carrying sarcophagi. In LSJ it is translated as a 'breastwork, parapet, or dwarf-wall of an enclosure.'[36]

topos (τόπος) – place, region. A territory around the tomb where construction was not permitted.

trapeza (τράπεζα) – among other meanings, can refer to a platform-like block monument (especially in Athens).

tymbos (τύμβος) – has a broad meaning; like *taphos*, frequently used of sepulchral mounds, barrows, or tombs in general.

It is important to understand that the meaning of these words was sometimes changed or modified with the passing of time and that some terms were restricted to certain geographic regions of the Mediterranean (e.g., 'thorakeion' occurs mostly in inscriptions found at Smyrna and Aphrodisias).

2

Monumental Tombs prior to the Fourth Century

In the following discussion selected examples of the main groups of funerary structures will be treated under separate headings. In section IA of built tombs a special emphasis is given to structures incorporating a pyramid in their design, a feature that in Hellenistic times frequently appeared in tomb architecture. In section IB other types of selected built tombs are discussed.

I Built Tombs

In the formation of Hellenistic monumental tombs, Greece proper played little direct role.[1] Even prior to the fifth century the role of the Greek mainland in the architectural developments of Asia Minor was rather passive. The activity of Attic artists in Asia Minor becomes more frequent only after the termination of the Periklean building program in Athens: for example, definite traces of mainland workmanship are detectable in Xanthian buildings, including the best-known tomb there, the Nereid Monument.[2] However, before discussing the Nereid Monument and its architectural impact on later large-scale tomb buildings, developments that preceded it should be examined.

The most important contribution to Greek tomb architecture probably comes from lands dominated by the Persians. During the sixth century the Ionian Greeks seem to have been the leading designers, artists, and craftsmen of the Greek world. Even before the Persian conquest of Ionia, they must have had a highly developed tradition in monumental architecture, which led to the creation of the huge Ionic temples at Ephesos, Didyma, and on the island of Samos. East Greek influence was strongly felt not only in Greek-speaking regions, but also among their non-Greek neighbours. Migrating (or sometimes exiled) Ionian workmen often appeared selling their services at the courts of greater and lesser monarchs in the territories controlled by Persians. Among other places, they left the trademarks of their workmanship not only in Lycia, where to the best of our knowledge the prototype of the Hellenistic monumental tomb was created, but also in other satrapies of the Persian kings.

Indeed the contribution of these Ionian Greek stonemasons to Achaemenid building programs at Pasargadai and later at Persepolis was indispensable, even if they did not set the overall style. In his study of the origins of Achaemenid masonry, Nylander concludes: 'It was possible to demonstrate the probable Greek origin of a number of technical solutions to the problems of stoneworking, not only in Achaemenid Persia but also in the ancient world as a whole. Apparently, some specialized stone-cutting tools, the anathyrosis principle, the elaborate setting procedures, the advanced bonding with a special type of reinforced iron clamp, and the ingenious lead sealing of dowels, some of which have remained in use for thousands of years, were either original Greek inventions or radical improvements of earlier, less practical solutions.'[3]

Besides Greeks, other nationalities also helped to create a characteristically Persian style of architecture. In dealing with Achaemenid buildings one cannot speak of a single prototype, because several sources often contributed to a single work; what made the work a stylistic whole was the underlying and pervading Persian spirit. An important inscription mentioning the international contributions to Darius's building program was found at Susa. This trilingual document (Persian, Babylonian, Elamite) leaves no doubt about the origin of the stonemasons: 'The stone cutters who wrought the stone those were Ionians and Sardians.'[4] The inscription also suggests that the Persians chose to adopt the cultural heritage of the defeated people after their continuing military successes.

On Persian art in general, H. Frankfort expressed well the essence of the dilemma of Persia: 'It had no native antecedents and was created to meet the unprecedented situation in which the Persians found themselves after Cyrus' conquest of Babylon (539 BC) ... it could either accept or destroy the cultural heritage.'[5] The Persians chose to blend the cultural traditions of the conquered lands of Media, Lydia, Babylonia, and other regions. The contributions of these lands were just as important as those of the Greeks.

With the gradual expansion of the Persian Empire, the absorption of new elements into Persian architecture took place with little hesitation. If nothing else, Persian architecture was flexible; and the rulers seem to have been always ready to improve or replace conventional methods and motifs with new ones. For example, the invasion of Egypt by Cambyses II took place in 525 BC, shortly after the death of Cyrus II (559–530 BC), who commissioned the Pasargadai complex; thus it is significant that Egyptianizing lintels, which are not found at Pasargadai, were employed in the structures of Darius I (521–486 BC) at Persepolis a couple of decades later.[6]

Alongside the formation of a Persian royal architecture, some regional styles also flourished. The relative calm and prosperity enjoyed under Achaemenid domination favoured more-ambitious building programs in certain regions; in fact, the conditions created by the Achaemenid conquests in many ways anticipate those that later prevailed all over the Mediterranean under the Pax Romana.

In the conquered territories, where established architectural traditions already existed, a twofold evolution can be observed. On the one hand, the old traditions continued, and occasionally even came into the foreground. For example, recent research indicates that in the Near East, with its long experience in building techniques, earlier methods of construction were revived.[7] On the other hand, the erection of splendid new complexes in the Achaemenid centres of power inspired local rulers to borrow and imitate the architectural forms and schemes of edifices in these capital cities.

In Achaemenid tomb architecture the same eclectic tendencies are noticeable in both private and public buildings. A. Demandt distinguishes three tomb-types with a definite chronological development: 'The "house type," such as the Meshed in Pasargadai, the "tower type," seen in the Zindan and the Ka'bah, and finally the rock-cut tombs at Naqsh-i Rustam.'[8]

Demandt's classification is acceptable in so far as he distinguishes built from rock-cut tombs; unfortunately, there is no definite evidence for his 'tower-type' of burial. Both the Zindan and the Ka'bah do have a sacred character, but even recent excavations on the sites have not revealed their specific purpose. As a matter of fact, the excavators of the Ka'bah observed that 'the evidence pointing to the use of the tower as the dynastic fire sanctuary of Persis princes and Sassanian emperors induces us to conclude that this edifice and its counterpart at Pasargadai were erected to shelter the royal fire in the two homeland capitals of the Achaemenids. The Zindan at Pasargadai was undoubtedly built by Cyrus the Great ... the tower at Naqsh-i Rustam was most probably built by Darius the Great.[9] Furthermore, we do not know what the tombs of the predecessors of Cyrus the Great were like. The existing rock-cut tombs of Median and Urartian origin may suggest, as one of the possibilities, that Persian nobles were buried in rock tombs even before the Naqsh-i Rustam period.[10] The overwhelming majority of the preserved Persian funerary monuments are rock-cut burials, which offer greater resistance to the forces of destruction; but the earliest dated and securely identified royal monument is the built Tomb of Cyrus the Great (fig. 4a, b, c, d). One of the most notable features of the structure was the incorporation of the pyramid motif in its design.

A *Use of Pyramidal Structures in Tombs*
before the Mausoleum at Halikarnassos

The first major Persian funerary monument to be discussed is the Tomb of Cyrus at Pasargadai.

Ancient sources tend to concentrate on the description of the interior of the tomb, with only a superficial description of the structure itself. The most explicit are Arrian (6.29.4) and Strabo (15.3.2), who derived their information mainly from Aristobulus and Onesicritus.

Mentioned in both texts is an important point that could hardly have been established from the remains now extant, even though in other respects the tomb is well preserved. Arrian states: 'The tomb of this Cyrus was in the territory of Pasargadai in the royal park; around it had been planted a grove of all sorts of trees; the grove was irrigated, and deep grass had grown in the meadow.' A similar landscape architecture reappeared in connection with later Lycian, Hellenistic, and Roman monumental tombs, probably more often than we are aware.

The actual Tomb of Cyrus[11] is a burial above ground, like all other Persian, and indeed most of the Lycian, tombs.[12] Above a rectangular 'plinth' rises a stepped platform, which in turn supports a gable-roofed building. The overall height of this section is approximately 11 m. The lowest part of the stepped pyramid starts out with an unfinished moulding; in earlier drawings this moulding is shown as cyma recta, but this cannot be more than a hypothesis. Above the moulding are three higher and three lower receding steps. Around the base of the actual burial building runs another decorative band, unfinished like the one below the steps; this band is followed by a high orthostate section and three courses of ashlar. The transition to the cornice under the gabled stone roof consists of an unfinished dentil course and a cyma reversa moulding between two narrow flat bands. The gable roof, which has an angle of 36°, is made of large, precisely cut slabs. In the centre of the front gable there is an eroded and hardly noticeable decorative rosette.[13] The small door of the burial chamber has a two-fascia frame with a (no longer recognizable) crowning moulding.[14] The chamber measures 2.1 × 3.2 × 2.2 m.[15] The edifice was surrounded by columns (eight on each side) that created a temenos-like enclosure.[16]

To sort out exactly the different artistic influences incorporated in this scheme would be a difficult, if not impossible, task. However, it is possible to distinguish the Greek elements from the others. The cyma-profiled mouldings, their use as a transition from vertical wall to horizontal geison, the unfinished dentils, and perhaps the pedimental shape of the cella roof show Ionian Greek influence. Moreover, the stoneworking technique, the clamps (swallow-tail), the fine joints, and the use of anathyrosis may also be Ionian/Lydian. The division of the entire structure into tripartite units also suggests Ionian Greek influence.

Despite these western traits the appearance of the complex as a whole is non-Greek. Herodotus (1.178ff.) reports Cyrus's attack on the Assyrian capital at Babylon, and describes as follows the most impressive buildings within the walls: 'In the centre of this enclosure a solid tower has been built, one of a furlong's length and breadth; a second tower rises from this, and from it yet another, till at last there are eight ... In the last tower there is a great shrine' (1.181). The inspiration for the Tomb of Cyrus, apart from possible local predecessors, probably comes from buildings such as this and other Mesopotamian ziggurats seen by the Persian monarch during his campaigns.

Similar conclusions may be drawn from another, but less pretentious, tomb known as Gur-e-Dokhtar and located at Buzpar (fig. 5a, b). Here, as in many Lycian tombs and Greek temple designs, the base consists of only three steps. The total height of the tomb is approximately 4.5 m; the interior chamber measures 2 × 2.2 × 1.5 m. The structure has a simplified form and lacks decoration of Greek origin; its date remains questionable.[17]

The pyramidal platform as found in the Tomb of Cyrus remained a rare architectural concept;[18] there are very few known funerary monuments that followed the ziggurat form. The so-called Pyramid Tomb at Sardis (fig. 6) is one of these. The tomb is located on a hillside near the river Pactolus among Lydian chamber tombs. In concept it is analogous to the Tomb of Cyrus; if Hanfmann is right in his assumption that this tomb 'may be the funeral monument for a Persian nobleman who fell in battle for Sardis (547 BC),'[19] the structure actually pre-dates the Tomb of Cyrus.

The tomb was reinvestigated in 1969 and reconstructed by S. Kasper as a twelve-stepped limestone structure, instead of the six or seven steps favoured by some earlier scholars.[20] It is approximately square on plan (ca 7.5 m per side). The rectangular tomb chamber, facing north, was placed within the upper seven tiers of the receding steps, a unique arrangement in funerary architecture. The steps are 0.34–0.35 m high, quite close to the length of the foot unit used in contemporary Ionia, for example at Didyma.[21] In technical execution there are resemblances to the chambers of some of the Bin Tepe tumulus tombs. The stone blocks, with their differently tooled surfaces, but all with drafted edges, can also be related to the recently exposed section of the city wall at Sardis.[22] In Persian royal architecture similar masonry techniques can be found as far away from Sardis as Daskylion and Pasargadai.[23]

The existence of an unexplored monumental stepped pyramid (fig. 7) at Is-Safiyeh in Syria is recorded by H.C. Butler. In the early twentieth century this tower-like structure still had two well-preserved stages forming a truncated pyramid. Inside the second storey there were two burial chambers reached by an exterior stair. Concerning the date of the tomb Butler states: 'I do not hesitate, however, to assume that this stepped pyramid is to be reckoned among the most ancient monuments of Syria, antedating the Roman and Nabataean periods by many generations.' This type of building was not a rarity in the region, for Butler adds: 'A similar structure was found at Damit il-Alya in the Ledja, and other massive structures, presumably in the same form, existed in various quarters of the Hauran, but have long served as stone quarries, and are consequently in no condition to publish.'[24]

For the sake of convenience, a rock-cut monument will be included here – the so-called Pyramid Tomb at Midas City in Phrygia (fig. 8). Above the tomb chamber, now largely obliterated, the outlines of a steep, smooth-sided pyramid are still discernible. E. Haspels dates the original structure to the period of Lydian peace, that is, the time of the second flourishing of Midas City, during the second quarter of the sixth century.[25]

At Amrith in Syria there are four curious monuments of which three are surmounted by pyramids of the smooth-sided type.[26] Two are next to each other; one is topped by a dome while the other culminates in a smooth-sided pyramid. Because no Greek type of decoration appears on the exterior of these two monuments, their date must be earlier than the fourth century, i.e., before any Greek architectural influence reached the region (fig. 9). The third structure with a pyramid at its summit is ca 200 m south of the above-mentioned two (fig. 10). The fourth, called Burdj el-Bezzak (fig. 11), is a short distance from Amrith. This tomb resembles an elongated cube which terminates in a smooth-sided pyramid. Both of the latter two structures have loculi in their interiors indicating a date in or later than the fourth century.[27] Whether Egyptian or Babylonian models inspired this form of building in Syria is hard to say; in either case the pyramids on top presumably have a similar symbolic significance.

In connection with pyramid-like structures the existence of stepped funerary monuments in Etruria ought to be mentioned. However, in Etruria the steps formed the upper part of the circular tumuli or constituted the entire structure above ground. A tomb of this type noted in the nineteenth century[28] had eight circular receding rows of cut blocks facing a rock-cut core that contained a half-sunken, hewn funerary chamber (fig. 12). No date has been suggested for the structure, but the form seems to imitate the stepped-cone altars known from archaic Greece, while the arrangement of the interior chamber is akin to examples found in the early period of Etruscan funerary architecture.[29]

With the passing of time the function of stepped pyramids gradually changed. The stepped pyramid of Djoser (fig. 13) was the resting place of the divine pharaoh. The uppermost stages of the Babylonian ziggurats housed shrines for the worship of supernatural beings.[30] To understand why Mausolos in the fourth century chose the pyramidal form for the top part of his tomb, it is worthwhile to dwell further on the symbolic significance of pyramids. It is very likely that stepped mastabas preceded pyramids as architectural forms. Reisner states: 'It was the layer mastaba which developed into the layer or step pyramid of stone and finally into the true pyramid.'[31] The Pyramid Texts help to clarify further the use and meaning of these structures. Basically they were symbolic elevations enabling the ruler to ascend to the sky and mingle with the stars.

A. Badawy very aptly summarized the ideological essence of pyramids: 'The ziggurat of Mesopotamia, resembling the stepped mastaba or pyramid even to its method of construction (accretion layers for enlargement at Ur-Warka), was also a "stairway to heaven" (name of the ziggurat at Sippar), and the term "ziggurat" probably meant "the pointed one" or "the high one." Further names of the ziggurat, "house of the link between heaven and earth" (Babylon), and the existence of one sanctuary on top and another at the bottom, have led scholars to consider this structure as an actual link, intended, according to Mesopotamian mythology, to connect heaven and earth. In this respect the pyramid would hove been for the pharaoh what the ziggurat was for the Mesopotamian gods.'[32] Furthermore, in Mesopotamia truncated pyramids surmounted by an obelisk or a chapel were built for solar cults. Obelisk-like victory (?) stelae with stepped pyramidal tops are known from the region of Shalmaneser III (859–824 BC) of Assyria (fig. 14). The iconographic significance of such monuments coincides with the broader meaning of tombs surmounted by pyramids, both serving for memorial purposes.[33]

This symbolic meaning of the pyramid survived and spread to other lands. In Egypt we find pyramids surmounting exposed private tombs as early as the New Kingdom. For example, representations of funerary naiskoi topped by smooth-sided pyramids are found at Deir el-Medineh near Thebes (fig. 15).[34]

The same idea later reappeared outside Egypt, e.g., in the so-called Tomb of the Pharaoh's Daughter (or 'Monolith of Siloe') at Jerusalem (fig. 16).[35] The structure is entirely rock-cut except for the pyramid on top. This pyramid was of the Egyptian type, with smooth sides, suggesting the influence of the land of the Pharaohs rather than that of Babylonia.

In connection with pyramidal monuments prior to the fourth century, the Tomb of Pythagoras in the Athenian Kerameikos cemetery deserves some attention. It is located at the foot of a small hill facing north and overlooking the Eridanos. Five receding limestone steps enclosed the burial chamber corresponding to the second and third courses; above the chamber stood a high (ca 1.19 m) commemorative stele. Hoepfner re-examined the monument and pointed out the underlying mathematical principles of its construction.[36] The inscription on the north side of the monument mentions that its commissioner, a certain Pythagoras, came from Selymbria.[37] On the basis of his examination of the inscription, Hoepfner shifted the date of the tomb from the early fourth century to not after the middle of the fifth century. From the archaeological evidence we know that by the first half of the fourth century the base of the monument was already partly underground. Taking all these facts together, we may suggest that this monument was inspired by a stepped design like that of the Sardis tomb, perhaps in the period before the Persian invasion of Greece.

In the Greek world there is no evidence for the inclusion of stepped pyramids as the uppermost part of monumental tombs prior to the fourth century. From the architectural point of view their role from the fourth century onward was to serve as roof structures, and at the same time to support statues and other trophies. The Greeks avoided placing a peripteral naos on a pyramid-like structure. Moreover, the pyramid would have lost its visual importance, and perhaps its symbolic meaning, if it was to be used as a substructure and not a superstructure. Consequently, in tombs where the symbolic pyramid form was retained, the pyramids were placed at the top of the structure, following the example of Near Eastern models.[38]

The Mausoleum at Halikarnassos is presumably the first instance of the reintroduction of the symbolic pyramid into the monumental tomb architecture of western Asia Minor in the fourth century. It is not known exactly what prompted Mausolos (377–353 BC) or his architect to incorporate the pyramidal form into the tomb building; but his oriental background and the symbolic impressiveness of such structures may have been factors. As indicated before, both stepped and smooth pyramids were known in Asia Minor, as well as in the Greek world proper.[39] However, before the time of Mausolos such forms were rarely employed in monumental architecture.

Only some monumental altars, like that in the sanctuary of the chthonian gods at Akragas (fig. 17) or the archaic Artemis altar in Sardis, utilized the stepped pyramidal scheme.[40] The existence of such altars at Amyklai (the Throne of Apollo) and especially at Olympia (Zeus altar) is questionable.[41]

In connection with pyramid-like structures of the later fourth century, it could be mentioned that Alexander the Great, during his campaign in the east, visited many different sites; like Cyrus before him, he (and his architects) may have derived ideas from eastern structures for their own buildings. Diodorus Siculus (18.4.5) tells us that among the written instructions left behind by Alexander there was one for a new burial-place for his father: 'A tomb for his father Philip was to be constructed to match the greatest of the pyramids of Egypt, buildings which some persons count among the seven greatest works of man.' From the same account we also know that the project was never carried out.[42] Alexander did, however, erect a magnificent pyre of six receding elevations in honour of his deceased general Hephaistion; the total height was 'more than one hundred and thirty cubits.'[43]

In later Hellenistic times, pyramids (stepped or smooth-sided) appeared in several geographically distinct regions. After the fourth century, regardless of their scale, they were most frequently the uppermost parts of built or rock-cut tombs. They can be called a sort of 'baroque' version of the ziggurat. No true stepped pyramids are known to have served as the lowest supporting section of any later monument. Three – very rarely four – stepped bases have little if anything to do with the original ziggurat form. They simply served as elevated supports or base courses, without having clear symbolic significance. The origin of these three-stepped bases is obscure. Greeks, Lycians, and others used them as a standard form for the crepidoma of many types of buildings.

B Other Types of Built Monumental Tombs

About two centuries prior to the creation of the Halikarnassian mausoleum, the existence of a number of monumental built tombs is attested to in both the eastern and western Mediterranean region. These structures are important for the record; they are the evidence of the search for expressive monumental built tombs as counterparts of analogous rock-cut tombs and tumuli. A famous example in the Peloponnesos is the so-called Throne of Apollo at Amyklai near Sparta (fig. 18). This building, now completely destroyed except for some of the substructures and fragments (in the Sparta Museum) of the superstructure, is generally dated to the second half of the sixth century. On the basis of Pausanias's description, scholars have attempted many reconstructions of the edifice; one of the latest is by R. Martin.[44]

Pausanias was mainly concerned with the large number of sculptural reliefs; and he also speaks in more detail about the huge idol (ca 14–15 m high) in the centre than about the architecture. His meagre evidence regarding the architecture is the following: 'Bathykles of Magnesia ... made the throne of the Amyklaian (god), ... I saw the throne and will describe its details. It is supported in front, and similarly behind, by two Graces and two Seasons. On the left stand Echidna and Typhos, on the right Tritons.'[45] Then comes the description of a number of reliefs: 'At the upper edge of the throne are wrought, one on each side, the sons of Tyndareus on horses ... On the top of the throne has been wrought a band of dancers, the Magnesians who helped Bathykles to make the throne. Underneath the throne, the inner part away from the Tritons contains the hunting of the Kalydonian boar ... The part of the throne where the god would sit is not continuous; there are several seats, and by the side of each seat is left a wide empty space, the middle, whereon the image stands, being the widest of them all ... The pedestal of the statue is fashioned into the shape of an altar (βωμός) and they say Hyakinthos is buried in it, ... they devote offerings to Hyakinthos as to a hero into this altar through a bronze door, which is on the left of the altar.'[46] This account is followed by a further description of sculptures. To this can be added a sentence from his description of the throne of the cult-statue of Zeus at Olympia: 'It is impossible to go under the throne, in the way we enter the inner part of the throne at Amyklai.'[47]

Naturally the archaeological and comparative evidence has to be included in any proposed restoration. The former comprises the (not entirely clear) foundation courses, Doric column fragments (free-standing, engaged, and three-quarter columns), Doric capitals, console capitals, and a few other architectural embellishments. The comparative material is much too extensive to be dealt with here in detail. It involves commemorative and cult buildings in Asia Minor, especially altars and tomb monuments, and their predecessor in the east.

As Martin points out, although the βωμός (bomos) of Pausanias has been understood as an altar, the word actually has a much broader meaning and can refer to a large socle or podium. Some of the Ionian altars with steps in the middle, such as those at Cape Monodendri near Didyma (fig. 19) and in the sanctuary of Hera on Samos, do in fact have elevated platforms.[48] Many of the Lycian and the later fourth-century monumental tombs in Asia Minor were also placed on elevated platforms. The large altars of ash also rose high above the ground, but because of their different function they had a different form.

Pausanias seems to mean by 'throne' the entire monument and by bomos the central part of it, housing the tomb and supporting the statue. The free-standing column fragments could have belonged either to a temenos around the monument or to a propylon, as Martin has suggested, though the latter seems less likely. A third possibility is that the columns stood on top of the high bomos, as was the case in the fourth-century altar of Artemis at Ephesos or in that at Magnesia,[49] where statues were placed in the intercolumniations (fig. 20). The arrangement of the engaged columns remains just as uncertain as that of the free-standing members. In all the proposed reconstructions they are shown as part of screen wall. However, they could have surrounded the massive podium section as attached columns – an arrangement known from a small-scale (0.62 m high) marble model of a shrine found at Sardis (fig. 21).[50] Here there were painted reliefs in three zones between the attached columns.

Another puzzle at Amyklai is the number and position of the Karyatid-like supports. Pausanias begins his description with the mention of these figures; they seemed to have been the first element to greet the approaching visitor. Thus they must have been clearly visible, as in all the other known examples of Karyatid arrangements. In this respect Fiechter's reconstruction perhaps comes closest to the truth (fig. 22).[51] From Pausanias's description we can also assume the existence of other free-standing statues.[52] However, we do not know whether they were placed on the throne or on the more secluded inner part of the bomos. They could also have stood between some of the columns, as in later tombs such as the Nereid Monument, or around the edge of the bomos (the burial place), as in the fifth-century heroon 'G' at Xanthos.[53] The position of the 'several seats' is also debatable. In any case they were near the pedestal, perhaps flanking it.

The architectural composition of the 'throne' as a whole must have had a pyramid-like appearance, with its different elevations culminating in the idol in the centre. Contributing to such an effect was the prominent setting of the edifice on the summit of a hill (like a mountain-top sanctuary).[54]

Another type of monumental built structure housing a tomb was the Tomb of Porsenna at Clusium in Etruria (fig. 23).[55] Unfortunately we are on even more shaky ground with this structure than with the Throne of Apollo at Amyklai. The only ancient literary source is the Elder Pliny, who relies on Varro's account (late second century), indicating that in his own day no more remains existed.

The relevant passage in Pliny is as follows: 'for it is appropriate to call

Italian, as well as Etruscan, the labyrinth made by King Porsenna of Etruria to serve as his tomb, with the result at the same time that even the vanity of foreign kings is surpassed by those of Italy. But since irresponsible story-telling here exceeds all bounds, I shall in describing the building make use of the very words of Marcus Varro himself: He is buried close to the city of Clusium, in a place where he has left a square monument built of squared blocks of stone, each side being 300 feet long and 50 feet high. Inside this square pedestal there is a tangle labyrinth, which no one must enter without a ball of thread if he is to find his way out. On this square pedestal stand five pyramids, four at the corners and one at the centre, each of them being 75 feet broad at the base and 150 feet high. They taper in such a manner that on top of the whole group there rests a single bronze disk together with a conical cupola, from which hang bells fastened with chains: when these are set in motion by the wind, their sound carried to a great distance, as was formerly the case at Dodona. On this disk stand four more pyramids, each 100 feet high, and above these on a single platform, five more. The height of these last pyramids was a detail that Varro was ashamed to add to his account: but the Etruscan stories relate that it was equal to that of the whole work up to their level, insane folly as it was to have courted fame by spending for the benefit of none and to have exhausted furthermore the resources of a kingdom; and the result, after all was more honour for the designer than for the sponsor.'[56]

Needless to say, this description has prompted many archaeologists to produce reconstructions, many of them quite fantastic. One of the last futile attempts was made by J.L. Myres.[57] If one follows the narrative carefully it becomes evident that the building presented to the reader is architecturally impossible. Yet, despite the exaggerated account of Varro, one cannot doubt that a magnificent tomb was raised for Lars Porsenna, a powerful chieftain, who threatened Rome's newly declared independence in the last decade of the sixth century.[58] The site of his sepulchre would naturally be at Clusium, his capital. One can also assume that if it had not been of extraordinary dimensions and splendour, historians would not have recorded its existence. It is also not improbable that it had a square basement of regular masonry, supporting five pyramids; an example of such a tomb is still extant on the Via Appia at Albano Laziale (fig. 24a, b). Although this tomb is of Republican date, the scheme, with a square basement and five conical pyramids on top, relies on a much earlier model: 'It seems to show that this kind of tomb of the reges atavi of Etruria was among the antique tombs which the grandees of Republican and early Imperial Rome imitated, in addition to mounds – as seen at the Via Appia – and perhaps, tholoi.'[59]

The Cucumella at Vulci (fig. 25),[60] with its circular walled base and pair of towers,[61] square and conical, inside the mound, also shows affinities with Porsenna's tomb. Further analogies can be found in Lydian mounds, especially the tomb of Alyattes near Sardis;[62] it is known from Herodotus (1.93) that five οὖροι marked the summit of this huge tumulus.

The labyrinth, another distinguishing feature of Porsenna's tomb, has also been the subject of controversy. It was in all probability underground, beneath the superstructure. No vestiges of it have been brought to light, though not far from Clusium (Chiusi), at Poggio Gajella, an underground maze of tombs was found in the late nineteenth century. It may or may not be connected with Porsenna's tomb.[63]

To summarize, the origins of Porsenna's tomb are just as obscure as its subsequent fate. If one looks for contemporary or earlier analogous schemes, one should not forget that, in addition to the obvious eastern parallels, the Bronze Age nuraghi of Sardinia (fig. 26) also present similarities to the Porsenna complex, both in elevation and in the maze-like interior plan.[64] Moreover, the existence of a bronze model (fig. 27) suggests that representations of the nuraghi appeared in smaller transportable art forms outside their region of origin.[65]

In looking for antecedents of Hellenistic monumental built tombs in the sixth century and after, we come finally to Lycia. In this mountainous district of western Asia Minor there is more evidence for 'proto-mausoleum' forms than anywhere else in the Mediterranean region. The early history of Lycia is practically unknown. The region came under Persian domination after 545 BC. The Persian general Harpagos managed to subdue the fiercely fighting Lycians, and at Xanthos killed all the inhabitants of that city saving eighty households ... these eighty families as it chanced were at that time away from the city, and thus they survived.'[66] Following the conquest, Xanthos was largely repopulated by foreigners, a fact suggesting that with the newcomers there came also an influx of new ideas.

The currently available evidence suggests that in Lycian architecture stone construction started to play a more important role only from the middle of the sixth century onwards. This is the time when the first stone tumuli and pillar tombs appeared. Previously timber had been the dominant material; if the wooden hut engraved on the Phaistos disc[67] indicates perhaps a Lycian building type (fig. 28), the forms had remained essentially unchanged since the later Bronze Age. Obviously, in the early stages of the development of cut-stone architecture, forms inherited from wooden construction played an important role. The essential supporting members of stone buildings were cut so that they closely imitated their wooden prototypes. Thus, in the early stages of the transition from timber to stone, there remained a clear visual link with the past, though this link later gradually diminished.[68]

Among the different varieties of Lycian funerary monuments the earliest are the tumuli and pillar tombs. Built house tombs appeared around the second quarter of the fifth century; shortly afterwards the schemes were reproduced in rock-cut architecture. The story is the same with built sarcophagi and their rock-cut versions, the former series starting around 400 BC. It can safely be assumed that all the different types existed simultaneously till about the early third century. Thereafter Greek forms predominated in the architecture of the region.[69]

It should, of course, be remembered that certain Greek decorative and technical elements were found in remote areas of Asia Minor, and farther inland, even in the sixth century. Lycia was no exception in this respect; but the full impact of the western influence was not felt before the end of the fifth century. To judge from the available archaeological evidence, there took place about this time a rather successful combination of local forms and ideas with others imported from the east and the west. One outstanding result of this combination was the Nereid Monument, a 'temple tomb' on a podium, the forerunner of the Mausoleum at Halikarnassos (or what we may call the mausoleum-form of tomb).

Both pillar tombs and sarcophagi can be dismissed as typological predecessors of the Nereid Monument. The pillar tomb, of which there are some thirty known examples, consisted (with a few exceptions) of a tall monolith with a burial chamber and crowning statue(s) on top (fig. 29). The origin of this type is obscure; Mesopotamian stelai, Assyrian obelisks, Persian towers, and high local beehives have all been suggested as prototypes. The existence of (elevated) sarcophagi (fig. 30) cannot be documented before the end of the fifth century; thus, these tombs are more or less contemporary with the Nereid Monument and its successors. Besides, like the pillar tombs, they belong to a typologically different category.

Only the house tombs remain to be considered; and here, indeed, one finds a major component of the later elevated 'temple tombs.' 'Temple tombs' are, in fact, house tombs raised on podia or platforms.[70] In the case of the two earliest, heroon 'G' in Xanthos (fig. 31) and a dynastic tomb in Apollonia (fig. 32), it would, perhaps, be even better to speak of house tombs on terraces. Other house tombs of roughly contemporary date had only a stepped crepidoma for additional height. The superstructure, i.e., the actual house tomb or cella, is basically the same in all examples, and was perhaps derived from Lycian granaries or some other type of native wooden building. The style is easily recognizable by the imitation of projecting log ends and recessed panelling, usually confined to the narrower front and back ends. In all instances the roof consisted of cut stone slabs, whether gabled (Xanthos, 'F' [fig. 33] and 'H' [fig. 34])[71] or of the flat horizontal type (as in heroon 'G' [fig. 35]), excavated and record published by the French in the 1950s and 1960s.[72]

Heroon 'G' occupied a prominent position partly inside the city walls, on a levelled rock surface in the southwest part of the Lycian acropolis. The walls were of ashlar masonry, except the one on the south where the structure formed part of the fortification wall. This section was built of huge blocks, all straight-sided, but some of them polygonal, others four-sided. The built terrace, about 3 m high,[73] formed a platform that covered about 159 m² (15.5 × 10.25 m). The retaining wall of this terrace started out with an orthostate course.[74] The uppermost section of the wall terminates in an unmistakably Greek astragal crowned by two rows of egg-and-dart embellishments. Exactly the same decorative composition crowned the podium of the Nereid Monument, but there the style is more advanced, the eggs are more elongated, and all the contours are better defined.

In the central section of the north side a stair or ramp, parallel to the wall, gave access to the top of the terrace, the outer perimeter of which was presumably lined by statues.[75] On the basis of comparative evidence from the Apollonia tomb, it has recently been suggested that there may have been a chamber within the high terrace of heroon 'G.'[76] The cella or cult building occupied a relatively small portion on the top of the terrace. It had a ground plan of 6.4 × 4.26 m above a one-step elevation. The height of the structure almost 5 m. The walls consisted of neatly fitted ashlars, 'framed' with the typical Lycian imitation of wooden beams and recessed panels. In the interior six free-standing pillars supported the flat Lycian roof, the entablature of which consisted of a row of close-set round 'logs' supporting two fasciae and a taenia.

Opinions are divided about the disposition of the friezes found nearby. Coupel and Metzger place the frieze of the 'coqs et poules' on the lowest section of the cella walls.[77] Some distance above this band they would place another (fig. 36), wider frieze, with a third frieze adorning the interior. In their restored drawing of the building[78] another frieze with a series of animals appears just below the egg-and-dart decoration on the principal east side of the terraced platform. They reject the more common combination of friezes, one immediately above the other, proposed by Bernard for the terrace wall.[79] According to Bernard's scheme, the 'coqs et poules' frieze would come between the larger animal panels and the profiled cornice of the podium.

Two technical features deserve attention: the constant use of dovetail clamps and the refined stoneworking. The latter feature is also found in the dynastic tomb at Apollonia and in several other Lycian buildings. In heroon 'F' the lowest portions of the east sub-basement are still in situ; 'the edges of these ashlars are carefully dressed, being bevelled with an oblique edge ca 1 cm. wide and deep, so that the blocks are separated by a groove ca 2 cm. wide, compared to the ca 5 cm. on the Apollonia tomb. In addition, the faces of the blocks are lined by a smooth margin (drafted edge) ca 5 cm. wide, inside which the surface is at a slightly higher level and seems worked only by a pointed chisel.'[80] As the Danish archaeologists have pointed out, on the basis of the Greek evidence these walls cannot be dated before the early fourth century. However, 'the dated Xanthian walls ... show the Greek evidence to be of doubtful value and use for the dating of the Lycian indigenous walls. We have seen that bevelling was well-known at least as early as ca 460 B.C. and that related oblique edge, which often was used to set a wall of a pillar-tomb off from a foundation or the bed-rock, already is seen c. 480/470 B.C. (the Harpy Tomb).'[81] Both heroon 'G' and the Apollonia complex have been dated on archaeological and comparative evidence to the second quarter of the fifth century.

In heroon 'G' one can already sense the diverse influences that also characterize many of the later more-complex and better-unified designs for the monumental built tombs of the region. One of these influences is Greek, as shown in the decorative details and the technical execution of the complex. The cella building is definitely Lycian. The origin of the terraced podium as well as the subject-matter of the friezes is debatable; they could be either oriental or local. Finally, the overall disposition of the two main elements, consisting of a platform below and a cella above, recalls the design of the Cyrus tomb.

Platforms or podia made of mud brick or ashlar also occur in Attica (and rarely elsewhere) as early as the archaic period. They imitated domestic architecture, but the burial-place lay beneath them, not inside. Built tombs of this type continued into the classical age. They were rarely free-standing and often give the impression of retaining walls built against a hillside. Moreover, these monuments never had a cult building on top or a hyposorion inside. They simply supported grave markers, such as stelai, funerary naiskoi, and vases. The development of the more grandiose peribolos tombs (enclosing a group of graves) does not pre-date the fourth century.[82] Consequently it is hardly conceivable that any of these Attic tombs could have been a formative influence in the development of the elevated 'temple tombs' of western Asia Minor.

Krischen's imaginative and intriguing idea – that we should see the Temple of Nike on the Athenian Acropolis as a possible predecessor for the design of the Nereid Monument – cannot be substantiated in the light of local Lycian evidence.[83] The transporting of this idea to Lycia is highly unlikely, especially because the known Greek contribution to this part of Asia Minor in general and in particular to its architecture was restricted to decorative motifs and workmanship and did not extend to overall composition. Only from the early fourth century onwards can we find a more significant transmission of building forms or frieze subjects to Lycia. Even then, the underlying ideological principles of the new creations, the organization and the combination of units, and their display in Lycian funerary architecture remain in essence non-Greek. The Lycians either misunderstood or did not care to follow the architectural guide-lines and principles employed in fourth-century Greece.

A find from Sardis known as the Pactolus pediment (fig. 37) has introduced a new and puzzling problem into the search for the origin of the broadly defined 'mausoleum' type of burial and, more particularly, of the 'temple tombs.'[84] The white marble pediment (ca 4.6 m long) is preserved in two sections; it represents a funeral banquet. The sloping sides of the pediment were decorated with a bead-and-reel below, and a Lesbian cyma moulding above. The cuttings on top of this cornice were probably for the attachment of a sima. On the basis of its high reliefs, which show a general affinity to the Satrap sarcophagus from Sidon,[85] the pediment has been dated to the third quarter of the fifth century, or more precisely to 430–420 BC. The form and appearance of the rest of the building remain largely unknown, 'it may have been a building in antis, ... what little architectural decoration is left argues for the Ionic order.'[86] The importance of the find is that 'the new pediment indicates that among the Lydian funerary monuments there was represented a type hitherto unknown in the Sardis area, – the mausoleum in the form of a temple-like shrine.'[87] The location of the building is also conjectural, though it was presumably in the same general area where the Pyramid Tomb was found. The find unquestionably adds a new dimension to Lydian funerary architecture, but until more is known about the overall architectural development in the region no conclusions can be drawn.

Here may be mentioned Butler's proposed restoration of a tent-like or triangular built façade above a Lydian chamber tomb (fig. 38).[88] Butler's description of this curious mixed construction is as follows: 'The entrance was approached by a broad flight of four steps composed of well wrought blocks of white limestone. At either end of the steps stood a tall stele, one of which, though perfectly plain in other respects, preserved a part of its ornamental akroterion ... the opening into the tomb chamber is now simply the end of a wide passage with double pitched ceiling; it probably was originally closed with a wall and doorway, since destroyed.'[89] The height of the façade, including the steps, was approximately 4 m, the width without the stelai ca. 2 m. The tomb can be dated ca. 500–480 B.C.'[90] The discovery of the Pactolus pediment certainly seems to support Butler's proposed restoration of a 'pedimental' crown for the façade of this tomb. Presumably the other chamber tombs overlooking the Pactolus valley had similar or perhaps even more elaborate façades: in the light of the advanced stoneworking techniques of Lydia, this situation would not be surprising.

II Rock-cut Tombs

The use of monumental rock-cut tombs with imposing façade was restricted to regions with appropriate geological formations. For smaller rough chambers and rock-cut sarcophagi, or for other architecturally insignificant tombs, irregular rock surfaces were sufficient. However, the overwhelming majority of rock-cut tombs to be discussed below present two-dimensional tomb façades of some architectural pretensions. There are only a few examples where the units are completely free-standing, i.e., not attached to the surrounding rock except at the base.

Although in the construction of built tombs the same methods were applied as in any other built structure, in rock-cut tombs different techniques were required, though the forms often copy built structures. Even if the thrust and support principle existed visually, it was irrelevant technically. First the sites had to be chosen. For groups of tombs where the emphasis was on the façades, extensive vertical rock formations served best. In most instances they provided a picturesque setting, a 'frame' for the funerary monuments. If there were no visible fissures in the rocks, then work could be started. After having outlined the design of the façade and roughly dressed the rock-face, the cutting could proceed from top to bottom. The workmen were lowered from above on ropes. At the appropriate level they erected temporary scaffolding from which to work. Around a number of tombs the square holes that once supported the scaffolding are still visible today.[91] As the unfinished façade of tomb B2 at Kaunos indicates (fig. 39), the work at each level was largely complete before the masons moved to the next lower section. The carving of finer details was probably left to another group of workmen. When the intercolumniations had been completely freed from the back, the hewing out of the pronaos (if there was to be one) and the chamber behind could have begun. P. Roos in his study of the Kaunos tombs has pointed out that 'stucco has been used in several tombs and for different purposes, coating, moulding and fastening.'[92] Furthermore, as in built architecture, painting played an important role.[93] Occasionally, too, painted ornament replaced carving as in the Amyntas tomb at Telmessos[94] or in numerous buildings in Macedonia.

For the treatment of the rock surfaces various tools were used at the different stages of work. First, for the preparation of the tomb site, the pickaxe was employed. This pickaxe was either pointed at both ends or had a flat butt at one end. It was employed to remove large quantities of stone. After this initial stage, points were employed. These long and narrow iron tools of various sizes could be used for both the coarser and the finer treatment of the rock surfaces. The various hammers with their blades (some with teeth) played an important role in making the desired planes, curved or flat. Chisels (pointed, flat, curved, and toothed) usually came in at the last stage of work, often being used to cut out reliefs or other architectural ornaments. Because in rock-cut tombs the finishing polish did not exist, paint was applied to these semi-smooth surfaces. Sometimes the above-mentioned stone-cutting stages were not fully carried out. Interment often took place even before the chiselling stage had been reached; in such cases, with a few exceptions, the façade was never completed.

Historically, the tradition of monumental rock-cut tombs and cult monuments goes back to the Bronze Age. These built structures occur in Egypt (fig. 48) as well as in the Near East. Some of the Hittite rock-cut sanctuaries, such as Yazilikaya, executed in the reign of Hattusili III (1275–1250 BC),[95] are still well preserved today. During the first half of the first millennium BC rock-cut tombs continued in use in Anatolia and the Near East. However, they were never so popular or as elaborate as they became after the custom had been revived by Darius I (521–486) BC). One isolated example has already been mentioned, i.e., the Tomb of the Pharaoh's Daughter of the first temple period in Jerusalem; in addition, Urartian rock-cut monuments also deserve attention.

The purpose of the Urartian chambers hewn out of the rock has only recently been recognized: 'The rock-cut chambers in the precipitous south side of Van citadel ... must be described not as shrines but as tombs.'[96] The three largest belonged to the royal house of Urartu. For the tomb of Angishti I (786–764 BC – the only identifiable one of the three) the entire upper section of a projecting cliff was reshaped. The exterior, with whatever applied architectural embellishments it carried, has completely disappeared. The tomb was approached by steps placed parallel to the cliff face. The interior was decorated with bronze stars of Assyrian pattern similar to those found in some of the Mycenaean beehive tombs.

The monumental Phrygian rock façades are another link, even if indirect, leading to the creation of monumental rock-cut tombs of western Asia

Minor. Their exact use was in question for a long time, though it is now believed that most of them were cult monuments.[97]

The so-called Midas Monument, near Eskişehir (fig. 40), is one of the largest and a typical example.[98] An architectural composition enclosed a relatively small recessed niche, intended for the display of a cult statue (of Kubila or Kybele). A succession of shallow frames enclosed the niche and helped to focus attention on this idol. Carved geometric patterns (mainly variations of the meander motif) cover the entire surface of the façade, which otherwise reproduces the front of a contemporary gabled building. Eighth-century line drawings on wall blocks found at Gordion support this view.[99] It is generally believed that the above-mentioned rectilinear patterns, as ornamental motifs, originated in the minor arts, such as terracotta tiles, textiles, and inlaid woodwork.[100] Here, they are reproduced rather skilfully and on a gigantic scale.

Among the Phrygian rock-cut monuments near Ayazin at Köhnüş the best preserved is the so-called Lion Tomb (fig. 41), locally known as Arslan Taş.[101] That it was definitely a burial-place is shown by the arrangement of the interior chamber. The monument was cut out of a cube of rock 11 m high. The disposition of the two huge lionesses, flanking and symbolically protecting the chamber high above the ground level, recalls the Hittite tradition; but these lionesses are 'more vigorous, more alive, less conventional than the Hittite.'[102]

In connection with these rock-cut monuments a number of observations can be made. The tombs of the group to which the Midas Monument belongs, with their low-pitched gable roofs and the double frames of the door openings showing the ends of cross-beams, all imitate wooden construction. Stone versions of timber buildings are also known from Lycia, but their existence cannot be documented before the end of the sixth century. The idea of possible cross-influences from Lycia to Phrygia, put forward by Akurgal, cannot be maintained from the chronological point of view.[103] E. Haspels also raised this possibility, but dismissed the idea, both on the ground that the styles differ greatly, each being individual and regional, and on account of the geographical separation of the regions.[104] Phrygian façades also demonstrate that free-standing monuments, regardless of their size, could be abstracted from their settings and re-created in their essentials as two-dimensional designs on a vertical rock surface.

The Persians seem to have adopted the form to the exclusion of others. From the time of Darius I to the fall of the Achaemenid dynasty all their royal tombs were rock-cut. It is not known exactly what led Darius I to change the form of the royal burial just introduced by Cyrus. However, the move has to be seen in the context of the new overall approach adopted by Darius I. He re-established the capital at Persepolis, and he also revived old religious and political ideas and applied them with some modifications in his own administration. In monumental architecture Darius I, like Cyrus before him, showed the Achaemenid ability to borrow and adapt features. In the introduction of the new type of funerary architecture it is conceivable that the decorative effect of the large 'spread out' rock-cut monuments (as in the Phrygian façades) was closer to native thinking than the more sophisticated built burials of developed civilizations. Picturesque façades effectively conveyed the idea of the superhuman nature of the king to the majority of the population whose background was rooted in the nomadic tradition. Textiles, metal works, etc. were highly developed in Persia, a heritage shared with the Phrygians, whose territory came under the control of the Achaemenids after the mid sixth century.

No securely dated rock-cut tombs with architectural façades are known before the time of Darius I. However, E. Herzfeld's supposition that the rock-cut tombs in the mountains of Kurdistan belonged to Median or early Achaemenid rulers may possibly be correct.[105]

Of the seven mostly cruciform-like (fig. 42) Achaemenid royal tombs, the earliest, that of Darius I, is securely dated by the inscription.[106] The sacred site of Naqsh-i Rustam was chosen for the tomb. The cutting of the central portion of the 64-m-high cliff started soon after 520 BC.[107] The height of the rock-cut façade is 23 m. The illusionistic composition has three registers. The bottom part (6.8 m high) is left blank. Above that the scheme expands horizontally. Four attached ('Persian') columns with double bull protomes as capitals support visually an Ionic architrave and a dentil course. In the central intercolumniation a doorway with an Egyptian lintel above leads to the hewn interior. The arrangement of this central section probably reflects in a simplified form the front of the Persepolis palace.[108] The top register is equal in width to the section at the bottom and accurately aligned with it but somewhat higher (8.5 m). Here, the king can be seen worshipping before the symbol of his god on a three-stepped pedestal. Opposite him, balancing the design, is a fire altar. The entire composition is raised on a monumental 'throne' supported by thirty figures in two tiers, each figure representing a separate nation.[109] Each tier is topped by a single row of archaic Ionic cyma decoration. The excavators have shown that at least some sections of the façade were painted.[110]

It is easy to realize that the scheme is the translation of a three-dimensional building on to a two-dimensional surface, resulting in a strangely tower-like appearance. For the plain bottom register no acceptable explanation has yet been found. Perhaps the blank zone represents a 'paved approach' to the complex, but now on a vertical surface.[111] The arrangement of the interior of the tomb lies outside the scope of this study; however, it is important to note that new studies suggest Urartian origins for the scheme.[112]

Returning to architectural façades imitating wooden construction, we should note one more series of funerary structures that needs to be discussed in this context, namely, the Phoenicio-Cypriot Royal Tombs at Tamassos on Cyprus.[113] Both the execution of the façades and the interiors show that the reproduction of timber forms in stone architecture was well advanced before the Lycian 'mass production' of such tombs started. Because all the Cypriote monuments are underground tombs and of mixed construction, more detailed discussion will be reserved for them in the following section.

A unique group of three little-known tombs near ancient Phokaia on the coast of western Asia Minor may be discussed here. These tombs were probably executed under Phrygian influence. All of them are dated in recent literature to the fourth century, though on the basis of architectural style they ought to be much earlier.

One of the tombs in question, referred to in literature as Taş Kule (fig. 43a, b, c), is a curiously cut structure of unique design and not readily classified. The date of the tomb, as well as the provenance of the stonemasons and that of the owner, remains a subject of dispute. For example, G. Bean has assigned it to the eighth century, while Akurgal advocates a date in the fourth century.[114] The monument is located in an open, slightly undulating landscape, about 7 km from modern Foça on the way to Izmir. A large outcrop of rock was shaped into the desired form, a rectangle measuring 8.8 × 6.25 m, and rising to a height of 2.5 m on all sides. Around the base of the otherwise vertical faces there are step-like cuttings arranged in an irregular fashion. Three sides were left plain; only the eastern , or principal, façade carried some ornamentation in the form of a slightly recessed false window surrounded by a double frame, the outer of which projects slightly. The top band is crowned by two more horizontal fascia-like bands. The ends of the lower fascia are shaped in a double curve, recalling a flattened cyma-reversa moulding; the upper fascia had ⌂-shaped corners in very low relief that were still visible in the last century.[115]

Corresponding to this 'cornice' section, the other sides, above the level of the main rectangular platform, have a three-stepped base measuring ca 3.1 × 3.4 m on the top step. A fourth step, on top of these, is continuous on all four sides, including the east. This stepped base, approximately 1.3 m high, is surmounted by a solid cube reaching ca 1.9 m in height. Here again steps start of which only two are still in situ with a broken surface above them. The reconstruction of this uppermost section remains conjectural. It may have ended simply in a pyramid or a stepped base surmounted by a phallus stone, as suggested by Bean and others.[116]

The interior of the tomb is reached by a small doorway in the eastern part of the north façade. An elongated forechamber (1.6 × 2.65 m) is followed by the roughly square burial-room opening off the west side of the antechamber and set at a slightly lower level. In this inner room is a sunken rectangular pit, 1.25 × 2.35 m and 1.3 m deep, for the actual burial. Both chambers have flat horizontal ceilings. Around the exterior of the monument there are rather irregular but straight channels that may have served to drain the rain-water. The tomb has been compared to a small village church with its projecting tower.[117] Certainly the play of elements is on the eastern side. It is a 'disturbingly' one-sided, asymmetrical design, both in its details and as a whole.

The other tomb, closer to Eski Foça, is known as Şeytan Hamami (Devil's Bath).[118] It was completely hewn out of the rock. Architecturally, the façade is not imposing. An arched rock-cut doorway, with sides and top stepped inward, gave access to two chambers, slightly off axis, one behind the other (3.00 × 4.12 m and 3.10 × 3.42 m). The inner chamber is entered by another arched doorway; as in the Taş Kule, there is a sunken pit for the burial.[119] In contrast to Taş Kule, the ceiling of this tomb was carved to represent a very low pitched roof.

The date of these tombs is controversial.[120] Architecturally, the complete absence of Greek decoration in fourth-century Ionian tombs is hardly conceivable. Moreover, there are no comparable monuments in the neighbourhood; neither are there any traits in these tombs that can be compared with buildings at Larisa, possibly the origin of the commissioners. Consequently, the source of inspiration must be sought elsewhere. After Harpagos's devastating campaign in the mid sixth century and the ill-fated Ionian revolt of 499–494 BC, Phokaia became impoverished, and never regained its former importance. However, in the decades just before the Persian invasion, Phokaians were famous navigators; and they also founded several colonies in the western Mediterranean, including Massalia, the present-day Marseille. Phokaia was a prosperous city, with contacts all over the Mediterranean world. What its people lacked in their native tradition could be imported from other places; this borrowing could well have included architectural forms and ideas.

In nearby Phrygian territory we find numerous rock-cut monuments ranging in date from the eighth (or even earlier) to the mid sixth century. Large natural rock formations were frequently utilized for the cutting of these Phrygian monuments. For instance, Midas City itself is nothing but a huge rock-cut establishment.[121] The still existing individual structures within the city testify to the great variety of rock-cut forms. Among others, stepped platforms and asymmetrical designs characterize the so-called Altar[122] and Step-Monument 'H.'[123] Window-like niches framed by recessed panels also appear frequently.[124] Phrygian interiors include some examples with flat ceilings, others with sloping sides. Moreover, among the two-roomed schemes we find cases both of axially aligned rooms and of inner rooms at right angles to the outer chambers.[125] These Phrygian parallels certainly suggest that the Ionian tombs under discussion may also have been executed under Phrygian inspiration at some date before the destruction of Phokaia by the Persians in the third quarter of the sixth century. A third Ionian rock-cut tomb of the region is of peculiar design; known as the Tomb of St Charalambos, it deserves mention here (fig. 44a, b). It is located near Manisa at the northeast foot of Mt Sipylus.[126] The imposing structure was created by a simple but clever method. The scheme is adjusted to the natural contours of the sloping hillside. First, a ca 5.7 m-wide dromos was hewn out of the rock all the way from the horizontal platform to the vertical, undecorated façade. The full width of this dromos is occupied by steps leading up to a landing 2.2 m deep, which in turn supports a smaller two-stepped 'crepis' right in front of the doorway of the tomb. The vertical façade rises 3 m above the threshold of this doorway. For the top, or 'roof,' section of the design (if one can speak of such a feature at all in this case), the approximately 45° slope of the hillside was smoothed out. The sloping surface of this 'lean-to roof' measures 9.50 × 6.24 m; it is set off from the surrounding hillside by a trench that marked the extent of the project and at the same time provided drainage.

The two-roomed interior resembles the axial arrangement of the Şeytan Hamami tomb; but the second room has a slightly lower floor level as in the Taş Kule tomb. Also, the opening between the two chambers is not aligned with the outer doorway. Both rooms have curved ceilings.

There is little evidence for the period of construction.[127] As with the other two tombs near Foça, and especially because of the lack of Greek architectural mouldings, it seems safe to assume that the Tomb of St Charalambos was cut under Phrygian influence before the Achaemenid invasion of the region.

All the rock-cut tombs discussed above belong to a period of negligible Greek architectural influence. It is appropriate to include here two groups of rock-cut façade tombs in Paphlagonia (Asia Minor) and in Cyrene (North Africa), in the latter of which, at least, entire schemes were derived from Greek sources. The Paphlagonian and Cyrenaican tombs can be treated as groups because individual examples show few variations in design; most of them follow a stereotyped pattern.

The earliest façade tombs of Paphlagonia can be dated to the early fifth century. They continued to be cut down to imperial times, though with the progress of time they became less and less pretentious architecturally. The façades are flush with the rock surfaces.[128] They all have a columnar treatment with a porch and burial-chamber(s) behind the columns. The façades were often, if not always, crowned by an incised gable and embellished by symbolic carvings in low relief (fig. 45). The number of columns can vary from one, as in the Direklikaya tomb at Alasökü, to a maximum of five, in the Kaya-dibi tomb at Asar;[129] the columns are generally short and heavy in proportion. A few of the columns lack bases; where there is a base, it generally consists of a high torus (or half torus), sometimes with a narrow plinth below. There is little carved detail; one can only agree with von Gall that 'the bases resemble forms known from late Hittite architecture.'[130] Interestingly enough, the type of base remained essentially unchanged, even in tombs that were cut in the late fourth century (i.e., Direklikaya tomb),[131] when Greek influence had become quite widespread in the Mediterranean. Perhaps the only exception is the Gerdek Boğazi tomb at Karakoyunlu,[132] of the late fourth century, where the anta-bases are reminiscent of the Asiatic-Ionic type (fig. 46).

The capitals too rarely have even a suggestion of Greek influence; their prototypes are generally to be sought in wooden architecture imitating simple "plinth" forms. However, once again the capitals of the Gerdek Boğazi tomb at Karakoyunlu (both those of the free-standing columns and those the two antae) show some Greek influence on the native Anatolian style.[133] In the design (palmette forms ending in volutes) there seems to be some reliance on Greek sources, as seen for example in an anta capital from the Hekatomnid Andron at Labraynda.[134] Otherwise, the form finds its closest parallel in the Tomba dei Capitelli at Caere in Etruria.[135] The monotony of plinth-like capitals in a few other instances was replaced by crouching bull figures; this idea was certainly borrowed from Achaemenid architecture.

In most tombs access to the burial chamber(s) was through window-like openings, framed by an embrasure with triple step-backs. Even the outer borders of the façade often show the same treatment.[136] Similar framing has been noted in some of the Phrygian rock-cut monuments mentioned above. This device has a long history prior to its occurrence in the Phrygian and Paphlagonian examples;[137] and the motif was also taken over by Ionic architecture, where we see it in the three-fascia architrave and the triple recessed bands of doorways (e.g., Erechtheion in Athens). As so often, all these schemes seem to have originated in wooden architecture.

The inspiration for the open 'colonnaded' porches remains debatable; however, it seems unlikely that they would have appeared without some knowledge of Greek peripteral or prostyle temple forms.

Much easier to recognize is the source of inspiration for the earliest rock-cut façade tombs in Cyrene.[138] They all show principles that are in general derived from Greek architecture. All the early, and rather roughly executed, façade-tombs occur in the northern necropolis, along the road to ancient Apollonia. Of these eight tombs standing side by side and numbered N_2–N_9 from east to west, the three easterly ones have pillars across the front of the porch, while the others have columns (fig. 47). They are similar in size: their width varies between 3 m and 5.5 m, and their height from 2.8 m to 3.3 m. Seven of the tombs have three supports between the side walls; there is only one example with a distyle in antis disposition. It is notable that in the original form of the local temple of Zeus (variously dated from 540 to 450 BC),[139] we find a tristyle in antis arrangement in the opisthodomus, and the possibility cannot be excluded that the tomb designers derived the idea from the plan of the temple – if in fact the latter belongs to the second half of the sixth century. The capitals of N_2–N_4 are Aeolic, N_8 is Ionic, and the rest (N_5–N_7 and N_9) are of the Doric order. All the column shafts are fluted, though the flutes are not regular in number.[140]

The rectangular burial-chambers were entered by a single door, more or less in the centre of the back wall. The interiors have been recut over the centuries; thus the original plans can hardly be determined.

In all but one of the tombs the section above the columns consists of nothing but a flat architrave; only N_8 has its carved pediment preserved. Presumably in all the other tombs the pediments were separately cut and attached to the entablature and could, thus, be easily carried off and reused.

The front of Tomb N_5 is raised on a two-stepped base, while Tombs N_6 and N_7 have a low narrow platform in front of the columns. In N_2–N_4 and N_9 the walls of the porches are lined with rock-cut benches, providing seating for visitors.[141]

For the date of the tombs the best clues are offered by the decoration. The most ornate, and probably the latest, of the group is Tomb N_8. The Ionic capitals have large archaic volutes, placed quite far apart. The slightly concave spirals of the volutes are connected by a canalis of archaic style, convex in profile with a sagging lower edge. A Lesbian cyma ornament embellishes the abacus of the capitals. In their main characteristics the capitals are certainly comparable to the capital of the so-called Column of the Sphinx in Cyrene, or with that of the Column of the Naxians in Delphi.[142] Yet the closest parallel to the Cyrene design seems to be an early fifth-century capital found at Halikarnassos;[143] a similar date is possible for

Tomb N_8,[144] Noteworthy are the Aeolic capitals of the pillars in Tombs N_2–N_4. They consist of two close-set volutes with concave channels, with a plant motif springing up in the centre of the capitals from the point where the spirals meet. These capitals are a rare type; perhaps the closest parallel to them is a capital from Eressos on the island of Lesbos. According to P. Betancourt, the date of the Eressos capital is problematical; it has been assigned to 'the sixth century B.C. (presumably in the second half) ... but an even later time is possible.'[145] The same type of Aeolic capital was found not far from Cyrene in a rock-cut sanctuary at Ain Hofra.[146] This capital, along with those of Tombs N_2–N_4, can also be dated to the second half of the sixth century, making them the earliest of the group. The Doric tombs should probably be dated somewhere between N_2–N_4 and N_8 (the Ionic tomb).

These eight façade-tombs, with a columnar treatment in front of the porch and with other Greek features, are the earliest known examples of their kind in the Mediterranean region. Cyrene was founded in 631 BC[147] by Dorian colonists from the island of Thera, who brought with them no established architectural tradition. It is likely that many of the earliest buildings of the new colony were at least partly built of wood. Cyrene was renowned for its hard and weather-resistant thyine wood; according to Theophrastos, 'Thyon, which some call thya, grows near the Temple of Zeus Ammon and in the district of Cyrene ... there is abundance of it where now the city stands, and men can still recall that some of the roofs in ancient times were made of it.'[148] However, within a few decades cut stone seems to have become the preferred building material in the city. One would expect that the strongest architectural influence would come from other Dorian regions, i.e., the Peloponnesos, the Dorian islands, and the Dorian settlements of southwestern Asia Minor; the two latter areas, of course, were increasingly subject to Ionian influences. The Aeolic capitals of Tombs N_2–N_4 and the Ionic capital of N_8 no doubt indicate such influence, though there are in the islands and in Asia Minor no known rock-cut façade-tombs of the sixth century that are analogous to those at Cyrene. The Persian royal tombs could have been known to Cyrenaican architects, especially because the district, along with Egypt and Libya, became the sixth satrapy of Persia during the reign of Arkesilaos III, ca 530–510 BC: however, these Persian tombs, as we have seen, are different in concept. In Greek architecture the building types closest to the Cyrene tombs are treasuries (e.g., the Massalian Treasury at Delphi) and shrines. Among other possible models outside the Greek sphere, the rock-cut tomb façades at Beni Hassan in Egypt (fig. 48), executed during the Twelfth Dynasty, 2000–1785 BC, seem to be the closest to the Cyrenaican rock-cut façades.[149] Cyrene had connections with Egypt all through its history; thus these early façade-tombs could be Greek versions of much earlier Egyptian models.

III Tumuli and Underground Tombs

Tumuli, because of their exterior form, constitute a separate category of funerary architecture. Structurally, tumuli, like underground tombs without visible exterior forms, can be constructed of different materials or can be rock-cut.

In describing the territory of Pheneos in Arkadia, Pausanias remarks: 'The grave of Aipytos I was especially anxious to see, because Homer in his verses about the Arkadians makes mention of the tomb of Aipytos. It is a mound of earth of no great size, surrounded by a circular base of stone.'[150] Obviously he is describing a simple type of tumulus; nevertheless, the form of all these circular earth mounds was basically the same, regardless of their size. Pausanias, who was probably a native of Magnesia-ad-Sipylum, must have seen in his native Lydia much more imposing tumuli, erected many centuries before his time. He also could have seen grandiose earth tumuli in the Roman Empire, where such mounds were no longer a novelty. Like the other major tomb-types, tumulus burials also had their periods of popularity, depending on the region and the times. In the Aegean, the most notable pre–Iron Age tumuli were the Mycenean beehive, or tholos, tombs and Trojan tumuli. In the eighth and seventh centuries a new upsurge of tumulus construction began in regions such as south Russia, Anatolia, Etruria, and the lands north of the Aegean.

In Phrygia the most significant concentration of tumuli (approximately one hundred) is to be found around Gordion, but the existence of the same type is also noted elsewhere in Anatolia, for instance at Ankara.[151] The Phrygian tumuli are in open terrain, not on hillocks or mountainsides. Only about half of the known mounds at Gordion have been explored. Certain features are common to them all. The so-called Great Tumulus incorporates all the characteristics of the smaller mounds, but naturally on a more imposing scale (fig. 49). Because of erosion, the tumulus is at present only 53 m in height but close to 300 m in diameter; 'the original diameter of the mound must have been about 250 m, and its height 70 to 80 m.'[152] The excavation of the mound started in the 1950s, after initial technical difficulties were overcome.[153] A tunnel was dug into the mound from ground level, creating a modern 'dromos' that was no part of this or any other Phrygian tumulus. In the case of the Great Tumulus, the tomb is built above ground level, rather than in a sunken shaft as in other known examples; it occupies roughly the centre of the artificial hill. Inside, concentric rings of different materials ensured the safety of the tomb chamber up to our times (fig. 50). The first protective inner 'belt' consists of a built wall, ca 3 m high and 0.8 m thick, of limestone blocks. About 2.5 m further on towards the tomb chamber, another wall of eight wooden logs – in alternating courses of two smaller and two larger logs of juniper (or cedar) – rose to a height of about 2.5 m. The space between the logs and the outer limestone construction was filled by rubble that was removed during the excavations. At 0.3 m inside the log-wall is another wall of precisely squared and fitted beams of pine that forms the enclosure of the actual tomb.[154] Except for the outer rubble filling, no clamps or any other artificial bonding was used to hold the whole structure together. The logs are carefully finished inside, with imperfections removed and the holes filled with stones. The tomb chamber measures 6.2 × 5.15 m, and 3.25 m in height up to the beginning of the double-sloped roof. The ends, connected by cross-beams, form triangular gables. According to the excavators, 'the roof is double, with an outer layer of round logs overlying the inner layer of squared timbers.'[155] Above that, 'an attempt was made to relieve, or rather to spread, the downward pressure of the stone mass by laying a series of long parallel logs in the rubble immediately above the ridge of the tomb-roof, at right angles to it and to its entire length. Above these, stones were piled to a depth of almost three meters, assuming the shallow dome-shaped mass natural to such a pile of loose stone. Over this again the clay of the tumulus was piled to a height of nearly forty meters.'[156] There was no door leading to the burial-place; thus it is assumed, no doubt correctly, that the walls enclosing the chamber had already reached the level of the roof before the interment took place. The rest of the mound was then built by piling materials toward the centre. The construction shows experience in building the wooden chamber and the tumulus above it.[157]

Despite the intact state of the burial-chamber in the Great Tumulus, the commissioner and the date of construction remain controversial. Obviously this tomb, and all others of similar nature, were intended to be used only once. The size of the Great Tumulus indicates that it was built by a king in a time of prosperity, in all likelihood before the Kimmerian assault on the Phrygian capital in the early years of the seventh century. R.S. Young assumed that the tomb was that of King Gordios and not of Midas. The latter was killed during the Kimmerian raids on Phrygia; 'since Midas was already on the throne in 717 his predecessor must have been dead and buried; our tomb then, must be dated before 717 at the earliest, and probably in the years between 725 and 720 B.C.'[158] Akurgal takes note of Young's suggestion, but says 'this date hardly agrees with the age of the Assyrian and Urartian objects found among the grave offerings.'[159] He concludes, therefore, 'that the great tumulus must be that of king Midas, who probably died in 696 B.C.'[160] Yet he assigns the Urartian cauldrons and the bronze situla found in the tomb to the Sargonid period (721–705 BC), a date that does not exclude the possibility that such objects were already used during the last years of Gordios's rule. The difficulty in connecting the tomb with Midas arises, of course, from the extent of the Kimmerian destruction. The question must remain unsolved till more is known about the chronology of the early Phrygian Kingdom.[161]

The Lydian necropolis at Bin Tepe near Sardis makes an impression similar to that of the Gordion countryside. The landscape is dominated by artificial mounds (over a hundred in number) of various sizes. However, in contrast to their Phrygian counterparts these tumuli, or at least the larger ones, have a stone crepidoma, a built dromos, tomb chamber(s) of neatly fitted ashlars, and a mound interspersed with chips of limestone. There is also evidence that many of them had grave markers on the summit.

Some of the most imposing of these mounds were noted by ancient authors. For the Ephesian Hipponax (second half of the sixth century), they seem to have been landmarks.[162] On his way to the west coast of Asia Minor he takes note of them briefly 'by the road to Smyrna; go through Lydia past the mound of Attales, the tomb of Gyges ... and the marker and memorial of Tos ... turning your belly to the setting sun.'[163]

Herodotus was just as impressed by the largest of the mounds, the tumulus of Alyattes (610–560 BC), as he was by the Egyptian pyramids. He gives a fairly detailed account of the tomb: 'Lydia does not have many marvels worth mentioning like any other country, except the gold dust brought down from Tmolus. But there is one piece of work which is more enormous than any excepting those of Egypt and Babylon. There is the tomb of Alyattes, father of Croesus; its retaining wall is built of large stones, and the rest of the tomb is a mound of earth. The merchants, the craftsmen, and the prostitutes built it, and five markers, on which written characters recorded the work contributed by each, survived till my day atop the tomb ... The circumference of the tomb is six stades and two plethra, and its breadth is thirteen plethra. A great lake is nearby the tomb which the Lydians say is ever full, and it is called Gygaean.'[164]

It is difficult to translate the ancient measurements into metres because the values of plethron and stadion are not known exactly.[165] However, a general correspondence can be deduced from the figures given by Herodotus and those of H. Spiegelthal;[166] the diameter at the base of the retaining wall (which has since been removed by stone robbers) was 355.20 m, the calculated circumference 1115.32 m and the height 61.46 m.

Strabo, relying on Herodotus, also draws attention to the tomb, but seemingly stresses its socio-economic background: 'The tombs of the kings are located close by Lake Coloe. Directly opposite Sardis itself is the great mound of Alyattes built within a high retaining wall by the city's populace, as Herodotus says. Prostitutes contributed most of the work, and Herodotus says that all Lydian women prostituted themselves; some call the tomb itself a monument to prostitution.'[167] Obviously the lake in Strabo is that known today as Marmara Gölü.

The re-examination of the Alyattes mound conducted by G.M.A. Hanfmann in the early 1960s could do no more than confirm the results of Spiegelthal's work, and make a few additional observations.[168] The complex could have started soon after Alyattes came to power in 610 BC. The known nucleus, about 30 m off-centre, consists of a marble antechamber and the marble chamber behind it. The former measure 2 × 2.24 m and 2.5 m in height, while the latter is 3.34 × 2.37 m and 2.08 m high. The masonry shows a very high quality of proficiency for seventh-to-sixth-century Lydia. 'The astonishing feature of the monument is the complete mastery of huge marble masonry fitted with hairbreadth precision ... the joints are razor sharp.'[169] The north or rear end of the main chamber has a double wall. Here, according to Hanfmann, a large iron clamp is still visible in the wall.[170] The block above the entrance weighs approximately sixteen tons. Another interesting observation of the reinvestigation of the mound is a sort of corbelled vault northwest of the chamber,[171] perhaps a relieving triangle over another room. There are other features inside the mound that suggest the existence of more structures within, but this possibility can only be confirmed by future investigations.

Above the ceiling of the main burial-chamber a thick layer of oak ashes was found, suggesting cremation rites. It indicates that the mound could have been completed only after the death of its commissioner. This would explain the extensive V-shaped built section and platform on the summit of the tomb.[172]

The excavation of the other mounds, including the second largest, that of the Gyges (680–645 BC) mentioned by Hipponax and Nicander,[173] has confirmed the advanced architectural techniques employed elsewhere in Lydian constructions. The mound was excavated by an American team in the 1960s.[174] Neither the burial-chamber nor its dromos was ever found; however, the identity of the commissioner has been ascertained. A dozen signs have been found carved into the wall of the crepidoma, referring to a certain GUGU, i.e., Gyges, who died near Sardis fighting against the Kimmerians.

The artificial hill, apart from chunks of limestone, consists of a combination of hard red and softer greenish clay. Rather remarkable is the crepis wall, forming a circle of about 210 m.[175] The original ring of stones is well preserved (fig. 51a, b), thanks to the fact that it was covered over in the later seventh century, when the mound was enlarged. It comprises two courses of rectangular ashlar masonry (almost 2 m high) and a huge round 'bolster' course on top. The arrangement is reminiscent of the retaining walls of tumuli built in Etruria. The masonry is advanced, not the work of first-generation masons. Its subtleties can be especially well observed where the round 'bolsters' meet. The central portion of each block is rusticated, with a drafted margin all around, while the joints have bevelled edges. As noted above, this technique reappeared (probably under Lydian influence) in the fifth century in Lycia.

Many of the other tumulus tombs show additional technical virtuosity. A smaller-scale tomb, possibly that of a nobleman, has a room in which the faces of the side walls incline inward slightly from floor to ceiling, especially in the uppermost of their height.[176] In another sixth-century tomb⊓ - shaped iron clamps were leaded into cuttings with triangular or circular heads.[177] In this tomb vertical anathyrosis is also found. In two other tombs one finds features that recur in the Belevi tumulus.[178] One of these is a chamber tomb of the sixth (or early fifth) century with a ceiling block that has a semi-circular hole in the centre, just as in one of the chambers in the Belevi mound. Presumably libations were poured into the interior through this opening. In the other sixth-century tomb triangular slabs were found, indicating a roofing system similar to that employed in the forechamber of the Belevi tumulus. If these observations are correct, a sixth-century date for the initial construction period of the Belevi mound cannot be excluded.[179]

Near Old Smyrna (modern Bayrakli) are the ruins of the so-called Tomb of Tantalos (fig. 52a, b).[180] The tumulus survived through the ages in a good state of preservation until the nineteenth century, when Texier, in order to examine the interior, destroyed it.[181] This monumental tomb, despite its smaller scale, ranks with the Great Tumulus at Gordion and the Alyattes tomb at Bin Tepe.

In this instance we are dealing with a mound entirely of stone, built on the summit of a rocky hill. Pausanias, in his frequent references to the west coast of Asia Minor, twice makes brief mention of the tomb of Tantalos: 'The grave of him who legend says was son of Zeus and Pluto – is it worth seeing – is on Mount Sipylos. I know because I saw it.'[182] Later he returns to the region: 'There is a lake called after Tantalos and a famous grave, and on a peak of Mount Sipylos there is a throne of Pelops.'[183]

The form of the edifice, as known from Texier's drawings, indicates a tumulus-like construction. It is almost as high (27.6 m) as wide (29.6 m in diameter). One can conceive of the construction as an enormous Mycenaean tholos or beehive tomb stripped of its exterior earth filling. In Texier's drawings the tumulus appears as a perfect circle of 33.6 m in diameter (or 106.53 m in circumference) with the tomb chamber in the centre. Miltner re-examined the ruins and gives 14.8 m for the radius (i.e., 29.6 m across).[184] The plan is oval, rather than circular, and the tomb chamber is somewhat off-centre, to the southwest.

The rectangular built chamber (3.55 × 2.17 m and 2.85 m high) has no dromos. It is corbel-vaulted, recalling Bronze Age designs of similar nature as has been recognized by Akurgal.[185] To these could be added the use of corbelling in the walls of Boğazköy, the corbel-vaulted passages at Tiryns and Mycenae, and the more contemporary tomb interiors in Etruria, such as the Cucumella at Gajolo in St Giulian and the late seventh-century Cucumella at Vulci.[186] The system also resembles the chamber of a tumulus tomb near Ephesos.[187] The course above the apex of the vault (and only this part) is fastened with dovetail clamps, the type noted in the Alyattes mound.

A series of protective concentric rings of different-sized stones enclosed the nucleus, ensuring the solidity of the structure.[188] The system of cross-walls meeting the radial sections extends all the way to the outer perimeter. Smaller stones were packed between these ribs to create a closely fitting 'web.' The idea of protective layers around the tomb chamber is found, as we have seen, in Phrygian tumuli; but there the concept was less sophisticated. In the tomb of Tantalos the exterior of the entire mound was faced with closely jointed polygonal stones. The cylindrical section at its base and top carried a profiled moulding, while the summit was crowned by a phallus stone.

Legend, supported by the passage of Pausanias quoted above, connects the tomb with the name of Tantalos: 'Tantalos is vaguely linked with the Hittite stage of culture, not only by his supposed approximate date (1300 B.C.) but by three traditions connecting him with Mt. Sipylos,' states Cadoux.[189] Certainly the tomb is much later, but probably still the first and largest in a series of some forty tumuli on the southeast slopes of the same mountain. The proposed dates, because of the lack of small finds, range from the seventh to the fourth century.[190] The masonry is certainly in the tradition that can be seen in some of the fortification walls erected before the Lydian destruction of Old Smyrna in 600 BC.[191] In addition, the seventh-century corbel-vaulted fountain house of Old Smyrna provides another obvious comparison, this time with the tomb chamber.[192] The presence of dovetail clamps makes the problem more difficult, because they 'appear to have been unknown in the Smyrna temple buildings of the end of the seventh century B.C.'[193] The mouldings of the cylindrical part do not provide a useful criterion for dating; nevertheless, their presence is remarkable just by their existence. Akurgal leaves the question of date open (either the end of the seventh or the second quarter of the sixth century). From the historical point of view, the later seventh-century date would appear more likely, for it was in this period that the city of Old Smyrna experienced its greatest prosperity.

As the sixth century advanced, tumulus burials seemingly became the most popular form of monumental funerary architecture around the Mediterranean. Their existence is documented in regions as far apart geographically as Illyria in the north, Olbia in the northeast, Etruria in the west, Cyrene on the north coast of Africa, and Attica in mainland Greece.[194]

Tumuli built entirely of ashlar were rather rare. A well-preserved example of the type is to be found on the island of Corfu.[195] From the inscription carved on the monument we know that it is the cenotaph of Menekrates (fig. 53), son of Tlasias, a citizen of Oianthia, a locality on the north coast of the Corinthian Gulf. The epitaph also tells us that Menekrates died in a shipwreck, and that the monument was erected by his brother Praximenes and the people of Corfu to honour his service to the islanders. The letter-forms of the Corinthian alphabet date the cenotaph with reasonable certainty to around 600 BC.[196] The structure, built of hard limestone, stands on a one-stepped socle. Five courses of masonry, of equal height and inclined inward 2.25°, form the drum section (4.69 m in diameter). The fifth course, with the inscription, contains the longest blocks. The slabs of the 'cornice,' approximately 1.4 m above ground level, project slightly. The present flattened dome is modern, but the original was probably similar to it, at least as far as one can tell from drawings of 1843, when the cenotaph was excavated.[197] The archaic statue of a crouching lion, found 7 m from the edifice, was in all likelihood the crowning feature of another funerary monument. There are no close parallels to the tomb from the archaic period, only from later times.[198]

A so-called Rundbau, recently reconstructed from spolia (fig. 56a, b) found in the Dipylon area of the Athenian Kerameikos and elsewhere, is a further development of the above-described type.[199] According to Koenigs the structure was approximately 5.5 m high. The base of the round building consisted of a two-stepped platform, topped by a 0.35-m-high torus. A slightly tapering drum (8.4 m in diameter at the base and 8.16 m at the top), presumably of five courses each 0.48 m high and of double thickness, constituted the main body of the cylindrical structure. The entablature consisted of a Doric frieze and a geison separated by a high Lesbian cyma. The roof was probably a very low conical dome. In the architectural composition and decoration Gruben sees a mixture of Ionic and Aeolic forms that were transmitted to Athens by Ionian workmen in the early years of the

Peisistratid rule.[200] The function of the building was similar to that of the Corfu tumulus: it was probably a cenotaph-heroon. Koenigs, in dealing with this 'rundbau,' echoes earlier views, according to which the 'Kuppel-gräber' (the corbel-domed tombs) disappeared at the end of the Mycenaean period in Greece, while the tumulus form survived.[201] In the archaic period circular buildings, even if not exclusively so used, became more and more frequently and closely associated with hero cults. As a matter of fact, in the Menekrates monument and in this Athenian rundbau we may have a transitional step from tumulus towards the creation of later tholoi. The underlying concept of the type becomes more evident in the fully developed tholoi, in which columns (borrowed from temple architecture) encircle the building. In such tholoi the idea of a temple is united with a tomb building to honour the heroes, who as mortals, became god-like. With the increase of hero cults in the classical period and later, the circular buildings became more and more sophisticated structures.[202] Their interiors could serve for different purposes, such as the display of statues or places for holding rituals. The rather austere exteriors of the sixth century changed in a generation or two into fields for architectural decorations, often with columns (as noted above) around the 'cella' walls. The original concept of the tumulus, as an impressive structure mainly because of its huge mass, was lost in the built tholoi.[203] Earth tumuli recalling the form of Phrygian or Lydian mounds continued to be erected throughout the Hellenistic period, along with built tholoi, but on a smaller scale. The subsequent history of the tumulus and the tholos, from the time when they became separated in the archaic age, cannot be traced here, simply because of the sheer quantity of the material.[204] However, it is interesting to note that the two concepts were once more revitalized and united in imperial Rome.[205]

Finally, a unique group of archaic tombs, noted before, is included here. At Tamassos in central Cyprus a number of built (sandstone) Royal Tombs have been excavated. All of them are underground burials, with no traces of a tumulus above them.[206] The most elaborate example of the group is known as Royal Tomb v (fig. 57). The entrance to this complex is reached by a stepped dromos, approximately 6 m long and widening toward the bottom. The walls flanking the dromos show fine workmanship, with carefully jointed ashlar blocks; the technique was to 'frame' large slabs, set upright as stretchers, by others laid either flat or upright as headers.

The façade is a rare feature in underground tombs and tumuli; the most notable buried tomb façades in the Aegean before this Cyprus group were those of the so-called Treasury of Atreus (fig. 58) and the Tomb of Clytemnestra at Mycenae. In later times the series of the so-called Macedonian tombs, starting in the later fourth century, employed a similar concept of burial.

The origins of the well-preserved Tamassian Royal Tombs have long been recognized; the group shows forms that recall the workmanship of a carpenter.[207] In Tomb v a three-fascia stepped-back frame encloses the door opening. Above that appears a plain lintel topped by a heavy dentil course. The gabled ceiling of the interior did not extend all the way to the entrance (unless it was indicated in paint?), as it does in Royal Tomb xi.[208] A singular treatment characterizes the sides of the entrance porch. Here heavy pilasters, one on each side, are crowned by Phoenicio-Cypriot capitals with a single 'Aeolic' volute. As P. Betancourt observes, 'Phoenician influence in the style seems certain ... It seems quite likely that the Phoenicians often used wooden Aeolic pilasters at the entrances of important buildings. Whether they are to be taken as decorations on the inner facings of antae or as simple doorjambs is not clear from the nature of the evidence. Either use is possible, since the structural origins would be the same – a wooden facing to strengthen and protect the ends of mud-brick walls and give needed support for a heavy wooden beam. The ceiling beams, visible ... as dentils, would then be laid across this horizontal member. Most of the surviving examples of the system used gable roofs.'[209]

In the antechamber there were two false doors opening in the side walls; it is interesting that even the locking system of contemporary doors has been precisely carved in the stone. There is a small sunken panel, serving as a false window, over the door leading to the actual funeral chamber; 'the sills of the windows are carved with elaborate sacred trees, a motif familiar from both Phoenician and Cypriote art.'[210] The second interior chamber had plain walls without any carved or illusionistic devices. Whether it was painted or not remains unknown. The saddle roof of both chambers is constructed of huge slabs resting on the side walls and leaning against each other. Certainly the pressure of the earth above was needed to keep the roof in place.[211] The inner surfaces of the slabs were carved to represent round logs, with a moulded beam running along the ridge-line of the roof. Members imitating timber work are often found in the tomb interiors of Etruria; and the same system can now be documented in archaic Asia Minor, in a tomb at Soma.[212]

Royal Tomb v and most of the others of the same series can be dated to the first half of the sixth century.[213]

3

The Development of Tomb Structures in Asia Minor from the Nereid Monument Onwards

As indicated in the previous chapter, there were many divergent tendencies in large-scale funerary architecture prior to the fourth century. Initially, the dominant type seems to have been the huge tumulus tomb. With the Phrygians and Persian there developed a new interest in rock-cut tomb architecture. Attempts were also made to erect monumental built tombs of cut stone; however, no really successful type of built funerary monument appeared before the end of the fifth century. At this time a special combination of circumstances helped to produce in western Asia Minor a type of built tomb that soon became very popular both there and elsewhere. The development of this new type of structure was evolutionary rather than revolutionary. It took centuries of experimentation with different types of grave monuments before a new form was created that was both grandiose and expressive in terms of architectural structure and sculptural decoration.

The achievement of such a satisfactory solution required a favourable political atmosphere. From the point of view of this study, the most important political development in the Mediterranean world was the Greek success in checking the westward advance of Persia. This hard-won victory must have greatly enhanced the reputation of the mainland Greeks in the eyes of the peoples of Asia Minor that remained under Persian domination. In Attica it also led to the spectacular building program on the Athenian acropolis.

Nevertheless, funerary architecture for the time being remained bound to earlier traditions, for funerary customs do not change overnight. This adherence to inherited forms is found in all regions. In Lycia, for particular religious reasons, interment above ground was the dominant custom, and the same was true in Persia. The function of the tomb building, however, was not so much to elevate the body (which in fact was often placed in a hyposorion, barely if at all above ground level), but rather to surround it with a glorified setting that could be expressed in clear visual forms. The Lycian pillar tombs are a good example of such an approach (fig. 29). The eastern idea of heroization after death, known to the Lycian nobles through Persian influence, seems to have appealed to Lycian rulers. They, too, wished to be venerated after their earthly existence as semi-divine heroes.

Thanks to their geographical location the Lycians also had connections with the Greek world. They must have had some knowledge of Greek temple architecture and the reasons for its existence, even if the true nature of Greek sacred buildings was not quite clear to them. In any case they welcomed Greek ideas, which were to their liking. Thus, as the Peloponnesian War dragged on in Greece, they readily opened their territories to refugees from the west. A number of the people who found shelter and employment in Lycia were craftsmen and artisans, whose activities were usually restricted by war. Acceptance of them created a situation that was favourable for modifications and new developments in various fields, including that of funerary architecture.

Tumuli, regardless of their size, could not adequately express the visual message that local rulers wanted to convey; they remained essentially 'silent' monuments. Rock-cut tombs were too restrictive in the choice of location. Only built structures could have all the qualities needed to fulfil the overall aims of the Lycian nobles. The majestic Greek temple form, especially if elevated well above ground and sumptuously decorated, was undoubtedly one that attracted attention: it was precisely what these well-to-do nobles wanted. They wished to remain part of the community after their death, in the same dominant position that they had enjoyed during their lifetimes. We now turn to the first known structure that fully expressed these ideas.

1 The Nereid Monument at Xanthos

This Xanthian structure was designed in accordance with Lycio-Persian customs, but clearly under Greek influence. It stands on a rocky hillside about 200 m west of the acropolis of Xanthos (fig. 59). It was set in a (walled) enclosure, and rose to a height of about 13.5 m.[1] The lower part of the rectangular podium, 6.80 × 10.17 m, consisted of limestone blocks, above which were three courses of marble; the two upper courses were carved with sculptural friezes.[2] On the larger lower frieze were generalized combat scenes. The smaller upper band depicted the siege and surrender of a city. A meticulously executed astragal, a double row of egg-and-dart, and a plain narrow band formed the crown of the high podium (fig. 60). In the interior

of the podium, almost 3 m above ground level, was a rectangular chamber
(fig. 61), accessible by way of a ramp leading from the paved platform of
the northern side of the tomb.

Above the podium stood a small peripteral Ionic temple, which, in contrast
to the high tower-like lower part, is purely Greek in concept (fig. 62). There
were four columns on the shorter east and west façades, six along the north
and south sides (fig. 63). The columns were 3.04 m tall, with monolithic
shafts of twenty flutes each; the height was eight times the lower diameter
while the intercolumniations measured 2.06 m on the shorter and 1.91 m
along the longer sides. The capitals imitated, though in a simplified form,
those of the Athenian Erechtheion, while the bases were of the Asiatic-Ionic
type, i.e., a double scotia topped by a torus but without the plinth. The
four-cornered, or diagonal, capitals at the corners are among the earliest
known examples of the type.[3] Nereids, or Aurae (sea breezes), stood in the
wide intercolumnar spaces, giving a certain flamboyance to the otherwise
conventional Ionic framework. Free-standing statues here appear for the
first known time in the intercolumnar spaces of a building of Greek form.[4]

The 'cella' within the peristyle of this upper structure contained four
kline beds, placed in pairs along the longer walls. From the 'cella' there were
doors giving access to the porches (the 'pronaos' and 'opisthodomos') at
each end. The elaborately carved lintels, framed by consoles, again betray
the influence of the Erechtheion. The necks of the anta capitals had rosettes
in relief, a widely used motif on the later rock-cut tombs of Asia Minor.[5]

The outer faces of the cella walls were crowned with a decorative frieze,
which dealt with such funerary themes as banquets and sacrifices. The
ceiling of the pteron and the naos consisted of three different sizes of marble
coffers, decorated with floral and figure designs. The architrave over the
peristyle was carved with a fourth frieze depicting hunting scenes; above
this frieze was a row of large dentils, surmounted by a cornice and a lion-
head sima. The gabled roof had an unusually heavy covering of stone tiles
(fig. 65). The west pediment contained a schematized combat scene between
horsemen and foot-soldiers; in the east pediment the dynastic couple were
shown seated among their attendants (fig. 66). This latter theme recalls the
east frieze of the Parthenon, or even the east frieze of the Athena Nike
temple in Athens. Large figured acroteria crowned the gables. As symbolic
guardians of the tomb, lions and sphinxes were also included in the ornamental scheme, but their place in the overall design is not clear.

The appearance of the monument, as reassembled in the British Museum
(fig. 67), is stylistically quite heterogeneous. The artists who worked on
this tomb were obviously familiar with the architecture both of the Ionian
coast and of the Greek mainland; in particular, they had a firsthand acquain-

tance with Athenian buildings, such as the Nike and Ilissos temples and the Erechtheion. Nevertheless, here on Lycian soil the rigid Greek temple form underwent a considerable change. The adaptation of the temple to serve as a tomb involved modification of a typical temple design, as a result of which only the 'distorted' outlines of an Ionic temple remain. The notion of constructing a tower-like grave monument, which at the same time served as a commemorative building, was Perso-Lycian.

The technical details of the building also display a mixture of indigenous Lycian and imported Greek traditions. In the limestone foundation the Lycian system of jointing was employed, except for the two top courses, where double-T clamps of Greek type were used. The door structures of the cella were Lycian, but the decoration was Greek. Furthermore, the sima on the north flank was Lycian in shape, that on the south was Greek.[6] In the stoneworking technique one can see either Ionian or Lydian influences. In course 'B,' still in situ, the vertical edges of the ashlar blocks are slightly bevelled; and the perimeter of each block has a smooth margin enclosing the rusticated central part. Such combinations indicate the mixed background of the artists who worked on the monument; yet its commissioner in all likelihood belonged to the local aristocracy.[7] The monument can be dated to the early decades of the fourth century.[8]

II Heroon at Limyra

The new form of tomb represented by the Nereid Monument became very popular in Asia Minor and elsewhere. One of the first of the series of later large-scale tombs was the heroon at Limyra, also in Lycian territory.[9] This building was discovered in 1966 on a rocky terraced promontory, 218 m above sea level, on the lower level of the acropolis of Limyra (fig. 68). The excavation of the complex was undertaken between 1969 and 1971. The site commands a spectacular view of the surrounding region. The actual tomb building, 6.8 × 10.4 m on plan was situated within an ample rock-cut temenos, 19 m wide and 18 m deep. Even after the structure had been destroyed by earthquake many of the scuputral and architectural fragments remained on the site because of the difficult terrain, making an accurate reconstruction possible (fig. 69).

The podium, 3.8 m high and built of large neatly fitted ashlar blocks, was placed on a slightly projecting base course (0.5 m high) laid immediately above the rock surface. Within this podium there was a hyposorion that could be approached through an opening from the south or main façade. According to the excavators there was (in contrast to the Nereid Monument) no relief decoration on the podium, which was crowned by a simple cyma reversa moulding.

For the superstructure the designer chose the amphiprostyle plan used in the late fifth-century Ilissos and Nike temples at Athens.[10] Instead of columns, four karyatids, (2.8 m tall), set on circular bases (0.9 m high), supported an Ionic entablature at the narrow east and west ends of the building (fig. 70). The composition is strongly reminiscent of the Karyatid Porch of the Athenian Erechtheion (fig. 71). However, in Limyra the female figures are not graceful, but heavy pillar-like supports (fig. 72). Each of them wears a peplos over a chiton and carries cult objects in her hands (e.g., libation bowls and rhytons), clearly indicating an association with funerary rituals. On their heads the karyatids wear a high headgear; their hair-style is oriental. Besides reminding the visitor to observe the cult of the dead, they may also have symbolized a promise of life after death.

At any rate, their symbolic function is unquestionable, even if we can no longer determine their precise role in an ancient funerary context. Borchhardt identifies them as Horae or Charites, and an analogous role might be suggested for related korai: the Erechtheion maidens,[11] those of heroon 'G', at Xanthos, and the female statues supporting the upper structure of the Tomb of Hyakinthos at Amyklai. Among these examples, the only extant representatives – the karyatids of the Erechtheion – deserve special attention. In the light of the Limyra discovery, the notion that the Athenian temple was erected over the legendary tomb of Kekrops, with the six maidens supporting a baldacchino over the grave, becomes once more the most plausible theory concerning the function of the building.

In this connection, questions also arise regarding the role of the female figures of the Knidian and Siphnian (fig. 73) treasuries at Delphi. However, no definite answers can be given without further research. The motif seems to have been derived from the Near East.[12]

An architrave of two fasciae constitutes the lowest section of the Ionic entablature. Again recalling the Karyatid Porch in Athens, the upper fascia was adorned with a row of carved rosettes, an appropriate decoration for funerary and commemorative buildings. The next element was a row of large dentils, followed by the geison and a lion-head sima on the long sides of the edifice. The south and north façades carried a pediment.

After some initial difficulty the central and corner acroteria of the north pediment have been convincingly reconstructed.[13] The central acroterion represents Perseus with the beheaded Medusa at his feet, while the corners show the sisters of Medusa, Stheno and Euryale, in flight (fig. 75). The theme was well known in Greek art. The southern acroteria, facing the sea, have disappeared, but according to the excavators the subject was Bellerophon's fight against the Amazons.[14] The height of the still existing central acroterion on the north came to 1.6 m, while the superstructure, from the capitals of the karyatid figures to the apex of the pediment, measured 2 m.

The cella (6 m long) behind the karyatid supports housed a second burial-chamber above the hyposorion of the podium. The outer face of the third course of the chamber (0.9 m high) was decorated on the east and west with sculptured reliefs. The west frieze is quite well preserved; it shows a scene reminiscent of a military parade. At the head of the procession is a quadriga, followed by attendants, mounted horsemen, and foot-soldiers in full armour. Although most of the east frieze is missing, it can be established from the remaining fragments that it was an almost exact copy of the processional scene on the west side. In both friezes the participants move from north to south.

The corners of the cella walls were adorned with pilasters; below the capitals appeared carved rosettes in pairs.

The main approach to the temenos of the heroon was from the east. The wide flight of steps in front of the south façade had no functional purpose but, rather, contributed to the monumental effect by increasing the apparent height of the structure as seen from below. The structure and its decoration stand out from the monotonous background of rock and further increased the brilliant and striking effect of the tomb, which perhaps also served as a landmark for sailors approaching Limyra.

As a measure of economy, both the architectural and sculptural members were executed in local stone, quarried in the course of preparing the ground for the heroon. The complex may have been the tomb of the Lycian dynast Perikles, who became ruler of the region during the decade 380–370 BC, and perished during the satraps' revolt of 362–360 BC.[15]

The building, although it reflects Attic influence in plan and Xanthian influence in the arrangement of the main units, is an independent creation showing a different form of the theme of the Nereid Monument, i.e., the 'temple tomb' on a podium. The architect must have been a Lycian who was also quite familiar with the strict symmetry of Persian architectural designs; for example, the mirror-image effect of the friezes is also found in the entrance ways of Achaemenid buildings.[16] The dramatic setting of the complex is its most remarkable feature. It is in the focal point of the projecting lower level of the acropolis of Limyra, which in an abstract way resembles the ornamental prow of a large ship. By combining the living quarters (which were located above the tomb) and the funerary complex, the residences of the living and of the dead, the person who commissioned the heroon made his presence in the community eternal.

III The Mausoleum at Halikarnassos

The largest and most magnificent tomb of the fourth century was undoubtedly the Mausoleum at Halikarnassos;[17] none of its Greek successors surpassed it either in scale or in fame. The city of Halikarnassos, Herodotus's birthplace, rose to importance under the Karian dynast Mausolos (377–353 BC). He spared no expense in refounding this coastal town as his capital.[18] Unfortunately, very little has survived either of his tomb or of his palace, probably the two most splendid buildings of the entire city. During the sixteenth century of our era, the Castle of St Peter was erected on the site of the palace, reusing materials from the mausoleum. The site of the tomb was rediscovered in 1856, and then excavated by C.T. Newton. Since that time numerous restorations of the mausoleum have been proposed, relying partly on the results of Newton's excavation and partly on the descriptions of ancient writers. A fresh campaign of study and excavation was started by Danish archaeologists in the 1960s.

Vitruvius (2.8.11) aptly described the location of the mausoleum as being in the middle of a natural amphitheatre, i.e., the curved and gradually rising ground level enclosing the bay of Halikarnassos. A section of an earlier necropolis was utilized for the new tomb; the soft rock was recut for the white marble floor of the actual tomb chamber, placed in the NW section of the enclosure. This chamber was directly connected with the wide western staircase through a vestibule and a short dromos. A huge portcullis blocked the entrance to the burial place. All the architectural ornaments have disappeared, but a sixteenth-century description suggests that the interior was lavishly decorated.[20]

To relieve the weight over the tomb chamber the architect probably relied on the well-tested system of corbelled vaulting that had been widely employed in funerary architecture since Mycenaean times.[21] Another rock-cut, but smaller, staircase was set obliquely to the SE part of the complex. It faced the south side of the tomb chamber and carried cuttings for offering-vases. A unique and extensive system of drainage channels and regularly placed pillars surrounded the entire foundation cutting. The latter, perhaps, served to support the lifting machines employed during the construction of the edifice.

There is little or no direct information concerning the podium of the mausoleum. However, the vague reference in Vitruvius may relate to the podium: 'For on the several elevations [i.e., perhaps indicating a stepped podium] different rival craftsmen took their share in decorations wherein they competed.'[22] Martial describes the mausoleum as 'hanging in vacant air.'[23] In speaking of the dismantling of the remains Guichard says that 'the deeper they went the more the structure was enlarged at its base';[24] these words may indicate some peculiarities of the high socle, perhaps suggesting again a stepped podium-like appearance for it.

Other literary sources emphasize that the mausoleum was regarded as one of the seven wonders of the ancient world mainly because of its sculpture.[25] The total number of statues could have been as many as 330. The large number of sculptural fragments found on the site seems to support this point; a certain number of these figures must have belonged to the high podium. The height of the podium, 19.2 m, probably equalled that of the pteron and the pyramid on top. It has been calculated that 'the podium contracted between its base and summit by 6.4 m on each long side, and 6 m on each short side, or 10 and $9\frac{3}{8}$ feet.'[26] Thus the podium was 'encircled' by a number of socles or parapets of blue limestone for the free-standing sculptures. These parapets were stepped back one above and behind the other (fig. 77). The sculptures included both groups and single figures. The groups at the base were life-size.[27] On the middle section were heroic or slightly over life-size figures, while the statues on the upper pedestal were of colossal size. Next followed a marble-faced wall, crowned on all four sides by a relief frieze, representing the familiar theme of an Amazonomachy on top, and perhaps a Centauromachy below.[28]

Above a crowning moulding and a one-stepped stylobate an Ionic peristyle enclosed the 'cella'. The thirty-six columns were set out in a 9 × 11 arrangement. Blue plinths supported white marble bases of Asiatic-Ionic profile. The column shafts measured 1.1 m at the base and had twenty-four flutes.[29] The capitals conformed to the type current in the mid fourth century. There is no evidence for a frieze-course between the architrave and the dentils; the crowning moulding of the former, an astragal under an egg-and-dart, provided the transition. Free-standing sculptures stood in the ca 3-m-wide axial spaces,[30] doubtless recalling such arrangements as the Nereid Monument, the fourth-century heroon at Limyra, and the sarcophagus of the Mourning Women from Sidon. Above the sima, and slightly set back from the edge, stood groups of heraldic lions. If the arrangement of the later Belevi Mausoleum is any indication, these lions faced ornamental motifs, while the four corners carried group compositions.

The description of the uppermost portion of the tomb in Pliny is fairly explicit, though not precise: 'Above the pteron there was a pyramid, equal in height to the lower part [i.e., the colonnade], contracting by twenty-four steps to a summit like that of the meta. At the top of all was a chariot with four horses.'[31]

The steps of the pyramid supported a rectangular pedestal. On this platform there was a huge chariot; it can be assumed that the chariot had at least one figure in it, that of Mausolos, perhaps in the disguise of Helios. The height of the pedestal including the chariot on top came to 6.6 m.

Information is scarce regarding the cella of the peripteral stage. This section, too, may have had a corbel-vaulted interior to provide support for the pyramidal roof (fig. 78). Because of its good state of preservation the chariot frieze, made of fine-grained white marble, must have been in a part of the building that was protected from the weather. It may have been placed at the top of the outer face of the cella walls. The coffers of the pteron were sculptured, providing an early example of this kind of ornament.

The artists employed to execute all these sculptures were among the most famous of the time. Scopas worked on the east, Bryaxis on the north, Timotheos on the south, and Leochares on the west side. In addition, a certain Pytheos made the marble quadriga, and in co-operation with Satyros of Paros published a study on the mausoleum; he is usually assumed to have been the architect of the whole building.[32]

In connection with the measurements and the numerical relationship of the component parts of the tomb, there arises the question of the module employed. According to the Danish excavators a foot-unit of ca 32 cm comes closest to Pliny's dimensions; however, the foot of ca 30 cm also played an important part in the design.[33] Jeppesen restores the total height of the tomb as 57.6 m, the circumference as 128 m, and the height of the middle colonnaded part as 12 m (fig. 79a, b, c).[34]

An extensive peribolos wall was planned to surround the terrace of the mausoleum (105 × 242.5 m). This spacious enclosure was to be used for festivals, though its south, east, and west sides were never finished. The enclosure was entered by a propylon in the east wall, but this gateway was left unfinished around 340 BC when work on the tomb itself stopped (figs 79b and c).

By this time both political and economic conditions had become unfavourable for the completion of the project. Mausolos, who must have conceived the grandiose design early in his reign, died when building activity was at its height. However, his wife Artemisia carried on the task till her own death in 351 BC. Thereafter the construction continued with interruptions until it came to a standstill about a decade later.[35]

Because of its size and prominent position the mausoleum not only dominated the city but also may have served as a familiar landmark for sailors. It was a monumental undertaking on the part of a local ruler designed to win him immortality. Here the earlier Asia Minor tradition of commemorative buildings and grave monuments was developed into an impressive, even awe-inspiring, 'heroon tomb,' or a true Syngonion on account of its portrait statues.[36] In place of a conventional roof like those of the Nereid Monument and the fourth-century heroon at the Limyra, the design terminated in a stepped pyramid. As indicated in the preceding chapter, this idea was probably derived from oriental sources.[37] The unusual height of the tomb itself, the excellence and variety of the sculptures (an almost 'Gothic' combination), and the large temenos made the mausoleum complex a source of inspiration for many later monuments; these included not only tombs and memorial buildings, but also lighthouses and altars.

IV The Large Tomb at Labraynda

The original capital of the Hekatomnid dynasts of Karia had been at Mylasa (modern Milas), some 14 km southwest of the Karian national sanctuary at Labraynda. The impressive ruins of Labraynda are located in mountainous terrain, about 700 m above sea-level. The necropolis around the sanctuary contains both rock-cut and built tombs of the fourth century. Most of these tombs are still little-known, including the largest example, which is relatively well preserved. The best (though not completely accurate) drawings of this large tomb are those of Le Bas (fig. 80), who visited the site in 1844. The structure was restudied and redrawn by a Swedish team in 1960.[38]

The lower sections of the multi-storied building are still in situ, about 30 m higher up the slope above the temple area (fig. 81). A small terrace was cut in the mountainside to provide a prominent site for the heroon. Fifty metres higher again is the former acropolis, known today as Hisar (fortress). A passage, partly stepped, connected the heroon with the lower-lying sanctuary. Thus, the siting of the tomb is roughly comparable to that of the fourth-century heroon at Limyra. Nearby are many traces of the quarries that provided building material for the tomb as well as for the other structures on the terraced areas below.

The complex, 15 m long, consists of three units. On the east is a dromos (or courtyard), more than 6 m long, followed by two chambers axially aligned with the dromos. The whole north wall, approximately up to the apex of the roof of the chambers, was built against the scraped rock surface on the uphill side of the terrace; the north wall of the dromos consisted of at least six courses of ashlar, laid as alternating headers and stretchers. On the east side the roughly cut rock surface was left unfaced. The south side, facing the sanctuary below, is still preserved to a height of 5.2 m. Here, two slightly projecting foundation courses support a base moulding, followed by a higher, then a lower, course of blocks, which might perhaps be regarded as 'orthostates' crowned by a 'string-course.' The next three courses, except for the long corner blocks, consist of headers. The fourth course consists of stretchers; above this level the still existing courses are stepped back in a scheme corresponding to that of the north side, where the Swedish excavations 'revealed three steps running along the whole of the north long side of the structure like a kind of stylobate, on which the tomb wall rises to a height of three courses of 1.30 m'[39]

The dromos was entered by a low door with tapering sides, set in the middle of the south side; the two large threshold blocks were fixed in place by a leaded-in iron clamp. According to the excavators, after the funeral the door was sealed and the open courtyard, or dromos, filled with sand and earth. A doorway similar to that of the dromos leads into the interior. A six-ton slab of gneiss, not unlike the one used in the tomb chamber of the Halikarnassian mausoleum, blocked the entrance to the burial-rooms. The lintel over this doorway measures 0.65 × 0.9 × 2.4 m; the block above it is 5.3 m long, thus transferring the weight of all higher courses to the solid wall on either side of the door. Two sarcophagi were placed in the forechamber, to the left and right of the doorway. The larger main room originally contained one sarcophagus, but at a later period was rearranged to accommodate three. The ceilings are corbel vaulted, but the soffit of the vault is shaped to give the impression of semicircular barrel vaulting (fig. 82). Both rear corners of the inner chamber were built of large L-shaped blocks that formed part of the side wall as well as of the rear wall.

Above the two chambers the design of the tomb is unusual, consisting of a single rectangular 'chamber' measuring 6 × 3.2 m, and ca 0.7 m in height; access to this space was through a trapezoidal opening in the east wall, i.e., the west wall of the dromos (fig. 83a, b). Its purpose is not known; persumably it was needed to relieve the pressure of the superstructure above. The roof of this 'clerestorey' consists of a series of ten huge slabs of gneiss, each ca 4.5 m long (fig. 84); these slabs also provided a base for the lost upper structure. No reconstruction of this superstructure has been proposed. One of the finds illustrated by Le Bas, a section of a marble Doric frieze with a metope between two triglyphs,[40] has since disappeared. The combined height of the architrave and frieze was approximately 1.05 m. The cornice block, also drawn in Le Bas (pl. II-9 nVIII), was 0.29 m high. The triglyphs are classical looking with their grooves showing elliptical profiles; the outer edges of the glyphs have curved tops. The moulding of the cornice, taken as a unit, have no really close comparable parallel. Separately, however, the cyma reversa geison bed-mould may be roughly compared with mid fourth-century designs, e.g., in the third Temple of Athena Pronaia and the new temple of Apollo at Delphi. The geison mouldings of the Temple of Alea Athena at Tegea and of the Thersilion at Megalopolis, both of the mid fourth century, also recall the Labraynda moulding. The hawksbeak of the Doric geison crown is once more classical in appearance, distantly echoing the form of the same moulding in the interior order of the Temple of Apollo at Bassae.

On the east part of the temple terrace fragments of a small Doric column and of a capital were found. Their size would be appropriate for a colonnaded superstructure rising above the chambers of the tomb. In the absence of any additional information, it can be tentatively suggested that the building was an elevated 'temple tomb' like the Nereid Monument or the fourth-century heroon at Limyra, though the possibility also exists that there was only a Doric parapet on the roof of the tomb.

The masonry is of the same nature as those of other buildings in the sanctuary executed during the reigns of Mausolos, Idrieus (351–344 BC), and Ada (344–341 BC). It is known that Idrieus dedicated a large number of buildings on the site, including the andron, the temple, the oikoi, and a gateway.[41] The closeness of the heroon tomb to the main sanctuary would indicate that it belonged to an important person of the region; this person may have been Idrieus, the brother of Mausolos.

v Tombs at Knidos, Alinda, and Antiphellos

A number of commemorative tomb structures used a large-scale lion as their epithema, or crowning element. Even if lions were rarely seen by the Greeks, the symbolic value of the king of beasts must have been well known to them, thus accounting for the standardized types. Some of these monuments (e.g., those at Thespiai, Chaeronea, and Amphipolis) employed the seated type, while the Knidian Lion Tomb (fig. 85) had a reclining lion on top. The evidence of the Chaeronea and Knidos examples indicates that they were erected to honour a number of individuals rather than a single person.

The limestone core of the Lion Tomb at Knidos is still standing (fig. 86) to about 6 m, or approximately one-third of its original height.[42] The rocky ground was carefully levelled to receive the foundation layers. The square lower part of the tomb, measuring over 12 m per side, consisted of a three-stepped crepis and a high socle finished in fine 'bossiert' style. Four engaged Doric columns, ca 5.5 lower diameters in height, adorned each side of the massive middle section of the building. According to the excavators, there were three triglyphs above the central intercolumniation, two above the lateral spans, with a complete triglyph at the corners. The arrangement of three triglyphs in the central interval is analogous to the Doric Portico of Knidos, datable perhaps to the late fourth or early third century.[43] The width of the metopes varied. The entablature terminated in a plain lion-head sima, only roughly blocked out.

To support the crowning lion figure and its hollow rectangular pedestal an oblong stepped pyramid was erected above the lower storey; the sides and bottom of each block of the risers were decorated with a band of drafting. Inside the podium and pyramid was a circular beehive-shaped chamber (fig. 87), built of 'concentric horizontal courses, overhanging each other so as gradually to converge to an apex.'[44] A huge circular slab, trapezoidal in section, closed the top of the beehive. The walls immediately above the paved floor were pierced by eleven radiating loculi plus a larger opening on the north side for the doorway.[45] These rectangular burial niches extended right to the external marble facing of the podium.

No architectural decorations were found, except for a broken relief shield, which, in all probability, was placed above the doorway of the central intercolumniation.[46] In addition to the above-mentioned limestone, greyish marble with purple and yellowish patches was employed for the external walls. The lion was of Pentelic marble (fig. 88), possibly indicating some sort of Attic connections for the monument.

The entire complex is located on the projecting tip of a small peninsula, about 4 km east of Knidos. An extensive walled temenos, a common feature of heroon tombs, surrounded the central structure. Traces of this enclosure are still visible on the north and west sides (fig. 89). Because of its prominent site overlooking the sea, it must have been a familiar landmark to mariners.

Remains of other elevated tombs, similar in nature to the Lion Tomb, are to be found along the ancient road to Knidos.[47] Their period of construction must fall within the years of the Lion Tomb, when such pyramidal structures were fashionable.

In the absence of inscriptions and small finds (except for a small vase of the shape known as a lagynos found outside the doorway),[48] there is no firm basis for dating the Lion Tomb. Many of its architectural details were left uncarved. However, its overall design connects it with the Halikarnassian mausoleum and its successors in the same region. The solution to the problem of roofing the interior chamber seems rather old-fashioned, recalling Mycenaean beehive tombs; but the corbelled construction is also comparable with some of the other roof structures on the Lelegian peninsula, at Gebe Kilisse (fig. 90) and Asarlik, and perhaps even with the burial-chamber of Mausolos's tomb.[49] Loculi are found in the late fourth century in the Charmyleion on Kos, as well as later, in the Hellenistic heroon at Miletos.

Representations of lions are often seen on Knidian coinage from the archaic period onward,[50] but they are of little help in dating the Lion Tomb. Knidos apparently enjoyed an upsurge of artistic activity in the second half of the fourth century, after the refounding, or at least enlarging, of the city at the end of the peninsula.[51] During this period the Knidians acquired a number of works of art created by famous Attic artists.[52] Thus, it would not be surprising if this Dorian city employed an architect who had acquired practical experience from various parts of the Mediterranean. Besides being familiar with developments in Attica and Asia Minor, the architect may also have had a firsthand knowledge of Macedonian architecture. Macedonian Doric architecture is of excellent quality, and engaged columns resting on a socle often appear in Macedonian designs.[53]

The Lion Tomb used to be associated with Konon's naval victory over the Spartans off the Knidian coast in 394 BC. However, a date in the late fourth or early third century now seems far more plausible. A similar design was employed in the less well preserved Lion Tomb at Amphipolis (fig. 91), which must belong to the same time.[54] Among their successors in Asia Minor are the early Doric constructions of Pergamon, the even more advanced buildings of the second century at Miletos (e.g., the Bouleuterion), and the still later tomb at Ta Marmara near Didyma.

Also related to the Lion tomb at Knidos is a much smaller built but now destroyed tomb at Alinda (fig. 92).[55] The main or middle section of the tomb was raised on a four-stepped crepidoma, approximately 1.2 m high. Each side of the square stylobate measured ca 3.9 m. All four faces carried an identical design of two Doric half-columns enclosed by boldly projecting corner pilasters. The lower diameter of the columns, 0.38 m, was equal to the width of the pilasters; the column height measured 6.5 times the lower diameter, or 2.47 m exactly. Architrave and frieze were Doric; there were two triglyphs above each intercolumnar space, i.e., ten triglyphs and nine metopes on each side. The architrave and frieze were equal in height (0.3 m each). No restoration has been proposed for the sections, if any, above the frieze; the Knidos and Amphipolis examples suggest that there may have been a pyramidal top, with some sort of a crowning finial. The date of the structure is probably within the fourth century, perhaps even before that of the Knidian Lion Tomb.

Somewhat different in design but still of the same genre is a largely rock-cut but free-standing tomb outside Kaş (ancient Antiphellos) in Lycia (fig. 93a, b). The monument has been noted briefly by a few authors but otherwise remains largely unrecorded in literature.[55] It is almost square on plan, the front measuring 4.7 m in width, the sides 4 m; the preserved height is about 4.5 m. The sides are plain; at the corners are pilasters. A Doric entablature crowns the cubical lower part of the monument. The rest of the superstructure has almost completely disappeared, so that its original form cannot be determined with certainty; however, a stepped pyramid again seems to be the most appropriate form for the crowning element, i.e., the Kaş monument would have resembled a small-scale Hellenistic tomb model found at Syracuse (fig. 94),[57] or another tomb at Turğut in Asia Minor (fig. 95).[58]

The burial-chamber was reached through a narrow doorway, with a 'Vitruvian Doric' frame, the outer edges of which are decorated all around by an astragal moulding. Inside the chamber three klinai served for the interment of bodies. Their ornamentation included a frieze (0.2 m wide) of rosettes alternating with stylized palmettes. Other decorative motifs found in the tomb are a small pilaster capital (0.18 m high), with floral ornament springing from volutes (the top of a kline leg?), and another small frieze (0.2 m high) of twenty-four 'dancing girls.'[59]

On the basis of the decorative details the tomb can be dated to the first half of the third century.

VI The Belevi Mausoleum near Ephesos

This monument is located about 14 km inland from Ephesos.[60] The tomb stands at the foot of a sloping hillside overlooking a fertile plain. In contrast to the Halikarnassian mausoleum, where the rock surface was hollowed out to receive the foundation layers, at Belevi the living rock was artificially shaped to provide a core for the high basement (fig. 96).[61] In other respects, however, the main outlines of the design clearly followed those of Mausolos's tomb. The ground plan was square, each side measuring 29.65 m; this figure probably represents 100 feet of 0.2965 m. Above the euthynteria a three-stepped crepidoma 1.18 m high supported the base mouldings, consisting of a plain band, torus, scotia, and Lesbian cyma. Above this base the podium was faced with ten courses of large neatly cut ashlar, 0.69 m to 0.88 m high. A low architrave (0.45 m) and somewhat higher Doric frieze (0.67 m) and a corona (0.45 m) ran around the top of the podium. The ratio of epistyle to frieze is a rather unique 2:3. Another interesting feature is that the top of the glyphs end in a gentle curve (as in classical times) instead of the conventional Hellenistic horizontal line. Furthermore, the side glyphs have 'ears'. Along the south side a deep recess was cut into the rock core for the burial-chamber (7.4 × 4.5 m and 8.25 m in height), which was placed off-centre and sealed from the outside so as to conceal its existence (fig. 97a, b). The actual chamber within the recess was barrel vaulted, and consisted of a small vestibule and a larger rectangular back-room for the kline-sarcophagus. The north or main façade of the edifice facing the street had an unfinished false door.

The second floor again started out with a three-stepped crepis, 1.12 m high, the top step serving as the stylobate for a Corinthian peristasis (fig. 98) with eight columns per side.[62] The Attic-Ionic column bases rested on plinths, as at Langaza in Macedonia and in one of the largest rock-cut tombs in Lycia at Telmessos.[63] In the entablature (fig. 99) the three-fascia architrave was crowned by an astragal, egg-and-dart, and a plain fillet moulding. Above the architrave were both a cyma-profiled palmette-and-lotus frieze and a dentil course. The Ionic cornice supported a plain sima with lion-head waterspouts.[64] The total height of the entablature was 1.7 m.

The ceiling of the pteron was embellished in a 'baroque' manner with large coffers. The panels of the principal north side represented funerary games, while the reliefs of the other sides dealt with a centauromachy.[65] The Austrian archaeologists restored on each side, above the sima, three pairs (twenty-four in all) of antithetic lion-griffin figures facing large stone vases; pairs of horses (2.25 m high) were placed at the corners. Little or no archaeological evidence is left for the reconstruction of the cella and the roof structure. The latter in all probability resembled Halikarnassos in having a stepped pyramid with a crowning element on top.[66]

From the surviving traces of the ground plan of the cella it may be conjectured that the inner face of the walls was adorned with pilasters and (or) with engaged Doric columns (fig. 100), not unlike those of the adyton walls of the Hellenistic Didymaion.[67] A block, perhaps belonging to the architrave of the inner order, was found; it bears the inscription: 'ΗΛΙ-ΑΔΕΣ.' Some fragments of a small palm-leaf capital and fluted Ionic drums may belong to the same section of the building. Perhaps they formed part of a two-tiered interior decorative scheme. The north side of the cella wall probably had a decorative door, while in the south wall there might have been a niche for a statue.

The sculptural finds inside the burial chamber included a large sarcophagus with an unfinished reclining figure on top, and a standing statue of a servant. The existence of other figures is indicated by fragments found around the site. The sculptures as well as the architectural members still bear extensive remains of their painted finish; frequently painting replaced carving on the architectural mouldings, a practice reminiscent of Macedonian architecture.

An estimated 2500 m³ of marble was extracted from the quarries of the neighbourhood for building the tomb. If the monument was ever completed to its summit it must have reached a height of about 35 m (fig. 101a, b).

(The calculated height of the three main units is 11.643 m + 11.362 m + 12.407 m = 35.412 m, or 119⅚ ft. To this can be added the height of a crowning quadriga or some other type of finial.) The unfinished architectural members indicate that work stopped rather suddenly; we are thus able to see the different stages in the progress of the stonecarving (fig. 102).

The problem of the identity of the commissioner and the date of construction remains unsolved. The high square podium and the pyramid (?) on top are non-Greek. Oriental influence is seen in some of the sculptural decoration, such as the statue of the servant and the heraldic lion-griffin figures and vases. The execution of the tomb chamber is Macedonian. The combination of different orders on the exterior of buildings appeared elsewhere in early Hellenistic work, e.g., in the Great Tomb at Lefkadia and the Propylon of Ptolemy on Samothrace.

From the time of the Nereid Monument onward, important tombs had often been richly decorated. The form of the capitals and the profiles of the mouldings find their closest parallels in buildings belonging to the first half of the third century, such as the Lysimachean projects on Samothrace and at Miletos, the Athena temple at Ilion, and, above all, the somewhat later Naiskos at Didyma.[68] Ultimately the decorative forms of the period go back to the fourth-century Temple of Athena at Priene: but the particular shapes became harder and less lively, e.g., as in the third-century Temple of Zeus in the same city. At the same time, some of the strictly technical details, such as the type of the foot unit and the form of the dowel holes, continue unchanged from the Athena temple at Priene.[69]

To make matters even more difficult, there is no uniformity in the corresponding details at Belevi. For example, the row of frieze blocks of the Corinthian order and the Lesbian cyma decoration show variations in the carving. Some sections are still executed in the late fourth-century manner, while others are more stiff and shallow.[70]

Perhaps there were two or more periods of construction at Belevi; the strongest indication of this possibility is given by a number of coffer plaques that resemble reliefs from the early second-century Hekataion at Lagina.[71] Otherwise the mausoleum seems to belong to the first half of the third century. Its commissioner was presumably a king. In choosing the site, the existence of the nearby tumulus tomb, perhaps also of royal origin but of an earlier period, must have been a decisive factor.[72] The design, the preparation of the ground, and the building itself required years of work that could not have been done in an emergency or on the spur of the moment. The order to erect this huge tomb perhaps came from the reorganizer of the nearby city of Ephesos, Lysimachos himself.[73]

The influence of the Belevi Mausoleum elsewhere in the Hellenistic world seems to have been widespread. Such monuments as the 'Tomba Ildebranda' in Etruria, the so-called Tomb of the Ptolemies on Rhodes, and the tower tomb at Ptolemais in North Africa are all directly or indirectly related to the Belevi building.[74]

In western Asia Minor proper this mausoleum is one of the last-known examples of a built tomb[75] of monumental scale that also included new features in its design. Not until the building of the so-called Ta Marmara tomb near Didyma, in the mid second century, do we again find a built tomb noteworthy for its size and architectural execution. This 'gap' in monumental tomb buildings may be attributed largely to the uncertainty of the times and the generally poor economic climate. In order to find a continuation of the trend established by the Nereid Monument one has to turn to the islands off the coast of Asia Minor. These islands were always receptive to the ideas popular in Asia Minor and often transmitted them to the western regions of the Mediterranean world.

VII The Charmyleion on the Island of Kos

One of the earliest edifices to show the influence of the monumental tombs of Asia Minor was the Charmyleion on the island of Kos (fig. 103).[76] The building was the product of Ionian provincial architecture, with some Doric elements in its design. An inscription found nearby, originally from some part of the edifice, identifies its owner as Chyarmylos and his family, who lived around 300 BC.[77]

The design is unusual because only the façade of the building is emphasized. The sides and back are devoid of architectural decoration. The tomb consisted of three levels, of which the lowest was underground. This crypt was approached from above by steps forming a short dromos (fig. 104). A wide shallow antechamber gave access to the vaulted burial-chamber, 5.58 m long. Along the west and east walls of this vaulted space were six loculi, each 2.45 m deep. This arrangement for burial in the basement is comparable in a general way with that of the Lion Tomb at Knidos, and especially with the heroon on the Theatre Hill at Miletos. These loculi were closed by large slabs depicting in relief the short end of a funeral kline with a tympanon on top.

Above the basement the narrow podium running along the north, or main, façade of the building was broken by two symmetrically placed staircases leading up to the doorways (fig. 105). The lintel of each door was topped by a slightly projecting band of Ionic decorations, consisting of egg-and-dart above a hanging palmette, cyma reversa, and astragal, with consoles closing the ends. The horizontal relief of each door-leaf was carved with rosettes, such as are found in Macedonian and Asia Minor examples. Behind this façade, which measured 9.5 m in width, there were two identical rooms, their floors supported on six parallel rows of poros blocks running N–S above the vaulted basement, not unlike the joists below a stage floor; this arrangement seems to have been designed simply to bring the floor level to the desired height. The exterior of the rather plain first storey terminated in an Ionic cyma profile.

The second storey was visually lighter and more open. Corner pilasters flanked the two Ionic columns in antis that formed the façade of a rectangular aedicula. The entablature had a row of dentils, but no frieze band. The crowning course of the wall of the central aedicula, or cult room, and the necks of the pilasters and antae were carved with a row of rosettes. The acanthus foliage of the pilaster capitals and the Lesbian cyma of their bases both indicate a close stylistic relationship with Priene, Didyma, and Belevi. The façade of the central aedicula was crowned by a 'relief' pediment, behind which a lean-to roof sloped down to the rear.

The masonry of the building was pseudo-isodomic. From the inscription it is known that the design included a temenos containing other buildings and gardens belonging to the Twelve Gods and the hero: 'Sacred is the land and the building on the land, the gardens and the buildings in the gardens to the Twelve Gods and to Charmylos, hero of the Charmyle(i)oi.'

VIII Tombs at Lindos and Rhodini

Rock-cut monuments generally imitated free-standing built edifices but were modified to suit the different method of execution. The prototypes of two monumental rock-cut tombs on the island of Rhodes were clearly built structures. The first example is only a rock-cut façade, though one of the largest of its kind and of unusual design; it is located at Lindos, some distance south of the city of Rhodes (fig. 106). Like many other funerary structures, the monument occupies a conspicuous site just above the western section of the city, in the region called Kampana.[78] From inscriptions found on the site we know that it was commissioned by one Archokrates as a burial place for himself and his immediate family, thus assuring their continued 'presence' in the community even after their physical death.

The façade of the tomb, 22.5 m long and approximately 9.5 m high, was cut from the living rock; it faced eastward, and was two storeys high (fig. 107). The lower storey consisted of an engaged order of twelve Doric half-columns. The fluted Doric shafts rested on a platform of three steps. The necking of these half-columns consisted of three annulets below a slightly curving echinus. The ratio of column height to lower diameter was 5.8:1;

the axial span was 2 m. The frieze had two triglyphs, with flat topped grooves, above each intercolumnar space. The lower order terminated in a projecting sima with antefixes. Above the sima was a wide decorative band on which elliptical medallions alternated with female figures emerging from acanthus foliage. The simplified second storey stood at the back of a narrow platform (maximum width 1.65 m) that could be reached from the sides by symmetrically placed staircases recalling the approaches to the proskenion of a Hellenistic theatre. In the centre of this 'stage' were placed four cylindrical marble altars with inscribed bases. Here the vertical lines of the ground floor were continued by flat pilasters, 2.2 m high, placed on a high socle. The crowning elements are missing, but in all probability a carved horizontal cornice and sima topped the façade of the monument.

To enhance the scenographic impression of the composition, decorative elements (painted, or sculptured, or both) probably played a considerable role. Only a few traces of these decorations have been found; but their positions, between the engaged Doric columns of the lower and in the pinax-like panels of the upper storey, can be restored by analogy with the Lefkadia tomb (see p. 107).

From the east, one could enter the interior through three centrally placed openings between the Doric columns. An approximately square chamber, preceded by a much wider but shallower vestibule, recalls the ground plans of Macedonian subterranean tombs. A remarkable feature of this rock-cut cult tomb is its western podium, approached by steps along the sides, with a T-shaped burial-place beneath. A centrally placed staircase led to this chamber. On the other sides of the cult room rock-cut benches lined the walls. Because the interior is badly damaged and somewhat altered by the addition of later loculi, its exact shape and decoration can only be conjectured. Originally the ceiling may have had a tent form, while the walls had polychrome painted revetments, composed of panels alternating with pilasters similar to those on the upper part of the façade.

Architecturally, the overall scheme of the Archokrateion can be compared with other local buildings, e.g., the lower stoa and the propylaia of the Athena precinct (both with imposing columnar façades), a monumental rock-cut tomb at Rhodini, and especially the temenos wall at Kamiros.[79] In turn the architectural scheme of the Archokrateion might have influenced the design of a number of local Rhodian tombs like the one at Asgourou.[80] Moreover, the monument is related to other two-storeyed structures, especially theatre and some other tomb façades, in which scenic effects were stressed at the expense of a more conventional design.

We know from the Lindian Chronicle that Archokrates became a priest of Athena in 225 BC. It can, therefore, be assumed that the tomb was executed during the last quarter of the third century.

In addition to the better-known Archokrateion at Lindos, there is another monumental Hellenistic tomb on the island of Rhodes – a huge rock-cut structure at Rhodini.[81] This tomb is situated in a spacious park a couple of kilometres southwest of the city of Rhodes. In contrasts to the Archokrateion, the Rhodini tomb is not merely a façade but a completely free-standing structure (fig. 108). A small natural hill of sandstone, located between two ravines, was chosen for the structure. The rock was cut to form a cube, ca 4.5 m high, each side being roughly 27.8 m long.[82] Of the four sides, only the north is relatively well preserved. Here, and presumably along the other sides too, the main body of the mausoleum was decorated with a row of twenty-one engaged half-columns, standing on a three-stepped crepidoma raised on a high base. Each of the three steps is ca 0.35 m high and 0.3 m deep. The columns lack bases and have very slender proportions. They project 0.3 m from the wall; the lower diameter averages 0.48 m. The interaxial span is 1.3 m. All the shafts are unfluted. Although not a single capital is preserved, the order was undoubtedly Doric, the most widely used of the orders on Rhodes during the Hellenistic age. No fragments of the entablature have been found. For the upper part of the tomb, Ross suggested a pyramid or simply a tumulus planted with trees like that of the Mausoleum of Augustus in Rome; Newton prefers (correctly, as I believe) the first possibility. In fact, among the numerous large masses of carved sandstone on the site is one that seems to have come from the upper part of the pyramid; it now lies close to the NE angle of the ruined structure.[83]

On the north side, between the fifth and sixth columns from the NW corner, a doorway (2.7 m high and 1.1 m wide) gave access to the hewn-out interior. As in the Archokrateion, a vestibule (here wide and shallow, 9.2 × 3 m) precedes the main cult room. This room is on axis with the exterior doorway; it is 6.75 m long and 4.4 m wide. The forechamber has two loculi of unequal depth cut into the long ends of the wall. The second room has three on the west side, two in the back (or south) wall; no two of these are the same size. In the east wall were five loculi, each 1.2 m deep and 0.65 m wide.

Both rooms show traces of a coat of whitewash; originally both were painted, but no traces of their decorative schemes have remained. Ross and Newton suggested that there might be additional burial-rooms inside the rock-core because the excavated room occupies only one-fourth of the complex.[84]

The closest parallel to the Rhodini design is the Belevi Mausoleum near

Ephesos, which can be considered as a kind of prototype of the Rhodini tomb. The rock-cut core faced with columns, the pyramidal top, and the burial-chamber opening off-centre from one of the sides indicate that the architect of the Rhodini project was familiar with the layout of some monument such as the Belevi Mausoleum. However, at Rhodini, to judge from the still extant remains, everything is simple in design and less meticulously executed than at Belevi. The two-storey arrangement of Belevi has been kept, but the supporting base (in place of a real podium) was included at Rhodini probably because of the unevenness of the ground line. Instead of a free-standing Corinthian order, Doric half-columns, like those of the Knidian Lion Tomb, were carved from the core of living rock. The tomb at Rhodini was a huge monolith that impressed by its overall mass rather than by its details, the execution of which is rather mechanical. In this respect it resembles other third- and second-century Rhodian projects, such as the large lower stoa at Lindos and the Colossus of Rhodes, overthrown by the earthquake of 227–26 BC.

The date and the owner of the huge tomb at Rhodini are both unknown. Dates from the fourth to the first century BC have been suggested; but no theories have been put forward regarding the identity of the owner of the tomb. In literature it is known as the 'Tomb of the Ptolemies,' or 'Ptolemaion,' probably a misnomer that goes back to medieval Frankish writers working on the island.[85]

Within the Hellenistic period the most flourishing years in the history of Rhodes began about 220 BC[86] and lasted for about half a century. During these years the Rhodians sided with the Romans and won a number of decisive sea battles against their enemies. Most remarkable was the sea battle off the coast of Chios, won by the combined Rhodian-Pergamene navy in 201 BC. The victory was mainly the result of direction by an energetic Rhodian politician and skilful admiral named Theophiliskos, who died as a result of this engagement. It would not be surprising if the tomb at Rhodini was made for this outstanding, and presumably wealthy, person.[87] Whether the interior rooms were originally designed as a family burial place with loculi or whether the loculi were a later addition can no longer be determined.

There are very few projects closely comparable with the tomb at Rhodini other than the partly rock-cut Belevi Mausoleum and the built Lion Tomb at Knidos. However, some resemblance can be detected between the monumental Rhodian structure and both the Algerian Medracen tomb (see p. 137) and Tomb w80 in Cyrene; the latter is dated by Stucchi to the first century BC.[88] The Absalom and Zachariah tombs in Jerusalem, and the Tomb of

Hamrath at Suweida, also show some similarities in concept.[89]

This tomb at Rhodini is the largest of the extant funerary structures in the vicinity and dominates the entire necropolis.[90] Only one other tomb deserves to be mentioned here. Located west of the so-called Ptolemaion, it is a rock-cut façade-tomb with three false doors between four fluted columns (fig. 109). The capitals are missing; according to Ross they were of the Corinthian order, though the Doric or even the Ionic order would be more appropriate for the tomb.[91] Below the façade (which is some 3 m high and 5 m wide) were three openings for the actual burial; an arrangement of this sort was common in Etruria, and to a lesser extent at Cyrene in North Africa. The other tombs in the neighbourhood were mostly simple chamber tombs; the few that had architectural decoration have been destroyed beyond recognition.

IX Ta Marmara near Didyma

About 11.5 km northeast and inland from the village of Didyma stand the ruins of the large Hellenistic tomb known in modern literature as Ta Marmara.[92] This structure, 12 m square on plan (fig. 110), was built on a hill some 40 m high, overlooking Akbük bay to the south. The building material was the local limestone, stuccoed and painted. A stepped socle, more than 1.5 m high, supported three courses of isodomic masonry, the total height of which was about the same as that of the socle. On this high platform stood a walled cella enclosed by Doric columns. The sides and back had a 6 × 6 arrangement of free-standing columns set close to the cella walls.[93] The front was tetrastyle with two half-columns between the corner supports; in the wide central span was a large doorway. The only relief decoration of the heroon consisted of carved and painted shields in the upper part of the intercolumniations. A Doric architrave and frieze,[94] and a low pitched roof with pedimental ends, completed the temple-like form of the monument. A small doorway in the lower storey gave access to a chamber divided into two sections, one behind the other. The interior of the upper floor repeated this plan, but here the ceiling was adorned with diamond-shaped coffers.

The Ta Marmara tomb provides another example of a temple form modified to serve as a burial-place; but it also has close affinities with the second-century bouleuterion at nearby Miletos, which was probably built a few years before the tomb. The Ta Marmara in turn may have had a formative influence on similar schemes of the Roman era.

x Diocaesarea Tower Tomb

The Ta Marmara tomb represents the end of the line, not only of Hellenistic 'temple tombs' on podia in western Asia Minor, but also of monumental tomb building in general, until the idea was revived in the later first century BC under Roman rule. There is only one large built tomb of the early first century BC that deserves attention, and this not so much for its peculiarities as for its good state of preservation. It is located in the mountains of Cilicia near ancient Diocaesarea (modern Uzuncaburç).[95] It is a high tower tomb (fig. 111), square on plan (ca 5.4 × 5.4 m), set on a three-stepped platform. Above a high orthostate course the upward tapering tower is built of pseudo-isodomic masonry. The four angles are articulated by Doric pilasters; above these is a Doric entablature consisting of a plain architrave and a frieze course with five triglyphs and four undecorated metopes on each side. A pointed stepped pyramid surmounts the scheme. Access to the interior is from the south, through a small opening less than one metre high, which could be closed by a sliding slab. Inside there are arrangements for three kline burials within a low vaulted chamber.

The tomb has been dated to the first quarter of the first century BC. According to Keil and Wilhelm, it was the burial-place of a priestly ruler of Olba or perhaps even the Seleucid king Philip I (ca 93–84 BC).[96] The tower structure betrays Syrian influence, while the interior almost certainly copies some Macedonian prototype. If, in fact, the grave monument was built for a Seleucid king, the Macedonian character of the interior is understandable; at the same time, Cilicia's geographical proximity to Syria would explain the tower form of the exterior. This type, with some changes, was later imitated in Roman Cilicia.[97] Outside Asia Minor its closest parallels in form (and time) are to be found in North Africa; these tombs will be discussed in some detail in a later chapter.

xi Heroa at Gölbaşi-Trysa, Miletos, and Termessos

These three monumental complexes, although related in size and pretentiousness to the tombs described earlier, show a somewhat different concept. In each of them the actual tomb building or burial-place was just one element of the overall design, and not necessarily the dominant one; the rest of the complex was given over to cultic purposes. Only a few details of the designs were derived from the Nereid Monument and related edifices. At Gölbaşi-Trysa the Lycian type of tomb house, imitating timber construction was retained for the actual burial building; at Miletos a tumulus was raised

above the central core containing the burial; and at Termessos the picturesque qualities in sixth-century monumental rock carvings reappear in the
carvings around the kline bed.

The earliest of the three complexes is the heroon at Gölbaşi-Trysa
(fig. 112).[98] The site is located in a wooded region 866 m above sea level;
the setting is spectacular. Falkner describes it as follows: 'The view that
presents itself from the peribolos, I consider as the most beautiful that I
have ever beheld. To the east one looks towards a distant promontory;
below you is the sea, with a row of rocky islands; on the north and west
rise mountains above mountains while the immediate foreground is grand
and striking.'[99]

The higher (by some three metres) of two natural plateaus on the east
side of the acropolis hill was chosen for the sacred enclosure, which was
scraped back into the rising slope on the west and built up on the east to
form a more or less horizontal surface. The limestone walls enclose a
trapezoidal peribolos. The south, or principal, side is 19.66 m long, the west
24.54 m, the north 20.7 m, the east 23.5 m. The walls are on the average
1 m thick; the original height of the inner face was about 3 m. The three
free-standing walls on the north, east and south were constructed of two
parallel rows of stretchers, the space between them filled with rubble. The
fourth, or eastern side, abutting against the scrap of the hill, had polygonal
blocks behind a single row of stretchers. Coping-stones ca 0.34 m thick
covered the tops of all the walls. The doorway on the south side was placed
slightly off-centre.

The masonry of the south wall is more sophisticated than that of the
other sides. The exterior, up to the level of the door threshold, consists'
mostly of rusticated blocks with smooth drafted margins. Above that level
there are two massive courses of plain trapezoidal blocks followed by two
superimposed friezes. The decorative band beneath the coping is found only
on the exterior face of this south wall; it consists of an astragal, and egg-
and-dart, and the cornice proper. The height (0.32 m) and disposition of
this decorative band is almost the same as in the Nereid Monument (0.325 m
in height), with its double row of egg-and-dart. However, at Gölbaşi-Trysa
the cornice projects more and the eggs are less rounded.

The heroon is justly famous for its low-relief friezes, of which ca 210 m
is preserved (now in Vienna). They were displayed in a double row on the
inner faces of all the walls, in addition to the exterior face of the south wall
(fig. 113). The subjects represented are almost exclusively derived from
Greek mythology;[100] but the disposition of the friezes, and the lack of
mouldings above and below them, are very un-Greek.

The themes are the following (A indicates upper frieze, B lower frieze):

1 South wall, exterior frieze east of the doorway:
  A Seven against Thebes (9.40 m long)
  B Battle at landing (9.70 m)
2 South wall, exterior frieze west of the doorway:
  A Amazonomachy (7.25 m)
  B Centauromachy (7.50 m)
3 South wall, interior, west of the doorway:
  A Slaying of the suitors (7.61 m)
  B Meleager hunt (7.61 m)
4 West wall, south section:
  A and B Battle scenes, mostly hand-to-hand combat (11.26 m)
5 West wall, centre section:
  A and B Siege of Troy (6.18 m)
6 West wall, north section:
  A and B Amazonomachy (7.10 m)
7 North wall, west section:
  A and B Abduction of the daughters of Leucippus (8.74 m)
8 North wall, eastern section:
  A Hunting scenes (11.96 m)
  B Centauromachy (11.96 m)
9 East wall, north section:
  A Deeds of Theseus and Perseus (11.75 m)
  B Centauromachy (11.75 m), a continuation of the scene from the north wall
     (8:B)

The southeastern half of the eastern peribolos wall and a stretch (6.92 m long) at the eastern end of the southern wall were taken up by scenes from a funeral banquet. In this south eastern corner of the temenos there was a two-roomed wooden cult building open along the sides (fig. 114); thus the friezes occupied the second and third courses from the top, instead of the two top courses. The remaining stretch on the interior of the south wall, 2.30 m long, was taken up by a representation of a quadriga (A) above a scene with Bellerophon (B).

The doorway in the south wall of the precinct could be reached by a path; but there must have been steps or a ladder in front of the entrance to overcome the difference in level of some two metres between the ground and the threshold. The exterior face of the lintel was carved with projecting bull protomes (and three rosettes) above four seated figures. These two couples were in all likelihood the commissioners of the monument. On each side the reveal of the doorway had a large-scale dancing figure; above these, on the soffit of the lintel, was carved a group of masked musicians and dancers. The symbolism of the door frames seems obvious. The bull protomes protect the people below them, the rosettes indicate the commemorative nature of the heroon, and the dance inside the entrance is of a religious nature, connected with the funeral or commemorative rites.

In the northwest sector of the complex stood a large stone tomb house of typical Lycian design (i.e., imitating timber construction), oriented toward the cult building in the opposite corner. Fragments of a number of other sarcophagi were found inside the peribolos wall, but their number and position is uncertain. The rest of the enclosure probably contained plants and trees.

The Gölbaşi-Trysa heroon is not a building in the conventional sense; the architectural components do not create their own three-dimensional space defined by walls and a roof. Here the circuit wall alone marks the limits of the sacred area. Within this enclosure existing natural features were not completely destroyed but rather adjusted to suit the new function of the site. In modern terminology the design could be described as a kind of landscape architecture. The hanging gardens of Babylon, the setting of the Tomb of Cyrus the adyton of the Didyma temple, Mustafa Pasha Tomb III at Alexandria, and the later Mausoleum of Augustus at Rome are all, in a sense, related to the Lycian heroon in that they all depended for their decorative effects on landscape gardening as well as on architectural ornament.

The Austrian excavators emphasize the relationship between the heroon and the temenos of a god with its sacred grove.[101] At the same time Benndorf points out the functional differences between funeral enclosures and those of other sacred places.[102]

The Gölbaşi-Trysa heroon, which can be dated to about 360 BC on the basis of the relief decoration,[103] invites comparison with other well-known heroa with courtyards, for instance the Epicteta heroon on Thera mentioned earlier, and that of Antigonos Gonatas near Knidos. An inscription found at Myra[104] tells us that caretakers were to live at the heroon there, to serve as guards and keep the place tidy. Similar arrangements were to be found in other places in the Greek world, even as far away as Ai-Khanoum in present-day Afghanistan.[105] Cyrene also has a number of large heroa;[106] and the late-sixth-century-BC 'El Maabad' ('place of prayer') complex near Amrith (Marathos) in Syria (fig. 115) was in all probability yet another heroon or cult place.[107] The latter consists of a large, rock-cut rectangular (ca 50 × 57 m) courtyard, with a monumental shrine in the centre. The concept of the design is certainly akin to some of the later Hellenistic heroa complexes.

By the late Hellenistic period heroa with courtyards are found over a wide area, often, as we might expect, with features peculiar to particular localities. The overall form also changed with the passing of time, as may be seen in the heroon at Kalydon, dating from the early first century BC (fig. 2).[108] While the general concept is the same as at Gölbaşi-Trysa, the courtyard is completely surrounded by rooms of varying sizes, and there was an underground chamber below the principal room.

The Gölbaşi-Trysa heroon remains unique in Lycia. Although its origins are disputed, the strong mainland Greek influence is beyond question.[109] A similar view is expressed by M. Robertson: 'We know that some Greek hero-shrines, especially those of Theseus and the Dioscuri at Athens, were adorned with wall-paintings ... the disposition of the pictorial reliefs at Gölbaşi-Trysa echoes this practice.' He notes further: 'We have seen that there is evidence for such an arrangement in a building possibly identifiable as the Theseion at Athens, where the cornice had the same deep projection as here.'[110] Yet we should not forget that already in the late sixth century, long friezes were a standard feature on both the exterior and interior of Achaemenid buildings; moreover the custom of 'decorat[ing] and protect [ing] gates and entrances ... is Mesopotamian.'[111]

The necropoleis of Miletos have not as yet been studied in detail, and many tombs (including some large ones) remain unexplored. The tombs discovered to date range from Mycenaean times to the Roman era. The largest concentration is in the region called Kazar Tepe. Among the Hellenistic structures a barrel-vaulted underground tomb approached by a short dromos is especially important from the architectural viewpoint.[112] The technique and execution are akin to those of Macedonian tombs; but the Milesian example has no antechamber or decorated façade preceding the actual burial-chamber.

At Miletos, as elsewhere, the only burials allowed inside the city walls were those of persons of outstanding importance. One such intramural Hellenistic complex, the largest of its kind in the region, is located on the northeastern slopes of the theatre hill (fig. 116a, b). The site was briefly explored in the early twentieth century,[113] and a few years later the central core of the heroon was restored under the direction of A. von Gerkan.

The complex originally measured 43.50 × 39.96 m. The entrance to the heroon was from the centre of the east side, through a vaulted dromos that opened into the burial-chamber. This chamber also has a vaulted ceiling spanning the width (4.17 m) of the room; its depth is 3.57 m. five loculi, each 1.95 m deep, were placed in the lower part of the west or back wall of the chamber. In the middle of the room is a sunken area (1.1 × 1.1 m) faced with marble slabs; originally this 'basin' was covered by a slab of which a section still remains in situ. The top surface of the slab is picked smooth, in a fashion indicating that something else was placed on top of it, perhaps an altar or a kline. From the sunken area came the only small finds of the complex, including a silver ring, a small gold plate, glass fragments, bones, and a relatively well-preserved skull.

According to the excavators, the entire circular central core was built of blocks of poros in a tumulus-like manner. The original form of this artificial tumulus (14.5 m in diameter) cannot readily be determined today. T. Wiegand's suggestion, that it perhaps resembled the conical superstructure of the tomb at Albano Laziale (fig. 24), is intriguing, but lacks supporting evidence. Along the shorter east and west sides of the courtyard were found remains of rooms, some of which, to judge from the preserved portions, were two storeys high. As one would expect, these rooms served for cultic purposes.

None of the architectural ornament has remained in situ; but fragments of Ionic columns, dentils, entablature, and pieces of sima, all of Hellenistic date, have been found. According to the excavators, all these elements belong stylistically to the late fourth century; a date in the last decades of the century is also indicated by the pebble mosaics found in two of the rooms.

So far no inscriptions have come to light; a small marble naiskos (0.90 m high and 0.54 m wide) is the only indication of a hero cult within the establishment. Though the identity of the person who commissioned it is not known, he must have been an important person in the history of the city. The size of the heroon, and its location half-way up the theatre hill, made it visible from almost all points of the city; as we have seen, such a conspicuous location is typical of structures of this type. We know from Pausanias that the founder of Miletos, Neleus, was buried outside the city walls;[114] consequently he could not have been honoured by this large heroon. The architecture of the vaulted burial-chamber, as well as the artificial mound above it, suggest Macedonian connections. The existence of loculi inside, as in the Knidian Lion Tomb, the Charmyleion on Kos, and the Sidi Gaber tomb at Alexandria, indicates that the tomb served an entire family.[115] Diodorus Siculus, in his account of Milesian affairs after the death of Alexander, mentions that in 314–313 BC the city was in the hands of a certain Macedonian named Asandros.[116] Because Asandros was a tyrant, he might have had enough money and manpower to build this monumental heroon for himself during his short reign; however, no definite conclusions can be drawn until the site is completely investigated.

The influence of the complex can be detected in later Milesian funerary architecture; for example, the plan of the largest Roman heroon (46 × 28 m), near the Faustina Baths, recalls that of its Hellenistic forerunner.[117]

At this point I should mention the small monument within the courtyard of the Hellenistic bouleuterion at Miletos, formerly labelled 'Ehrengrab.' Tuchelt has now shown conclusively that this structure was a monumental altar of the Augustan period, as had been originally believed.[118]

The largely unexplored site of Termessos in Pisidia is located about 30 km northwest of modern Antalya, on a small natural shelf, or plateau, enclosed by mountains. Its elevation, averaging 1000–1100 m above sea level, and the natural defences provided by the local rock formations, made the city isolated and difficult to reach.[119] The earliest rock-cut tombs, probably dating from the fourth century, are cut into the vertical cliffs along the western side of the plateau. Many of these tombs recall Lycian or Karian rock-cut examples that imitated timber construction;[120] however, the largest and most interesting tomb in this western necropolis is of a rather different character (fig. 117). The monument in question is not a façade-tomb; rather, it is a natural hollow that seems to have been enlarged and cut back so as to provide an enclosure for the tomb. The two extant rock-cut walls form an angle of approximately 90°. The east and south sides are now open, but presumably were closed by some sort of a built wall. Perhaps future excavations will reveal more about the nature of these destroyed sections.

The north, or principal, wall contains the sarcophagus partly broken, the front of which is carved to represent a kline. This projecting sarcophagus-kline is 1.8 m long, 0.6 m wide, and 0.4 m deep. In front of it is a bench, 0.38 m deep, recalling arrangements elsewhere with funerary tables in front of a kline, e.g., on the sarcophagus of Athienau from Cyprus,[121] or the Satrap sarcophagus from Sidon.[122] Palmettes rising between volutes decorate the legs of the kline-sarcophagus; Kleiner notes their resemblance to 'late classical palmettes.'[123]

Above the actual burial arrangement appears a relief screen wall, 1.64 m long, enclosed by pilasters. The bases of these pilasters have a torus-scotia-torus profile above a plinth; the neck of each of the capitals was originally ornamented either by a rosette or a disc. The pilasters support a friezeless Ionic entablature, consisting of an architrave of three fasciae (the width of the bands increasing from bottom up) and a dentil course. The composition is crowned by a low pediment.

Obviously this section, ca 2.4 m high, is a representation of a three-dimensional structure on a two-dimensional surface, such as occurs earlier in Persian or Phrygian rock-cut monuments; the entire scheme above the kline-sarcophagus seems to be derived from a baldacchino supported by four pillars, with a trellis work between them. The basic idea is similar to that of the funeral carriage of Alexander the Great described by Diodorus Siculus: 'The colonnade that supported the vault was a golden net, made of cords the thickness of a finger, which carried four long painted tablets, their ends adjoining, each equal in length to a side of the colonnade.' On top of this, 'on each corner of the vault on each side was a golden figure of Victory holding a trophy.'[124] Above the summit of the gabled roof in the Termessos relief, i.e., corresponding to the victory figures on Alexander's carriage, there is an eagle with spread wings holding a snake in its talons. The eagle indicates the royal rank of the person buried there, rather than an apotheosis scene.

To the right of the kline-sarcophagus there are a number of broken rock-cut containers, which were used for offerings. Further to the right is a large vessel in which water was collected from a lion-head waterspout above. Not far from this lion head there are two small relief figures, perhaps representing Hermes (or Dionysos) and Aphrodite (or a Nymph).[125] Next to this large container appears a segment of a circular relief, the edge of which is decorated by a wide plain band followed by a row of egg-and-dart and an astragal moulding. To the left of the kline-sarcophagus is a broken ostotheke with a false door on its front.[126]

Roughly in the centre of the west wall is a carving of a mounted warrior approximately 2 m high. His head was deliberately smashed in antiquity. In the northwest corner of the same wall are weapons and pieces of armour in relief: a round shield with a short sword behind it, a pair of greaves below, and a helmet above the shield.

The reliefs and the arrangement of the interior (fig. 118) of the tomb are unmistakenly Macedonian. Burial on a kline is also a standard feature of Macedonian tombs. The armour of the horsemen closely resembles that worn by Alexander in the scene from the battle of Issus (333 BC) represented in the Naples mosaic.[127] The short sword and the helmet-type[128] are Illyrian in origin; a similar shield and helmet appear on an Illyrian rock-cut tomb near Pogredace in Albania.[129] The depiction of mounted warriors was a popular theme with the Macedonian nobility. Outside of Macedonia the so-called Alexander Sarcophagus from Sidon,[130] a tomb relief at Kadyanda in Lycia,[131] and a painted stele from Shatby in Alexandria[132] all show analogous representations of horsemen. Finally, in the territories adjoining Macedonia there are a number of other comparable horsemen reliefs, long overlooked, in Epirus,[133] in Thessaly,[134] and in a Thracian rock relief[135] (perhaps the closest in style to the Termessos horseman).

The date and identity of the person buried in this tomb is less of a problem than in other instances. Diodorus Siculus gives a detailed account of Termessian affairs after the death of Perdikas in 319 BC.[136] Antigonos, in his bid to gain power in Asia Minor, had to defeat other Macedonians who were aiming at the same goal. One of them was a certain Alkestas, a former general of Alexander. After losing his army in a series of minor engagements with Antigonos, Alkestas retreated to the mountain stronghold of Termessos. The older Termessians, wishing to save the city from a siege, plotted to capture Alkestas and deliver him to Antigonos. They acted while the younger men, who were ardent supporters of Alkestas, were outside the city; however, Alkestas committed suicide before they could capture him alive. His body was mutilated and left unburied by Antigonos, when he departed from the region: 'But the young men of Termessos, still preserving their goodwill for the victim, recovered the body and honoured it with splendid obsequies.'[137] The imposing tomb under discussion can be plausibly associated with the burial of Alkestas, for there is nothing in the still-preserved portions that conflicts with the date of 319 BC implied by such an association.

XII Simple Façade-Tombs

Among the façade-tombs that are less elaborate than the Archokrateion at Lindos, there are a large number of examples in Lycia. Individually these tombs show little variety in design. Like the sixth- and fifth-century tombs of Cyrene and the somewhat later Paphlagonian rock-cut façades, most of them follow a stereotyped scheme.

In western Asia Minor the fourth century witnessed the development of entire necropoleis of rock-cut tombs, all reflecting Greek architectural influence. While the existence of such burials depended in part on local geological conditions, economic considerations also played an important role. It was cheaper to cut a façade out of the face of the cliff than to build a free-standing structure of equal dimensions.

The most common arrangement was that of an imposing façade masking a small (and often summarily executed) burial-chamber, with rock-cut klinai (imitating wooden prototypes) along the walls. The number of columns on the façade varied from one to four, though the most common arrangement was distyle in antis. In contrast to fourth-century temples, tomb façades with uneven numbers of columns were not uncommon because in tomb architecture the obstruction of the entrance was not always considered a serious matter.

The best sites for rock-cut façade-tombs, which were meant to attract attention, were vertical cliffs visible from a number of different directions. The Doric order was less commonly employed, except at Cyrene; and there is only one known example of a Corinthian tomb, at Sovana in Etruria.[138] In proportions and details no strict rules were applied by the designers; the result was a non-canonical, 'free-style' imitation of established Greek principles.

Of the numerous façade-tombs, two large examples, both Ionic, will be chosen for discussion from the Lycian series. Following that, we shall turn to the few extant monumental rock-cut tombs from Phrygia and Kappadocia. Of the very few Doric façades in western Asia Minor the best preserved are at Kaunos in Karia (fig. 39); these tombs, including the Ionic designs (fig. 119), have been studied and recorded in great detail in publications by P. Roos.[139]

The façade of the so-called Tomb of Amyntas at Telmessos[140] (modern Fethiyeh) stands in a large niche, approximately 11 × 13 m, hewn out of the limestone rock (fig. 120). As in numerous other tombs of similar nature, the sides of the façade are flanked by shallow recesses. Four high steps, perhaps taking the place of a podium, lead up to a rather deep (ca 2.6 m) porch, ca 6 m in width.[141] The front is distyle in antis; the unfluted columns are ca 6.15 m high, with a lower diameter of 0.73 m. The Ionic capitals have heavy prominent volutes, in some respects recalling those of the Temple of Apollo at Bassae.[142] The bases are also unusual in possessing a plinth; the scotia between the upper and lower torus is extremely elongated. Each of the antae has three carved rosettes beneath the capital. The left-hand anta also has an inscription, AMYNTOY TOY ΕΡΜΑΓΙΟΥ (of Amyntas son of Hermagios), which probably identifies the owner of the tomb. The simplified entablature, a common feature of rock-cut tombs that is very evident here, consists of a rather bulky dentil course supported by a two-fascia architrave. The pediment is quite low; it carries no sculpture but was probably painted. The apex and corners are ornamented with acroteria.

A high stone door with four panels masked the burial chamber. In design it faithfully copied Greek wooden prototypes, even including their bronze ornaments. Here, however, only the lower right-hand panel could be opened to allow access to the interior. The door lintel has a series of carved bands, painted with decorative motifs and enclosed by unfinished consoles. In the interior, three rock-cut benches projected from the walls of the small (ca 2.5 × 2.7 m) burial-chamber.

The date of the Amyntas tomb, like most of the rock-cut tombs, remains an enigma. All these burials have been robbed of their contents, and what remains in the way of supplementary evidence is meagre. The unorthodox execution of the architectural forms makes them difficult to date on stylistic grounds, the more so because many of the tombs were never completed. In the rock-cut tradition of Asia Minor, and especially Lycia, the introduction of Greek architectural elements was a gradual process. Following a period in which Lycian rock-cut tombs imitated wooden construction, mixed designs with some Greek mouldings began to appear. Completely Greek façades must then have been created under the influence of such monumental free-standing tombs as the Nereid Monument.

The Tomb of Amyntas can probably be assigned to the later fourth century, a period that saw an upsurge of monumental building activity.[143] By the time of the Macedonian conquest of Asia Minor many of these tombs were already standing, and new rulers continued to erect them.[144] Because Amyntas is a Macedonian name, it is conceivable that the Amyntas tomb belonged to a prominent Macedonian who died at Telmessos.[145]

In the necropolis at Myra two large concentrations of rock-cut tombs occupy the almost vertical slopes of the local acropolis.[146] The southwest group, facing the sea, is also known as the seaward necropolis while the other cluster of tombs is referred to as the river necropolis, because it faces the Demre-Çay. The large majority of these very picturesque burials are of the familiar 'Lycian type' (fig. 121), imitating local wooden construction. Among the few of the 'Greek type,' Tomb no. 69 of the river necropolis, about 50 m up the cliff-face, is perhaps the most remarkable (fig. 122).[147] The façade, raised on a low socle, was carved completely free of the surrounding rock to a depth of about 2.5 m; it measures roughly 6 m across and 4 m in height. The porch, with three unfluted Ionic columns (no longer extant), was rather unconventional. There is a friezeless entablature, with an architrave of three fasciae surmounted by a heavy dentil course. The tympanon is occupied by low relief, a rather rare feature of rock-cut tombs in Lycia. It shows a lion attacking a bull. The plan recalls the arrangement of a prostyle temple.

In the centre of the back wall is a doorway framed all around by three fascia-like bands; above the lintel there is a relief band representing a funeral banquet. (The painted blue background of the frieze was still visible a few years ago.) Flanking the doorway are two pilasters and two engaged Ionic columns; each pilaster supports a large lion head, placed at the level of the capitals over the exterior columns. Next to the lion head of the right hand anta are two identical 'plant goddesses' carved in low relief (fig. 123a, b).

On the left side of the doorway there is only one goddess between the lion head and the engaged Ionic capital, so that the design of the door wall becomes unsymmetrical. On the upper part of each anta are three large rosettes placed one above the other. The engaged Ionic columns stand free of the wall for three-quarters of their diameter; the bases have a torus-scotia-torus profile, with no plinth.

In the mid-nineteenth-century publication record of the tomb by Texier, the funeral chamber appears to be perpendicular to the façade, with three klinai along the walls.[148] However, Borchhardt correctly notes that the tomb has only one kline (in the east wall), and the axis of the chamber is at an oblique angle to the façade.

In the absence of inscriptions and small finds it is hard to assign a date to the tomb. The large volutes of the Ionic capitals are set fairly close together, with a high canalis between them. Designs of this type seem to occur most frequently in late archaic and early classical times (i.e., first half of the fifth century); the volutes of later capitals are often large in proportion to the eye-to-eye width, but the canalis is very low. The occurrence of large volutes with high canalis in Lycian territory may have been the result, in part, of the influence of wooden prototypes. In the present case the line of the column's outer circumference, if extended, would cut through the eyes of the volutes, as is the case in capitals of the Hellenistic age. In built architecture there are no readily available parallels for the capitals under discussion; but the tradition seems to be that of Bassae, and its influence is noticeable in other rock-cut Ionic tombs in Lycia (e.g., Telmessos) and Karia (e.g., Kaunos).[149] If Roux is correct in identifying the Ionic forms at Bassae as the work of a Peloponnesian, and specifically of the Argive school, we must then assume some degree of Peloponnesian as well as Attic influence in Lycia.

According to Borchhardt, many of the decorative details are stylistically akin to other examples from the fourth century, to which Tomb no. 69 may also belong. Although there is no room here to discuss the origin of the decorative motifs or to analyse their style, their strongly symbolic nature should be noted, because most of the tomb ornaments of the fourth century are analogous in this respect. The meaning of the funeral-banquet scene is obvious. The animal fight is symbolic of an old oriental notion, the 'cycle' of life and death. Lions are often represented as protectors and guardians of tombs; here the two large lions heads seem to fulfil the same function. The goddesses emerging from plants are probably representations of Artemis; besides being protectors of vegetation and animals, they are also rulers over the realm of the dead.

In the fourth century, meanders, along with rosettes, frequently occur on tomb monuments. However, their symbolic significance has long been ignored.[150]

In Phrygia, where there was a long and well-established tradition of rock-cut monuments, one might expect to find an abundance of large Hellenistic rock-tombs. Yet there are only a few known examples that are clearly derived from Hellenistic Greek architecture.[151] The best preserved and the most interesting of these is the so-called Gerdek Kaya tomb near Çukura (fig. 124).

The façade of this tomb, approximately 8 m wide and 6 m high, stands about 4 m above ground level; it is flush with the surrounding vertical rock surface, except on the top and the right side, where the rock forms a slightly projecting 'frame.' Two slender, unfluted Doric columns (now mostly destroyed) were set far apart between the corner antae. The entablature, too, is Doric, with a narrow architrave and a somewhat wider triglyph-and-metope frieze. There are four triglyphs and five metopes over the central intercolumnar space, with two triglyphs and three metopes over each of the corner intervals. The façade is crowned by a low pediment with central and corner acroteria. The porch behind the columns is 3.6 m deep and widens inwards to a maximum breadth of 8.5 m. The flat ceiling clearly imitates a wooden construction of rafters laid over lengthwise beams that are parallel to the ridge-beam. The interior of the tomb was altered during the Roman period; originally it had two burial rooms, arranged as triclinia with three benches in each room.

The façade, unusually for a two-dimensional rock-cut tomb, was surmounted by a colossal lion figure (one foot measures 1.1 m across). According to Haspels, the lion was shown in the same position, with legs stretched forward, as the Hamadan lion in ancient Ekbatana.[152]

The low, wide façade, and the increased number of triglyphs over the central intercolumniation, can be compared to the Knidian monument; however, at Gerdek Kaya the widening of the central span is much more pronounced.

The date of the Phrygian tomb must surely be later than the Knidian Lion Tomb; to judge from the architectural details, it can hardly be earlier than the second century.[153]

Kappadocia is best known for its numerous rock-cut churches of the Byzantine era, but among the earlier architectural remains there are a number of little-known Hellenistic rock-cut tombs.[154] Near the modern village of Mazıköy there are four Doric tombs, with columns in antis, cut into the vertical north (three tombs) and south (one tomb) sides of a rocky plateau. The façades either are all flush with the irregular rock surface or project slightly from it (fig. 125). All the northern tombs are crowned by a low pediment. The superstructure of the southern tomb (fig. 126), above the columns, resembles the frieze-like band in the recently discovered (1977) Doric Tomb II at Vergina in Macedonia. In the centre of this wide 'frieze' stands a human figure with outstretched arms.[155]

The three tomb façades (also Doric) at the nearby village of Maçan are closely related to the preceding monuments. The largest, now destroyed, even attracted the attention of Texier.[156] The site is known as Dikili Taş. The façade measured 14.36 m in width, but only about 3 m in height (fig. 127). In the middle of this façade were two heavy-set columns flanked on each side by a free-standing square pier and a corner anta. The capitals of the columns and piers are derived from the Doric order; none of the supporting members has a base. Above the façade was a low pediment. The ceiling of the interior room, off which opened three spacious loculi, imitated barrel vaulting. Presumably in Roman times, when the tomb was reused, a funerary column (as seen for example next to the Kara Kuş tumulus in Kommagene)[157] was added to the grave monument. H. von Gall has compared the scheme to that of the small Asagi Güney tomb in Paphlagonia.[158] As a matter of fact, these seven Kappadocian tombs are all closer in concept to those of Paphlagonia than to any other group. However, the Greek influence seems to be somewhat stronger in Kappadocia than in Paphlagonia. The date of the tombs must fall within the period of the Kappadocian kingdom, which lasted from the third to the first century BC.

Mithradates I. Ktistes was the first king of Pontus to achieve substantial military successes. Even before 281 BC he managed to conquer most of Paphlagonia and a large portion of Kappadocia. In his capital, at ancient Amaseia, there are a number of niche-like rock-cut façade-tombs that must date from the period before the king's residence was moved to Sinope in the middle of the second century.[159] These tombs are interesting, inasmuch as none of them has a columnar treatment; the scheme is that of an aedicula or perhaps the vaulted interior room of a tumulus, represented in rock-cut form (fig. 128).

4

The Development of
Hellenistic Monumental Tombs
outside Asia Minor

It is well known that, as a result of Alexander the Great's campaigns, Greek language and culture spread over a very large area. The use of a single language greatly encouraged the exchange of ideas between the different regions of the Mediterranean. Before the rise of the Macedonians, contacts and trade connections between the Greek and non-Greek populations of the Mediterranean had generally been on a more restricted scale. The Macedonian dynasties acted as a unifying influence by establishing many new colonies in non-Greek regions, such as Alexandria in Egypt. The Graeco-Macedonian settlers brought with them fresh ideas that certainly influenced the local cultural outlook and provided the basis for new developments in architecture as well as in other fields.

In Asia Minor and the offshore islands very few new monumental tombs were built after the third century; however, the earlier grandiose examples remained to impress all who saw them. Thus, the architectural novelties of each region could be studied (especially by military engineers), and later reproduced or imitated elsewhere, whenever the political and economic situations were favourable. Imitation did not necessarily mean the mechanical copying of an entire building; as a matter of fact, in really monumental structures, direct copying never occurred. Instead, parts or sections of earlier buildings that appealed to those who designed or commissioned later tombs were borrowed and incorporated into the new monuments; sometimes ideas derived from several different places were united in a single building. At sites where there was an existing tradition of built, rock-cut architecture, or tumuli, established local customs and forms often played a dominant role, even in the execution of new types of funerary monuments that had been previously unknown in the region.

The tombs discussed in the following pages can be regarded as a continuation, or rather a further development, of the monumental tombs erected in western Asia Minor. As the construction of monumental tomb buildings spread to other regions, the variety of forms increased. In a few projects the direct influence of Anatolian models can be detected; more often, however, Anatolian influence was indirect and was transmitted through intermediaries. In still other cases the inspiration for the building (or cutting) of monumental tombs may have come from other forms of sacred or utilitarian architecture.

The large Anatolian 'temple tombs' on podia were familiar to the fourth-century designers of mainland Greece, including the Peloponnesos; indeed mainland artists actually worked on several of the east-Greek monuments. Yet neither at Athens nor elsewhere on the mainland do we find tombs closely related in scale and decoration to the monumental funerary buildings of Asia Minor. The tombs of the early fourth century along the West Road of the Athenian Kerameikos, or the larger monuments on the Academy Road between horoi 2 and 3, are of little interest from the architectural point of view.[1] Somewhat more sumptuous tombs seem to have appeared in Attica and elsewhere in mainland Greece only after the mid fourth century.[2]

1 Funerary Monuments in Greece

A *The Tomb at Kallithea*

One of the largest tombs of the later fourth century, betraying at least some influence of prototypes from Asia Minor, was found at Kallithea in 1968.[3] The ruins of this tomb came to light next to a gateway in the long walls that once connected Piraeus with Athens.[4] The structure is reconstructed in the Piraeus museum.

A three-stepped platform supported a high limestone podium, which presumably carried two superimposed friezes separated by an inscribed course. The lower frieze (fragmentary) represents an Amazonomachy, the upper (almost 4.5 m long) an animal fight. Above the geison course that crowned the podium, the superstructure was raised on a two-stepped base. It was probably in the form of a large naos (ca 3 m high) with a façade of two Ionic columns (with Attic-Ionic bases) in front of the antae – a distyle-prostyle aedicula arrangement. The antae were richly painted in brilliant shades of red, blue, and yellow. Inside the naos were statues of a young, a middle-aged, and an old man. E. Tsirivakos, the excavator of the site, suggests that they were perhaps father and son with a servant. The overall height of the monument was about 8.3 m. The tomb can be dated on the basis of its relief sculpture to the third quarter of the fourth century, just before the enactment of the sumptuary laws of Demetrios of Phaleron in 316 BC.

By the second half of the fourth century there were other structures in Athens that echoed the tripartitie division of the monumental tombs of western Asia Minor (e.g., the Lysikrates Monument). Yet the Kallithea tomb in general still adheres to the tradition of the Kerameikos grave plots of the earlier fourth century, e.g., the Dexileos tomb of 394 BC. Only the presence of a decorated podium (if the proposed reconstruction is correct) indicates possible influence from Asia Minor.

B The Tombs in Arkadia

During the third and second centuries few large new tombs seem to have been built either in Attica or in most other regions of mainland Greece. The obvious exceptions are the Macedonian, or Macedonian-inspired, grave monuments; there were also a few tombs with architectural façades at Alipheira in Arkadia.[5]

The Alipheira tombs had large forecourts in front of the actual tomb façades, of which one of the largest one was ca 5 m wide (fig. 129). A number of openings separated by piers faced the lower parts of the façades, behind which were installed long, narrow compartments. The façades supported pediments crowned by acroteria. The Arkadian tomb fronts vaguely resemble the simpler Macedonian tombs with pedimental façades. However, the interior arrangements in Arkadia followed a concept quite different from that employed in Macedonia; they were simple rectangular shafts with a flat ceiling.

C The Tombs in Macedonia

During the fourth century a special tomb-type evolved in Macedonia; in modern literature they are known as the 'Macedonian tombs.'[6] The vaulted burial-chambers, often masked by imposing façades, were covered by earth tumuli or mounds. The design of the façades shows great variety, both in the use of the columnar orders and in the subsidiary decoration. The most pretentious tombs resembled (to some extent) the façades of temples, with Ionic or Doric members engaged in the outer face of the entrance wall, which was crowned by a pediment. Among the finest Ionic examples are those at Vergina (fig. 130), Langaza, and Lefkadia-Naoussa,[7] each with a tetrastyle front of engaged columns.[8] The large akroteria-anthemia surmounting the pediment of the Lefkadia-Naoussa tomb are unusual (fig. 131).

Among the Doric tombs is one, at Laina, in which two free-standing columns stood between the antae.[9] Otherwise the columns were generally engaged, as in the so-called Haghios Athanasios Tomb (fig. 132)[10] or in the above-mentioned Ionic tomb at Vergina. Moreover, some façades had no columns at all, e.g., the so-called Soteriades tomb at Dion[11] (fig. 133), where, however, there are engaged Ionic columns in the interior (fig. 134). No tomb of the Corinthian order has yet come to light; presumably Corinthian was never really accepted in the otherwise eclectic architectural style of Macedonia.

Most of the tombs in Macedonia were constructed of local lime stone; marble was rarely used.[12] The decoration, whether plain panels, relief figures, or applied architectural elements with hardly any structural function, was executed in painted stucco. Klinai are found in virtually all the burial-chambers, which were often approached by a short dromos leading to the entrance.[13]

All the 'Macedonian tombs' with decorated façades and vaulted interior(s) were constructed during the 150–200 years immediately preceding the Roman conquest of the region in 168 BC; the 'group' has close to 100 known examples.

The tumulus type of burial has a long tradition in Macedonia. For example, in the region of Vergina there are numerous small tumuli some of them dating back to about 1000 BC. It is also in the area of Vergina where presumably Aigai, the ancient capital of Macedonia, is located.[14]

The excavations of the Great Tumulus[15] at Vergina up to 1977 did not reveal any substantial buildings below the mound. It was in the autumn of that year that the team of M. Andronikos located the first structures near the southern edge of the tumulus: 'Three structures were found at the time, one of them, a Heroon (sanctuary), was destroyed except for the foundations. The other two were intact and were underground graves. The first of these, Tomb I, is rectangular, measuring 3.50 by 2.09 meters, and 3 meters high; it has no entrance. The burial was effected through an opening at the top, which was later sealed up with big oblong blocks ... The pottery dates the tomb to around the middle of the fourth century B.C., perhaps to about 340 B.C.'[16] In the burial-chamber of Tomb I was found a painting of excellent quality: it depicts Pluto seizing Persephone. The composition is executed on a plastered wall surface, 3.5 m long and 1 m high.[17]

Tomb II is located a short distance northwest of Tomb I. It was an

undisturbed large barrel-vaulted structure, measuring approximately 10 ×
5.5 m and 6 m in height (fig. 135). The plastered[18] and painted façade is of
a single storey of the Doric order, but with a high decorative Ionic frieze
above the Doric entablature. The 5.56-m-long and 1.16-m-high frieze is
protected by a projecting cornice on top and below. It carries a remarkable
painting of a hunting scene.[19] The Doric entablature is painted in a conventional colour scheme: blue for the triglyphs and red for the horizontal
members.[20] Below the undecorated epistyle is a centrally located marble
doorway framed by two Doric half-columns and pilasters at the sides. The
doorway was protected by a wall of limestone blocks against the pressure
of the earth filling. Behind the imposing façade both the forechamber and
the main chamber carry a barrel vault. The interior walls of the main
chamber have only a coarse coating of stucco and do not carry any figural
or other type of decoration. The antechamber is 3.66 m long, while its width
and height are exactly the same as for the main chamber. It has a very fine
stuccoed wall surface – white for the lower section and red for the upper
part. The springing of the vault is indicated by mouldings that had pegs for
suspending objects. Everything deposited in the chambers was found in situ
as had been left at the time of the burial(s). The exterior of the barrel
vault has a thick layer of waterproof stucco, an exceptional feature of the
Hellenistic monumental tombs in Macedonia. On top of the vault were
located the remnants of an altar built of sun-dried bricks.[21]

A third intact tomb came to light in 1978 a short distance to the northwest
of Tomb I.[22] It also has an antechamber and a main chamber behind it, but
its dimensions are smaller than those of Tomb II. The painting of the façade
has disappeared, because it was executed on a panel of wood or leather and
then fastened to the background. But in the forechamber there is a relatively
well-preserved narrow frieze of a two-horse chariot. It is not of the high
quality of the exterior frieze of Tomb II but is, nevertheless, the work of a
gifted painter. The objects found inside Tomb III indicate that the structure
belonged to a less important person than the 'owner' of Tomb II.

All three burials are probably to be associated with members of the
Macedonian royal family. The largest and the most pretentious of the three
structures, Tomb II, could have served for the burial of Philip II.[23] Among
all the known barrel-vaulted examples in Macedonia, Tomb II has the
greatest length and height. The care taken to protect the exterior two-leaved
marble door and the fine waterproof stucco on top of the vaulting suggest
that the designer(s) of the structure had previous experience with such
technicalities and/or relied on prototypes known to them. Its date, as indicated above, would fall in the third quarter of the fourth century after the
construction of Tomb I but antedating Tomb III. Consequently the barrel

vault of Tomb II would be the earliest known example of such a technique employed in Greece. Its well-developed form seems to underline the controversial testimony of Plato that the principle of the true arch was probably known to the Greeks all throughout the fourth century or perhaps even before.[24]

In 1981 three more large tumulus tombs were discovered in the region of Vergina.[25] In this group Tomb no. I has a façade decorated with four Doric half-columns and a regular entablature (fig. 136). The remarkable feature of this tomb is the unusually high raking sima, which seems to be a 'replacement' for the Ionic frieze found in Tomb II of the Great Tumulus. The structure is datable to the second half of the third century.

Tomb no. II of the group has a simple façade and a huge sarcophagus inside the chamber. In Tomb no. III there are no architectural elements applied to the façade. Here, the space between the pediment and the lintel of the doorway is occupied by a group of painted figures (fig. 137). The structure can be assigned to the early years of the third century.

The most splendid example of all the tombs uncovered in Macedonia is the so-called Great Tomb at Lefkadia (fig. 138), discovered and excavated during the 1950s.[26] Local limestone was employed for the entire structure, including the platform, a half-metre thick, that served as the only foundation for the tomb building. Unlike the other known tombs in Macedonia, the façade of the Lefkadia building has two tiers of columns, although the interior is one-storeyed. The height of the façade (8.55 m) is almost the same as its width (8.68 m). Four fluted Doric half-columns, 3.35 m high, stand between the corner pilasters; there is a large doorway in the central span of this lower order. The height of the Doric columns is six times the lower diameter. The stuccoed intervals are divided into two sections. The lower part imitates coursed masonry; the panels above (1.29 m high and 1.55 m wide) carry paintings of the deceased person and Hermes on the left of the entrance, and of Aiakos and Rhadamanthys on the right.[27] All the figures turn towards the doorway, indicating that behind it lay the focal point of the whole building, i.e., the burial. The figures are placed on a ground-line consisting of a painted-egg-and-tongue.

Above the central intercolumniation there are two triglyphs.[28] The eleven metopes represent fights between Lapiths and Centaurs; they were covered with a light wash, but had no colour except for the strongly emphasized dark-brown shadow lines to give the illusion of relief sculpture.[29] A Doric cornice crowns the lower storey; its topmost section has a lively leaf-scroll decoration, painted in black, yellow, green, red, and white, on a blue background.

A particularly striking element in the decoration of the façade is the insertion of a continuous frieze, 0.7 m high, between the Doric lower and the Ionic upper storey. This stuccoed and painted relief band depicts a battle between Greeks (Macedonians) and Persians, a subject that must have enjoyed a considerable popularity after the conquests of Alexander the Great in the east. The frieze is surmounted by an Ionic cornice, above which a stylobate course supports the upper order, consisting of six engaged Ionic columns, 1.46 m high, between corner antae. The intercolumnar spaces are filled by seven false doors. The idea of a row of columns set on a high socle seems to have come from the podium tombs of Asia Minor. Here, however, the compression of the façade into one plane does not have the same 'stage' effect found, for example, in the Archokrateion at Lindos. Yet there is a certain theatrical quality to the design; the scenographic impression is emphasized by setting the Ionic half-columns of the upper storey against a brightly painted background, thus creating the illusion of a real portico. The entablature of the upper order consists of a two-fascia architrave with a narrow band on top, followed by a Lesbian-leaf course, dentils, and a painted pediment. The paintings of the pediment have almost completely eroded, except for the faint outlines of a (portrait) head.

Behind this extremely decorative front wall, the more modest vestibule and funerary chamber were laid out in a T-shaped plan (fig. 139a), the former wide and shallow (6.50 × 2.12 m), the latter square (4.8 m per side). Both are barrel-vaulted; the vaults reach a height of 7.7 m and 5.4 m respectively. The anteroom has little ornament apart from the two relief shields flanking the doorway of the partition wall. The walls of the burial-chamber, however, are richly decorated in stucco relief. The lowest element consists of three horizontal fields of varying widths, forming a 'podium' 1.5 m high. Above this 'podium' are fourteen engaged pilasters supporting a continuous Ionic entablature.[30] The scheme as a whole (fig. 139b) seems to echo the second storey of the façade.[31]

In the design of the façade the upper portion (including the Ionic frieze) may be compared with monumental altars as well as podium tombs. High decorated podia surmounted by columns, such as are found in the Hellenistic altars at Priene, Magnesia-on-the-Maeander, and Pergamon, are certainly related in concept to the upper level of the Lefkadia façade. At the same time, no known Hellenistic building is close enough to the overall design of the Lefkadia tomb to have served as a prototype. Temples do not have multi-storeyed fronts. Such combinations were reserved for certain types of public and private buildings. Stoas, the scene-buildings of theatres, and some parts of palaces and larger private houses all show a predilection for two-storeyed designs. Some large-scale tombs (e.g., those at Cyrenaica [fig. 141], Canosa [fig. 142], and Kandyba in Lycia)[32] and gateways (e.g., the

Gate of Zeus and Hera on Thasos [fig. 143])[33] also had two-storeyed façades. However, none of these structures was as elaborate as Lefkadia, and all lacked the intermediate frieze.

We must conclude, therefore, that in this Macedonian tomb elements derived from various contexts were blended into a unified and original composition. Combinations of different orders, or of their component parts, are by no means unknown in Macedonian monuments, as attested by the Vergina palace and the Philippeion at Olympia.[34] Clearly Macedonian expansion in the eastern Mediterranean during the latter part of the fourth century resulted, among other things, in the modification of the traditional tombs in Macedonia. Some of the new influences can already be discerned in the description by ancient authors of Alexander's funeral carriage.[35]

The reasons for building most of the tombs in Macedonia underground are obscure; probably religious beliefs and customs were the major factors. It is possible that by raising a tumulus over the tomb, the builders ensured that the burial-chamber could not be seen by mortals, but only by gods and supernatural beings.

The Great Tomb, along with the other known burials of the 'Macedonian type' in the Lefkadia region,[36] is not far from modern Edessa, where some scholars place the old national capital of Aigai;[37] and Aigai also served as the burial-place of the native kings from Perdikas onward. Consequently, the owner of the tomb may have been a prominent member of the Macedonian aristocracy, who died around 300 BC to judge from the stylistic details of the façade of his tomb.[38]

II Funerary Monuments in Albania (ancient Illyria)

Among the monumental rock-cut tombs of the Hellenistic age, special interest attaches to the series of Illyrian monuments located in the mountainous eastern region (called Basse-Selce) of present-day Albania. In Illyria, unlike in some other regions of the Mediterranean where Hellenistic rock-cut tombs are found, there was no earlier native tradition of such structures. The tombs in question are cut along a ridge of a precipitous limestone cliff, approximately 1000 m above sea-level. Only three of them were finished; the others were never completed and are thus less interesting architecturally. The three finished tombs are the earliest in the entire group. The investigation of the site as a whole was carried out by Albanian archaeologists in 1970–1.[39]

Tomb 1[40] occupies the central position among the three finished tombs (fig. 144a, b). It consists of a straight façade 2.4 m high and 4 m long, raised on a ledge, 0.25 m high. The door, tapering slightly towards the top, is located in the centre of the façade; it is 1.02 m wide and 1.98 m high, and is framed by a flat relief band. The lintel is crowned by two narrow fillets under a moulding that vaguely resembles the profile of a Greek egg-and-dart. The overall design recalls the exteriors of the Langaza and Palatitza tombs. Two slender unfluted Ionic columns, without bases, flank the central opening; their height is slightly more than ten times the lower diameter. According to the excavators, the capitals were decorated with rosettes in the middle of the canalis.[41] The ends of the façade are closed by pilasters with simple rectangular capitals. The surfaces between the pilasters and the columns once carried frescos. The actual funerary chamber behind the façade measures 3 × 2.8 m. Along the left side and across the back of the room are two rock-cut benches (ca 0.5 m high) on which the corpses were laid. The ceiling of the chamber is cut in the shape of a barrel vault. An interesting feature of the tomb is the level rock-cut area, with benches along the sides (3.8 × 3.5 m), in front of the façade; there are some indications of supports for a timber roof over this area.

Tomb 2 stands a few metres north of Tomb 1, but 1.5 m higher; it is the only known specimen of its kind in Hellenistic funerary architecture (fig. 145a, b). It is laid out on two different levels; the lower contains the actual burial-place, while the upper part was intended for commemorative ceremonies. This upper section, horseshoe-shaped and 1.32 m high, consists of three steps forming seats like those in the cavea of a theatre. Around the outer circumference of the uppermost step there is a channel to collect rainwater, thus preventing it from getting into the interior of this 'theatre' tomb. Beneath the 'orchestra' were sunk two rectangular shafts, the upper 1.78 × 1.68 m and 0.77 m deep, the lower somewhat smaller, 1 × 1.22 m and 0.87 m in depth. These shafts served to hold the funerary urns of the deceased; they were covered by a flat slab that formed the floor of the 'orchestra.' The 'skene' is formed by a wall (0.45 m thick), pierced by a small central door that was originally blocked and sealed by lead. Around the 'cavea,' which undoubtedly served for commemorative ceremonies, there are cuttings indicating the existence of some sort of a wooden roof for protection against sun and rain.

Tomb 3, the largest of the group (fig. 146a, b), occupies a ridge above and to the south of Tomb 1. The façade, 3 m high, has the form of a portico with a semicircular recess in the middle containing the doorway. A continuous two-stepped base, 0.4 m high, supports eight engaged Ionic columns with a door in the centre. Six of these eight members are half-columns; the central recess is framed by three-quarter columns. In contrast to Tomb 1, all the columns have bases and fluted shafts. The capitals are separately carved and inserted in spaces left between the tops of the shafts and the architrave. These capitals (fig. 147c) have much the same form as those of Tomb 1, with a rosette in the centre of the unusually wide canalis; but here the workmanship is more careful and refined. The bases (fig. 147d) are rather unorthodox. The apophyge is hardly noticeable, but the bases are strongly splayed; the profile consists of a concave bottom member above a narrow fillet, and two superimposed cyma bands crowned by a second narrow fillet. Both the capitals and the bases recall those of the Temple of Apollo at Bassae. The architrave has two fasciae of equal width, crowned by a third, and much narrower, band (hardly to be called a fascia). The profile of the cornice forms an elongated 'S' curve. In the centre of the façade above the cornice there are the remains of a rectangular built niche (0.98 × 0.43 m). Probably the niche contained a statue, or an inscription, or both. The panels (2.2 m high and 0.7 m wide) flanking the doorway in the central semicircular section of the façade were evidently painted; unfortunately no traces of the paintings have survived. The scenographic effect of the whole design was further enhanced by reliefs carved in the intercolumniations of the straight wing sections. On the spectator's left side is a shallow rectangular niche (fig. 147b), once containing the head of a bull in high relief; a Hellenistic helmet, displaying some Thracian features, is carved above this recess.[42] On the right side (fig. 147a) a round shield (0.7 m in diameter), also in relief, is placed in the intercolumnar space; half its design has been broken away, including the central portion. The still existing upper part of the shield has a relatively wide rim and a swastika decoration enclosed by three ellipses – the type of shield that is used in Illyria but also occurs in Macedonian contexts.[43]

The central door (2 × 1.1 m) is similar to that of Tomb 1, with a relief frame around it. The lower part of the door-leaves were found in situ; they closely resemble Macedonian examples. The interior of the room was never finished because of technical difficulties resulting from the faults in the rock. Instead, a second funerary chamber was hewn below the open courtyard in front of the façade of the tomb; this chamber is almost square (2.77 × 2.72 m and maximum height 1.85 m), with a ceiling imitating a barrel vault. Two klinai were placed inside the chamber; the one along the back wall (fig. 147e) has decorative carvings. The decorative patterns and especially the general form of the legs of this kline are once more closely related to Macedonian examples such as those found in the Pydna tomb.[44]

The courtyard in front of the façade deserves special attention, not only on account of its size (ca 6.5 × 4 m) but also because of its decoration. The floor was completely covered by mosaics, further enhancing the picturesqueness of the entire complex.

Tomb 4, to the south of the above-mentioned monuments (fig. 148), was never completed. As far as can be determined from its incomplete state, it was meant to have a pediment supported by either columns or pilasters, with a doorway in the centre of the façade. Somewhat to the north of this façade six lines of an inscription were found. Each line mentions a certain Mηκος, who doubtless commissioned the tomb. The name and the way it is spelled are local Illyrian; the letter forms suggest a date in the second half of the third century for both inscription and tomb.

Because of their unfinished state, the other tombs of this rock-cut cemetery are devoid of architectural interest. However, only about 40 m from Tomb 4 is a well-preserved built tomb with a barrel-vaulted interior (fig. 149a, b). The rectangular tomb measures 4.25 × 2.5 m overall; the vault reaches a height of 2.4 m. Local stone was used for the construction and clamps were employed to ensure the stability of the vaulted interior. As in the typical 'Macedonian tomb,' this interior is divided into two compartments, a vestibule (1.8 × 1.2 m) and a burial-chamber (1.85 × 1.85 m). In the burial-chamber, a kline was found, there were also benches along the side walls. The Albanian archaeologists make no mention of evidence for a tumulus above the built chamber.

Vaulted construction seems to be almost as widespread in certain parts of Illyria as it was in Macedonia, as shown for instance by several examples in the valley of Vjose.[45]

The ceilings of rock-cut tombs in Illyria also imitated barrel vaulting; the source of inspiration was undoubtedly Macedonia. Thus, the Illyrian examples must be later in date than the Macedonian models. Illyria was always receptive to outside influences, especially from the Greek peninsula and Asia Minor. A good example is a little-known relief of warriors from Apollonia (fig. 150), 0.6 m high and executed in archaic style.[46] The relief, recalling a similar scene from the treasury of the Siphnians from Delphi, shows strong Ionic influence, and can be dated to the early fifth century. The type of building to which it belonged is hard to determine. L. Rey posed this question: 'Faut-il y voir le soubassement de quelque monument analogue à ceux de Lycie?'[47] Because there is no evidence in Illyria for buildings like the Nereid Monument at Xanthos, the question must remain unanswered. In contrast, the source of inspiration for the Hellenistic tombs discussed above is much easier to detect. The interiors are clearly based on the vaulted tombs of Macedonia, though in the case of rock-cut tombs the outer chamber, or prodomos, of the Macedonian prototype is transformed into an open-air courtyard, or covered only with a light timber construction. The façades of Tombs 1 and 4 rely directly on Macedonian models, such as the Ionic tomb at Vergina;[48] but they are now exposed to view, after the fashion of the rock-cut tombs of Asia Minor, which probably also provided part of the inspiration for the buried tomb façades in Macedonia. The design of Tombs 2 and 3 is based on secular buildings (e.g., theatre and portico), as was often the case with grave monuments. The character of the design was determined to a certain extent by the rock formation, or at least by the fact that the tombs were carved from the living rock, not built; thus the forms were simplified and reduced in scale. The courtyards, with closed sides, of Tombs 1, 3, and 4, are a feature rarely, if ever, encountered in the rock-cut tombs of Asia Minor; but such a scheme was quite widespread, for example, in the necropoleis of Cyrene.

The period of construction of the rock-cut tombs of Hellenistic Illyria must lie between the late fourth and the last quarter of the third century. During this period the region enjoyed political stability land relative prosperity. In Tomb 3 the majority of the small finds date from the second half of the third century; however, they might belong to a secondary burial, rather than to the period of the original cutting of the tomb. From the point of view of architectural style, a date in the first half of the third century cannot be excluded, and the same is true for Tombs 1 and 2, the former being perhaps the earliest in the entire necropolis. The unfinished tombs constitute a second chronological group; they must have been started only in the later third century. They were commissioned by military personnel, as shown for example by the relief decoration of Tomb 3, and by wealthy citizens who owed their prosperity to Macedonian influence in their territory.

III Funerary Monuments in Italy

A *The Tombs at Canosa*

The Greeks of southern Italy and the Etruscans of central and northern Italy constituted an integral part of Mediterranean culture. Their burial monuments had a distinctive mark from archaic times on, but not without eastern influences. By the Hellenistic period, and especially beginning with the third century, the 'temple tombs' of Asia Minor and their underground variants in Macedonia and other types elsewhere must have been known to architects on the Italian peninsula. For example, the Great Tomb at Lefkadia has a closely related design at Canosa in southern Italy. Of the three tombs placed side by side and known as the 'Ipogei Lagrasta,' one (no. 3) had a two-storeyed façade (figs. 142 and 151).[49] Unfortunately the tomb, though still relatively well preserved up to the 1850s, has almost completely disappeared during the past century.[50]

Drawings from the middle of the last century show a lower storey with plain corner pilasters and two fluted Doric half-columns flanking a central doorway.[51] The upper half of the intervals between the half-columns and the pilasters was decorated with false windows. A regular Doric entablature followed, with a low architrave and a much higher frieze course; the metopes carried figured scenes. In contrast to the Lefkadia Great Tomb, there was no Ionic frieze band separating the upper storey from the lower. Instead, a series of mouldings (their total height less than that of the Doric frieze) provided a narrow base for the upper storey. The drawings of Bonucci and Gerhard in general agree in their representation of the lower storey. Both drawings show engaged Ionic columns, but Gerhard has six (fig. 142), Bonucci only five (fig. 151), with pilasters at the corners.[52] Both scholars assumed, probably correctly, that the upper storey was surmounted by a pediment. The column bases shown in the drawings were of regular Attic-Ionic type.

A long dromos preceded the elaborate façade. In addition to the central door of the façade there were two entrances in the side walls of the dromos leading to separate burial-chambers. Each of these side entrances was framed by two engaged Doric columns supporting an entablature crowned by a pediment.[53] In plan, the complex closely resembles the cruciform arrangement of Etruscan tombs rather than that of Macedonian and other eastern Hellenistic examples.

The same may be said of the plan of the neighbouring tomb, no. 2, located northwest of Tomb no. 3. An interesting feature of this tomb is the back wall of the antechamber, behind which was one additional room. This wall, still well preserved and 3.85 m wide, has four Ionic half-columns (each with eight flutes) and a doorway in the middle (fig. 152). The capitals have a sagging lower section to the canalis; the spirals of the volutes are incomplete.[54] The upper half of the wall between the columns was painted with false windows, as on the façade of Tomb no. 3. In the top portion of these panels, traces of wings can be made out; these may have belonged to Harpies or Sirens. Above the columns there is an architrave and a dentil course. The flat ceiling was carved in imitation of wooden construction in the manner familiar from Etruscan tombs at Caere and elsewhere.[55] Along the base of the walls there is a high, painted socle. The decorative scheme, as will be seen below, is surprisingly similar to that of some rock-cut tombs in Alexandria, e.g., the hypogeum at Shatbi. However, as Bertocchi points out, by the third century, tombs such as those of the Canosa group are found over a wide area, with similarities in plan as well as decocration.[56]

The five exterior doorways, one in the centre of the façade and two in each of the side walls of the dromos, have no special interest; each of the lateral entrances has a columnar frame similar to those of the lateral entrances of Tomb no. 3.

The date of the tombs at Lagrasta can be fairly definitely fixed in the first half of the third century. We know from Diodoros Siculus and Livy,[57] that Canosa enjoyed a period of relative prosperity during the later decades of the fourth and the first half of the third century. The pottery found in the tombs also supports a date in the early part of the third century.

B The Tombs at Sovana and Norchia

During the Hellenistic period, Etrusco-Italic tomb designs generally continued to follow local patterns that had been developed during earlier centuries. Tumuli and rock-cut cubic tombs (the so-called dadi) seem to have been the most popular forms; in these, special attention was given to interior design. Nevertheless, there are a number of monumental tombs, with elaborately decorated exteriors, that at least suggest the possibility of direct influence from eastern Mediterranean prototypes. The fame of the fourth-century 'temple tombs' of Asia Minor gradually spread to many other regions of the Mediterranean world. Travellers, military men, and merchants must have seen at first hand tombs such as the Mausoleum at Halikarnassos and related structures in the Hellenistic east. Imitations, or adaptations, of these monuments may then occasionally have replaced more traditional forms of burial. For example, the overall design of the so-called Tomba Ildebranda[58] at Sovana (fig. 153a, b), about 100 km northwest of Rome, was perhaps derived from one or the other of the tomb-types of Asia Minor. The tomb site, on a cliff-face overlooking a vast valley below, is visible from a considerable distance. Three sides of the tomb were carved entirely free of the rock, thus creating the illusion of a free-standing monument. The front is over 12 m wide, while the depth and height of the hewn-out section each measures approximately 10 m. The podium, 3.5 m high, consists of two sections, of which the lower projects slightly. The upper section is crowned by a large torus moulding, not a leaf- or egg-moulding in the Greek fashion.

The front originally had six fluted columns, more than 4 m high, with three more on each return. The intercolumnar spaces varied from 1.52 m to 1.73 m. Such variations are common in rock-cut tombs, where technical requirements played a secondary role.

Today, only one column remains in situ (lower diameter 0.83 m); most of the others have completely disappeared, except for some of the bases. The bases are relatively high (0.47 m), with a central drum-like section (fig. 154) (which can hardly be called a scotia) enclosed by two narrow tori. The design is similar to that of some rock-cut tombs in Asia Minor, for example the Amyntas tomb at Telmessos. The capitals (fig. 154), 0.77 m in height, have a band of acanthus foliage around the bottom; the corner leaves spring boldly up to form volutes, while in the middle of each face there is carved a human head.[59] The flanking colonnades are continued backward by walls faced with pilasters. The ceiling of the pteron was carved to imitate a complex scheme of coffering. The section corresponding to the pronaos and cella of a Greek temple is a solid rectangular block, the front of which had a false door apparently decorated with lozenges in low relief, in imitation of a metal grille.

Above the columns there were two friezes (fig. 154); the lower band (0.47 m high) has juxtaposed griffins between plant motifs, while the upper (0.8 m high) consisted of foliage patterns. The crowning element was a series of dentils, with large rosettes at regular intervals replacing the conventional antefixes.[60] There was no pediment, only a stone cippus, 0.77 m high, placed in the centre of the façade above the horizontal roof line. The impressiveness of the façade must have been enhanced by its polychrome effect; stucco fragments with traces of red, green, blue, yellow, and white paint were found in the tomb.

Two stairways flanking the podium led up to the colonnade. In front of the podium is a rock-cut platform, in the middle of which a deep dromos (5 m long and 1.9 m wide) leads to the burial-chamber, a large room of cruciform shape (maximum depth more than 7.5 m), with the ceiling sloping down from the 'ridge-beam' on either side. Along the back wall is a bench decorated with two rosettes.

Bianchi-Bandinelli, who excavated the site and studied the architectural elements in detail, came to the conclusion that the Tomba Ildebranda reproduces in rock-cut form the design of an Etruscan temple. His theory has generally been accepted without reservations; and indeed the plan does resemble those of Etruscan and Italic temples dating from the end of the fourth down to the first century BC. Examples include the Temple of Diana at Ariccia, Temple 'C' in the Largo Argentina at Rome, the Corinthian-Doric temple in the forum at Paestum, and the temple at Gabii.[61] He notes that the plan of the Tomba Ildebranda resembles that of a typical Etruscan temple as described by Vitruvius.[62] The podium is of course another characteristic element of Etruscan temple design.[63]

At the same time, the prominent gabled roof of the Etruscan temple, with all its component parts, is missing in the design of the tomb. The omission of this distinctive feature of Etruscan temples cannot have been due to lack of space or (as far as we can tell) to any other practical reason; it was simply not part of the design. As will be seen below, whenever the Etruscans wanted to imitate temple façades in rock-cut architecture, they included a conspicuous pediment above the columns.

If one looks elsewhere in the tomb architecture of the Hellenistic period for possible prototypes for the Tomba Ildebranda, the Belevi Mausoleum seems to provide an obvious parallel.[64] There is a striking correspondence between the main components of the two monuments: both have a high podium supporting a colonnaded middle section with a flat roof-line. It is true that at Belevi the original place probably included a crowning section in the form of a stepped pyramid, like that of the Mausoleum at Halikarnassos; however, this part of the tomb seems never to have been built.

A double frieze, with one band above the other as in the Nereid Monument, also occurs on the podium in a number of tomb designs in Asia Minor. At Sovana the double frieze appears above the columns; but this arrangement may be compared on the one hand with the sculptured architrave of the Nereid Monument, on the other with the sculptured architrave surmounted by a triglyph-and-metope frieze of the early Doric temple at Assos. Of course, all exposed wooden parts of Etruscan temples were normally faced with terracotta slabs, bearing either figured or floral and geometric ornament; and these terracotta revetments doubtless provided part of the inspiration for the rock-cut design at Sovana. However, Etruscan terracotta revetments are themselves derived from archaic Greek models; and it was apparently only in Hellenistic times, long after the step had been taken in Asia Minor, that Etruscan architects thought of transferring the architectural and structural forms of temples to the design of tombs. Thus, it is hard to believe that the new development was not inspired by Aegean prototypes – the more so because the development of later Etruscan sculpture and painting remains closely tied to that of the eastern Mediterranean. The Etruscans were almost always imitators rather than originators in the fields of art and architecture; and the unique character of the Tomba Ildebranda, among known examples of Hellenistic Etruscan tombs, must surely suggest a foreign rather than a native source of inspiration.

The lower and narrower of the two friezes at Sovana represents juxtaposed griffins, as mentioned above; at Belevi there is a free-standing version of the same theme, placed along the roof-line of the monument. The block-like entablature, filled with reliefs, with columns below but without a pediment or pyramid above, was rare in funerary architecture. However, such a feature is readily explained if it was in fact copied from the unfinished monument at Belevi.

Bianchi-Bandinelli, in discussing the individual architectural elements of the decoration of the Tomba Ildebranda, mentions possible outside influences from the eastern Mediterranean in matters of detail, but never raises the possibility of foreign influence for the design as a whole. He regards the design as a local development, based on Etruscan temple projects of the second century, a few decades before strong influences from Asia Minor reached central Italy.[65] Although the Tomba Ildebranda embodies many local Etruscan architectural elements, the end result is not really comparable with any other known Etruscan building. We may therefore suggest that the tomb is actually an Etruscan version of the Belevi Mausoleum, remodelled and executed in a manner that shows little regard for accepted conventions of Greek temple architecture.

If this view is correct, the buildings at Belevi and Sovana add one more proof of the existence of active connections between central Italy and Asia Minor.[66] Nevertheless, the dating of the Tomba Ildebranda remains problematic. If we could demonstrate the existence of strong and direct connections between the architecture of Etruria and that of Asia Minor as early as the third century, it would be reasonable to assign the tomb to this period. Yet such connections do not really seem to begin before the early second century, when Rome, and with her all of central and south Italy, was increasingly involved in affairs east of the Adriatic. The initial trickle of Anatolian influences became a flood only after 133 BC, when the 'Provincia Asia' was formed out of the Pergamene kingdom; but Italic familiarity with, and imitation of, the monuments of western Asia Minor is possible at any time following the campaign that culminated in the victory of Rome and Pergamon at Magnesia in 190 BC.[67] Thus, Bianchi-Bandinelli's dating of the Tomba Ildebranda to the earlier second century can be retained without dismissing the possibility of a direct connection with Belevi.[68]

The Grotta Pola, also at Sovana,[69] is a 'temple tomb' design with a pediment over the colonnaded façade (fig. 155). In contrast to the Tomba Ildebranda, no attempt was made to produce the appearance of a three-dimensional building. There are no returning sides; and the podium does not stand out clearly, but rather forms part of the surrounding vertical cliff. Only one of the row of eight columns, set in front of a continuous wall, is now standing. The height of this column is just under 4 m, its lower diameter 0.8 m; the thirteen flutes are separated by wide fillets. The bases consist of two large tori enclosing a narrow scotia. The capitals resemble those of the Tomba Ildebranda, with human heads in the centre of each face. Behind the corner columns fluted pilasters were carved on the wall; the pilaster capitals were also adorned with human heads. The façade measures 12.5 m in width, and could be approached by a flight of steps on the right side. More than two-thirds of the pediment has broken away; no traces of decoration have been detected on the remaining section. As in the Tomba Ildebranda, there is a large hypogeum, preceded by a dromos, about 6 m below the middle of the façade. The hypogeum is extremely long (18.5 m) and of cruciform plan. The bodies were laid out on benches along the walls. The date of the complex must be close to that of the Tomba Ildebranda; in neither case do we know who commissioned the tomb.

It is much easier to recognize the prototypes of two entirely rock-cut tombs at Norchia south of Sovana. Dennis noted that their 'peculiarity consists in this: that while all the sepulchres around are of the severely simple style of Castel d'Asso, approximating to the Egyptian, these two are highly ornate, and of Greek character.'[70] They are generally referred to as Doric, or as temple tombs. The façades, carved very closely side by side at the end of a series of cube-like tombs (fig. 156), overlook the valley of the Aqualta stream. Because of the softness of the local tufa, neither tomb is well preserved.

Tomb A, the more westernly of the two, is slightly larger (9 m wide) and more elaborate than Tomb B (7 m wide). Curiously enough, in both tombs the characteristic podium of Etruscan temple architecture is missing. All the supports of the pediments have disappeared. However, it can be established with certainty that Tomb B had an arrangement of two columns standing on a low parapet that rose above the floor of the portico; Tomb A, to judge from the remains, had pillars instead of columns.

The superstructure is more or less the same in both monuments. Above a plain architrave there is a Doric frieze slightly set back, then a projecting dentil course in two bands (the upper of these could be called a 'dentillated cornice'), and a pediment (of which the sloping sides are framed by large cyma leaves, recalling archaic Etruscan examples).[71] The decoration of the friezes is quite unusual. Each metope had a single carved human head;[72] each triglyph had only three guttae, which were of a peculiar downward-tapering shape. Also noteworthy are the volutes at the junction of the raking and horizontal geisa. In Tomb A these are adorned with Gorgon heads; those of Tomb B probably had lion heads. Traces of acroteria were also found. The corner acroteria had seated animal figures cut in the living rock, while the central figures (now completely lost) were carved separately and then attached. Although the figures in both pediments are partly preserved, the subject-matter cannot be clearly determined. The scene in tympanon A remains disputed;[73] tympanon B seems to represent the story of the Niobids.

The pronaos wall of Tomb A is decorated with remarkable reliefs representing a processional scene of warriors and the soul of the deceased. In addition to the figures, there are also ornamental motifs: a convex round shield, greaves, two helmets, two daggers, and a lance. As Demus-Quatember has pointed out, the topics are related to tomb paintings in Tarquinia, especially to the Tomba del Tifone.[74]

In front of the façades there was a platform for the funeral rites; here the remains of an altar have been found.

The hypogaea of these tombs are approximately 8 m below the level of the pronaos. The western tomb has the larger chamber, with only three loculi; the smaller burial-chamber beneath Tomb B has eleven loculi and two sarcophagi. Both tombs show signs of burials from different periods.

The style and execution of the sculptural decoration of Tomb A indicate that it slightly pre-dates Tomb B; however, the reliefs of the pronaos wall (which somewhat overlap into Tomb B) were evidently executed sometime after the completion of the eastern tomb. The architectural ornament, as well as the sculptural reliefs, was stuccoed and painted over in a polychrome scheme. A cippus with a few roughly carved letters was found in Tomb A. The inscription mentions a family name, Vel, that was very common in the region; but there are no other clues to the identity of the persons buried in either tomb. To judge from the style, these two tombs at Norchia were probably executed about the same time as the Tomba Ildebranda at Sovana.[75] They have no real predecessors or successors in Etruscan Italy. Consequently, prototypes for the façades must be sought outside Etruria, and perhaps outside Italy altogether. The borrowed elements, however, were combined with native forms; and even without these it must be admitted that no façades of exactly this type are known in the eastern Mediterranean. The most that can be said is that some of the inspiration may have been provided by classical or Hellenistic 'temple tombs' in Lycia or Karia.[76] The theory of Anatolian influence is of course all the more plausible if the suggested association of the Tomba Ildebranda with the Belevi Mausoleum is accepted.

The other large rock-cut tomb of unusual design at Norchia is the so-called Tomba Lattanzi.[77] The façade of this monument must have had a really splendid appearance when approached from the plain below (fig. 157). It reached a height of some 16 m, while its width increased from 13 m at the bottom to 15 m at the summit. Rosi restores this huge tomb with two superimposed colonnades above a high podium.[78] On the (spectator's) left of the façade is a flight of eleven steps, each 0.42 m high.

Two large Tuscan-Doric columns supported the floor of the upper storey. A column fragment found on the site, probably from one of these two columns, measures 1.55 m in diameter and has twenty-eight flutes; its estimated height was ca 5.5 m. The base consists of a large bell-profiled section topped by a narrow torus moulding. Behind these two columns there was a false door carved in the middle of the back wall. On the left side of the portico was a fluted pilaster set on the back of a standing monster figure. This feature is strikingly similar to an earlier rock-cut tomb, presumably of the fifth century, at Terlik Kayasi in Paphlagonia, where again only the left anta is placed on a summarily executed lion figure.[79] About 1 m behind the pilaster of the Etruscan tomb is a circular hollow that once held a cippus. To the left of the pilaster the lower stairway continues upward, but reduced to a width of only about 1 m. A frieze, 0.9 m high with griffins alternating with rosettes and four-petalled flowers, separated the lower floor from the upper.

In the second storey an open platform, more than 4 m deep, preceded a colonnaded porch (fig. 158). This storey consisted of three compartments divided by walls which terminated on their fronts in four fluted columns, 2.7 m high. The remains of the capitals suggest a variant of Corinthian. There is a second stairway on this level, continuing all the way up to the summit of the tomb; but it is placed on the right of the façade, instead of on the left, as in the lower storey. The burial-chamber, as in the other Etruscan tombs described above, is placed well below the floor of the pronaos (7 m down).

Unfortunately many of the ornamental features of the tomb are unknown, being either destroyed or not yet recovered; but according to Rosi, 'the architecture of the tomb is ostentatious in its decoration, and shows an uncouth jumble of monstrosities.'[80] The coloured stucco fragments, some of them still in situ in the last century, indicate that much of the tomb was painted. The monument has been variously dated from the fourth to the second centuries.[81]

Bianchi-Bandinelli concluded that in the elevation of the tomb one can see the imitation of two-storeyed porticos as they appeared in the Hellenistic east and later on in Rome.[82] Rosi saw in the superimposed orders of the Tomba Lattanzi a Hellenistic, if not a Roman, architectural innovation; but he does not suggest a source for the design. There is some truth in both these views. Seen from in front and from a distance, the tomb did indeed resemble a two-storeyed portico; however, the painted recesses of the second floor are also reminiscent of the pinakes of the proskenia of Hellenistic theatres. During the third century two-storeyed façades certainly became fairly common in stoas; but they were also used in theatres, at least in the west.[83] Gateways and private houses, too, employed such features, though rarely with colonnades on both levels. Even in altars there is evidence for the existence of similar designs, and on Italian soil. An altar model from Capua, 1.14 m high, and probably of third-century date, has a podium-like base on which stand two engaged Tuscan-Doric columns supporting a Doric frieze; above this, in turn, is a much smaller second 'storey' with engaged columns.[84]

Some tombs with two-storeyed columnar façades are perhaps as early as the fifth century. We have already noted, at Barka in Cyrenaica, a rock-cut tomb façade with two tiers of vertical supports (fig. 141). On the façade of the porch of the lower floor at Barka there are two short, thick Doric columns, while the upper storey has three piers, each with a bowl-shaped capital, described to be Aeolic by Stucchi.[85] Behind these supports there is another true porch. The façade measures over 5 m in both width and height. Another example of the two-storeyed arrangement, but later in date, is the well-known Great Tomb at Lefkadia.[86]

With the exception of the theatre proskenia, the above-noted two-tiered façades, including the non-funerary ones, are almost all in a single plane. A striking exception among the tombs is the upper storey of the Tomba Lattanzi, which is set back from the line of the lower storey, rather in the manner of a Hellenistic skene in relation to the proskenion; thus, an open space for the performance of funerary rites was left in front of the columns of the upper storey. In funerary architecture there is only one other rock-cut tomb of monumental scale with an analogous treatment of the façade, namely, the Archokrateion at Lindos (fig. 107). A comparison of these two tombs shows that they were conceived along similar lines, despite differences in details and the unsymmetrical execution of the front of the Tomba Lattanzi. It is possible, therefore, that the designer of the Tomba Lattanzi drew his inspiration from the Archokrateion; if such was indeed the case, the Etruscan tomb is another example of direct influence in Italy of the eastern type of monumental tomb. The suggested relationship between the two monuments would also provide a firm terminus post in the early second century for the Tomba Lattanzi.

c *Middle and Later Republican Tombs in Italy:*
Some Hellenistic Influences

As a result of the expansion of Roman power and ever increasing influence, not only in Italy, but also in other regions of the Mediterranean world, wealthy Romans of the later Republic, like their counterparts elsewhere, became increasingly interested in constructing large funerary monuments commemorating deceased members of their families. One of the earliest and best known of the large Republican family tombs in Rome is that of the Scipios, whose family became increasingly prominent in the third century.[87] This tomb, hewn from the local tufa, is located beside the Via Appia, just inside the Aurelian Wall. The identification of the tomb is certain, because it contained both painted and engraved inscriptions referring to the family. It was first discovered in 1614 and investigated during the following centuries. The remains of the complex were partly restored in 1926. The original third-century aspect of the façade is not known; the rebuilt version of the second century can be reconstructed with some accuracy (fig. 159a, b). Ancient references to the tomb are scarce; Livy's text is the most explicit, though he says more about the tomb sculptures than about the architecture. He also mentions that there were tombs of the Scipios at two different locations: 'In both places tombs and statues are shown; for at Liternum there is a tomb and a statue placed upon the tomb, which I myself saw recently, shattered by a storm, and at Rome, outside the Porta Capena, in the tomb of the Scipios, there are three statues, two of which are said to represent Publius and Lucius Scipio, the third the poet Quintus Ennius.'[88]

The façade added to the rock-cut background was probably constructed in the third quarter of the second century, when the Scipio family was again politically prominent. For example, Cornelius Scipio Hispanus was praetor in 139 BC. The new ashlar façade, in contemporary Hellenistic style, consisted of a high podium with a columnar superstructure. The podium, ca 27 m long and 2.2 m high, had three arched openings, the central one being the largest. The prominent moulded cornice of the podium consisted of a large cyma reversa moulding between two fasciae. Above this rather plain podium rose a much more decorative superstructure.[89] Three pairs of either Ionic or Corinthian half-columns, ca 6 m high, flanked three large niches containing statues, as mentioned by Livy. The entablature probably supported a low attic that formed the uppermost element of the façade.[90]

The spacious rock-cut interior (ca 14.5 × 13.5 m) housed the sarcophagi of the members of the family; the most notable of these is an elegant Doric-Ionic sarcophagus (fig. 264) in the mixed style of the second century.[91]

The materials used in building the screen-like painted façade included Grotta Oscura tufa for the podium wall, peperino tufa for the podium cornice, the decorative wall with its half-columns, and the bases of the arches, and Anio stone for the actual voussoirs. The use of Anio tufa is helpful in dating the façade to the second century, because the earliest known occurrence of this material is in the Aqua Marcia, of 144 BC.[92]

The tripartite division of the façade, as described above, is reminiscent of other monumental tombs in which the design was based on the elevation of a Hellenistic stage-house; it remained unique in Rome until late Republican times, when monumental tombs, in a variety of forms, became more and more widespread.

The tomb of the Sempronii (fig. 160), discovered in 1863 on the slope of the Quirinal, belongs to the end of the republican era shortly after 50 BC.[93] It is a rock-cut tomb that was faced with neatly assembled travertine blocks. Surmounting the high podium the superstructure was pierced by a single large arch, with an inscription above it identifying the owners of the tomb:

'Cn(aeus) Sempronius Cn(aei) f(ilius) Rom(ilia)/Sempronia Cn(aei) f(ilia) Soror/Larcia M(anii) f(ilia) mater.' An Ionic entablature, its frieze richly carved with palmette motifs and an egg-and-dart course above a row of dentils, formed the crowning element.

Although both these tombs were large in scale, they were merely façade-tombs, restricted in their embellishments and thus a far cry from some of the great monumental tombs of Asia Minor, or even from those of the Etruscans discussed above. Free-standing built structures, of tower form with Hellenistic architectural decoration, appeared in Rome only in the second century.[94] The archaeological remains, as one would expect, indicate that the new tower tombs were built for members of the high aristocracy. However, the new form of funerary monument seems soon to have given way to round tombs or tumuli. Thus Sulla, the most powerful Roman of this day, was buried in a tumulus (imperatorius), believed to be fitting for 'royalty.'[95] By the time of Augustus, tumuli were the preferred form of tomb for the leading members of Roman society. Whereas earlier examples of tumuli are plentiful in Italy, there are few if any significant prototypes for free-standing multi-storeyed tombs of tower form; and we have seen that even the few existing tombs that come closest to the 'temple-tomb'-on-podium concept (e.g. Tomba Ildebranda) were based on models in other regions of the Mediterranean. In fact, while the construction of tumuli seems to have been motivated by their 'political' symbolism, the multi-storeyed tomb form was probably chosen in recognition of the many-faceted nature of these structures already tested elsewhere.

Perhaps the earliest funerary monument of tower-type in Rome is the tomb of Caius Poplicius Bibulus, a Roman tribune (fig. 161).[96] This Republican tomb occupied a much-frequented site at the northern foot of the Capitoline Hill outside the Porta Fontinalis of the Servian Wall, at the head of the Via Flaminia. According to inscriptions on the exterior of the tomb, it was erected by the People and the Senate free of charge for the person buried within: 'C(aio) Poplicio Bibulo aed(ili) pl(ebis) honoris/virtutisque caussa Senatus consulto populique iussu locus/monumento quo ipse postere-ique/eius inferrentur publice datus est.' Today only the southwest wall and south corner remain standing, though not to their full height; the other sides have almost completely disappeared. Although the ruins were not excavated until 1907, the existence of the monument had long been known.

The tomb was originally four-sided; a high podium supported the 'cella,' which was decorated with pilasters. The materials employed were tufa and travertine (the latter for the whole exterior facing). The eight ashlar courses of the podium (4.74 m in height) stood on a slightly projecting euthynteria course. The width of the side still extant is 6.57 m; here, slightly off-centre to the left, is cut the above-quoted inscription on the two uppermost courses of the facing. An analogous inscription appeared on at least one of the other sides of the monument.[97] The funeral chamber was located in the podium, apparently without any indication of its presence on the exterior. The upper storey, 3.71 m high, is set back somewhat from the edge of the podium, standing on a two-stepped socle 0.47 m in height. The preserved southwest wall is treated like the façade of a small shrine or temple, with four Doric pilasters and a central false door in the form of a niche that in all probability housed a statue. In the narrower outer intervals tablets were placed half-way up the wall; both tablets and niches are also found in the tomb of the Scipios. The anta-bases consist of a torus and fillet set on a plinth; the mouldings continue along the foot of the wall as a decorative socle, inter-rupted only by the 'threshold' of the central niche. An architrave of two fasciae, an Ionic frieze with bucrania linked by garlands beneath rosette-bowls, and a cornice constituted the entablature of the second storey.

On the basis of letter forms and spelling, the tomb inscription has been dated to the second quarter of the first century BC. The difficulty involved in this dating is that no official by the name of Caius Poplicius Bibulus is known at this time. There was, however, a Caius Poplicius Bibulus, Tribunus Plebis in 208 BC. Thus, it is possible that the tomb was originally erected sometime in the first half of the second century, and later restored in the the time of Sulla, when a new inscription was carved on the upper part of the podium. Certainly the architectural vocabulary does not exclude a second-century date for the structure.[98] Designs related to the tomb of Bibulus became more widespread in the first century BC, occurring in various forms in a number of funerary monuments around Rome.[99]

D The Tomb of Theron in Sicily

The so-called Tomb of Theron at Agrigento (Greek Akragas) in Sicily (fig. 162) is a unique structure in the region of Magna Graecia.[100] Its form has affinities with Punic tombs in North Africa, though it is also closely related to the tomb of Bibulus at Rome. As we see it today, the tomb consists of a high podium resting on a projecting socle, and supporting an upper storey with engaged Ionic columns. Above the socle is a toichobate crowned by a cyma recta moulding. The main portion of the lower storey, or podium, is of plain isodomic construction. Above this is a complex cornice terminating in a pronounced cavetto profile. The total height of the socle, including base and crown, is 3.91 m; each side measures 4.81 m. The 3.73-m-high upper storey has a large false door placed in the middle of each side; at the corners are three-quarter Attic-Ionic columns. A Doric architrave and frieze are the highest elements still preserved today; the strong taper of the podium and the storey above suggest that the crowning element was probably a pyramid, such as we find in most of the related Punic monuments. The now undivided interior must originally have had a lower and an upper chamber, corresponding to the two levels of the exterior. The commissioner and the date of construction of this monumental tomb remain unknown; dates from the third to the first century BC have been suggested for the structure.[101] However, it was probably built in the course of the second century for an important local person.

E The Tomb of M. Vergilius Eurysaces in Rome

The first century BC witnessed the appearance of a great variety of tomb designs, sometimes quite eccentric in character, such as the tomb of the baker, M. Vergilius Eurysaces (fig. 163).[102] This well-preserved structure stands today immediately outside the Porta Maggiore in Rome. To commemorate his profession the wealthy owner deliberately chose an unusual form for the tomb, a panarium, or receptacle for storing bread. The inscription, presumably added by his wife Atistia, states: 'It is the tomb of Marcus Vergilius Eurysaces who was an entrepreneur and civil servant.'

The structure is trapezoid on plan by the necessity of its location. The exterior is unique inasmuch as it is decorated with rows of large vertical and horizontal tubes, apparently representing corn measures. It has a conventionally placed figure frieze depicting the daily activity of a commercial baker. The crowning element has completely disappeared but it was probably in the form of a pyramid. Although the exact date of the erection of this attractive funerary monument is not known, it is to be placed in the last years of the Roman Republic around 30 BC.

Outside Rome, in the cemeteries of Ostia, Pompeii, Aquileia, Sarsina, and elsewhere, most of the well-documented large-scale funerary monuments are Augustan or later. Their style and technique of construction belong to the imperial age, and thus fall outside the scope of this survey, even though many of them still have some clearly recognizable Hellenistic features.[103]

IV Funerary Monuments in North Africa

A Tombs at Cyrene and Ptolemais

The extensive and well-preserved necropoleis of Cyrene offer many examples of the tomb types found in the eastern Mediterranean. To the fourth century may be assigned a number of stone tumuli that are best seen as descendants of archaic stone mounds,[104] such as the tomb of Menecrates on the island of Corfu. One of the best-preserved examples is Tomb N_1 (fig. 54).[105] A square platform, of three steps above a euthynteria course, supports a cylindrical superstructure. The drum is 8.07 m in diameter and 1.72 m in height; it has a neatly carved base moulding consisting of a cyma recta crowned by an astragal. The top section of the drum imitates a Doric architrave course with Ionic decorative mouldings above. Inside the tomb were two rectangular compartments covered by flat slabs. The roofing blocks of the tumulus itself were arranged in a fan-shaped pattern, sloping downward and outward. On the exterior of the monument the masonry is carefully cut and fitted; toward the interior the blocks were only roughly dressed.

Although Tomb N_1 remained an unusual exercise in funerary architecture, nevertheless its form was imitated in a number of later small-scale stone tumuli scattered throughout the Mediterranean.[106]

Among the long rectangular cella-like 'temple tombs,' the best specimens are those at Messa and Zawani near Cyrene. At Zawani there are two well-preserved examples, one behind the other.[107] One of them is of single-cella type; the other has a double cella (fig. 164). In each case a low platform supports a rectangular superstructure rising from a stepped socle. The general effect is reminiscent of the Tomb of Cyrus at Pasargadai, where a stepped pyramid supported a rectangular building. At Zawani, however, the stepped section is 'contracted,' so that it forms the base of the outer walls of the cella itself. On top of the tomb there was a platform framed by low pediments at the shorter ends; on this platform stood statues or stelai. At Zawani, as elsewhere, a large decorative doorway occupied much of one of the short ends of the building. The entablature, as in the built tumuli at Cyrene, carried a Doric architrave with taenia and regulae, surmounted by a series of mouldings. Tombs of the Zawani type, with some local variations, appeared in the Cyrene region during the fourth century and were still being constructed in the third century.

The giant elevated sarcophagi of Cyrenaica are related to the 'temple tombs,' though they do not give the impression of a shrine, or of the built cella of a temple. These sarcophagi frequently stand on a socle and stepped base;[108] well-preserved examples are located at Gasr Gebrà, a few kilometres southeast of Cyrene (fig. 165).

More sophisticated are the 'mastaba tombs' developed from a local North African tradition of funerary architecture. An example of the fourth or early third century is Tomb E19 in the eastern cemetery of Cyrene (fig. 166). The exterior walls reproduce the form of an Egyptian mastaba with sloping sides; these walls enclose a plain rectangular sarcophagus with two compartments that contained wooden coffins.

Among the more elaborate rock-cut funerary monuments, a popular type was the 'courtyard tomb,' i.e., the type found in the Mustafa Pasha cemetery of Alexandria.[109] In almost all the examples at Cyrene only one side, with a short return at each end, was fully executed (fig. 167);[110] yet this is enough to give the impression of a courtyard. The dominant order is Doric; only occasionally do Ionic decorative elements occur in the otherwise purely Doric façades. The majority of these tombs belong to the period of direct Alexandrian influence in Cyrenaica.

The design that most clearly resembles the 'mausoleum type' developed in Asia Minor is perhaps that found in Tomb N_{180}, in the northern cemetery of the city (fig. 168).[111] This monument is of 'mixed' construction. The podium is rock-cut, while the stepped socle, the lower storey, and the crowning pyramid were built of ashlar blocks. The masonry portion of the tomb has collapsed, but can be almost completely restored on the basis of the extant blocks lying on the site. The podium, slightly over 1 m high and 4 m wide, contains three rock-cut burial compartments, closed by doors. Above them is a narrow platform, at the back of which a four-stepped socle led up to the square middle section of the monument, which measured 3.7 m per side. In the Lion Tomb at Knidos, to which N_{180} is closely related typologically, the sharp corners of the cube are softened by engaged columns; at Cyrene the corners are emphasized by flat pilasters enclosing plain panels. The outer edges of these panels, framed by the corner pilasters and the architrave, were enlivened by a decorative cyma leaf pattern. The architrave supported a Doric frieze and a cornice with ovolo and Lesbian cyma ornament. Above the cornice there was probably a twelve-stepped pyramid, crowned by a statue or a stele.[112]

The composition of Tomb N_{180}, with its tripartite division of the main elements, clearly presupposes some acquaintance with the mausolea of Asia Minor. In the local Cyrenaican context, the articulation of the middle section shows similarities with the late fourth-century (308–305 BC) Strategeion.[113] The marked 'frontal' aspect of the tomb, which stands free on all sides above the four-stepped base, and the multiple compartments resembling loculi, suggest a date not earlier than the third century.[114]

Tombs N_{57}, N_{58}, and S_{185} in Cyrene show a vague resemblance to Tomb N_{180}. As indicated above, however, from the third century onward Cyrenaican tombs were influenced by Alexandrian rather than Anatolian designs.

Farther west along the coast there is a massive tower tomb at Ptolemais.[115] The tomb still stands on its solid rock foundation to a height of 14 m; the original height was ca 27 m, while the still existing base is a 12 m square (fig. 169). On top of a stepped platform the first storey is decorated with a Doric frieze above plain corner pilasters; there are three false doors on the north, or main, façade. The second storey has a Corinthian order, with five engaged columns per side supporting the entablature. The upper part of the second storey has disappeared. For a long time it was believed to have been decorated by Ionic columns (fig. 170). However, the still existing necking ornament of acanthus foliage seems to indicate the use of the Corinthian order.[116] On the north façade in the intercolumniations appeared blind windows corresponding to the false doors below. The third storey was rather squat. There, the upper sections of the three intercolumnar spaces on the north façade were presumably decorated by shields, a custom often found in Macedonian-inspired tombs. The cornice was of the cavetto type. The monumental three-storeyed structure was perhaps surmounted by a stepped pyramid and not by a pedimental roof as had been suggested earlier.

Provisions were made for multiple burials in the interior, which could be reached through an opening on the south side. The different elevations were connected by an interior staircase. The combination of architectural elements, the beautiful ashlar construction, and the foot unit employed (36.5 cm) serve to date the tomb to the Hellenistic period, perhaps to the second half of the third or the first half of the second century.[117]

B *Tombs in Alexandria*

The history of the Greek city of Alexandria that supplanted the Egyptian fishing village of Rhakotis begins only with Alexander the Great. Thus the 'Greek tombs' in its various necropoleis are all of Hellenistic date. The more elaborate of the preserved Hellenistic examples are, in most cases, cut into the soft bedrock of the region.

As the town expanded, especially eastwards, the cemeteries also moved outward, because they were normally situated outside the inhabited areas. In the eastern part of the city, where most Greeks and foreigners lived, are the cemeteries of Shatbi, Hadra, Ibrahimiya, Sidi Gaber, and Mustafa Pasha; the last-named constitutes the largest and richest Hellenistic burial complex so far discovered in Alexandria. The western necropoleis of Gabbari, Wardi-an-Mafrusa,[118] and Mex came more and more into use from the later second century onward. The Anfushi and Ras et-Tin cemeteries are located on the Pharos island. Southwest of the city centre, near the Sarapeion, lie the later catacombs of Kom es-Shogafa. The so-called Alabaster Tomb, southwest of the Shatbi cemetery, is a unique fragment of a sumptuous built funerary monument of the Ptolemaic age. A rock-cut bed was prepared for a series of meticulously constructed rooms (one still exists) (fig. 171), which were probably surmounted by a tumulus in the Macedonian manner.[119] In the vicinity of the Alexandrian Eleusis, southeast of the Hadra area, lay the so-called Antoniades Tomb. In ground plan it was comparable to Greek dwelling houses of the second and first centuries BC, with a series of rooms arranged around a central nucleus.[120]

Unfortunately the Sema of Alexander, mentioned by ancient authors along with the royal burials of the Ptolemies, has not yet come to light; in all probability it occupied a focal point in the layout of the city.[121]

It is reasonable to assume that the Macedonians who settled in the Nile delta after 332 BC initially buried their dead according to their own customs. However, local geological and climatic conditions, the Pharaonic heritage, and the earlier traditions of rock-cut tomb architecture in Asia Minor and the Cyrene region soon led to modifications in the funerary practices and architecture of Alexandria.

The Shatbi tombs seems to be among the earliest of known Hellenistic funerary complexes, datable to the first generations of the history of Alexandria.[122] They were discovered during the nineteenth century near the coast and east of the ancient Nile canal that opened into the royal harbour. The original plan was altered over the years by the addition of new sections, until the ever-expanding city absorbed the site. However, the original form of the main tomb can still be traced. An open courtyard, 6.75 × 8.2 m with a pseudo-peristyle of half-columns (fig. 172a, b), was preceded on the north by a wide, shallow vestibule and an adjoining corridor. To the east opened an antechamber leading to the burial-room proper (fig. 173).

Architecturally the most intriguing parts of this rock-cut sunken tomb are the walls with engaged orders. Against the northern wall of the large court stood six partly fluted Doric half-columns, with a central doorway.[123] In the upper sections of the intercolumniations were false windows above a string course; the right-hand panels, painted sky blue, were slightly set back. Obviously the intention was to create the effect of vistas through the wall, such as later appeared in wall paintings of the Second Pompeian Style. The entrance to the kline chamber reflects the same concept. In this case, the wall is decorated with a small tetrastyle Ionic temple façade supporting a low pediment; this scheme recalls the façades of Macedonian tombs. Presumably the same kind of illusionistic treatment was accorded to the now destroyed wall surfaces of its central court. In addition to the loculi of the antechamber, a number of later burial niches were added to the east and west of the main complex, at the time when the original family burial-place became a public cemetery.

Tombs I and IV in the well-preserved necropolis of Mustafa Pasha, as well as the Antoniades hypogeum, all belong to the same class of burials as

Shatbi; a central open space formed the nucleus of the design. In other respects, each of these monuments has its own special features.

Mustafa Pasha Tomb I (fig. 174) is approached by a staircase set along the western side of a pseudo-peristyle courtyard.[124] The openings on each of the four sides of the court are framed by pairs of Doric half-columns; in each corner two quarter-columns form a relief version of the cordiform pier (fig. 175). The frieze had three triglyphs over each intercolumnar space; the corner triglyphs were bent around the internal angle. Above the lintel of the middle doorway on the south side of the court a remarkable painting, imitating Macedonian models, depicted three horsemen and two standing female figures (fig. 176).[125] Only a few traces remain of the rest of the painted decoration; one panel represents the upper part of a tholos building.[126] Behind the somewhat Egyptianized doorways an extensive vestibule with loculi opening off the sides gives access to the kline chamber. Corinthian pilasters (fig. 177) and a plain pediment framed the entrance, providing one of the earliest examples of such an arrangement. The remaining two rooms on the south, along with those of the north and east sides, served for loculus burials.

The complex has generally been assigned to the second half of the third century, mainly on the basis of the style of the paintings.[127] However, the architectural members do not exclude an earlier period within the same century.[128] Closely related, but later in time, are some rock-cut tombs at Nea-Paphos on Cyprus (fig. 3) and others at Cyrene.[129]

Much more original is the somewhat later Mustafa Pasha Tomb III (fig. 178). Some effort is needed to detect the architect's source of inspiration. The semicircular exedra for funerary rites on the south side of the central court was probably suggested by the cavea of the theatre. At the opposite end of the court, the kline chamber-like arrangement is preceded by a square room with an altar in the middle. Taking up the full width of the courtyard is a simple raised 'stage' with a decorative back wall; this 'skene-building' constitutes the principal element of the design. The 'scaenae frons' is adorned with four Doric half-columns, plus two quarter-columns in the corners; the scheme is reminiscent of Shatbi. In the three middle intervals there were real openings; in the corner bays of the returning wings were false doors (fig. 179a, b). Unlike Tomb I, the corners of the courtyard of Tomb III were filled by pilasters; the corner spans had only one triglyph, while the other intercolumniations had two. Most of the painted surfaces, along with other decorative details, have long since disappeared.

This tomb complex was partly built above ground; with its different levels and variety of shapes and forms, including the central court, it is a unique product of the funerary architecture of the Hellenistic era.[130] The imaginative organization of space and the frequent use of purely decorative non-structural architectural members, particularly half-columns, give a clearer notion of the character of the residential architecture at Alexandria than any other monuments discovered in the Ptolemaic capital.

Tomb IV, datable to the second century, lies north of Tomb III. It is remarkable in having a true peristyle, with two free-standing Doric columns between antae on each side of a square courtyard (fig. 180).

Among the excavated tombs of the Mustafa Pasha cemetery, Tomb II (fig. 181) clearly reproduces the so-called oikos-type of house plan, with various compartments disposed along a central axis. A staircase along the east side, parallel to that of Tomb I (fig. 182), gives access to a hypaethral court decorated on all sides with a triglyph-and-metope frieze 3.85 m above ground level. Two smaller compartments, one for a painted kline, the other for a well, are cut in the western wall of the court. At the northern end an annex used for funerary banquets faces the main compartments. On the south a tripartite entrance with two Doric columns in antis leads to a vestibule. At the back of this vestibule another distyle-in-antis colonnade forms the approach to the cult room, which was provided along the longer sides with benches in front of loculi. At the far end of the complex is an offering table with a small chamber behind it. The tomb has been dated by coin finds to the first half of the second century; but the architectural and decorative details suggest that it may actually have been cut in the late third century.[131]

The hypogeum at Sidi Gaber, of which virtually nothing now remains, lay a short distance west of the Mustafa Pasha cemetery. The plan shows a strict axial arrangement of the various components (fig. 183) of an open court, vestibule, and kline chamber with a loculus at the back.[132] The ceiling of the antechamber in the form of a segmental vault is an interesting feature of this tomb. The wall surfaces of this room were divided into a tripartite system of painted horizontal zones. A wide passage way, flanked by inward-facing Doric half-columns attached to the antae, preceded the actual oikos. At the back there was a large kline painted with an Amazonomachy. The walls were decorated with garlands hung between pilasters, such as are found in some Macedonian tombs. The relative scarcity of Egyptianizing features and the combination of a single loculus with a real kline, as opposed to false couches in relief or painting, suggest a date in the third century, possibly earlier than Mustafa Pasha Tomb II.

Of the six large tombs in the Anfushi district, the two most important were discovered in the early twentieth century.[133] Both have a plan similar to that of Sidi Gaber. They exhibit numerous Egyptianizing features, including two segmental pediments; these may be either originals or additions of a later period.[134] Some of the stuccoed and painted walls imitated marble incrustation; the ceilings have geometric patterns. The date of these tombs is conjectural, but the small finds and the absence of kline burials seem to indicate the later Ptolemaic era.

Brief mention may be made of two more large Hellenistic hypogea of oikos type found in Alexandria. The Mafrusa tomb is interesting for its wall paintings recalling the First Pompeian Style.[135] The Wardian tomb (no. 1) of the mid second century was discovered in the 1960s;[136] it has a painted false kline, with a niche placed behind it for the actual burial.

c Taposiris Magna, Lighthouse Tomb

In connection with Alexandrian developments some mentions must be made of the 'lighthouse,' or Pharos, type of funerary monument. The biggest and most famous of all ancient lighthouses was undoubtedly the Alexandrian Pharos, built in the early third century at the northeast entrance of the Great Harbour.[137] It was near, and may even have occupied the site of, an earlier building, perhaps a tomb connected with the worship of the local sea god Proteus.[138] The influence of the Pharos was substantial in both the Graeco-Roman and the Arabic world. It inspired the designs of many smaller lighthouses, watch-towers, tombs, 'trophies,' and minarets. One such building is the tower-like structure, of Ptolemaic date, only about 50 km west of Alexandria at Taposiris Magna (modern Abusir in Egypt).[139] Above a low base, 10.75 m square, stands a high octagonal middle section, which is surmounted by a cylindrical top (fig. 184). The entire edifice was constructed of neatly cut and well-fitted ashlar blocks, without architectural decoration. An interior staircase led to the summit. The existence of a hypogeum below the tower seems to indicate that the latter served as a funerary monument in the form of a lighthouse.[140]

d Tombs in Northwestern Africa

In the western Mediterranean many of the larger tombs were clearly influenced by eastern Hellenistic prototypes; known examples are all later than the most imposing types in Asia Minor. The 'obelisk' or 'pinnacle' tombs of the Punic-Numidian regions of North Africa (i.e., present-day Libya, Tunisia, Algeria, and Morocco) form a special category.[141] Their slender, tower-like appearance distantly echoes the design both of Semitic 'nefesh' monuments and of Lycian elevated sarcophagi and pillar tombs; and the 'multi-level' elevations perhaps suggest a link with the Halikarnassos mausoleum and its descendants. Yet there are also elements derived from local traditions, as well as borrowings from the architecture of the urban centres along the southern shore of the Mediterranean, e.g., Alexandria.

As one might expect, Alexandrian influence was filtered through Carthage and other Punic cities to the more westerly regions of North Africa. Unfortunately the extent of specifically Carthaginian contributions in architecture and decoration is difficult to assess, because Carthage was completely destroyed by the Romans in 146 BC. However, the existence of tower-like funerary buildings in the Punic region is proved by wall paintings found in the necropolis of Djebel Mlessa in Tunisia (fig. 185). Furthermore, a spectacular Graeco-Punic tower tomb has recently been excavated and reconstructed west of modern Tripoli, at Sabratha in Libya (fig. 186). It is the most remarkable, as well as the oldest, known Graeco-Punic tower tomb. The sandstone structure is referred to either as Mausoleum B or as the mausoleum of Beş or Bisu.[142] This slender building is approximately 24 m high, giving a ratio of width to height 1:2.4.[143]

The structure stands on a three-cornered base, and resembles a monumental tripod-like design. The stepped platform (3.2 m high with concave sides) supports a lower storey framed by squat engaged Ionic columns (4.6 m high). The necking ornament of the diagonal capitals is reminiscent of the Erechtheion capitals in Athens. On the eastern or principal side, the engaged column in the centre is almost entirely masked by a false door of wholly Egyptian design; such doors are a common feature of Punic architecture. A plain architrave surmounted by a large cavetto cornice supports the podium of the second storey, which is 6.82 m high, and has a lavish decoration including free-standing sculptures; at the corners three seated lions support projecting consoles on which stand colossal kouroi, each ca 3 m high.[144] The concave fields of the three sides of the upper storey are framed by tall slender pilasters with Phoenicio-Cypriot capitals.[145] The lower section of each face, between the seated lions, is decorated with reliefs;[146] the zone between the capitals carries a band of stylized palmettes. A second cavetto cornice and a steep pyramid (combined height 7.33 m) crown the monument. The entire structure was covered with painted stucco. The tomb was probably built in the course of the third century.[147]

Only a few years later than the mausoleum of Beş is the typologically related, but even larger, structure at Siga in western Numidia (fig. 187);[148] presumably it was the burial place of Vermina (201–191 BC), the last king of the Massylians, and of his family. The mausoleum at Siga is similar to the Sabratha example; the blunter angles, however, produce a hexagonal plan, with three flat (3.9 m each) and three concave (7.2 m each) sides. Three steps support the still partly preserved socle, which terminates in a series of mouldings. The middle section above the socle contained three false doors, one in the centre of each concave side. These false doors were flanked by Ionic columns supporting a projecting lintel. Another series of mouldings surmounted by three steps and a second, rather squat, socle form the transition to the topmost storey. A steep six-sided pyramid served for the crowning element of the design, again with three flat and three concave faces. The monument, more than 30 m in height, was surmounted by a statue or some other finial. Fragments of decorative sculpture were found during the excavations, but their place in the overall design remains obscure. The exterior of the structure, like that of Mausoleum B at Sabratha, was stuccoed and painted. There was no burial-chamber inside this huge monument; instead, the burials were made in ten rooms excavated beneath the perimeter of the commemorative tower (fig. 188). They were approached from the north, south, and west by arched doors below ground level. An interesting and unique feature of the structure is that in place of iron clamps and wooden pegs customary in Hellenistic architecture the joints were mortared, a most unusual procedure in late third- or second-century architecture of North Africa.

Another large tomb of Graeco-Numidian inspiration still stands at Dugga in Tunisia (fig. 189).[149] It has long been regarded, on the monument of a certain Ateban, believed to be a Numidian chief of the time of king Massinissa (201–149 BC). However, recent re-examination of the inscription indicates that it names a number of Numidian craftsmen who helped to build the tomb, among them Ateban, who was the architect. The identity of the actual owner is thus unknown, though he was certainly a Numidian prince or king.[150]

The tower tomb, approximately 21 m high, consists of three square storeys, each level stepping inward from the one below it, because each stands on a stepped base. The lowest storey, or socle, measures 9.14 m per side and 5.74 m in height. It has the largest number of steps (five), and is decorated with corner pilasters topped by 'bent' Phoenicio-Cypriot capitals. The intervals enclosed by the corner pilasters on the north and east sides contain real openings that could be blocked by movable slabs, while those on the south and west sides are false windows. The second storey, 5.21 m high and 6.72 m wide, and resting on three steps, has four engaged Ionic columns per side; on the north and east sides there is an opening in each of the central intervals. The third stage, 6.21 m in height and 3.04 m in width, is more elongated than the others; at the corners are pilasters with 'bent' Phoenicio-Cypriot capitals, surmounted by an architrave and cavetto cornice similar to those of the second storey. At the angles the three steps of the base abutted on high pedestals, which once carried statues of horsemen; in the middle of each side, above the stepped base, there are archaizing reliefs of quadrigas. The crowning element, as in Mausoleum B at Sabratha, is pyramidal (3.75 m high); at the corners of the base of the pyramid were winged female figures and at the apex a seated lion. In all sections below the pyramid the masonry is pseudo-isodomic.

Direct contact between Numidia and the Hellenistic Greek monarchies became more tangible in the later second century, after the final defeat of Carthage, and resulted in increasingly Hellenistic influence in some later Numidian structures, including tombs. A good example of a thoroughly 'Hellenized' funerary monument is to be found near the modern Algerian town of El Khroub, about 14 km from the Numidian royal residence at Cirta (Constantine) (fig. 190).[151] As in other Numidian tower tombs, the site of the so-called Es Souma is not on the summit of a mountain but further down the slope. Nevertheless, the monument still stands on a conspicuous site; even today the ruins (fig. 191) can be seen from a distance of 25 km.

When complete, this multi-storeyed tomb was almost 30 m in height. It is square on plan, measuring 10.56 m per side. A still preserved low socle and three steps (combined height 2.8 m) support a podium. The podium is 1.7 m high and has a moulded cyma base and cornice on top. The first storey above the podium was approximately 4.5 m high and had a false door flanked by round shields on each of the four sides. Another podium, 2.05 m high, with a profiled base and cornice, supported the second storey consisting of twelve free-standing (4.05 m high) Doric columns, four per side. The columns had moulded bases; the shafts and capitals were cut from a single block. Above the entablature four pediments, one on each side, completed the Greek temple-like design of the second storey. The columns enclosed a solid 'cella block,' the upper sections of which emerged behind the pediments; its four sides terminated in a cavetto cornice. This cornice is the only non-Greek decorative feature in the entire design; and even here the profile is quite close to some Hellenistic simas.[152] The projecting top of the 'cella' served as the pedestal for a steep, four-sided pyramid ca 9 m high. The form of the apex cannot be determined with certainty, but if it was blunt rather than pointed, it could have supported an over-life-size statue of which parts were found in the last century.

The relatively small barrel-vaulted tomb chamber (1 m square on plan and 0.9 m high) is located at the centre of the structure, but below ground level. The chamber has no access; after it was closed, following the first interment, there was no possibility of further burials. It provides one of the very few instances in which the tomb furniture was found intact. Unfortunately, because of careless treatment in the early twentieth century, the contents have partly disappeared; as well, the tomb chamber and its architectural surroundings were destroyed in the process of excavation.[153]

The identity of the person who commissioned the Es Souma remains questionable. Typologically, the design seems to be the latest in the series of known Hellenistic tower tombs in northwestern Africa.[154] The decorative elements, with the exception of a single cavetto cornice, are Greek. The incorporation of a regular temple front into the scheme is also Greek and is without precedent in Numidian architecture. At the same time, the peculiar assemblage of the heterogeneous details is native; and the dry masonry structure also seems to be indigenous. Although clamps were used in certain sections of the building to secure the blocks in place, they were not consistently employed. For example, the columns and false doors were not fastened to anything, but were kept in place by the pressure of other elements, perhaps indicating an unfamiliarity with the use of free-standing columns above ground.

It is known that following the death of Massinissa in 149 BC, Micipsa ruled the kingdom till 118 BC. During his reign direct contact with both eastern and western Hellenistic centres became stronger and more extensive; the influence of these new contacts is evident in some of the tomb furnishings as well as in the architectural forms.[155] The location of the tomb near the capital of Cirta, its monumentality, and its strongly Hellenistic character may indicate that it was the royal tomb of Micipsa himself.

Large-scale tumuli entirely in stone were rare in the Hellenistic world. In Numidia a huge stone tumulus, known as the Medracen,[156] seems to pre-date all the examples of built tower tombs cited above (fig. 192a, b). As a matter of fact it may well be the earliest example of Numidian monumental architecture of any sort. The structure has been dated as early as the late fourth or early third century;[157] at least it was probably constructed no later than the second quarter of the third century.[158]

The tumulus, measuring 58.86 m in diameter at the base (ca 198.8 m in circumference) and 18.5 m in height, occupies a site at the northern edge of the Aures range in eastern Algeria. The lower cylindrical portion of the tomb is adorned with sixty Doric half-columns, 2.65 m high with unfluted shafts; these stand on a socle, and support a prominent cavetto cornice 5.25 m above ground level. The columns are rather squat, with axial spans of 2.9 m; their monotonous effect is somewhat relieved by three false doors, which have no relation to the actual tomb chamber, but are equidistantly placed around the perimeter.[159] In the central field of each niche-like door there may have been a statue, as was customary on Punic funerary stelai. The cavetto cornice is also Egypto-Punic in origin; but the squat proportions of the columns seem to be derived from earlier Sicilian Doric, e.g., Segesta. Above the cornice rises a 'conical pyramid,' with twenty-four steps, as in the Mausoleum at Halikarnassos. This 'conical pyramid' terminates in a platform, 11.4 m in diameter, which may once have supported a second pyramid, smooth-sided and steep, or some other epithema (e.g., a sculptural composition). In the centre of the tumulus is built a single tomb chamber (3.30 × 1.59 m), approached from the east by a corridor 17 m long (fig. 193). The outer end of the corridor is in level with the third step of the pyramid and could be blocked by a stone trapdoor. Unusual is the excellent preservation of the seventeen cedar logs that were still in situ in 1970; originally some forty-five beams formed the ceiling above the plastered walls of the corridor. The tomb chamber, with its long corridor, faced a built area (14 × 25 m) attached to the east side of the tumulus. This arrangement recalls the mortuary temples of the pyramids at Giza and the temenos of Anatolian tombs and heroa and probably served a cultic purpose.

The beautifully executed masonry of the tomb and the precise clamping and fitting of the blocks rival examples in the eastern Mediterranean, and also bear witness to the technical capability and good organization of the local workshop.

Less remarkable from the technical point of view, though equally impressive visually, is another Hellenistic stone tumulus located west of modern Algiers, near Tipasa, long known (inaccurately) as the Tombeau de la Chrétienne, but referred to in recent literature as the Kbour-er-Roumia tumulus (fig. 194a, b).[160] On a low, square socle measuring 63.4 m each side is a cylindrical drum with a diameter of 60.9 m. A three-stepped crepis supports the sixty slender Ionic half-columns that decorate the outer face of the drum. Each column has an Attic-Ionic base, without a plinth; the capitals recall forms used in archaic times. The entablature is simple with a very slightly projecting cyma moulding in its central section; the profile is quite far removed from the prominent cavetto cornice of the Medracen. Four of the intercolumnar spaces have axially placed false doors, each 6.9 m high. The decoration of the door-leaves forms a cross pattern, thus giving rise to the earlier name of the tumulus, Tombeau de la Chrétienne. The door lintels are richly carved in low relief, with Greek decorative motifs such as egg-and-dart, astragal, and dentils. Unlike all the other Ionic capitals, those flanking the doors, and only those, are of the four-cornered, or diagonal, type. The conical pyramid surmounting the drum consists of thirty-three steps. Here, as in the Medracen, the pyramid terminates in a circular platform, 32.4 m above ground level; the crowning element has, as usual, disappeared without trace.

The tomb chamber (4.4 × 3.60 m and 3.43 m high) is preceded by an outer room that was meant to be approached by a complex circular corridor, 141 m long (fig. 195). This barrel-vaulted corridor, 2 m wide and 2.4 m high, is entered from the east through an opening under the eastern false door. Shortly after entering, one reaches a vestibule beyond which the corridor starts in a westerly direction, spiralling inward from the outer vestibule. Fifty-one niches were cut along the sides of the corridor to hold the oil lamps that lit the passage on certain (ceremonial) occasions. On the east side of the tumulus an area 6 m wide and 16 m long housed a now ruined tomb altar or a cult building. The facing of the tumulus, like that of the Medracen, was fastened together by clamps; this type of construction is largely responsible for the relatively good preservation of both monuments.

Pomponius Mela, a Roman author of the mid first century AC, perhaps refers to this monument when he talks about a tomb of a royal family who lived near Iol/Caesarea (modern Cherchel).[161] Because the tomb chamber was robbed in antiquity, and no inscriptions were found in or around the structure, only the architectural style helps to date the Kbour-er-Roumia tumulus. The architect undoubtedly used the Medracen as his immediate model, but employed Ionic columns and other purely Greek ornament in place of the mixed style of the earlier building. The interior is more intricate, with a circular, 'labyrinth-like' ambulatory, such as had been used, for instance, in earlier and smaller tumuli (bazinas) in the region.[162]

A date in the first century BC or the time of Augustus is the most likely.[163] In that case, the Kbour-er-Roumia tumulus could have been constructed for either the younger or the older Bocchus, who ruled the kingdom in the first half of the first century BC, or more likely for Juba II, King of Mauretania (30 BC–AC 19) in whose reign the region enjoyed a relatively long period of peace and prosperity.

Among the monumental tombs in northwestern Africa described above, the tower-like design dominates. These 'pinnacle' tombs are rather far removed versions of the fourth-century funerary buildings of Asia Minor. Here, as elsewhere, the columnar orders never regained their long-lost classical function: they served merely decorative purposes. In the absence of evidence to the contrary, it can be assumed that the Punic type of mausoleum eventually reached Italy by way of Sicily (e.g., the so-called Tomb of Theron), and later influenced the design of Roman tombs in southern France (fig. 196) and elsewhere in the northern and western provinces of the Roman Empire.[164]

The large stone tumuli, as noted above, are unique in the architecture of the last three centuries BC. In Asia Minor there is hardly anything comparable with these Numidian monuments; the huge funerary monument at Rhodini on Rhodes, partly rock-cut and partly built, is perhaps closest in concept (see page 83ff). The impressiveness of the Numidian tumuli lies in the combination of Egyptian and Greek features. Whereas the awesome quality of the Egyptian pyramid lies in its mass and the simplicity of its lines, a Greek building has its beauty in the use of mouldings and architectural elements, and in the harmonious proportions of the parts to each other and to the building as a whole. The Numidian tumuli are a blend of these two major artistic traditions, which lived on in the Roman Empire, though under different technical conditions and thus in new forms (e.g., Mausoleum of Augustus in Rome, (fig. 197).

v Funerary Monuments of the Near and Middle East

The tradition of monumental funerary architecture was generally established in the Near and Middle East long before any Hellenistic influences were felt there. In Syria the well-constructed underground tombs at Ugarit (Ras-Shamra) [165] (fig. 198) date from about the beginning of the Iron Age; and some of the Phoenician monuments at Amrith (Marathos) are probably not later than the fourth century. Even as far afield as present-day Saudi Arabia and Yemen, mausolea of considerable size were already being constructed in the fifth century (fig. 199) for the rulers of the local kingdoms. [166]

A Tombs in Jerusalem

In Jerusalem the so-called Tomb of the Pharaoh's Daughter (fig. 12), and related monuments, especially in the Silwan necropolis, [167] provide evidence for the existence of large-scale funerary architecture during the period of the First Temple (tenth to sixth centuries). From the sixth to the third century there is little evidence for monumental tomb building in Jerusalem itself. Such activity reappears only in the second century often as a revival of old forms (e.g., cubes, pyramids) adorned with Hellenistic architectural ornament. As time progressed, tombs betraying Greek influence became more and more sumptuous. In general, the architectural vocabulary of the new tombs attempted to follow developments in important Hellenistic regions such as Asia Minor and Alexandria. The series of monumental tombs continues uninterrupted down to the destruction of Jerusalem in AD 70. As in other cities, cemeteries gradually developed all around the city, wherever the conditions were suitable for burials. The majority of the Jerusalem tombs are located north, east, and south of the city walls (fig. 200); the western outskirts have few examples, doubtless because of the prevailing western winds (causing odour) and the brittle nature of the rocks. Nevertheless, one of the earliest known Hellenistic tombs of monumental proportions was discovered in 1956 just west of the Old City.

This tomb goes under the name of the Tomb of Jason (fig. 201), [168] who is mentioned in an Aramaic inscription found on a plastered wall inside the tomb.[169] The complex is of mixed construction (i.e., partly rock-cut and partly built); it consists of a 'central porch' from which open two burial-chambers (fig. 202). Both chambers are rock-cut; the one on the left has eight roughly cut loculi, or kokhim in Hebrew terminology. The façade is a rare example of a single column (Doric) in antis.[170] The base of the column was partly covered by plaster when the floor was subsequently raised, to provide better drainage.[171] Two pilasters (the antae), constructed of small stones and plastered over, flank the central column. The architectural fragments found in the process of the excavation suggest that the anta capitals were Corinthian.[172] Above the lintel of the doorway there is a prominent cavetto cornice. Surmounting the porch is the usual nefesh, an important element of Semitic tombs, here consisting of a square podium crowned by a smooth-sided pyramid.

The 'central porch' to the south opens off an inner court, which in turn is preceded by an outer court and forecourt; all these elements are laid out on the same axis. The three courtyards run almost horizontally into the gentle slope of the hill, and are walled along their entire length; they thus form a sort of 'dromos.' The walls and floors were plastered, with the exception of the forecourt where the bedrock was dressed smooth and left uncovered. All three courtyards were open to the sky and separated by built walls. Centrally placed doorways provided access from one court to the other. Voussoirs found in the area of the doorway leading from the forecourt to the outer court indicate that this opening took the form of a true arch.

The complex, approximately 22 m long, is almost unique among the known funerary monuments in Jerusalem. It has an elaborate plan, with the columned porch as the focal point. Such a plan, though reminiscent of a long dromos (with divisions), also recalls some Alexandrian tomb plans of the Ptolemaic period,[173] or the layout of Tomb no. I and no. II at Marissa in Palestine itself.[174] The existing architectural ornament is meagre, perhaps indicating the rather restricted use of applied decoration at the time of construction. The extant fragments of the Corinthian pilaster capitals find their closest parallels in designs of the second century, such as the Temple of Hyrkanos at Araq-el-Emir or the Temple of Zeus Olbios at Diocaesarea (Uzuncaburç).[175] Rahmani, the excavator of the structure, has assigned the first burial in the tomb to the period of Alexander Jannaeus, in the early first century BC. However, the pottery finds and inscriptions, as well as the architectural ornament, suggest an earlier date, probably in the first half of the second century. Thereafter, at least three generations were buried here till the tomb was partially destroyed, about the time of the founding of the Herodian dynasty.

Of the pretentious funerary monuments of Jerusalem, the closest to Jason's tomb chronologically is the Tomb of Bene Hezir (sons of Hezir).[176] In contrast to Jason's tomb, where we have a combination of Corinthian and Doric elements, the Bene Hezir façade is purely Doric (fig. 203). It is situated in the Kidron Valley east of the Old City, just a few hundred metres north of the so-called Tomb of the Pharaoh's Daughter. The Bene Hezir tomb is one of a series of four monuments placed on a high rocky scrap at the foot of the western slopes of the Mount of Olives. The façade is distyle in antis, with two Doric columns supporting an architrave and a triglyph and metope frieze. On the architrave is a three-line inscription, which first informs the visitor that 'this is the grave and nefesh of Eleazar, Hania ...,' followed by the names of other family members who were buried there. Above the slightly projecting cavetto cornice the rock surface is cut back perpendicularly; the superstructure (if there was any) has disappeared without trace.[177] The nefesh mentioned in the text stood immediately next to the façade on the north. Its lower rock-cut section is still in situ, but the upper built portion has been dismantled. The form of the now non-existent crown is conjectural; however, it can be assumed that it took the usual form of a pyramid, as in much earlier Egyptian models at Thebes, and in the Tomb of the Pharaoh's Daughter and the Tomb of Jason at Jerusalem itself. Behind the two-columned porch of the façade there are a series of five burial chambers, some with loculi, and one in the back with arched niches. The complex is connected, through a rock-cut stairway to the south, with the so-called Tomb of Zachariah. The Bene Hezir tomb was for a long time assigned to the early first century BC or later, mainly on the basis of the inscription on the architrave. However, it is now believed to be a structure of the early Hasmonean period, dating from the second half of the second century. The overall design, the treatment of the architectural details, and the character of the mouldings[178] certainly do not exclude such an early date for the tomb.

Only a few metres south of the Bene Hezir structure is the Tomb of Zachariah.[179] It is a well-preserved monolith carved entirely free of the surrounding rock (fig. 204), which encloses the tomb on three sides; the fourth side faces the valley below. The cubic middle portion (7.5 m in height and 5.5 × 5.6 m on plan) stands on a four-stepped crepidoma; a pyramid (4.7 m high) served as the crowning feature. Excavations in the 1960s revealed a small irregular chamber below the level of the steps on the east; this feature is rarely found in the tombs of Jerusalem. Most of the applied architectural ornament occurs on the face of the main cubic element; it consists of engaged half- and quarter-columns, the latter attached to corner pilasters. Below the pilaster capitals there are four carved discs in a position corresponding to the placing of rosettes on antae in many of the rock-cut tombs in Asia Minor. The capitals are Ionic, with a straight canalis between the volutes. Below the capitals appears the beginning of fluting; flutes were never carried all the way down the column shafts. The bases were also left largely unfinished, or perhaps the details were executed in plaster. Although the decoration of the main cube is purely Greek, along the lines, for example, of the Lion Tomb at Knidos, the monumental tomb at Alinda, or the Tomb of Theron, the entablature is more in the native tradition, with a plain architrave surmounted by a prominent cavetto cornice, a common feature of the funerary monuments of North Africa as well as of the Near East.

The structure, because of the stairway connecting it with the Bene Hezir tomb, has mistakenly been said to have been part of a single complex; in other words it was to be the nefesh of the Bene Hezir tomb. This view is rarely accepted today, because both tombs have their own nefesh and burial arrangements.

The association of the tomb with Zachariah is also without any historical foundation, but the name is still used today for the sake of convenience. In the absence of small finds or epigraphic evidence the date of the tomb is problematic. The relative purity of its form is still largely in the local tradition of a square funeral chapel crowned by a pyramid. The novelty of the design is in the application of Greek architectural ornament to the main cube; in other respects the style shows little innovation or variety. Thus, a date in the second half of the first century BC is reasonable;[180] it was at this time that a local Hellenistic style began to flourish in Jerusalem and in the Palestine region in general.

The so-called Tomb of Absalom is located a short distance north of the two preceding monuments.[181] It is free-standing and of mixed construction, the lower section (approximately 8.5 m high) being carved out of the bedrock, while the remainder is constructed of ashlars (fig. 205a, b). The total height of the monument was ca 20 m. In the lower part a socle (1.5 m high) supports a cubic section (6.8 m per side at its base), the four faces of which are decorated with Ionic half-columns and quarter-columns engaged in corner pilasters, i.e., the same scheme as has been seen in the Tomb of Zachariah. The column shafts below the capitals are smooth, without any indication of fluting, a form that must have been thought to be proper for rock-cut architecture.[182] The bases are fully carved, consisting of a plinth, a torus, and a cyma reversa moulding. Typically of the local eclectic Hellenistic style, the entablature is Doric with a cavetto cornice surmounting it. The intermediate built element is a plain square podium (2.15 m high and 6 m per side) with a cornice of its own; it is constructed of large blocks, and has an opening in its southern side. Then follows a drum, 2.65 m high and 5.82

m in diameter; this, in turn, supports the concave conical roof (5.85 m high; lower diameter 6.1 m, upper diameter 0.8 m). This drum is divided into a larger lower section, with a profiled base and moulded cornice, and a smaller upper element ornamented by an unusual carved rope pattern. The finial at the apex of the structure is in the form of a lotus calyx with six large leaves (0.8 m high and 0.72 m wide).

The tomb chamber, with two arcosolia, is hewn down into the upper part of the rock-cut cube (fig. 206).

Its size and the combination of a number of different geometric elements make the Tomb of Absalom the most impressive in the Kidron Valley. Its designer went a step beyond the concept seen in the Tomb of Zachariah. The most important change occurs in the built upper parts, where the conventional pyramid is replaced by a Graeco-Roman 'tholos'; as Avigad rightly points out, only the columns are omitted, probably in order to avoid any resemblance to a pagan temple. At the same time, the symbolic significance of the crowning elements remains, even in their new form; the cylindrical structure is to be understood as the nefesh of the tomb below it.[183] By the end of the first century BC the tholos form was widely employed for tombs and commemorative buildings in different regions of the Mediterranean, e.g., the funerary Monument of the Julii at St Rémy (fig. 196) and the structure known as Rundbau at Ephesos (fig. 207).[184]

Often associated with the Tomb of Absalom is a burial cave erroneously labelled the Tomb of Jehoshaphat (fig. 205b). It lies immediately behind the Tomb of Absalom to the northeast. Architecturally it is of little significance. From the decorative point of view, it is to be noted for its floral motifs carved in relief in the pediment above the wide doorway. Inside, eight rooms provided ample space for burials. In view of their close proximity to each other, the two complexes presumably belonged to the same family; but they are not necessarily contemporary as has frequently been assumed. There is no resemblance in design or in the style of the architectural decoration. If the Tomb of Absalom dates from the late first century BC, or the early first century AC, the so-called Tomb of Jehoshaphat must have been an afterthought, cut somewhat later when additional space for burial was needed.

Of the other large funerary monuments in Jerusalem, several façade-tombs with Doric entablatures should be mentioned here. These tombs are in the tradition of the Bene Hezir structure but are more elaborate and sophisticated in design and execution.

The rock-cut tomb known as the Cave of Umm el-Ammed (fig. 208) is located north of the Old City in the Wadi el-Ammed.[185] The distyle-in-antis façade opened off a spacious courtyard. The width of the façade is

13.50 m, the height, including the cornice, is 4.37 m. Excavations carried out in the 1940s revealed a detailed picture of some of the lesser-known features of the design. Both the free-standing columns and the antae have Attic-Ionic bases placed on plinths. The capitals of both columns and antae are missing; the former were presumably Ionic, for Ionic capitals were often combined with a Doric entablature in the monuments of Jerusalem. Moreover, the Deir ed-Derb[186] tomb, which is very similar in every respect to the Umm el-Ammed example, has a well-preserved Ionic capital (fig. 209). The form of the Umm el-Ammed anta capitals was probably the same as that of the capitals of the pilasters at either end of the decorative façade. A narrow architrave-band, surmounted by a much wider Doric frieze decorated with rosettes, runs across the entire length of the façade. An interesting and unusual feature of the entablature is the row of Ionic dentils on top of the frieze, followed by Doric guttae on the soffit of the cornice. The occurrence of guttae in this context is unique in Palestine and rare in the Mediterranean world as a whole; among the few known examples of similarly placed guttae are the theatre of Marcellus in Rome and the Corinthian-Doric temple at Paestum. Above the slightly projecting cornice the rock-surface is cut back to form a ledge; if there were any additional elements here, they have completely disappeared. All wall surfaces (façade, returning ends of court-yard, and porch) are carved in imitation of evenly spaced drafted masonry. This treatment of the wall shows clearly that the architect was following the fashion established in private and public architecture. Real drafted masonry of comparable style had occurred as early as the first half of the second century in the 'Hyrkanos complex' at Araq el-Emir in Jordan (fig. 210).[187] Even closer in style to our tomb is the drafted masonry found in buildings of the early Herodian period (37–4 BC), such as the Phasael tower (Tower of David) in Jerusalem and the outer walls of the Haram el-Khalil in Hebron.[188]

The interior of the tomb can be approached by a low undercoated opening cut in the centre of the back wall of the porch. Inside there are two burial-chambers with loculi.

The monumental Deir ed-Derb tomb (fig. 211),[189] though in Samaria rather than in the Judaean highlands, is included here because of its close stylistic resemblance to the Umm el-Ammed and other monuments in Jerusalem. A large court, 17 m a side, precedes the façade, which is also approximately 17 m wide. Above the two Ionic columns of the porch is an incomplete Doric frieze (the ends remain uncarved); fifteen triglyphs and fourteen rosette metopes are surmounted by a row of dentils. Unlike the Umm el-Ammed tomb, each rosette is of a different design (fig. 212). The arrangement is comparable to a number of funerary and other types of monuments in Italy.[190] To articulate the wall surfaces, the walls were again carved to represent drafted masonry. Unfortunately, the tomb was left unfinished; thus the representation of headers and stretchers appears only inside the porch. On the exterior, to the right of the porch, a flight of steps leads up to a rock-cut platform. The interior contains three burial-chambers (fig. 213) approached by a small door. This door was closed by a large rolling stone, a method often employed to seal tombs in Palestine.

Less than 1 km north of the walls of the Old City lies the largest tomb of the Jerusalem necropolis, commonly known, though not on any historical grounds, as the 'tomb of the Kings (of Judah).' In actuality it probably belonged to Queen Helena of Adiabene (born in north Mesopotamia) and members of her family, who were buried in Jerusalem shortly after AD 50.[191] A corridor of twenty-three steps (30 m long and 9 m wide) leads from the southwest to the entrance of the enclosed courtyard in the northeast (fig. 214). Along the sides of this corridor water channels brought rain-water to two cisterns used for the ceremony of purification. The courtyard measures 26 × 27 m in area; its walls are about 8 m in height. The large monumental façade (27.5 m long) has a distyle in antis arrangement of two Ionic columns (fig. 215). The execution of the decorative framework above the column capitals is unusual. Instead of a regular Greek superstructure, there is a carved relief band of fruits and pine-cones, with a large rosette in the centre. This band is followed by a plain surface that was perhaps thought of as an architrave; above this plain band comes the Doric frieze. The central triglyph is replaced by a bunch of grapes, the flanking metopes by wreaths, and the next triglyph on either side by acanthus leaves; these motifs might have served a commemorative purpose. A prominent moulded cornice surmounts the frieze course. Everything above the cornice has completely disappeared, but it is known from Josephus that after the death of Queen Helena, 'Monobazus sent her bones and those of his brother to Jerusalem with instructions that they should be buried in three pyramids.'[192] These three pyramids may refer to the nefesh that probably surmounted the façade.[193] The interior of the tomb consists of a main room and eight burial-chambers with loculi and acrosolia. The entrance to the tombs was closed by a rolling stone operated by an intricate device of ropes from pits in the courtyard.

The date of the tomb, around the middle of the first century AC, agrees well with the late Hellenistic style of the façade. In no other tomb in Jerusalem do we see such a stage-like arrangement of the entablature. The Doric frieze is purely ornamental and freely composed. It seems to be 'glued on' to a neutral surface, rather than resting on a firm support;' consequently it only vaguely recalls the conventional setting of a Doric frieze. In this respect the frieze is quite different from some of the earlier designs discussed above.

There is no definite evidence for a second storey in any of the rock-cut façade-tombs at Jerusalem discussed above. Nevertheless, the existence of two-storeyed funerary monuments is attested by the dismembered remains of a façade-tomb in the northern necropolis (fig. 216). The ruins of this structure were investigated by K. Galling in the 1930s;[194] it has subsequently been variously described as the Two-storied Tomb or Pilaster Tomb. The lower storey is 5.5 m wide. The arrangement is in-antis, with widely spaced, ca 2.5-m-high columns; the capitals are perhaps best described as 'tubular' in form. There is only a vestigial architrave; most of the height of the entablature is taken up by a prominent Doric frieze. The metopes, as in the Tomb of Queen Helena, were decorated with discs, called unfinished 'double rosettes' by Galling.[195] Immediately above the cornice were four evenly spaced pilasters, portions of which were still in situ in the 1930s. These pilasters were very squat in proportion; the bases, related to the Attic-Ionic type, were quite high in relation to the height of the shafts. The two central pilasters were set closer together than the free-standing columns below them. The restoration of the topmost part of the façade is conjectural; with a gable roof, the height of the building would have reached 6.5 m. The interior of the tomb has not been explored.

The façade of this monument appears to be rather simple, by comparison with other examples of two-storeyed tombs discussed previously. The design is certainly not native to the region; presumably it was imported from the west, probably around the end of the first century BC. As will be seen below, imposing two-storeyed tombs were frequently constructed in the Nabataean kingdom from the late first century BC onward. This double-storeyed tomb in Jerusalem thus provides an important architectural link between the two regions; unfortunately we have no way of knowing whether the type appeared first in the Nabataean or in the Palestinian tradition.

Of the numerous large tombs in the 'funerary belt' around Jerusalem, the royal tomb of Herod's family is unique in being west of the Old City.[196] Architecturally the exterior is insignificant; the interior, however, is quite elaborate, with a central hall and four surrounding chambers. The walls of the interior rooms were faced with ashlars of excellent quality. Access to the interior was blocked by a huge rolling stone, which is still in situ (fig. 217). Near the entrance to the tomb remains of a nefesh were found.

The complex known as the Sanhedrin Tombs,[197] located near the modern Sanhedria quarter in northern Jerusalem, includes a large number of funerary monuments. Of these, the only example of a columnar façade is the structure known as the Two-columned Tomb (or Tomb no. 8).[198] The columns of the distyle-in-antis façade have no bases (fig. 218); the capitals recall those of the above-described Two-storied Tomb. The width of the entire façade is 9.18 m; its height up to the top of the columns is 2.57 m. The only existing decorative motifs are the parallel fillets of the anta capitals. A rock-cut court lined with benches along the sides precedes this rather austere-looking façade. The date of the structure must be close to that of the Two-storied Tomb.

The main entrance to the Sanhedrin Tombs complex has an elaborate carved pediment (fig. 219a, b), analogous to that of the 'Tomb of Jehoshaphat.' Pediments, indeed, are often found in plainer and less costly, though still pretentious, tombs of other than columnar design; and one relatively small façade-tomb, ca 3.5 m high and 3 m wide, has an elaborate Doric entablature carried by two antae (fig. 220).[199] Its source of inspiration seems to go back to decorative doorways such as that of the Erechtheion in Athens and the Tholos at Epidauros.

Outside Jerusalem the evidence for monumental funerary architecture in Palestine is scanty, partly because of the lack of excavations and partly a result of the destructive force of time. That sumptuous funerary buildings once existed is amply attested by the ancient literary evidence. One example from Josephus will suffice here: he mentions that at Modeei (ancient Modin in Palestine) a certain Simon 'built for his father and brothers a very great [funerary] monument of polished white marble, and raising it to a great and conspicious height, made porticoes around it, and erected monolithic pillars, a wonderful thing to see. In addition to these he built for his parents and brothers seven pyramids, one for each, so made as to excite wonder by their size and beauty; and those have been preserved to this day.'[200] This grandiose commemorative complex has either not yet been found or has disappeared without trace.

B *The Tomb of Hamrath, Suweida (Syria), and the Monuments at Hermel and Kalat Fakra (Lebanon)*

The locality of Suweida (Soada, Dionysias) is in the Hauran district south of Damascus. Travellers of the last century noted, among the ancient ruins of the town, a large and relatively well-preserved funerary monument on a hill overlooking a ravine (fig. 221a).[201] The structure, now destroyed, stood at the western edge of the ancient city. The association of the tomb with Hamrath is based on a bilingual inscription in Greek and Aramaic: 'Tomb of Hamrath, which was erected for her by Odainath her husband.'[202] On the basis of the lettering of this inscription the monument has been dated to the first century BC. The quadrangular building stood on a low stepped platform, measuring ca 11 m per side on the lower step. Above the stylobate was a large podium decorated with six engaged Doric columns on each side (three-quarter columns at the corners). The columns were 4.61 m high, with a lower diameter of 0.89 m, giving a ratio of ca 1:5.18. Furthermore, the columns leaned slightly inward, recalling the illusionistic device widely employed in classical Greek architecture. In the upper sections of the intercolumniations (1.84 m in width, reduced to 1.80 m at the corners) arms and armour were carved in relief, a rather strange feature in a tomb built for a woman. The entablature (1.23 m high) is in the tradition of later Hellenistic architecture, with a low architrave and three triglyphs per intercolumniation. Both mutules and guttae were omitted on the cornice, doubtless because of the difficulty of carving them from the hard basalt. Above the corona rose a stepped pyramid, of which the two lowest steps were still in situ in the nineteenth century. The estimated total height of the monument (without the finial, if such existed) was about 12 m. In the main, central section of the monument (built of neatly fitted isodomic masonry), there was no doorway, nor was any provision for a burial found. However, the area beneath the structure was not properly explored; the interment could have been below ground level, as in some of the above-discussed tombs at Amrith.[203]

The building in its essentials is Greek, of a type already seen in Asia Minor. In its main outlines it is especially close to the Lion Tomb at Knidos; to a lesser extent it also resembles the huge, partly rock-cut tomb at Rhodini on Rhodes. The stepped pyramid perhaps suggests eastern rather than local or western influence; stepped pyramids, however, had been well known in the Aegean and Asia Minor since the time of Mausolos. The relief carvings of armour between the columns was popular in buildings associated with Macedonians, though with the progress of the Hellenistic age this form of decoration became quite widespread in the Mediterranean.

In the Near and Middle East few known buildings of similar nature and type existed. Among the examples, which are still strongly Hellenistic in character, are the monuments at Hermel (fig. 222) and Kalat Fakra (fig. 223).[204] Unlike the Tomb of Hamrath, both of these are two-storeyed buildings surmounted by a smooth-sided pyramid. The structure at Hermel in northern Lebanon is ca 28 m high. Four corner pilasters decorate the lower storey (just over 9 m each side); low reliefs of hunting scenes are carved between them. The upper storey is ornamented with four pilasters on each face. Here, too, there was no doorway anywhere in the outer face of the building, and there are no discernible arrangements of any sort for a burial; the function is therefore assumed to have been non-sepulchral.

Yet much the same thing is true of the Tomb of Hamrath, where the inscription alone attests the funerary nature of the building; thus at Hermel, too, a funerary/commemorative function seems likely.

The monument at Kalat Fakra in central Lebanon must have been one of the largest of all built specimens of commemorative/funerary nature.[205] The tower-like structure measured approximately 16 m each side; the estimated total height was in the neighbourhood of 37 m. The lower storey, or podium, was plain, except for a stairway leading to a large door placed in the middle of the east side. The second storey had columnar treatment with a porch behind the free-standing central columns on the east side. Above the Cypriot-Phoenician capitals there was a regular Doric architrave and frieze course crowned by a cavetto cornice over a large 'torus'; the roof consisted of a steep, isosceles type of pyramid. The dedicatory inscription on the door lintel indicates a date in the reign of Claudius (AD 41–54).[206]

c Tombs of the Nabataeans

The development of the spectacular rock-cut tomb complexes of the Nabateans is a late phenomenon in Hellenistic funerary architecture. However, Nabataeans appeared in history in early Hellenistic times.[207] Our best ancient literary sources regarding this semi-nomadic people are the writings of Diodorus Siculus and Strabo.[208] The former based his account largely on the work of Hieronymus of Cardia (364–260 BC); Strabo's information came from Artemidoros, though Strabo himself also travelled in the Near East.

The territory of the Nabataeans in the late Hellenistic period embraced much of northern Arabia and the Sinai: 'After one has sailed past this country the Leanites Gulf comes next, about which are many inhabited villages of Arabs who are known as Nabataeans. This tribe occupies a large part of the coast and not a little of the country which stretches inland, and it has a people numerous beyond telling and flocks and herds in multitude beyond belief.'[209] The golden age of the Nabataean kingdom came during the reigns of Obodas II (30–9/8 BC) and his successor Aretas IV (9/8 BC–AD 40); this period presumably also produced some of the most magnificent rock-cut tombs. As in many other regions (e.g., Phrygia, Persia, and Lycia), readily accessible rock formations provided a convenient medium for the execution of conspicuous and imposing funerary monuments.

The administrative centre and the seat of the Nabataean royal family and ruling aristocracy was Petra (fig. 224), situated in the Negev region: 'The metropolis of the Nabataeans is Petra, as it is called, for it lies on a site which is otherwise smooth and level, but it is fortified all around by rock, the outside parts of the site being precipitous and sheer, and the inside parts having springs in abundance, both for domestic purposes and for watering gardens. Outside the circuit of the rock most of the territory is desert, in particular that towards Judaea.'[210]

The numerous rock-cut tombs around Petra have often been visited and surveyed since their discovery in 1812. The most comprehensive study of these tombs was undertaken by R.E. Brunnow and A. von Domaszewski in 1897 and 1898; they recorded 512 funerary monuments, which they classified on stylistic grounds.[211] Since that time more tombs have been added to the list; by far the largest number of these additions are simple 'pylon tombs.' However, for our purposes the most elaborate funerary monuments are also the most significant, for they clearly derived many elements of their design from the Hellenistic Greek architectural vocabulary. The finest of all the Petra tombs is known as the Khazneh ('Treasury') (fig. 225a, b).[212] The tomb is cut rather dramatically into a narrow gorge (called es Siq) at a point where it widens, so as to give a certain vista to the monument. The façade, cut back some 7 m into the face of the cliff, is 24.9 m wide and 38.7 m high. It consists of two storeys, of which the lower is a hexastyle colonnade of unfluted Corinthian columns (12.65 m high) standing on Attic-Ionic bases. The lateral pairs of columns are engaged; between the two free-standing columns in the centre a short flight of steps gives access to the vestibule and the burial-chambers (fig. 226a, b). The closed intercolumnar spaces at either end carry reliefs of horsemen, probably the Dioskuri. The Corinthian capitals (1.40 m high) have richly carved floral motifs. The entablature (2.87 m high) recedes slightly above the two end intercolumniations; a pediment with carved tympanon and acroteria crowns the three central spans. The frieze course has rinceaux pattern alternating with antithetic griffins facing craters. The foliage of the frieze is carved as minutely as that of the capitals; in this respect it recalls the love of decorative details found on the Tomba Ildebranda at Sovana in Etruria. The tympanon is filled with vine scrolls. Both horizontal and raking cornices have dentils, as is often the case in Hellenistic designs; the central acroterion is in the form of the crown of Isis. The entablature breaks forward above the end columns; the 'frieze' has carved heads, and there are 'corner acroteria' above the cornice. Behind and above the pediment is an attic (3.2 m high) crowned with a band of rosettes, above which a cyma and fillet form a 'podium' for the second storey. This second storey consists of a central tholos in bold relief (though not cut completely free from the background), flanked on either side by columns supporting a pair of quarter-pediments bent at right angles to each other. This arrangement in some ways recalls among other things Athenaeus's account of the tholos of Aphrodite 'opposite a peristyle' on the boat of Ptolemy IV[213] or a number of Pompeian wall paintings of the

Second Style, such as can be seen in the House of the Labyrinth (cubiculum 16). The interesting composition of the various architectural elements can be conceived as an illusionistic peristyle court, perhaps of a private villa or palace rather than a sanctuary.

The Corinthian columns (8.95 m high) are similar to those of the lower order, but smaller in size; their capitals have only one row of leaves in place of the two in the lower order. The wall surfaces between the engaged columns have carved figures: Tyche in the 'central' span of the tholos, with Amazons on the sides; Nikai between the tholos and the side 'pavilions'; Amazons again in the front spans of the 'pavilions.' The richly carved frieze course of the entablature of the second storey has floral motifs alternating with masks. A row of close-set antefixes gives a crown-like appearance to the conical roof of the tholos; at the apex of the cone there is a floral capital topped by a (funerary) urn. Surmounting the broken pediments of the lateral 'pavilions' are acroteria in the form of birds of prey (eagles). Truncated obelisks rising behind the broken pediments form the uppermost element of the imaginative design, recalling perhaps the nefesh of Semitic tombs.

The interior of the Khazneh (fig. 227) is reached from a rock-cut terrace leading to the vestibule (14 m wide, 6 m deep, and more than 12 m high), which rises about 1 m above the level of the terrace. In the centre of the back wall, steps lead up to a very ornamental doorway, behind which is the nearly cubical (12 m) main room.[214] In each of the three walls of this room there are secondary openings leading to small chambers. Side rooms also open off the vestibule by means of richly decorated doorways. To emphasize, at least visually, the architectural 'solidity' of the vestibule, there are Corinthian pilasters in the rear corners.

The disposition of the main interior room on the axis of the façade, and the lateral chambers opening off the sides of the vestibule, both recall the 'oikos' type of plan encountered in Alexandrian funerary architecture and described in connection with Alexandrian monuments. The vestibule behind the façade is also rare in Petra, but often occurs in Alexandria. Furthermore, the decorative details, especially those of the Corinthian capitals, show affinity with Alexandrian practice, suggesting foreign influence in the execution of the project.[215] The possibility of architect and artisans having been imported to work on the project is strengthened by the fact that the Khazneh had no known antecedents in Nabataean architecture; its decorative scheme (though not its design) remained unique in Nabataean practice even after the completion of this splendid tomb.

Stylistically, the façade has been regarded as a 'baroque' composition. It is certainly of a composite style; a rather restrained and classical lower storey, dominated by straight lines, is combined with a variety of concave, convex, and rectilinear elements in the upper level. The architect must have planned every element of the design with care, leaving nothing to chance. The location is commanding, producing an immediate effect on the visitor; the details of the carving are not lost, because only a close-range view of the tomb is possible.

It has also been suggested that the design represents the transposition to a vertical plane of a series of architectural entities that originally extended horizontally one behind the other. A similar possibility has been noted in connection with the rock-cut royal tombs of Persia. The large north palace complex at Herodian Masada, if viewed from below, would appear as a series of elements in a single vertical plane, though they are, in fact, located on different terraces receding in a step-like fashion (fig. 228). Alternatively, the architect of the Khazneh may simply have wished to 'lengthen' the apparent load supported by the lower storey, hence the breaking up of the classical forms.[216] In either case, the Khazneh certainly differs in design from other multi-storeyed tombs discussed earlier, with the exception of some of the North African mausolea, in which similar contrasts of concave and convex forms are introduced to achieve the desired visual effects. In North African architecture curvilinear designs also occur in the upper orders of non-funerary monuments, e.g., in the Palazzo delle Colonne in Ptolemais of the late Hellenistic or Augustan period.[217] At Petra there is little or no local comparative material from non-funerary architecture.[218] The only design that recalls the Khazneh façade appears in a stucco relief on the temple complex known as Qasr el-Bint Faraun.[219] This project is dated to the reign of Aretas IV (though it might have started under Obodas II), on the basis of an inscription of Aretas IV, found on a bench in the temenos of the complex.[220] Unfortunately, there is no inscription on the Khazneh itself, or indeed on most of the other tombs in Petra; nor are there datable grave-goods, because the tombs were plundered in antiquity. Thus, the criteria for dating are stylistic. In view of the eclectic nature of the Khazneh design there has been a considerable controversy regarding the period of construction; suggestions range from the early first century BC to the second century AC. Such a stately and magnificent tomb must surely have belonged to a king,[221] who could afford to finance such a splendid memorial to himself. The royal personage was most probably Aretas IV, Philodemos (9–40 AC), an identification also supported by historical data.[222]

Two other monumental rock-cut tombs in Petra vaguely resemble the general outlines of the Khazneh. The earlier of these, perhaps the resting-place of Malichus II (40–70 AC), the son of Aretas IV, is the monument known as the Corinthian Tomb (fig. 229), one of a group of large-scale funerary establishments approximately 1 km north of the Khazneh. The lower storey consists of eight engaged columns with Corithianizing capitals,[223] standing on a high podium. In the two intervals, at the left end of the façade, ornamental doorways lead to small burial-rooms; other openings remain unfinished, suggesting that all these apertures were an afterthought, rather than part of the original design. A (now badly damaged) central doorway, cut through both podium and colonnade, leads into the main burial-chamber (9 × 12 m). The entablature of the lower order is surmounted by an attic decorated by eight short pilasters; in the middle section of this attic a curvilinear pediment surmounts the central pair of columns of the lower storey, while the four central pilasters of the attic, in turn, support the broken pediment that terminates the narrow second, or middle, section of the design. The third level, though less pretentious in decoration than the upper storey of the Khazneh, is basically of the same design, i.e., a tholos flanked by two pavilions. In the Corinthian Tomb the arrangement of the planes 'one behind the other' is perhaps even more evident than in the Khazneh. The pilasters of the middle section, though continuing the lines of the 'Corinthian' columns of the lower storey, at the same time appear visually to be behind them, thus forming a second monumental entrance behind the first colonnade. Transposed to a horizontal plane, the whole design culminates still farther back in the tholos. Such a three-fold division of units appears in a number of Nabataean temple designs; besides the above-noted Qasr el-Bint Faraun, it is also found at Moab (biblical Dibon) and at Seeia, in the temple of Baal Shamin.[224]

While the architect of the Corinthian Tomb obviously based his design on the façade of the Khazneh, he also introduced modifications. In the process the lower storey became wider and was surmounted by a 'semi-storey' of equal width, while the crowning tholos section remained essentially unchanged. This 'building up' of the architectural units produces a roughly triangular design; the balance between the various levels that is so conspicuous in the Khazneh façade is consequently lost.

More in keeping with the architectural principles of the Khazneh is the largest tomb of Petra, referred to in literature as the Deir (the Convent) (fig. 230a, b). It is located on a high rocky plateau about 2 km northwest of Petra proper. An entire projecting section of a cliff was chosen for the site of the tomb, with ample vistas from every direction. The huge façade (47 × 42 m) is relatively well preserved. In contrast to the Khazneh, the complex projects from its background rather than being hewn into a 'niche.'[225] It consists of two storeys, the lower having six half-columns plus two quarter-columns attached to pilasters that close the corners of the façade. In each of the outermost intercolumniations there are blank niches surmounted by curved gables. A doorway adorned by a pediment leads from the centre of the front to a single large chamber with a niche cut in its back wall. A low entablature dominated by the frieze band supports the upper storey; the fairly conspicuous mid-section found in the Khazneh and the Corinthian Tomb was omitted. The disposition of the main elements of the second storey is the same as in the two tombs described above: a cylindrical central element (tholos) flanked by pavilions. However, in the Deir each pavilion is flanked by an additional intercolumniation, closed at the corner by a composite member above, and exactly like those of the lower order. Also, the vertical lines established by the columns of the lower order are neatly continued in the upper storey with little interruption, except for those of the tholos, which are more closely spaced than the central columns of the lower storey. There are three blank window-like niches in the central intercolumniations of the flanking pavilions. These niches were probably intended for statues, to judge from the treatment of the corresponding spaces in the upper storey of the Khazneh. In keeping with the rather austere character of the façade, the frieze course above the columns is Doric, with large plain discs in the metopes. Broken pediments flank the low conical roof of the tholos, which in turn supports a prominent finial. In the finial, as elsewhere in the façade, the design consists of plain geometric forms, rather than plant motifs or similar organic type of ornament. By and large, the same conclusions can be drawn from the carving of the capitals. These of both orders have been described as hybrid, or pseudo-Ionic and pseudo-Corinthian. However, they are perhaps best designated as Nabataean, even if their origin can be traced back to one of the canonical Greek orders. The shape of a typical Nabataean capital is trapezoid; the surface of the upper section is concave, with a U-shaped, dot-like projection in the centre of the uppermost part of the capital (fig. 231).

Although the Deir was not entirely finished down to the last decorative detail, it is quite evident from the entire façade that, even in its complete state, it would have produced a simpler and more serene effect than the Khazneh. Besides the lack of carved detail, the heaviness of the second storey distinguishes it from the Khazneh. Yet it still has a certain appeal, stemming from the overwhelming mass of the monument, in which the elements are correctly composed without being extremely elaborate[226] – an approach that has been revived in our own era, but is so often carried to an extreme under the slogan that 'less is more.'

The date of the tomb is uncertain; nevertheless, on stylistic and historical grounds it seems to be later than the Khazneh and the Corinthian Tomb.

Thus the Deir could have been commissioned by Rabel II (70–106 AC) at the end of the first century AC, just before the establishment of the Roman Provincia Arabia in AD 106.

Of the other elaborate Petraean monumental tombs of the second half of the first century AC, the Palace Tomb, the Tomb of Sextius Florentinus, and the Urn Tomb are perhaps the most interesting architecturally. The first of these (fig. 232a, b) adjoins the Corinthian Tomb, and is again a multi-storey design on a huge scale. The ground floor contains a series of four doorways, each flanked by pilasters, with engaged quarter-columns; the two end doors are surmounted by segmental pediments, the central pair by triangular pediments. The doors give access to four burial-chambers of varying dimensions. The second storey consists of a row of sixteen half-columns with a quarter-column and a pilaster at each end. The central intercolumniation is the widest; the width of the others varies in an intricate pattern. In some of the intercolumnar spaces there are shallow niches. The uppermost portions of the façade are poorly preserved; because of defects in the rock-formation, these portions were in part built of ashlars. The sections still in situ suggest a high superstructure above the columns that can be regarded as a third storey, with rows of short flat pilasters one above the other, the spacing corresponding to that of the columns below.

The façade is enormous but has little coherence; it is simply a broad, high surface with densely packed architectural ornament.[227] The units constitute an entity in themselves, as if they had been derived from a number of different sources and then set side by side on a single vertical plane, constituting a monumental scaenae frons. Perhaps because of this theatrical backdrop concept of the design, the composition does not have a focal point in contrast to the other Nabataean tombs seen before.

The controversial Sextius Florentinus tomb (fig. 233a, b) is only a couple of hundred metres north of the Palace Tomb. It was cut, along with the Corinthian Tomb and others, in the northeast wall of the el Kubtha cliff formation. The lower storey is raised on a ledge, or podium, except for the centrally placed doorway (cf. the Corinthian Tomb). It is tetrastyle, the corner elements being pilasters with engaged quarter-columns, while two half-columns flank the doorway. The doorway has pilasters of its own, supporting an entablature and pediment; on the apex of the pediment there is a badly weathered Victory figure (not a pilaster as seen in the reconstruction). Above the central half-columns a segmental pediment breaks upward into the second storey. The field of this pediment is carved in relief, with a Medusa head flanked by an octopus on each side; an eagle perches on the apex. The arch partly covers two of the four Nabataean 'compressed pilasters' that decorate the upper storey, which terminates in an entablature and pediment occupying the entire width of the façade. The central acroterion is in the form of a (funerary) urn.

The date of the tomb is controversial mainly because of a Latin inscription carved above the doorway[228] identifying its owner as Sextius Florentinus, who is known to have been posted to the Provincia Arabia around AD 127. However, the architectural vocabulary of the façade consists entirely of elements, or combinations of elements, that occur in the first-century tombs discussed above. It is thus quite possible that the tomb is earlier than the time of Florentinus by a half-century or more and was simply reused, and the inscription cut, at the time of his death. Inscriptions are rarely found on the tombs of Petra; the Florentinus inscription may have been specially cut in order to indicate the change of ownership of the tomb.

The Urn Tomb (fig. 234a, b) is seemingly no more than an over-elaborate temple façade, but the form also recalls tombs at Hegra. However, in contrast even to the most complex Hegra tombs (fig. 235),[229] the tetrastyle lower, and the compressed upper, storey are crowned by a Greek pediment, rather than the stepped or crenellated cube above a large cavetto cornice normally found in Hegra tombs. The Urn Tomb has a more grandiose setting, with a series of built arches below the façade and rock-cut colonnades along the sides of the enclosing niche in which the design is hewn.

Of the many hundred rock-cut tombs of the Nabataeans not treated here, the majority are simple pylon tombs (fig. 236) without any Hellenistic features. Chronologically they seem to be the earliest (starting in the first century BC), but their construction did not cease with the appearance of the more ornamental funerary monuments. All the tomb-types of the Nabataeans existed side by side, the scale and complexity probably depending on the wealth of those who commissioned them. The majority of the rock-cut tombs belong to the first century AC, a date also supported by comparison with the dated Nabataean tombs of 'Hegra' (el Hegr in present-day Saudi Arabia), approximately 500 km south of Petra.[230] The first hundred years of our era were a period of relative prosperity in the Nabataean kingdom, when large undertakings could be carried out without difficulty. In the Petra region the tombs constituted a 'continuity' with other architectural forms; as a matter of fact, the other architectural forms may have existed because the tombs were there.[231] In any case, the large necropolis of Petra enlivened the surrounding landscape (even if it was not a conscious effort in the beginning), and in a sense provided a commemorative/decorative setting for the inhabitants in a manner similar to the painted walls of a house or palace.

VI The 'Temple Tomb' at Ai-Khanoum (Afghanistan)

Lastly a unique example of a built monumental tomb should be mentioned that is located far beyond the 'boundaries' of the Greek-speaking world, in present-day Afghanistan. The site of Ai-Khanoum, discovered in the 1960s, is a settlement built under strong Hellenistic influence in the wake of Alexander's expansion into the east. Besides the spacious burial place of a certain Kineas, the remains of a large peripteral temple tomb came to light within the city limits.[232]

The structure consists of a combination of cut stone and baked brick. Only the foundation courses (fig. 237) and the elaborate underground burial arrangements survive. The crepis of three 'steps' measured 1.50 m in height, while the stylobate was 29.75 m long and 20 m wide. No traces of the peristyle columns (10 × 6) have been found, but they were presumably of baked clay, or perhaps even of wood, like the rest of the superstructure; their estimated height was 6 m. Exceptional features are the carefully carved Ionic capitals, which are modelled on Aegean prototypes. Although no exact parallel for these capitals can be found, they show close stylistic affinities with capitals from the Seleucid Kingdom.[233]

The actual cella measures 21.5 × 11.75 m on plan (fig. 238) and consists of a distyle-in-antis pronaos, a naos, and a back room. From the eastern part of the naos a twelve-stepped, 4.46-m-long stairway ('dromos') leads down to the actual main burial-chamber (4.54 × 2.32 m) placed under the back room. This dromos-like stairway was covered and sealed after each interment in order to 'conceal' its existence. The chamber itself is constructed of well-cut ashlars, fitted without the use of clamps or dowels, and roofed by a barrel vault in the Macedonian manner. Inside, two sarcophagi were found (one well preserved), and bones belonging to five skeletons.

The 'temple tomb' must have been used for the burial of a number of generations, as suggested by the addition of a later secondary chamber north of the stairway. The naos was obviously used for funerary cults, while sacrifices must have been made outside the building. An altar was discovered in front of the east façade next to a central stairway giving access to the naos.

According to the French excavators, at least two major stages of construction can be distinguished, the first in the early third century and the second in the late Hellenistic period.[234]

The design of the structure is based on Greek Hellenistic models, as is the case with most of the other buildings at Ai-Khanoum. Using the plan of the temple for a funerary purpose was nothing new and followed a tradition established in western Asia Minor. The novelty in the present case seems to be that a Greek temple plan was little, if at all, modified, and the high prominent podium, known for instance from the Nereid Monument, was reduced to three high steps. The actual burial arrangements were completely allocated to the basement (as in the Charmyleion on Kos), and unless the now-lost decoration had funerary character, the appearance of the building was more like that of a temple than of a tomb or a 'temple tomb' on a podium.

Conclusions

It is difficult to draw detailed conclusions concerning the relationship of Hellenistic monumental tombs to their predecessors, because in all periods these structures were likely to be highly individualistic creations. In contrast to other types of building designs, tomb designs emphasized variety; we need only recall the large number of tombs and tomb designs surveyed to appreciate multiplicity of sources behind the various types. Nevertheless, within the limits of specific periods or geographical locations, it is possible to distinguish certain major trends and 'fashionable' forms.

The appearance and subsequent popularity of the 'temple tombs' on podia during the fourth century was not so much the result of religious practices or beliefs as of political and economic conditions. These huge tombs, whether built or rock-cut, were effective displays of wealth and political power within their respective communities. As has often been emphasized, conspicuous and magnificently decorated tombs fulfilled several different functions. Besides serving for interments, they were also shrines for the worship of the heroized dead and were, thus, related in function to other commemorative buildings. They could also be conceived as victory monuments, keeping the glorious achievements of the deceased fresh in the minds of his or her own generation and of later ones. Of course, similar ideas had existed in monumental funerary architecture during the archaic age and even before, but they were not as dramatically expressed as in later monuments. Because monumental tombs were to be the 'surviving substance' of the deceased, the emphasis was on permanence and on designs that commanded the attention and respect of the living. For this purpose, all aspects of the architectural vocabulary current at a given time might be utilized in a single tomb; the type thus created, if successful, might then be further developed by later architects.

In tumuli and underground tombs the exterior forms changed little over the centuries. Perhaps the chief 'novelties' of Hellenistic examples lay in the small scale of the mounds and in the erection of a number of tumuli entirely of stone. The addition of a masonry crepis, to keep the piled-up earth (and other materials) of the mound in better shape, is already found in early examples but seems not to have been as widespread as in Hellenistic times. Inside the mound, the most significant modifications took place in the roofing of the burial-chamber and, in the case of the tumuli in Macedonia, in the addition of elaborate architectural façades. By the third century true barrel-vaulting, which appears in Macedonian tumuli during the last third of the fourth century, was widely used throughout the Hellenistic world. In certain territories (e.g., Macedonia proper) barrel vaulting was the principal technique for roofing tomb-chambers.

With built tombs of monumental proportions the question of ancestry is more complicated. There is no clear 'line of descent' for the 'temple tomb' on a podium before the construction of the Nereid Monument at Xanthos in Lycia. The sources of the Nereid Monument and of analogous projects seem to go back to the archaic period. It is at this time that the search for an effective form of a large-scale tomb – exposed to view and expressing other than just funerary aspirations – can be clearly documented within our general area of interest. However, despite their elaborate designs, neither the Tomb of Hyakinthos (known as the Throne of Apollo) nor the burial monument of Porsenna (i.e., the two that were discussed above in some detail) achieved an overall 'expressive' quality worthy of imitation in later structures.

Two important aspects that later proved to be the decisive factors in the popularity of 'temple tombs' on podia were missing: first, the sacred nature of the building, expressed in clear and simple visual terms by borrowing the peristyle of the Greek temple and, second, the extensive sculptural decoration celebrating the 'heroization' of the person(s) who commissioned the tombs. At least in the Tomb of Porsenna a third feature of the 'temple tomb,' i.e., the podium, was presumably present; if so, the idea was perhaps derived from some external source. In non-funerary monuments podia were already utilized in the earlier sixth century. The podium of the Temple of Athena at Miletos[1] was constructed around 580 BC; and there were doubtless statues around the precinct, even if not in any regular pattern. In the palace complex of Croesus at Sardis there were supporting terraces, but not on the scale of 'the Assyrian-Persepolis type of palace on one grandiose terrace.'[2]

In tomb architecture an early example of an elevated platform appears in the Tomb of Cyrus at Pasargadai. Here, a pyramidal podium (perhaps with a symbolic meaning attached to it) was used to increase the overall height.

However, the gradually narrowing platform could hardly have supported an elaborate structure such as a Greek peristyle enclosing a cella.

The custom of elevating tombs on podia must have spread from the neighbouring regions to Lycia, where the existence of raised terraces in tombs is documented from the first half of the fifth century onwards. The peripteral second storey of Lycian and other tombs is Greek in origin, as noted previously. It was only in the sixth century that Greek temples regularly began to use stone for the columns of the peristyle that enclosed the cella; thus, the idea can hardly have been copied in tombs until a later period. Perhaps not too surprisingly in view of the eclectic nature of funerary architecture, designers of tombs were quick to take advantage of the idea, as can be seen in the sarcophagus from Samos (see page 173).

It is far from clear when, where, and why the two separate architectural elements (i.e., podium and peristyle) were first combined in a single tomb. In the present state of our knowledge, which in many respects is admittedly scanty, Lycia, in the Nereid Monument of ca 400 BC, provides the first datable example of a tomb consisting of a supporting podium and a Greek cella with an enclosing peristyle. Several factors may have encouraged the appearance of this feature in Lycia at an earlier date than elsewhere. The Lycians had no established native tradition of monumental stone architecture, with fixed conventions and rules. Moreover, tombs were not utilitarian structures, so that easy access to the upper storey was not a practical necessity. It may be argued further that the extra elevation gave a better view of the monument, and may have been thought to provide some extra protection for the burial. The local Lycian custom (in all likelihood of Persian origin) of often burying the dead above ground may also have played a part.

Of course, the lavish sculptural decoration of Lycian tombs, from the late fifth century onward, required modifications in the conventional Greek temple plan. One consequence of these modifications was the breaking up of the serenity of Greek temples and the introduction of a certain flamboyant, or 'baroque,' quality that appeared in many other buildings during the Hellenistic period. In western Asia Minor, where there has been competition in erecting self-glorifying tomb monuments, the 'temple tomb' on a podium reached its zenith in the Mausoleum at Halikarnassos. This structure was carefully thought out, and the site well prepared; a great part of the resources of a powerful local ruler was used to achieve a sort of immortality. In fact, new elements were added to those of earlier designs, e.g., the pyramidal third storey (an architectural form that was certainly not without symbolic significance), crowned probably by the figure of Mausolos in his chariot.

Naturally, once the ground was broken new trends soon appeared in the development of Hellenistic monumental architecture. The 'temple tomb' on a podium lived on in many variants and in many different regions of the Mediterranean world; but the Hellenistic architects realized that several other types of large-scale building theatres, houses, altars, and so on) could be modified to produce some new variety of monumental tomb structure. As the larger tombs became more famous, their designs were borrowed and adopted for more modest graves, such as sarcophagi, cinerary urns, and naiskoi, as well as for other religious or secular projects.

From the technical point of view, built tombs, like temples, had to conform to certain mathematical and technical standards. In the large tombs, modules were used to determine the overall measurements and the relation of the component parts to one another and to the project as a whole. Clamping was extensively used when needed; unusual or new forms of cuttings sometimes appear on blocks, for example, on the column drums of the Belevi Mausoleum. Tombs also provided an excellent opportunity for the decorative styles of masonry and for the use of materials of different colours. The existence of masonry with drafted edges is now documented in Lycia as early as the first half of the fifth century; and we can also see (page 168ff) sophisticated rustication of the blocks in a kourgan in the Kimmerian Bosphorus that has been dated to the fourth century. In the excavations of the Mausoleum at Halikarnassos a large number of differently coloured stones came to light; presumably all these materials were actually used in the building.

Landscaping, especially in connection with elaborate tomb complexes, also seems to have been an important aspect of the overall design.[3]

The history of rock-cut funerary architecture runs more or less parallel to that of the built tombs. Often rock-cut monuments were simplified, and thus they were cheaper versions of built tombs. The most popular form was the façade-tomb, which from the visual point of view was 'two-dimensional' in character. The origins of Hellenistic rock-cut designs go back at least to the archaic age. The Phrygians, and later the Persians, were among the first to demonstrate the effectiveness of large decorative façades that included both architectural and sculptural elements. We have noted the existence of earlier rock-cut tombs in Urartu and Egypt, and the possible influence of these early tombs on isolated examples of later times; however, the extent of these influences remains questionable. Here again, acquaintance with Greek temple designs must have provided the main impetus for the development of entire rock-cut necropoleis in which most of the tombs employed the Greek orders (e.g., in Paphlagonia, Cyrene, and Lycia).

Large tombs were likely to be constructed anywhere in the Hellenistic world where money was available and political conditions were favourable. In the fourth and early third centuries western Asia Minor was the centre of monumental tomb-building activity; later, the emphasis shifted to other regions of the Mediterranean. New centres – all with their own particular antecedents – arose, producing not only strongly modified versions of the tomb-types of western Asia Minor but also almost completely new forms. Moreover, new non-funerary types of building, such as the triumphal arch, soon found their way into the vocabulary of funerary architecture, as can be seen, for example, in the Monument of the Julii at St Rémy in the Provence (fig. 196). Such interaction was especially likely to occur where non-funerary forms symbolized ideas that were also relevant to tomb architecture.

In Roman imperial times, employment of concrete, in connection with arches, vaults, and domes, eventually revolutionized all types of architectural design, including that of monumental tombs, and made it possible to discard the Greek post-and-lintel system as an essential structural element. However, by the first century BC–AC larger Hellenistic tombs and their Italo-Hellenistic offshoots had already provided the inspiration for a number of important funerary monuments of the Roman Empire, such as the monumental tomb of Augustus (fig. 197).

Technical Aspects of Some of the Roof Constructions of Tumulus Tombs

The following section looks at a number of examples of the roof-construction methods in tumuli. The selection of the monuments is not according to geographical regions. Examples from a wide range of tumulus type of tombs will be included, such as the tombs in Macedonia or the kourgans from the Black Sea region.

Tumuli, a widespread form of monumental tombs before the fifth century, were unimpressive structures from the architectural point of view, even when gigantic in scale. Their exteriors conveyed no specific 'messages,' such as could be derived, for example, from the exterior of the Nereid Monument. At the same time, while the interiors of tumuli and underground tombs might be spacious and elaborate, and might contain a rich collection of furnishings, these interiors remained hidden from mortal eyes after the burial had been completed.

Tumuli have a long history that goes back well into the Bronze Age. In certain regions the tradition of tumulus burials was so widespread and firmly rooted that such burials were preferred even in Hellenistic times, e.g., in Macedonia and Thrace. The Macedonians retained unchanged the exterior form of the tumulus, as a 'protecting cover,' concentrating instead on elaborating the façade of the actual burial-chamber, even though this façade was never meant to be seen after the burial. The Macedonian façades seem to have been inspired by examples in Asia Minor, e.g., façade-tombs, in which monumental fronts masked much smaller burial-chambers. The barrel vaulting of the burial-chambers was probably derived from oriental models, e.g., in Mesopotamia.

The suggestion that the chamber tombs of Olynthos (datable before 348 BC) served as prototypes for the Macedonian series[1] is hardly tenable; the Olynthian tombs are too simple in design and execution to be comparable with those of Macedonia. The Olynthian interiors, painted to imitate marble facing, were probably derived from domestic architecture; in any case such decoration is not peculiar to these tombs or to the Chalkidike region. The fact that the Olynthos tombs were also covered by tumuli is perhaps their strongest link with the Macedonian monuments; both regions were probably following an old, presumably Bronze Age, concept of burial. The same may be said of the chamber tombs of the fifth and fourth centuries on Rhodes (at Pontamo) and Aegina, or of the corbel-vaulted interiors of some Thessalian tombs, e.g., at Pharsalos and Krannon (fig. 239). All these monuments are of simple design and lack elaborate architectural façades, though they do have a dromos of varying length and are sometimes stepped in front of the entrance to the burial-chamber.[2]

In connection with the 'hidden' façades of Hellenistic Macedonia, we note that, with a few exceptions such as the Palatitza tomb (fig. 240) or the newly discovered Doric Tomb II at Vergina (fig. 135), the overwhelming majority of the known examples were crowned by a pediment.[3] It may well be that there was some special significance attached to the pediment, because it occurs even in a two-storeyed façade i.e., the Great Tomb at Lefkadia, the design of which cannot have been derived from temples. In this connection it is interesting that the pediment (fastigium) over the house of Julius Caesar was regarded by Cicero as a great mark of distinction, almost a sign of heroization: 'What greater honour had he obtained than to have a couch, an image, a pediment to his house, a flamen?'[4] Perhaps in the Hellenistic world of the eastern Mediterranean a similar significance was sometimes attached to pedimental façades, even in two-storeyed designs, such as in the propylon of the Athena precinct at Pergamon.[5]

1 True Arches and Vaults

For roofing the chambers of large tombs in Macedonia, constructed between the later fourth century and 168 BC, barrel vaulting was the preferred technique. Perhaps the earliest example of a barrel vault, not only in Macedonia, but anywhere in the Greek world east of the Adriatic, comes from the recently (1977) discovered Doric Tomb II at Vergina, if one accepts the thesis of the excavator of the site that it was the tomb of Philip II, and is thus datable to the third quarter of the fourth century.

The widespread use of the true arch in Macedonia should not be surprising; as already noted, the use of the barrel vault was perhaps known even before Macedonian military engineers became thoroughly acquainted with the technique during Alexander's eastern campaigns.[6] In the Aegean world early examples of barrel vaulting seem to be restricted to tombs, gate openings, passageways, and drainage systems. Only after an initial period of experimentation, in which the the technical aspects of vaulting became better known, did it find a more widespread acceptance;[7] and even then, arches and vaults never replaced the columnar orders on monumental façades. Besides the Macedonians, Pergamene architects seem to have been among the first to use barrel vaulting more widely. Actually, one of the extant Pergamene tumuli employs the principle of intersecting cross-vaulting (fig. 243).[8] The stones of the barrel vaults meeting at the same level were cut so as to conform to the curves of the joint vaults. This vault might be of Augustan date, but the intersecting vaults found in the theatre at Alinda in Karia probably date from the time of Pergamene control during the second century.[9]

To employ the new technique extensively the traditional Greek post-and-lintel system would have required extensive modifications and a considerable length of time.[10] However, in funerary architecture, especially in the case of tumuli and underground tombs, barrel vaulting was relatively widespread by the third century. Thus, the new technique was certainly regarded as an alternative to more traditional methods of roof construction, at least in many of the tombs in Macedonia.

II Corbel Vaulting

In the northeastern frontier regions of the Greek world (e.g., Thrace, the Kimmerian Bosphorus, and northern Anatolia), tumulus burials remained the dominating form of monumental funerary architecture throughout the Hellenistic period. It has been estimated that in Thracian territory alone there are 15,000 tumuli,[11] a large number of them of Hellenistic date.

The Thracian tribes, like the Scythians, must have profited a good deal from trade with the Greeks; and their new-found wealth was spent, among other things, on more sumptuous burials for their chieftains. Thracian tombs lacked ornamental façades, although their interiors might be very richly painted, as can be seen in the well-preserved decoration of the early-third-century Kazanlik tomb in present-day Bulgaria.[12] The technical execution of the domed tomb chamber at Kazanlik (and in others in the surrounding region) is notable for the use of baked bricks.[13] The bricks for the domed chambers were made in special moulds that were segments of circles; those used in the antechamber were rectangular. Outside this single course of corbelled bricks, the structure was strengthened by a string of stones set in mortar upon which the earth was piled (fig. 244). This form of a 'layered' tumulus is not unlike some of the large mounds in the Gordion region of central Anatolia, where, however, timber was used extensively for the actual tomb chamber(s).

As Hoddinott states, the source of the unique technique of construction found in Thrace cannot be determined exactly, but it should perhaps be sought in the southeastern Mediterranean: 'The origin of the craftsmen with the skill not only of brick-making but of building circular domed chambers is, as is their fate, an unsolved mystery. Perhaps a consequential benefit of Seuthes' relationship with Antigonos was a visit from Graeco-Syrian craftsmen who took their secret with them when they departed or died.'[14]

Corbelling had been extensively employed in tomb chambers, both above and below ground level, from archaic times onward and continued to be used by Hellenistic architects. This technique could be adopted to any form of ground-plan, whether round, square, or rectangular. The Lion Tomb at Knidos, many of the 'Lelegian' tombs in Karia,[15] the Mausoleum at Halikarnassos, most of the Thracian tombs, the kourgans of the fifth to the third century in the Kimmerian Bosphorus[15] (Ukraine), and many archaic (seventh- to sixth-century) Etruscan tombs (e.g., in the necropoleis at Populonia [San Cerbone], Cortona [fig. 245], and Caere) all made use of corbel vaulting.[17]

Most of the kourgans lie in the vicinity of ancient Pantikapaion (Kerch), but some have been found on the Taman peninsula and near Anapa. Immediately northeast of the region of the Kimmerian Bosphorus a flourishing tradition of timber construction, with burials in which a tumulus was erected over a simple wooden chamber (fig. 246), had existed from about 1800 BC onward.[18] However, the inspiration, at least, for the cut limestone tomb chambers of the kourgans, came from the west.[19] The remains of one of the most important mounds, the Gold Kourgan, are located near Pantikapaion. The mound, elliptical in plan (E-W: 88 m; N-S: 67 m), rose to a height of 15–16 m; the circumference measured 265 m. Inside, three separate tomb chambers were found, two rectangular and one circular. The latter is a unique example of the circular plan in this region; it measured 6.30 m in diameter and 11 m in height, and was approached by a dromos, 18 m long, 2.22 m wide, and 6.80 m high.[20] The exceptional height of the dromos results from the fact that the corbel vault started ca 3 m above the floor and then stepped gradually inward, toward the top (fig. 247). Interestingly enough, the floor of the circular main chamber was at a much lower level than that of the dromos and entrance way.

The circular chamber has been dated to the late fourth century. The other two, also corbel-vaulted rooms but of rectangular plan, are considered to be somewhat earlier. It has been assumed, probably correctly, that each of the earlier burials originally had its own separate mound, and that the large tumulus covering both of them and the circular chamber was erected only at the time that this main chamber (undoubtedly of royal origin) was built. At the same time, the entire complex was enclosed by a large retaining wall of huge 'cyclopean,' or polygonal blocks; this retaining wall is unique among the kourgans.[21] Gajdukevic rightly states that the form of the circular tomb must have originated outside the region, perhaps in Thrace.[22]

Even more intriguing is the design of another huge tumulus tomb located some 4 km northeast of Pantikapaion and known as the Czarskij Kourgan or Royal Kourgan,[23] Like the Gold Kourgan, this mound was excavated in the 1830s. Its height reached ca 17 m, the circumference ca 250 m. The dromos is 36 m long; for the last 20 m in front of the entrance to the chamber it was covered by a corbel vault, 2.80 m wide and 7.14 m high. The corridor was faced with beautifully fitted drystone masonry; the blocks had a rusticated panel surrounded by smoothly drafted margins (fig. 248). This sophisticated masonry was probably intended to increase the impressiveness and monumentality of the design. The tomb chamber is virtually square on plan (4.22 × 4.37 m), and was covered by a corbelled dome. Unlike many Mycenaean corbelled domes, in which the corbelling begins at floor level, in the Royal Kourgan the vertical face of the wall is clearly set off from the springing of the corbelling. The problem of erecting a circular dome over a square floor plan was ingeniously solved. Starting with the fifth course from the bottom, the corners of the chamber have blocks, set diagonally, so that each course slightly overlaps the one below until a complete circle is formed at the level of the tenth course (fig. 249). The next thirteen courses are corbelled inward to form a conical roof, the apex of the cone rising 8.73 m above the floor.

The Royal Kourgan, like most of the others, can be dated in the second half of the fourth century i.e., in the most prosperous period in the history of the Kimmerian Bosphorus; it was perhaps the burial-place of one of the two most venerated kings of the region, Parisades I or Leukon I, who according to Strabo 'were called tyrants, although most of them, beginning with Parisades and Leuco, proved to be equitable rulers. And Parisades was actually held in honour as god.'[24]

The roof of the chamber of the Royal Kourgan is designed to carry a great load and represents a technique of construction the possibilities of which were not realized until Byzantine times, when pendentives of brick began to be widely employed in the Mediterranean area. Curiously enough, prior to the building of the Pantikapaion tomb, structures of pendentive type seem to be found only in the peripheral regions of old Greece. For example, the tombs at Praesos in Crete (Tombs B and E)[25] have corner solutions reminiscent of pendentives. Some of the finds from these tombs can be dated in the geometric period; however, the actual construction of the tombs might be a couple of centuries earlier. On the island of Thera, two small square tombs with domical roofs supported on pendentive-like corner projections have been found.[26] Similar constructions existed at Assarlik in Karia; these were even simpler in character, for 'the consequent difficulty of roofing [was] met by the simple device of bracketing out the last few courses of the wall, and laying the roof slabs across the narrower opening which is thus left.'[27] Especially close to the pendentives of the Royal Kourgan is a chamber tomb discovered near Populonia at San Cerbone (fig. 250).[28] However, the technical execution of the 'pendentives' in the corners of the San Cerbone tomb is less refined; the rough character may have been due to the early date (around 600 BC).

Closely related to the above examples of corbel vaulting, but without pendentives, are a large number of Hellenistic tombs in the eastern Mediterranean. In these tombs the blocks of the ceiling narrowed gradually in an overlapping fashion from the four sides until the opening could be closed without difficulty. A good example of such construction above ground occurs in the already mentioned tomb of the early first century BC near Olba-Diocaesarea in Cilicia. In south Russia (Ukraine) the majority of the smaller tombs have similar pyramid-like roofs, though entirely underground. In most cases the top of the false vault was closed by a large slab. The well-preserved Melek-Česme kourgan is an important example of the type.[29] The mound itself is almost 8 m high and 200 m in circumference. The roughly quadrangular tomb chamber (ca 3.7 m) is approached by a dromos, 9 m long and ca 13.5 m wide. The corbel vault starts above the fifth course and consists of seven courses (fig. 251), narrowing in the manner described above, until the opening could be closed by a wedge-shaped slab; this solution recalls some of the less-sophisticated archaic Etruscan tombs, e.g., at Caere.[30] On the basis of the red-figured pottery found in the Melek-Česme kourgan, the burial has been dated not later than the second half of the fourth century.

III 'Lantern' ('Diagonal') Roofing

During the Hellenistic period the 'lantern,' or 'diagonal,' roof[31] was especially popular in Thrace and in tombs erected in Galatia from the late fourth century onward. This type of roof is made up of long flat slabs forming a series of superimposed 'frames' of more or less square shape; the slabs of each 'frame' were laid diagonally across the corners of the 'frame' below.

The squares gradually decreased in size from one course to the next, until the remaining opening was small enough to be closed without difficulty. The origins of this technique are to be sought in timber construction. For instance, 'lantern' roofs of wood have been used in Afghanistan down to the present.[32]

Good early examples of the 'lantern' roof have been found in Bulgaria. The Kurt-Kale tomb in the Mezek region, dated to the late fourth or early third century, is a well-preserved specimen of the type.[33] The tumulus contained two chambers without a dromos. A rectangular antechamber, 2 × 2.6 m, preceded the larger circular main room, covered by a false dome 3.57 m in diameter and 3.45 m in height; this circular room was the burial-chamber. The antechamber has a 'lantern' ceiling of four superimposed frames as described above (fig. 252).

Also from Bulgaria is the so-called Filibe tomb near Plovdiv,[34] in which the same type of roof appears in a tomb that has only a single chamber (fig. 253a, b); the masonry of the walls is pseudo-isodomic. The 'lantern' roof, the pseudo-isodomic masonry, and the size and shape of the chamber all suggest some connection between this tomb in Bulgaria and a number of examples in Turkey. Some at least of the diagonally roofed Anatolian tombs were presumably erected by people of the same stock as the builders of the Bulgarian examples; probably these people were the Galatians, who could have brought this type of roof from Thrace to Asia Minor. In western Asia Minor the 'lantern' roof appears in the vestibule of the rather puzzling tumulus at Belevi.[35] There is also an example, rare for the region in question, in a side room of the rock-cut Gerdek Boğazi tomb at Karakoyunlu in Paphlagonia.[36] Also interesting, although much later, is the 'lantern' roof of the free-standing Gümüş Teken tomb at Mylasa in Karia (fig. 254a–c).[37] This tomb, built in the second century AC, consists of a podium surmounted by an open pavilion with pilasters at the corners; it has often been compared with the Halikarnassian mausoleum.

In Asia Minor Hellenistic examples of single chambers covered by a lantern roof come from Gemlik, the ancient Kios on the Propontis[38] (fig. 255) (where, uniquely, the tomb was built entirely of marble), Mudanya,[39] Kepsut,[40] Iğdir,[41] and Hierapolis.[42] At Belevi (mentioned above), Musahoca-köy,[43] Gordion,[44] and Karalar[45] (Tomb c) the tombs have two chambers; however, only the last two have a 'lantern' roof over both chambers.

The tomb at Gordion (fig. 256), covered by a small tumulus, was excavated in the 1950s. A rectangular antechamber (2.47 × 1.67 m) precedes a square inner room (2.47 × 2.48 m). The masonry of the walls is of carefully fitted limestone blocks; the 'lantern' roof was built of a very hard type of limestone. According to the excavators, a specific module, or unit of measurement, occurs repeatedly in this tomb, suggesting 'that the unit of measurement in use in Phrygia in Hellenistic times was a foot of about 0.33 m.;[46]

Tomb C at Karalar (fig. 257) is one of three roughly contemporary Galatian royal burials found in the area northwest of Ankara. In construction it is related to the tomb at Gordion, but is probably somewhat later in date; in one of the three tombs (though one with a different type of roof) there was found an inscription relating to King Deiotares II, who died around 40 BC. This inscription suggests a date in the first century BC for all of these stylistically and technically closely related burials at Karalar.

In connection with the different types of Hellenistic vaulting we may mention another technique of roofing that resembled barrel vaulting in appearance but was much simpler in execution. Monolithic lunettes were placed above the door wall and the wall opposite; these lunettes, in turn, supported the ends of the long wedge-shaped stone beams with radially cut joints that formed the roof of the chamber. This system of roofing could be used only for chambers of modest size; relatively few examples are known, and the length of the beams seems normally to have been less than 3 m. At Hierapolis in western Asia Minor the technique was used (with rather flat slabs) to roof the chambers of a number of small tumuli[47] (fig. 258a, b). Curiously enough, the closest parallel for such roofing comes from Italy. The chamber of the so-called Tanella di Pitagora at Cortona[48] (fig. 259) (2.57 × 2.05 m) is roofed with similar wedge-shaped, but heavier, stone beams set over lunettes. The Hierapolis and Cortona examples also resemble each other in having a stone crepis to support the earth mound above the chambers.

From the point of view of roof construction, another Italian tomb at Faggeto[49] near Perugia can be included here (fig. 260). According to M.M. Chiari, the tomb at Faggeto is related typologically to some of the Etruscan tombs.[50] Apart from the tombs at Cortona (Tanella di Pitagora) and at Faggeto, the others cited by Chiari do not use monoliths to cover the entire span of the burial-chamber. In the tomb at Faggeto five wedge-shaped beams were employed to cover the small chamber (1.26 × 1.12 m); because of their relatively modest length they resemble elongated voussoirs. According to Chiari, the tomb can be dated before the middle of the second century.[51] The 'Tanella di Pitagora' and the tumuli at Hierapolis in Asia Minor, because of the analogies of the roof construction, may date from about the same period. Schneider Equini, in a study of the Hierapolis tumuli, has suggested a date in the first century BC;[52] however, we know that the city was under strong Pergamene influence by the time of Eumenes II (197–159 BC), and one would expect the earliest burial monuments erected in the second century to follow the Pergamene custom of tumulus burials.

The Relationship of Monumental Sarcophagi, Tholoi, and Other Buildings to Monumental Tombs

I Monumental Sarcophagi

The tendency to monumentalize sarcophagi by the addition of architectural elements from large-scale buildings, both sacred and secular, has a long history. The idea existed centuries before the first Greek examples were created.[1] Sarcophagi, like monumental tombs, might imitate many architectural forms. Altars, houses, adaptations of temple forms, and sometimes a mixture of elements from different sources are evident in the design of sarcophagi. From our present point of view, sarcophagi with columnar treatment, or those imitating in some degree the fourth-century 'temple tombs' on podia, are of special interest, though the Klazomenian series of sarcophagi must also be mentioned briefly.

One of the earliest known examples of a Greek sarcophagus with applied architectural decoration comes from the island of Samos.[2] The sarcophagus, measuring 2.10 m in length, 0.92 m in width, and 1 m in height including its lid (fig. 261), is made entirely of bluish marble. The form is that of a chest with a gabled lid. The exterior shows engaged Ionic pilasters in a low relief – three on the long sides and two on each of the ends. On the long sides the architectural members are enclosed by a frame of flat carved bands, a feature probably borrowed from the design of wooden sarcophagi. Around the lower border of the gabled lid the vertical faces have an incised decoration resembling long vertical cyma leaves; the same motif adorns the 'raking cornice' of the pediments. The central and side acroteria were carved to imitate palmettes. The 'pseudoperipteral' design of the sarcophagus, with its Ionic pilasters (or columns) and pedimental roof, seems to have been inspired by local monumental architecture, such as the famous Rhoikos Temple designed around 570–560 BC.[3]

On the west coast of Asia Minor similar attempts to monumentalize the designs of sarcophagi occur at Klazomene and the neighbouring region. The series of Klazomenian sarcophagi starts around the mid sixth century, probably under Egyptian influence,[4] and lasts for about 70–80 years.[5] The material of these sarcophagi was the local reddish clay; extensive painted ornament was applied to the flat top and sides of the 'coffin.' The earliest of these flat caskets were rectangular but with the passing of time they changed to a trapezoidal form in order to fit the shape of the human body. According to R.M. Cook, 'the strips at head and foot were usually painted with figures, the long sidepieces with cable and palmette, and panels at each end of the sidepieces with figures or ornaments.'[6]

Architectural decoration, whether painted or in relief, is not characteristic of Klazomenian sarcophagi, but is occasionally found. In an example from Izmir[7] there is a small Ionic column in the centre field under the end of the gabled roof; the column is represented as though it were supporting the curved roof line (fig. 262). Analogous representations of supports under the apex of the pediment are known from earlier rock monuments in Phrygia,[8] and the motif can actually be traced back to Hittite times or to designs such as that of the Lion Gate at Mycenae.

The same motif of a column under the apex of a pediment appears in the western Mediterranean, though as a purely decorative feature. The top of a funerary cippus in the Syracuse museum has the form of a gable roof with carved roof tiles of Sicilian type.[9] Beneath the central acroterion of the pediment there is a small engaged fluted column standing on a two-stepped base (fig. 263). The capital is closest to the so-called Aeolic form, with a large palmette springing from the centre where the volutes meet. The rounded top of the palmette is fully developed; obviously it is decorative only and has no supporting function. On either side of the central acroterion a horn-like feature of the type found in earlier Phrygian monuments rises from the top of the raking cornice.

Beneath the rather heavy roof is a Doric triglyph-and-metope frieze (three triglyphs per side); the rest of the cippus below this section is missing. Mainly on the basis of an archaic inscription found on the pedimental section, G.B. Gentili dated this small monument to the middle of the sixth century;[10] this date is in keeping with the style of the architectural features.

Other sixth- and fifth-century sarcophagi with columnar decoration have been found in Sicily. A number of richly painted examples from Gela[11] deserve special attention, because architectural ornament was applied to both the interior and the exterior; curiously enough columns appear only on the interior. One of the most impressive sarcophagi in this group has small engaged Ionic columns in the four corners of the interior of the casket (fig. 264).[12] The columns lack bases, and the capitals, above the echinus, are rather abruptly continued in relief rather than in the round. On the exterior of the sarcophagus the only 'architectural' decorations are the mouldings at the bottom and top. The sarcophagus is similar in size to the others of the Gela group, measuring 1.85 × 0.67 m and 0.78 m in height. Some other sarcophagi from Gela are more simple; in these examples the interior corner columns sometimes lack proper capitals.[13]

The source of the decorative schemes found on these sarcophagi remains a matter of dispute. P. Orsi compared the Gela examples with Klazomenian sarcophagi and stated that the idea might have originated in the art of the Mycenaeans.[14] He does not exclude the possibility that the more immediate source of inspiration for the Gela sarcophagi may have been Asia Minor.[15] Yet there are no known sarcophagi or monumental tombs in archaic Asia Minor with columns placed in the interior of the structures. At the same, time, some sixth-century Etruscan chamber tombs that imitate houses do have internal supports, as seen for example in the Tomb of the Doric Columns at Caere.[16]

From the fifth century onward, sarcophagi with architectural decoration became more and more popular, both among the western Greeks and in Asia Minor. From the necropolis of Montelusa near ancient Akragas comes a monolithic non-columnar sarcophagus, the exterior of which imitates a Doric entablature.[17] The lower half of the exterior was left undecorated, except for a moulded base; the upper half has a regular Doric frieze course surmounted by a narrow 'cornice' section above. Such decorative imitations of Doric entablatures became more elaborate and widespread in Hellenistic times. There are a number of Etruscan sarcophagi[18] of this type; but the best-known example is probably the sarcophagus of Scipio Barbatus, which has Ionic dentils above the Doric frieze (fig. 266).[19]

In Asia Minor there appeared in the mid fifth century the first of a series of Lycian elevated sarcophagi. These tombs are monumental in form and scale but lack columnar decorations of Greek type; even the use of Greek mouldings or dentils under the ogival roofs is not common. The aim was to reproduce the forms of local timber architecture in a more durable material. As far as architectural ornament (and especially the decorative use of the columnar orders) is concerned, the completion of the Nereid Monument in the early fourth century had little effect on the typical Lycian sarcophagi, which continued to imitate wooden construction. Perhaps the most readily discernible innovation in the elevated sarcophagi of the fourth century is their large size, greater elevation, and the more and more extensive use of relief sculpture, sometimes of Greek inspiration (fig. 267).

The representation of the Graeco-Persian columnar sarcophagus, on a stele from Daskylion,[20] may be briefly noted. One of the scenes on Stele no. 1 from this site shows a funeral procession in which a sarcophagus is placed on a horse-drawn carriage (fig. 268). Along one of the long sides of the sarcophagus are shown three crudely carved Ionic columns, apparently supporting the upper part of the sarcophagus with its ogival roof. Dates from the sixth to the fourth centuries have been proposed for the stele; the period around 500–480 BC is perhaps the most likely.[21] Whether the sarcophagus was designed under the impact of one of the 'temple tombs' on a podium is hard to say; in any event it belongs in the same tradition with the Samian sarcophagus discussed above, in which the design is derived from a Greek peripteral structure.

The influence of the 'temple tombs' on podia is clearly discernible in a number of non-elevated sarcophagi of the fourth century, both in the eastern Mediterranean and elsewhere. These sarcophagi were used as burials in underground chamber tombs.

The so-called sarcophagus of the Mourning Women from the royal necropolis at Sidon[22] is an excellent example of the adaptation of architectural forms of a large-scale monumental tomb to the decoration of a sarcophagus (fig. 269). Here, however, the high podium seen in the Nereid Monument or the fourth-century heroon at Limyra is reduced to a one-step base, above which follows a Lesbian cyma moulding and a continuous frieze of hunting scenes. The position of the frieze seems to correspond to that of the frieze(s) along the top of the podium on some of the monumental tombs, e.g., the Mausoleum at Halikarnassos. As in the mid-sixth-century Samian sarcophagus, the main, or central, section of the sarcophagus of the Mourning Women has a peripteral-like arrangement, with pilasters at the corners. The engaged columns are small-scale copies of the Attic-Ionic type; in the intercolumniations are eighteen weeping women placed in front of a balustrade between the columns. There is no figure-frieze above the three-fasciae architrave, as in the Mausoleum at Halikarnassos, but only an astragal moulding and a dentil course. The ends of the sarcophagus are crowned by pediments and acroteria. On the long sides the cornice is crowned by a sima embellishment with small lion heads, as was customary in the large-scale architecture that provided the model for the sarcophagus. Between the pediments, in place of a gable roof there is an 'attic' carrying a continuous frieze depicting a funeral procession with mourning male servants at regular intervals. While the mourning or weeping female figures wear a long chiton comparable with the type shown in mid-fourth-century Athenian sculptures, the scene on the attic shows carriages of Persian type and long Persian garments. The winged sphinxes of the corner acroteria may also betray oriental influence in the otherwise purely Greek decorative forms of the sarcophagus.

On the basis of style, the sarcophagus can be assigned to the mid fourth century. It was presumably the final resting place of the Phoenician king, Straton I, who died around 360 BC. From historical sources it is known that 'he led a life of debauchery surrounded by courtesans imported from the Peloponnese. The eighteen women depicted on the sarcophagus presumably represent those courtesans mourning their lord and master.'[23]

In the so-called Alexander Sarcophagus[24] of the late fourth century, the central section of the body of the sarcophagus is filled with relief sculpture (fig. 270). Thus the work is more decorative and less 'architectural' in appearance than the sarcophagus of the Mourning Women. However, V. von Graeve has aptly observed that the design of the sarcophagus resembles a Greek temple.[25] As far as the origins of the actual decorative elements are concerned, the style seems to point to a Peloponnesian rather than an Attic source, such as lay behind the sarcophagus of the Mourning Women. Indeed in the selection and richness of the ornamental features the Alexander Sarcophagus stands quite close to the Tholos at Epidauros. The sarcophagus was probably made for Abdalonymos, a local king in Sidon and a supporter of Alexander the Great. He died around 310 BC.

Among the very few known wooden sarcophagi there is a beautiful example from Pantikapaion.[26] It was discovered in 1874 on Mount Mithridates and has been referred to ever since as the Niobid Sarcophagus (fig. 271). Along the sides and ends there are engaged columns; thus the sarcophagus is related to the archaic example from Samos, and even more closely to the sarcophagus of the Mourning Women. The slender Ionic columns stand on a continuous four-stepped base or 'podium.' There is a balustrade in the lower section of the intercolumnar spaces; the corners are closed by quarter-columns engaged in plain pilasters. The treatment of the ends is especially interesting; the 'columns stand in front of pilasters with imposts from which arches are turned across.'[27] In the intercolumnar spaces, above the balustrade, were figures of coloured plaster; some of these (a Niobid and a Paidagogos) were found in situ. There is no architrave or frieze (in the traditional sense) above the columns; instead, a number of architectural mouldings form the transition to the dentil course along the top of the sarcophagus. Unfortunately the lid, which perhaps imitated the roof of a temple, was never found.

This wooden sarcophagus was dated by the excavators to the early Hellenistic period. However, the presence of an apparently true arch supported by corner piers, the use of quarter-columns engaged in pilasters as a decorative

corner motif, the slender proportions of the columns, and the combination
of architectural elements in purely decorative schemes, divorced from their
original functional role, all seem to argue against a date earlier than the first
century AC.[28] Perhaps the best basis for dating would be to determine the
earliest appearance of such features in the architecture of the Aegean world
and in the Seleucid and Ptolemaic kingdoms, then add 25–30 years to allow
for the penetration of the new ideas to the distant northern shores of the
Black Sea.

Other wooden sarcophagi from southern Russia also were quite pretentious in design; unfortunately the few remaining examples lack columnar
decoration.[29] One relatively well-preserved sarcophagus of the first or second century AC has panels inlaid with figured scenes along its central section
(fig. 272), i.e., in the position of the continuous frieze on the Alexander
Sarcophagus.[30]

Mainland Greece, as already noted, has produced no monumental tombs
of the types seen in Asia Minor and elsewhere; it is not surprising, therefore,
that there should be no monumental sarcophagi imitating such tombs.
However, an unusual example of a sarcophagus-like cist-grave, with 'columns' inside, was discovered in 1962 near Volos in Thessaly.[31] According
to the excavator, the grave has seven slabs, 'one at each of the 4 sides, one
at the bottom and one larger [slab] in 2 pieces at the top [and the arrange-
ment] looks [like] a sarcophagus.' Furthermore, 'the surfaces of the slabs are
rough outside; inside, they bear an incised decoration of columns supporting
friezes.'[32] The overall workmanship is rather crude and the decorative Ionic
'columns' appear to be pilasters in low relief, with incised capitals (fig. 273).
The find has been dated to the Hellenistic period, possibly to the third
century. The design may imitate some sort of a monumental building, e.g.,
the interior of a Hellenistic peristyle court. Yet it seems more likely that
the architectural decoration was placed inside simply because the exterior
was not intended to be seen at all. It is also conceivable that the arrangement
imitated in a simplified form interiors such as the Lefkadia Great Tomb.

Columns were applied not only to sarcophagi but sometimes also to
cinerary urns. The use of the forms of monumental architecture in such a
context begins at least as early as the fourth century, as seen on a limestone
urn now in the Museo Barracco in Rome (fig. 274).[33] The urn, measuring
0.60 × 0.33 m and 0.47 m in height including its lid, is much smaller
than a sarcophagus. The form of the urn again recalls the earlier Samian
sarcophagus with its applied Ionic decoration, and pilasters closing the
corners. There are two engaged Ionic columns in antis along the sides, one
in the middle of each end. These columns 'support' a gabled roof with
pediments and acroteria, as was customary in temple architecture or in

tomb structures of temple form. Numerous other Hellenistic ash-urns with figured sculpture along the sides of the urn are derived from types such as the so-called Alexander Sarcophagus. However, the discussion of such works is beyond the scope of the present study.

To return to sarcophagi, the columnar type, the origins of which are to be sought in peripteral temple plans, continued in use in later Hellenistic times. Sometimes, but rarely, the original forms and appearance of the Samian sarcophagus were retained, e.g., in a Hellenistic example in Iznik (fig. 275).[34] However, in Roman imperial times, if not before, the type became extremely elaborate, with complex decorative schemes and iconographic 'messages.'

Some Hellenistic sarcophagi outside Asia Minor, perhaps as the result of Lycian influence, were elevated on pedestals or podia. A number of such second-century sarcophagi were found on the island of Paros.[35] One of the best-preserved specimens of the Paros group has a rectangular podium (fig. 276), placed above a three-stepped base. This podium consists of neatly cut ashlars above an orthostate course; the corners are closed by pilasters. The podium was filled with rubble, and its back, i.e., one of the longer sides, was left rough. A simple gabled sarcophagus was set on top of the podium; in the middle of the roof-line was a pedestal for the display of portrait busts.

Closely related to the Parian example, but larger and more elaborate, is an elevated sarcophagus monument found on the island of Rheneia (which served as cemetery for Delos) in 1898 (fig. 277).[36] The structure was built for one Tertia Horaria and consisted originally of three 'storeys.' The lowest of these was a podium measuring 2.64 × 1.60 m, and 1.58 m in height; above a plinth and a base course there were three Corinthian half-columns along the main face, while the corners were closed by pilasters. Both columns and pilasters had Attic-Ionic bases. The entablature was Doric, with two triglyphs over each intercolumnar space: above the Doric frieze was a row of Ionic dentils and a projecting cornice. This podium, of highly eclectic style, supported the gabled sarcophagus, which in turn carried in the centre of the roof a small but richly carved funerary 'naiskos.' The total height of the monument was 4.43 m.

The tripartite arrangement of the tomb undoubtedly reflects the influence of the large tombs of western Asia Minor. However, in the monument described above the order of the different sections has been changed, so that the 'peristyle' now supports the sarcophagus; this arrangement is certainly more effective in view of the form and scale of the units involved. The combination of elements from the different orders in the decoration of the podium is striking, though far from unique. The detailed analysis of this feature is not the subject of our study; but it should be noted that Tertia

Horaria is an Italic name, and that she was doubtlessly a member of one of the many Italian merchants and families resident at Delos from the second century onward. Thus, there may well have been western influences at work in the design of this tomb; at the same time, combinations of elements from different orders are also found in second-century Asia Minor, e.g., the bouleuterion at Miletos. This tomb from the Delian cemetery and other structures of similar nature, including the Parian sarcophagi, can probably be dated to the later second century.[37]

II Tholoi

The relationship between tumuli and tholoi in the archaic period has already been briefly discussed. With the passing of time, built tholoi acquired their own architectural forms and functions. It is clear from the known examples that by the early fourth century the tholos built above ground had become a separate and very popular architectural type; virtually every locality of any importance had at least one tholos building.

Tholoi varied in size and architectural elaboration as well as in function. Most of them were commemorative structures and were often used as functional buildings for rituals or ceremonies on special occasions. They were rarely, if ever, utilized for actual burials, though some of them, like the Tholos at Epidauros, may have been conceived as a cenotaph.[38] Yet even in the case of this well-known, highly decorative, and extremely puzzling building the presumed funerary association (i.e., as the cenotaph of Asklepios) is just one of a number of possible roles of the structure, and not necessarily the primary one. The Nereid Monument and its successors, though they could and did convey other than funerary connotations, were built and employed in the first place as tombs; their other functions were secondary and resulted from the increasing elaboration of the tombs themselves. Fourth-century and Hellenistic tholoi, in contrast, should in general be considered as related to, but different from, funerary buildings, and thus a separate type of Greek structure.

Nevertheless, there are a number of tombs in which the tholos form appears to be the dominating element of the overall design, though examples are rare in the Hellenistic period. One such tomb is a third-century funerary monument that seems to imitate the design of the Lysikrates Monument at Athens. In 1974 the remains of a tomb, 5.8 × 5.9 m on plan, built entirely of local tufa and stuccoed over, came to light at Marsala in Sicily.[39] Fragments of Corinthian columns and capitals, painted screen walls and parts of the sima, cornice, and a 'cupola' were found. According to the excavator of the grave monument, the collected material suggests an early-third-century date for the structure.[40]

III Choragic Monuments and Monumental Altars

The 'temple tomb' on a podium, the most pretentious of the varieties of Hellenistic monumental tombs, was also influential outside the sphere of funerary architecture. Buildings of commemorative nature and monumental altars with columnar decoration seem to have been the types of structure likely to be influenced by the design of the Nereid Monument and its successors. The monument of Lysikrates at Athens or the Arsinoeion on Samothrace (essentially a form of tholos raised on a high podium) certainly betrays such influence. The architects of some non-circular choragic monuments, such as the one found on the island of Thasos[41] or the Monument of Thrasyllos[42] at Athens, may also have borrowed elements from built or rock-cut monumental tombs.

The Thasian choragic monument, in the northeast corner of the local sanctuary of Dionysos, stood on a high, stepped platform; a tetrastyle prostyle Doric porch gave access to the 'cella,' with its curved platform for the display of statues. The plan is reminiscent of the Temple of Athena Nike in Athens or the Athenian Temple on Delos, the latter of which also had a semicircular platform in the cella. However, both lacked a podium, a feature that was, perhaps, borrowed from the design of podium tombs. In the case of the Monument of Thrasyllos (fig. 278), in which a rock-cut chamber has a simple Doric façade set against the foot of the southern cliffs of the Athenian Acropolis, both location and execution are reminiscent of the rock-cut façade-tombs of western Asia Minor, some of which also have a single column in antis.[43]

As far as monumental altars are concerned, Şahin, in his study of the subject, sees rightly the Mausoleum at Halikarnassos as the actual predecessor of large columnar altars.[44]

The influence of monumental tomb architecture upon other types of building, and vice versa, is difficult to assess, and it becomes more and more complex in the course of the Hellenistic period. In this study, it seems sufficient to indicate the existence and scope of the sometimes puzzling problems, involved in establishing this influence.

NOTES

The abbreviations used in the text, captions, notes, and bibliography follow the system of the *American Journal of Archaeology* 90 (1986) 381–94.

INTRODUCTION

1 See page 19ff.
2 The site was investigated by M.K. Rhomaios. See 'Chronique des fouilles et découvertes archéologiques,' *BCH* 44 (1920) 393.
3 For Fyfe, Lawrence, and Kurtz and Boardman, see bibliography; for F. Matz, 'Hellenistische und römische Grabbauten,' *Die Antike* 4 (1928) 266–92.
4 M.I. Rostovzeff, 'The Mentality of the Hellenistic World and the Afterlife,' *Harvard Divinity School Bulletin* 18 (1938–9) 14
5 For further bibliography, see A. Pekridou, *Das Alkestas-Grab in Termessos IstMitt-BH* 32 (Tübingen 1986) 52–4.
6 See A. Negev, 'The Nabataean Necropolis at Egra,' *RBibl* 83 (1976) 203–6.
7 J.J. Coulton, *Ancient Greek Architects at Work* (New York 1977) 71–3

CHAPTER 1 TYPES OF MONUMENTAL TOMBS AND TERMINOLOGY

1 See page 66ff.
2 Fellows *Discov* 128
3 Ibid. 130
4 Ibid. 130
5 Benndorf and Niemann *Reisen* 95
6 Ibid. 113

7 Dinsmoor 66, 68; P. Demargne, P. Prunet, and P. Coupel, *Tombes-Maisons, Tombes Rupestres et Sarcophages* FX V (Paris 1974); K. Kjeldsen and J. Zahle, 'Lykische Gräber,' *AA* 90 (1975) 312–50

8 Borchhardt *Myra* 102

9 Use of timber was in general restricted to interior furniture, or doors and framing. However, there are a few examples in Phrygia, where beneath tumuli almost the entire tomb chamber consisted of timber (see R.S. Young, *Gordion: A Guide to the Excavations and Museum* [Ankara 1968] 39).

10 Damp or unstable sites were unfit for any kind of building, whether tombs or other edifices.

11 Ceka 167–216

12 At least as we see the tumuli today; in antiquity the cone must often have been somewhat higher, though we have no way of telling the exact original height.

13 See especially E. Kornemann, 'Zur Geschichte der antiken Herrscherkulte,' *Klio* 1 (1902) 51–146, and G. Wissowa, 'Heros,' *RE* 8 (1913) 1111–45. A heroon and thus the site of the subsequent cult of a buried person – in contrast to the cult places of the gods – was often tied by history or otherwise to certain memorable location(s). When a large heroon or monumental tomb was built within the city walls, it conceivably could have provided a protection for the city as a whole.

14 *IG* 3.330. See also H. Dragendorff, 'Theraeische Graeber,' *Thera* 2 (Berlin 1903) 239.

15 Excavated and published by Benndorf-Niemann *Gjölbaschi*. See also page 88ff.

16 H. Usener, 'Ein Epigramm von Knidos,' *RhM* 29 (1874) 29

17 E. Dyggve, F. Poulsen, and K. Rhomaios, *Das Heroon von Kalydon* (Copenhagen 1934)

18 Homer *Odyssey* 1.241, 4.584

19 V. Karageorghis, *Salamis in Cyprus* (London 1969) 151 and figs 85–100

20 J. Borchhardt, 'Ein Kenotaph für Gaius Caesar,' *Jdl* 89 (1974) 217–41

21 J. Roger, 'Le Monument au Lion d'Amphipolis,' *BCH* 63 (1939) 4–42 and O. Broneer, *The Lion Monument at Amphipolis* (Cambridge 1941) 84

22 For the Throne at Amyklai, see page 37ff. for the others consult, M. Lauter, 'Die Koren des Erechtheion,' *AntP* 16 (1976); G. Roux, *Architecture de l'Argolide aux IVe et IIIe siècles avant J.C.* (Paris 1961).

23 See *The Princeton Encyclopedia of Classical Sites* (Princeton 1976) Marathon 550; Chaeronea 215–16.

24 For a recently discovered typical fourth-century funerary peribolos at Rhamnous, see *BCH* 110 (1986) 680 fig. 24.

25 Heuzey-Daumet 239

26 K.G. Vollmoeller, *Griechische Kammergräber mit Totenbetten* (Bonn 1901)

27 Heuzey-Daumet 259 and Vollmoeller (supra n26) 4

28 H. Thiersch, *Zwei antike Grabanlagen bei Alexandria* (Berlin 1904)

29 A. Adriani *Annuaire* (1933–5) 72 is the first to describe the oikos type of arrangement at Alexandria: 'Sur le même axe de la cour s'alignent les chambres l'une après l'autre. Le point d'attraction de tout le tombeau est la dernière et la plus petite de toutes les pièces contenant généralement le lit funèbre ou, au moins, la sépulture principale.'

30 Dinsmoor 394

31 According to G. Wissowa, 'kamara' *RE* 10² (1919) 1800, 'der Name bedeutet etwas gewölbtes, ist ein Lehnwort dunkler Herkunft.' See also J. Kubinska, *Les monuments funéraires dans les inscriptions grecques de l'Asie Mineure* (Warsaw 1968) 94.

32 Kubinska (supra n31) 15

33 H.G. Liddell, R. Scott, and H.S. Jones, *A Greek-English Lexicon* 2 (Oxford 1948) 1249

34 Kubinska (supra n31) 90

35 W. Peek, *Attische Versinschriften*, Abhandlungen Akademie Leipzig (1980) lxix.2. For further explanations of *sema*, see *DarSag* 1213 and P.M. Fraser, *Ptolemaic Alexandria* 2 (Oxford 1972) 32 n79.

36 Liddell, Scott, Jones (supra n33) 813. Kubinska (supra n31) 88 in connection with the *thorakeion* remarks, 'Il pouvait servir aussi comme un socle pour l'héroôn. Le thorakeion n'est nulle part attesté comme un monument isolé, mais il fait toujours partie d'un ensemble funéraire.'

CHAPTER 2 MONUMENTAL TOMBS PRIOR TO THE FOURTH CENTURY

1 See chapter 4.

2 See page 66ff.

3 Nylander *Ionians* 70

4 G.M.A. Richter, 'Greeks in Persia,' *AJA* 50 (1946) 25; see also Nylander *Ionians* 18ff., 95

5 H. Frankfort, 'Achaemenian Sculpture,' *AJA* 50 (1946) 6

6 See, for example, S. Moscati, *Persepolis* (Milan 1980) figs 82, 91.

7 E. Stern, 'the Excavation at Tell Mevorach,' *BASOR* 221 (1977) 18: 'It became apparent that our finds at Mevorach were by no means unique, but agreed well with other discoveries, which, though few and sporadic, nevertheless show clearly that all of the well known "Phoenician" elements of the finest architecture of the tenth and ninth centuries reappeared in the region during the Persian and early Hellenistic periods (up to the third century).'

8 A. Demandt, 'Studien zur Kaaba-i-Zerdoscht,' AA 83 (1968) 539

9 Schmidt *Persepolis* III 49

10 For some of the rock-cut tombs at Urartu, see M. Charlesworth, 'Three Urartian Tombs at Palu in Turkey,' *AMIran* 13 (1980) 91–7. The author discusses three curiously placed rock-cut tombs that could be seen only from a distance, and not immediately from above or from below the cliff. These tombs can be dated to the time of Menua (ca 810–786 BC).

11 H. von Gall, 'Bemerkungen zum Kyrosgrab in Pasargadae und zu verwandten Denkmälern,' *AMIran* 12 (1979) 271–9) with further bibliography

12 In Lycia an exception is provided by the stone tumuli (Zahle-Kjeldsen *Centr Lycia* 29–46), which, however, may date from a period before the Persian influence became felt there.

13 For the possible symbolic meaning of this rosette, see H. von Gall (supra n11) 72.

14 For a more detailed description of the door, see D. Stronach, 'Excavations at Pasargadae: Second Preliminary Report,' *Iran* 2 (1964) 23.

15 According to S.M.T. Mostafavi, *The Land of Pars* (Chippenham 1978) 6, inside the burial chamber 'there are two grave-like cavities in the thickness of the stone ceiling, one of which has been assumed to be for the body of Cyrus the Great, and the other to be the burial place of his wife, Cassandana, the mother of Cambyses. The dimensions of one of the two graves are 2 × 1 m, and the other 1.95 × 0.95 m, and they are connected together by a passage 1 m long and 0.35 m wide. The depths of the graves and the passage are the same, 0.85 m.' Obviously these spaces were cut in a secret place between the ceiling of the room and the sloping roof of the tomb.

16 The colonnade around the tomb, as it is known today, was built in the twelfth century AC. The date of the column bases is questionable. According to J. Boardman they 'need not be contemporary, but must be quite early (by Ionic standards), for their plumpness and their shallow flutes with sharp arrises' ('Chian and Early Ionic Architecture,' *AntJ* 39 [1959] 217).

17 Stronach prefers a post-Achaemenid date. Mostafavi (supra n15) 245 suggests an early dating and adds: 'Perhaps this building belonged to one of the ancestors of Cyrus the Great, such as Teispes, or Cyrus I. The last named king was the grandfather of Cyrus the Great, and according to an inscription of Ashur-Gani-apal in 639 B.C. he was king of Parsuash or Pársa.' Nylander *Ionians* 93 prefers a late fifth- or early fourth-century date for this unique structure.

18 Nevertheless, the use of the pyramidal form must have been much more widespread than we realize today; among other examples it was used

for pyramidal seals. See J. Boardman, 'Pyramidal Stamp Seals in the Persian Empire,' *Iran* 8 (1970) 19.

19 G.M.A. Hanfmann, *Letters from Sardis* (Cambridge, MA, 1972) 261 fig. 192. See alsy Nylander *Ionians* 91.

20 Butler *Sardis* I 169. Butler proposed two reconstructions for the tomb, one having a twelve-stepped pyramid, the other resembling the Cyrus tomb at Pasargadai. Recent excavations on the site have confirmed the accuracy of the first of these two proposals.

21 See G. Gruben, 'Das archaische Didymaion,' *Jdl* 78 (1963) 84 n12.

22 See R. Gusmani, *Neue epichorische Schriftzeugnisse aus Sardis (1958–1971)* (Cambridge, MA 1975) fig. 44.

23 Daskylion: G.M.A. Hanfmann, The Fourth Campaign at Sardis (1961),' *BASOR* 166 (April 1962) 28 n49; Pasargadai: G.M.A. Hanfmann, *From Croesus to Constantine* (Ann Arbor 1975) fig. 38

24 Butler *Syria* IIA 125

25 Haspels 127, 136

26 Perrot-Chipiez *Hist* III 154. M. Gawlikowski, *Monuments Funéraires de Palmyre* (Warsaw 1970) 16–17. M.M. Dunand, N. Saliby, and A. Khirichian, 'Les Fouilles d'Amrith en 1954,' *Les Annales Archéologiques de Syrie* 4 and 5 (1954/5) 189–204. The authors suggest a fourth-century date for all the tombs on the basis of some of the pottery found inside the chambers. Despite these finds, it is possible that some of these tombs were constructed earlier, and then later reused for new burials.

27 For an earlier date of the two tombs next to each other, see J. Odenthal, *Syrien* (Cologne 1982) 243. The author says that 'die Grabdenkmäler müssen also vor dem 4. Jh. enstanden sein. Es handelt sich folglich um die frühesten phönizischen Grabbauten, die als Erinnerungsmale Vorläufer der hellenistischen und römischen Mausoleen sind.' It also should be noted that the existence of loculi before the fourth century is not documented.

28 *Monumenti Inediti* I (Rome and Paris 1829–32) pl. XLI, 13c

29 G. Dennis, *Cities and Cemeteries of Etruria* I (London 1883) 217 noted the existence of such structures a century ago in his comprehensive work on Etruscan cemeteries: 'Among the sepulchral varieties of Bieda, two claim particular notice. One of these, which lies in the glen to the east of the town, is a cone of rock, hewn into steps, or a series of circular bases, and opening upwards. Of these, four only now remain, and the cone is truncated, but whether this was its original form, it is not easy to say. Like the conical tombs of Vulci and Tarquinii, it was probably surmounted by a sphinx, lion, pinecone or some other funeral emblem, or by a cippus, or statue.'

30 R. Pagenstecher, *Nekropolis* (Leiden 1919) 11 expresses the same idea in connection with the Cyrus tomb: 'Die Stufenpyramide, der Zikkurat, ist der Thron der Gottheit. Wenn Cyrus sein Grab auf hohem Stufenbau errichtete, glich er sich damit der Göttern an.'

31 S.A. Reisner, 'The History of the Egyptian Mastaba,' *Mélanges Maspéro* I (Cairo 1935–8) 580

32 A. Badawy, 'The Ideology of the Superstructure of the Mastaba-tomb in Egypt,' *JNES* 15 (1956) 183. Here could be mentioned the cult of the pyramidal stone in Egypt, called ben-ben. It was believed that the spirit and power of Re, the sun god, resided in the ben-ben. In fact the pharaohs from the Fourth Dynasty on considered themselves to be the sons of Re. Consequently they could have believed that their divine body and soul would have been better preserved in the shape of the ben-ben than in any other form.

33 See H. Schaefer and W. Andrae, *Die Kunst des alten Orients* (Berlin 1925) 163.

34 J.P. Lauer, *Le Mystère des Pyramides* (Paris 1974) 149

35 C. Dalman, *Petra und seine Felsheiligtümer* (Leipzig 1908) 77. See also N. Avigad, 'Architectural Observations on Some Rock-cut Tombs,' *PEQ* (January-April 1947) 112–22. On the basis of its architecture and the type of inscription found on the tomb, Avigad dates the structure to the time of the kings in pre-exilic Jerusalem, i.e., the seventh century or before.

36 Hoepfner 145–63. He also drew attention to the foot unit, which seems to be close to that employed in the archaic Artemision at Ephesos, or to the temple of Apollo at Didyma.

37 Although Hoepfner says that Selymbria is in the Pontus region (145), there is only one Selymbria (Silivri) and it is on the Propontis on the Sea of Marmara.

38 G. Möbl, 'Agyptischer Einfluss in der griechischen Architektur,' *Öjh* 55 (1984) 15

39 Here could also be mentioned a curious three-sided pyramidal tomb stone (0.33 m high) from Sinope. One side has a very flat relief with an inscription above it. It is a provincial work datable to the second quarter of the fifth century. See E. Pfuhl and H. Möbius, *Die ostgriechischen Grabreliefs* (Mainz on the Rhine 1977) 1. 6n22; P.A. Hansen (ed.), *Carmina Epigraphica Graeca* (Berlin and New York 1983) 94.

40 G. Gruben, *Die Tempel der Griechen* (Munich 1976) 300. For Sardis see G.M.A. Hanfmann, 'On Lydian Sardis' *From Athens to Gordion* (Papers of a Memorial Symposium for Rodney S. Young 03/05/75, Phila-

delphia 1980)⁵ 125, fig. 22. See also M.J. Mellink, 'Archaeology in Anatolia,' *AJA* 91 (1987) 22–3.

41 See Şahin 28–35.

42 Tomb no. II, discovered in 1978 at Vergina under a tumulus, does not match the description of Diodorus Siculus. However, it is possible that the tomb was constructed for Philip II as the excavator of the site believes. See Andronikos *MacedTomb* 76 and M. Andronikos, 'Some Reflections on the Macedonian Tombs,' *BSA* 82 (1987) 1–16.

43 Diod. Sic. 17.115.1–4

44 R. Martin, 'Bathyclès de Magnésie et le 'trône' d'Apollon à Amyklae,' *RA* (1976 1) 205

45 Pausanias 3.18.9

46 Ibid. 3.19.1–5

47 Ibid. 5.11.4

48 A. Bammer, 'Der Altar des jüngeren Artemisions von Ephesos,' *AA* 83 (1968) 400

49 Şahin 91 figs 20 and 97

50 Hanfmann (supra n23/1975) 12 figs 23–26

51 E. Fiechter, 'Der Thron des Apollon,' *JdI* 33 (1918) 107–245

52 Pausanias 3.19.4, where he states 'now this statue of Hyakinthos ... '

53 H. Metzger *FX* II (1963) 51

54 Fiechter (supra n51) 242; and Martin (supra n44) 218

55 See G.A. Mansuelli, 'Il Monumento di Porsina di Chiusi,' in *Mélanges offerts à Jacques Heurgon* 2 (École Française de Rome, Palais Farnèse, 1976) 620.

56 Pliny *NH* 36.19.91–3

57 J.L. Myres, 'The Tomb of Porsenna at Clusium,' *BSA* 46 (1951) 117; see also E. Alföldi-Rosenbaum, *Anamur nekropolü: The Necropolis of Anemurium* (Ankara 1971) 95 n31.

58 For the history of the period, see A. Alföldi, *Early Rome and the Latins* (Ann Arbor 1965).

59 Boethius and Ward-Perkins 70

60 J. Martha, *L'Art Étrusque* (Paris 1889) fig. 159; G. Caputo, 'Sulla gradinata della Cuccumella di Vulci e la genesi della curia romana' in *La civilta arcaica di Vulci e la sua espansione* (Convegno nazionale di studi etruschi e italici, 10th, Grosseto 1975; publ. Florence 1977).

61 See Myres (supra n57) 118.

62 See page 58ff.

63 The suggestion cannot be entirely dismissed, as has been done as recently as 1975 by F. Boitani, M. Cataldi, and M. Pasquinucci, *Etruscan Cities*

(London 1975) 59.

64 Boethius and Ward-Perkins 12

65 A. Moravetti, 'Nuovi modellini di torri nuragiche,' *BdA* 65 (July–September 1980) 65–84

66 Herodotus 1.176

67 See Y. Duhoux, *Le Disque de Phaestos* (Louvain 1977) 59 n24 'edifice.'

68 In Greek columnar orders we also have echoes of earlier wooden prototypes, e.g., in the members of the entablature; but in the overall design they are less conspicuous than in Lycian buildings.

69 J. Borchhardt, 'Zur Herrschaft der Achaimeniden in der Bildkunst Lykiens,' *AMIran* Supplement 6 (Berlin 1979) 239–40. Borchhardt distinguishes two main periods in the funerary architecture of Lycia: 540–470/460 and 400–360 BC. However, there can be no definite conclusions about Lycian architecture until more research is carried out in the region. Perhaps we shall then have a clearer picture of the chronological developments as well.

70 In Phoenicia, podia or socles were used as ritual pieces of furniture for extra elevation. Naturally the idea was to isolate and to elevate the distinguished person above the common people. See M. Dunand and R. Duru, *Oumm el-Amed* (Paris 1967) 166.

71 *FX* II (1963). For 'F,' see 74 and for 'H,' 63.

72 *FX* II (1963) 49

73 Zahle-Kjeldsen *CentrLycia* 40

74 *FX* II (1963) 87. According to the excavators these blocks 'ne font point partie de l'édifice proprement dit et servent plutôt à délimiter un socle ou un terre-plein.'

75 See *FX* II (1963) 60: 'On fera valoir aussi le luxe de décor dont s'entourait le bâtiment, décor possible de la terasse, elle-même, fait de Corés d'un type purement grec, se dressant de place en place et montant une garde symbolique, décor du socle où se pressaient satyres et fauves.'

76 Zahle-Kjeldsen *CentrLycia* 41

77 See P. Coupel and H. Metzger, 'La frise des "coqs et poules" de l'Acropole de Xanthos,' *RA* (1976 2) 247.

78 *FX* II (1963) fig. 28

79 See P. Bernard, 'Remarques sur le décor sculpté d'un édifice à Xanthos.' *Syria* 42 (1965) 261–88 fig. 2.

80 Zahle-Kjeldsen *CentrLycia* 40

81 Ibid. 44

82 R. Garland, 'A First Catalogue of Attic Peribolos Tombs,' *BSA* 77 (1982) 127–76

83 H. Oelmann, 'Über das Mausoleion von Halikarnass als Denkmaltypus,' *AA* 45 (1930) 240

84 The pediment was found in two sections, one-half in 1969 and the other in 1976 (G.M.A. Hanfmann, 'A Pediment of the Persian Era from Sardis,' *Mélanges Mansel* [Ankara 1974] 289–302). See also C.H. Greenewalt Jr., E.L. Sterud, and D.F. Belknap, 'The Sardis Campaign of 1978,' *BASOR* 245 (Winter 1982) 24 fig. 25.

85 Kleemann *Satrapensark*

86 Hanfmann (supra n84) 295

87 Ibid. 290

88 Butler (supra n20) 116

89 Ibid.

90 For the date of the tomb, see G.M.A. Hanfmann, 'On Lydian and Eastern Greek Anthemion Stelai,' *RA* (1976/1) 36.

91 Roos *Caunus* pl. 19, n3

92 Ibid. 63

93 See ibid. 65: 'On the whole I think that the painting of the façades was of the same extent as, for example, that of the tomb at Leufkadhi in Macedonia with the exception of the painted frieze. This means that the shafts and the bases of the columns as well as the fronts and the bases of the antae, and the architrave, were unpainted.'

94 See page 97.

95 Akurgal *Ruins* 306

96 C. Burney, *From Village to Empire* (Oxford 1977) 164 and pls 27, 28

97 Akurgal *Anatolien* 70 and Haspels 73

98 Haspels 73

99 R. Young, 'Gordion: Problems of Western Phrygia,' *Huitième Congrès International d'Archéologie Classique* (Paris 1963) 482 fig. 3. There is evidence at Gordion that these megarons were covered by gable roofs: 'An acroterion; pictures of houses scratched on wall blocks; a gable-roofed wooden tomb under a tumulus.'

100 See R.M. Boehmer, 'Phrygische Prunkgewänder des 8. Jahrhunderts v. Chr.,' *AA* 88 (1973) 149 and esp. figs 7–9.

101 Haspels 118–19. See also P.Z. Spanos, 'Der Aslantaş in Phrygien,' *ZA* 65 (1975) 133–54. The author is of the opinion that the monument was not a tomb but a cult place. The rock-cut façade has been dated from 1116 to 548 BC.

102 Haspels 135

103 Akurgal *PhrygKunst* 88. The same idea is repeated in his *Anatolien* 108–9.

104 Haspels 101

105 E. Herzfeld, *Archaeological History of Iran* (London 1935) 204; also idem, *Iran in the Ancient East* (London and New York 1941) 205. H. von Gall, 'Zu den "Medischen" Felsgräbern in Nordwestiran und iraqi Kurdistan,' *AA* 81 (1966) 19 and D. Stronach, 'The Kuh-i-Sharrah Fire Altar,' *JNES* 25–6 (1966–7) 221. The authors are of the opinion that these rock-cut tombs, with their carved architectural members, were made in the wake of the royal tombs rather than before them. In contrast, L. Vanden Berghe, *Archéologie de l'Iran Ancien* (Leiden 1959) 58 dates the tombs between 640 and 560 BC.

106 Schmidt *Persepolis* III 80. The Naqsh-i Rustam tombs are in the area of the Hájiábád mountain, which was a sacred site even before the Achaemenid period. See Mostafavi (supra n15) 23: Religious scenes in relief belonging to the Elamite age – 2nd millennium B.C. – were carved there for devotional purposes.'

In the main group of tombs there are four façades, that of Darius I (the Great), Artaxerxes I, Darius II, and Xerxes I, the best preserved, which faces southwest and is higher than the others. The other three are at Persepolis: the unfinished tomb of the last Persian king Darius III, and those of Artaxerxes II and III.

107 The date around 520 BC is seemingly safe assumption, also supported by Ktesias's writings (*Persica* 38–9).

108 Schmidt *Persepolis* III 83

109 A remarkably similar treatment of this theme is to be found in a Neo-Assyrian rock relief; see R.M. Boehmer, 'Die neuassyrischen Felsreliefs von Maltai (Nord-Irak),' *Jdl* 90 (1975) 49 fig. 10.

110 Schmidt *Persepolis* III 84

111 E.F. Schmidt (*Persepolis* III) 81 says that it 'was presumably cut to prevent easy access to the funerary compartments.'

112 F.W. König, *Die Persika des Ktesias von Knidos* (Graz 1972) 67 and P. Calmeyer, 'Zur Genese altiranischer Motive,' *AMIran* 8 (1975) 99

113 H.G. Buchholz, 'Tamassos, Zypern, 1970–1972,' *AA* 88 (1973) 332 with additional bibliography. According to the author, these underground burials are 'die wichtigsten archaischen Zeugnisse der Insel für die monumentalisierende Nachbildung einer gemischten Stein-Holz-Architektur.'

114 Bean *Aegean* 125; Akurgal *Ruins* 118; see also G. Weber, 'Trois tombeaux archaiques de Phocée, *RA* ser. 3, 5 (1885) 129–38; Perrot-Chipiez *Hist* v 68; F. Sartiaux, *De la Nouvelle à l'Ancienne Phocée* (Paris 1914) 29; N. Cahill, 'Taş Kule: A Persian-Period Tomb near Phokaia,' *AJA* 92 (1988) 481–501.

115 No writers mention such features, and in the reproductions the mouldings are not visible except in Weber's fig. 10 (supra n114).

116 Bean *Aegean* 124

117 Weber (supra n114) 132

118 Bean *Aegean* 124; Akurgal *Ruins* 118; Perrot-Chipiez *Hist* v 64; Weber (supra n114) 129

119 Bean *Aegean* 124 notes two rectangular graves let into the floor in both of these chambers. In Weber (supra n114) fig. 2 there is no indication of such an arrangement.

120 Akurgal *Ruins* 118 has assigned both of these tombs to the fourth century BC, though on dubious evidence. He sees Lycian, Lydian, Phrygian, and Persian influence in the monolith of Taš Kule. The pattern on the front entrance (?) – which was actually left plain – suggests to him Lydian inspiration; the two-storeyed arrangement and form are Lycian, while the presence of a stepped section between the 'floors' is indicative of Achaemenid influence. Akurgal is probably right in saying that concept of design is native Anatolian, and that it was a princely tomb. However, whether it can be attributed to one of the tyrants who lived at nearby Larisa (granting that the site at Burunçuk is actually that of ancient Larisa) during the fifth and fourth centuries remains questionable. In the Şeytan Hamami tomb, Akurgal found some Greek sherds that 'may be dated to the end of the fourth century, and confirm the date suggested for the tomb lying near Foça.' It is worth recalling his earlier observation (Akurgal *Anatolien* 329 n41) concerning the find: 'In der Grabstelle haben wir einen ganzen aber zerbrochenen Lekythos hellenistischer Zeit gefunden. Der Lekythos mag dennoch aus einer späteren Verwendungszeit des Grabes herrühren.'

121 Haspels 139

122 Ibid. pl. 528

123 Ibid. pl. 529

124 Ibid., see pls 118, 185, 209, 245.

125 Ibid., see pls 541 n8, 542 n3, 543 n3 and 4.

126 Weber (supra n114) 136; Perrot-Chipiez *Hist* v 64; Bean *Aegean* 61

127 Bean *Aegean* 62 simply concludes: 'It is undoubtedly very ancient and may well be Pausanias's tomb of Tantalus.'

128 See A. Gökoğlu, *Paphlagonia* (Kastamonu 1952); von Gall *Felsgräber* with earlier bibliography.

129 Von Gall *Febsgräber* 98 and 108

130 Ibid. 114

131 Ibid. 57

132 Ibid. 73
133 For the Anatolian influence, see R. Naumann, *Architektur Kleinasiens* (Tübingen 1971) 139.
134 K. Jeppesen, 'The Propylaea,' *Laraunda* I¹ (Lund 1955) 42 fig. 27
135 Demus-Quatember *EtGrab* 49 pl. 30
136 Von Gall *Felsgräber* pl. 2 n3
137 See R.D. Barnett, *The Nimrud Ivories* (London 1975) 99.
138 For further bibliography, see Cassels 17 and Stucchi 38.
139 Stucchi 24
140 In the unfinished tomb N_9 the maximum is sixteen; however, J. Cassels says 'eighteen seems to be the number aimed at' (Cassels 18).
141 The benches in Tomb N_3, for example, might be later additions. The pillars have 'bases' as the result of recutting (see A. Rowe, *Cyrenaeican Expedition* [Manchester 1959] pl. 16a).
142 For both, see Stucchi 30.
143 R. Martin, 'Chapiteau Ionique d'Halicarnasse,' REA 61 (1959) 65 pl. 1
144 Cassels 18 sees in the mouldings of its pediment 'affinities with the sixth-century treasuries at Delphi, although being rock-cut they are much cruder.' Furthermore, 'the door, too, is perhaps a simplified version of the type represented by that of the Siphnian Treasury.'
145 P.P. Betancourt, *The Aeolic Style in Architecture* (Princeton 1977) 88. However, Betancourt did not include the Cyrene tomb capitals in his publication.
146 Stucchi 43 fig. 32b
147 Ibid. 3–4, with further bibliography on the early history of Cyrene.
148 Theophrastos *HistPlant* 5.3.7
149 A. Badawy, *A History of Egyptian Architecture* (Los Angeles 1966) 128 pl. 14
150 Pausanias 8.16.3; see also *Iliad* II.592 and II.604.
151 Akurgal *Ruins* 283; K. DeVries, *From Athens to Gordion* (Philadelphia 1980) 101
152 R.S. Young, *Gordion: A Guide to the Excavations and Museum* (Ankara 1968) 39. See also R.S. Young, *Three Great Early Tumuli* (Philadelphia 1981) 79–176 and DeVries (supra n151) 99.132
153 R.S. Young, 'The Campaign of 1955 at Gordion: Preliminary Report,' AJA 60 (1956) 264
154 At this point it should be mentioned that the data given by Akurgal *Ruins* 282 do not always correspond with those of the excavators.
155 R.S. Young, 'The Gordion Campaign of 1957: Preliminary Report,' AJA 62 (1958) 148
156 Ibid. 149

157 R.S. Young, The Gordion Campaign of 1959: Preliminary Report,' *AJA* 64 (1960) 228 n6

158 Young (supra n152, 1968) 42.

159 Akurgal *Ruins* 283

160 Ibid.; K. Ayiter, 'Treppen und Stufen bei phrygischen Felsendenkmälern,' *Festschrift für F.K. Dörner* (Berlin 1978) 99; the author is of the opinion that Midas died between 685 and 676 BC.

161 Haspels 142 seems to prefer Midas for the king who commissioned the tomb, but leaves the question open. See also Young (supra n152, 1981) 272.

162 O. Masson, *Les Fragments du Poète Hipponax* (Paris 1962) 11

163 Hipponax F42

164 Herodotus 1.93. The measurements given by Herodotus do not fit the tumulus of Alyattes.

165 W. Zschietzschmann, *Wettkampf und Übungstätten in Griechenland*, Stuttgart (1960) 7, gives for the stade 191.39 m at Priene, 192.27 m at Miletos. The stade in the Greek world varied a great deal.

166 H. Spiegelthal in J.F.M. von Olfers, 'Über die lydischen Königsgbräber bei Sardes und den Grabhügel des Alyattes,' *AbhBer* 16 (1858) 545

167 Strabo 13.4.7

168 See especially G.M.A. Hanfmann, 'The Fifth Campaign at Sardis (1962),' *BASOR* 170 (April 163) 52.

169 Ibid. 55

170 Ibid. 55; see also Spiegelthal (supra n 166) pl. III.

171 Hanfmann (supra n168) fig. 40 section A-A

172 Spiegelthal (supra n166) pl. IV. The platform could have served as a 'lid' after the burial. Perrot-Chipiez *Hist* v 272 describes it as follows: 'A' 26 mètres audessus du riveau de la plaine, commencait le tertre proprement dit; celui-ci était revêtu de briques, au moins dans le voisinage du sommet, et se terminait par un aire sur lequelle gisait encore, au moment des fouilles, renverséé, mais en place, une des bornes dont parle Hérodote; elle mesure a sa base 2.85 m. de diamètre.'

173 Hipponax F42; Nicander *Theriaca* 630–5

174 G.M.A. Hanfmann reports on the Sardis campaigns in *BASOR*: 174 (1964) 52; 177 (1965) 27: 182 (1966) 27; 186 (1967) 43.

175 Hanfmann (supra n168) 147

176 A. Ramage, 'The Fourteenth Campaign at Sardis 1971,' *BASOR* 206 (April 1972) 11

177 Hanfmann (supra n168) figs. 42–3

178 Hanfmann (supra n174, 1967) 48

179 The excellent masonry of its retaining wall would not necessarily indicate a Hellenistic date. It is also possible that the tumulus was repaired and

reused at a later time (see H. Vetters, 'Ephesos,' *Österreichisches Archäologisches Institut, Grabungen 1971/72* [Vienna 1974] 42).

180 See C. Texier, *Asie Mineure* (Paris 1862) 229; Perrot-Chipiez *Hist* v 48: F. and H. Miltner, 'Bericht über eine Voruntersuchung in Alt-Smyrna,' *Öjh Beibl* 27 (1932) 149; E. Akurgal, 'Smyrne a l'époque archaique et classique,' *Belleten* 10 (1946) 72; E. Akurgal, *Bayrakli: Die Ausgrabungen in Alt-Smyrna* (Ankara 1950) 81; R.V. Nicholls, 'Old Smyrna: The Iron Age Fortifications and Associated Remains on the City Perimeter,' BSA 53–4 (1958–9) 64.

181 Texier (supra n180) 231: 'J'ai été obligé de le dèmolir, ainsi que la majeure partie du soubassement, pour bien saisir ce système ingénieux de construction.'

182 Pausanias 2.22.3. It is rather difficult to reconcile Pausanias's location with that of the structure near Bayrakli.

183 Pausanias 5.13.7

184 Miltner (supra n180) 150

185 Akurgal (supra n180 1950) 133: 'Das Tantalos-Grab weist eine Grabkammer vom Typus Isopata auf, wie er auch in der Gräbern von Ras Şamra und in Mittelanatolien bei Câvurkale in einem Grabmonument der hethitischen Zeit vorkommt.'

186 Demus-Quatember *EtGrab* 68

187 For a short description and pictures, see ibid. 71 and figs. 42–3.

188 Perhaps such a construction made the tomb also shock resistant and thus capable of surviving the numerous earthquakes in the region.

189 C.J. Cadoux, *Ancient Smyrna* (Oxford 1938) 35

190 For the various dates, see Akurgal (supra n180, 1950) 81

191 Compare Akurgal (supra n180, 1950) fig. 18 n2 with Nicholls (supra n80) pl. 18b.

192 See Nicholls (supra n180) fig. 15.

193 Ibid. 65 n125. Nicholls also states that there is 'no certain evidence for the practice of tumulus burial at Smyrna before the Lydian period.' At the same time, there is no certain evidence to support either of his objections, both of which are tied to the presence of Lydian conquerors in Smyrna.

194 M. Djunič and B. Jovanovič, 'Illyrian Princely tombs in W. Serbia,' *Archaeology* 19 (January 1966) 43; E.B. de Ballu, *Olbia* (Leiden 1972) 29; Demus-Quatember *EtGrab* 15; Stucchi 12; B. Schlorb-Vierneisel, 'Eridanos-Nekropole,' *AM* (1966) 19

195 See J. Dörig, 'Frühe Löwen,' AM 76 (1961) 70, J.F. Crome, 'Löwenbilder des siebenten Jahrhunderts,' AM 76 (1961) 112, and *Kerameikos* 12 (1980) 42, n140; *Carmina Epigraphica Graeca* (Berlin and New York 1983) 78, ed. by P.A. Hansen.

196 Hansen (supra n195) 78–9

197 Crome (supra n195) pts 17 and 18

198 Among the structures that resemble this archaic cenotaph the closest well-preserved parallels – in size, form, and construction – are the early fourth-century stone tumuli at Cyrene (fig. 54) and the still later Tomb of Kleobulos at Lindos (fig. 55) (Stucchi Tomb N_1, fig 73–74; E. Dyggve, *Lindos* III-2 [Berlin and Copenhagen 1960] 487–9; H. Lauter, 'Kunst und Landschaft, – ein Beitrag zum rhodischen Hellenismus' *AntK* 15 [1975] 49–59). The tomb is placed on a natural rocky promontory, called Agios Milianos. Its structure expresses the architectonic form of the hill by being round with a low conical roof. The authors date the tomb to the late third or early second century.

199 The building has been reconstructed by W. Koenigs from fragments, some of which have been known for decades (see W. Koenigs, *Ein archaischer Rundbau in Kerameikos zu Athen* (diss. Munich 1974) and idem, 'Ein archaischer Rundbau,' *Kerameikos* 12 [1980] 1–55).

200 G. Gruben, 'Untersuchungen am Dipylon, 1964–1966,' *AA* 84 (1969) 32

201 For examples of surviving Mycenaean forms, see Koenigs (supra n 199, 1974) 7; H. Dragendorff, *Theraeische Graeber* (Berlin 1903) 98, where Dragendorff indicates that Mycenaean techniques have survived down to the sixth century. Koenigs (supra n199, 1974) 7: 'Die älteste aus dem Steinkreis um den Tumulus entwickelte monumentale Einfassungsmauer umzieht den Hügel über einem Kuppelgrab, dem sog. Grab der Klytemnästra in Mykene. Von den mykenischen Tumuli und Kuppelgräbern zum griechischen Heroenkult bestand eine literarische und kultische Verbindung die auf der Vorstellung des Grabhügels als Heroengrab beruhte.'

202 See F. Seiler, *Die griechische Tholos: Untersuchungen zur Entwicklung, Typologie und Funktion kunstmässiger Rundbauten* (Mainz 1986).

203 One of the few exceptions is the Arsinoeion on Samothrace, of the second decade of the third century.

204 The subject would easily fill a volume by itself. Therefore reference will be made only to built tholoi that have funerary connotations.

205 N. Valmin, 'Tholos Tomb and Tumuli,' *Skrifter Utgivna av Svenska Institutet* (Rome 1932) 227 n2

206 See H.G. Buchholz, 'Tamassos, Zypern 1970–72,' *AA* 88 (1973) 322 and 'Tamassos, Zypern, 1973,' *AA* 89 (1974) 578, with further bibliography.

207 G. Jeffrey, 'Rock-cutting and Tomb Architecture in Cyprus,' *Archaeologia* 66 (1914–15) 166; V. Karageorghis, *Cyprus* (London 1982) 1952 suggests that these tombs 'may have been constructed by itinerant masons from Anatolia.'

208 Buchholz (supra n206, 1973) pl. 25

209 Betancourt (supra n145) 48; for the possible origin of these tombs, see also
  A. Westholm, 'Built tombs in Cyprus' *OpArch* 2 (1941) 29–58.
210 Betancourt (supra n145) 48
211 The same approach was used (perhaps for the same reason in the Hellenistic
  period, when barrel-vaulted tomb chambers appeared (especially in
  Macedonia). As will be be seen later, such a 'safety device' suggests the
  inexperienced handling of true vaulting in its beginning stage.
212 S. Kasper, 'Eine Nekropole nordwestlich von Soma,' *AA* 85 (1970) 71
213 For other tombs with stepped dromoi and vaulted ceilings in the Amathus
  region, see *BCH* 103 (1979) 723, figs 100, 101.

CHAPTER 3 THE DEVELOPMENT OF TOMB STRUCTURES IN
ASIA MINOR FROM THE NEREID MONUMENT ONWARDS

1 A comprehensive publication of the monument appeared in *FX* III; see also
  W.A.P. Childs, 'Prolegomena to a Lycian Chronology: The Nereid Monument
  from Xanthos,' *OpRom* 9 (1973) 105–6; A.S. Shahbazi, *The Irano-Lycian
  Monuments* (Teheran 1975) 75; G. Roux, 'Le Monument des Néréides
  de Xanthos,' *RA* 88 (1975) 182–9; M.P. Demargne, 'Le Fronton Oriental
  du Monument des Néréides à Xanthos: Archaismes et Provincialismes,'
  CRAI (April 1982) 582–91, and idem, 'L'iconographie dynastique au monument des Néréides de Xanthos, 'Recueil Plassart, ed. Society of 'Les
  Belles-Lettres' (Paris 1976) 81–95; J.-F. Bommelaer, 'Sur le Monument
  des Néréides et sur quelques principes de l'analyse architecturale,' *BCH* 110
  (1986) 249–71.
2 The socle is of six courses on the south side, measuring 5.15 m in height.
  On the north side there are only three courses measuring 2.8 m in
  height. The change of technique in the construction of the socle indicates
  perhaps a change of workmen; they used the technique they were
  familiar with.
    If there was a high walled enclosure to the monument, then only the two
  uppermost courses (with the friezes) could have been seen from the outside.
3 The so-called 'Attic-Asiatic type of pulvinus with a central balteus, bordered
  by roundels and decorated with imbricated leaves,' according to
  P. Hellström and T. Thieme, *Labraunda: The Zeus Temple* (Stockholm
  1982) 52 n48
4 The mid-fourth-century sarcophagus of the Mourning Women from Sidon
  but now in Istanbul comes closest to such an arrangement (see fig. 267). A
  similar concept appeared in the fifth-century temple of Zeus at Agrigento
  (ancient Akragas). There, however, only the upper sections of the

intercolumnar spaces were decorated by human figures engaged into a continuous back wall (fig. 64).

5 Borchhardt *Myra* 135 has noted the possible symbolic significance of rosettes: 'Auch den drei Rosetten, die die Löwen tragenden Pilaster zieren, kommt sepulkrale Bedeutung zu. Diese Ornamente, die wir seit dem Beginn des Jahrhunderts an attischen Grabstelen und an Anten und Pilastern bei den vornehmlich griechisch beeinflussten Grabdenkmälern Lykiens beobachten können, sind Ausdruck einer freudigen Jenseitserwartung.'

6 See *FX* III¹ pl. 86; for the door, see 124–32 and for the sima 157–8.

7 Shahbazi (supra n1) 72, 108, considers the Nereid Monument as the heroon of Kheriga, who was active in the last quarter of the fifth century. W.A.P. Childs, 'Lycian Relations with Persians and Greeks in the Fifth and Fourth Centuries Reexamined,' *AnatSt* 31 (1981) 71–2, suggests (as does Demargne) that the Nereid Monument was built for Erbinna, the son of Kheriga and the successor of Kherei. Erbinna's rule seems to fall in the first quarter of the fourth century.

Demargne (supra n1 1982) 582 indicates that the Hellenization of Lycian architecture started around 400 BC. The Inscribed Pillar is still in the local tradition: 'On, il n'y a qu'une generation, tout au plus, entre Gergis, possesseur du Pilier inscrit (autour de 410–405) et le monument des Néréides qui s'il n'est pas celui l'Arbinas, fils de Gergis, appartient à un dynaste de la même génération.'

8 The French excavators dated the monument around 400–390 BC on the basis of its architecture; however, the style of the sculptural decoration might suggest a slightly later date (see Childs [supra n1] 105–16; J. Borchhardt *Bauskulptur* 137).

9 Borchhardt *Bauskulptur* and consult also the review of the publication by W.A.P. Childs, *AJA* 81 (1977) 399.

10 Concerning the date of the Ilissos temple, see C.A. Picon, 'The Ilissos Temple Reconsidered,' *AJA* 82 (1978) 47–81.

11 For a comprehensive study of the Karyatid Porch, see H. Lauter, 'Die Koren des Erechtheion,' *AntP* 16 (1976). On karyatids in general, consult E. Schmidt, *Geschichte der Karyatide* (Würzburg 1982).

12 The provenance of the karyatid figures is discussed at some length by Borchhardt *Bauskulptur* 42 and 118. Closest in date among the Near Eastern examples are the monumental anthropomorphic figures from Tell Halaf (fig. 74), dating from the eighth century (A. Parrot, *The Arts of Assyria* [New York 1961] 83). These three large standing figures of basalt, mounted on animals, supported the lintel of a doorway, 9.5 m wide,

in the temple palace. From here, perhaps through some Persian intermediary, the motif may have reached Greece, where, with the passing of time, a more and more functional role was atrributed to the karyatids – so much so, that by the time of Vitruvius their original symbolic role was not clearly understood (Vitruvius 1.1.5).

13 On display in the Antalya Museum (Turkey)

14 For the theme of the missing south acroterion, see Borchhardt *Bauskulptur* 88–97.

15 See ibid. 99

16 See Parrot (supra n12) fig. 243.

17 See K. Jeppesen, 'Neue Ergebnisse zur Widerherstellung des Maussolleions von Halikarnassos,' *IstMitt* 26 (1976) 47–99, and his later article with further bibliography, 'Zur Gründung und Baugeschichte des Maussolleions von Halikarnassos,' *IstMitt* 27/28 (1977/8) 169–211; G.B. Waywell, *The Free-standing Sculptures of the Mausoleum at Halicarnassus in the British Museum* (London 1978) and the review of the book in *JHS* 100 (1980) 277; S. Hornblower, *Mausolos* (Oxford 1982) 223–74; K. Jeppesen and A. Luttrell, *The Maussoleion at Halikarnassos, Vol. 2: The Written Sources and Their Archaeological Background* (Aarhus University Press 1986).

18 Vitruvius 2.8.10

19 The longer N–S sides are between 38.15 m and 38.40 m and the shorter E–W sides between 32.50 and 32.75 m. Accordingly, the foundation measures ca 39 × 33 m, giving a circumference of ca 141 m, or 440 feet, as stated by Pliny. Some of the foundation slabs are still in situ at the NW and SW corners.

20 Guichard's sixteenth-century account is as follows: 'They saw an opening as into a cellar ... found that it led into a fine large square hall, ornamented all around with columns of marble, with their bases, capitals, friezes, and cornices engraved and sculptured in half-relief. The space between the columns was lined with slabs and bands of marble of different colours, ornamented with mouldings and sculptures, in harmony with the rest of the work, and inserted in the white ground of the wall, which was all covered with histories and battle-scenes sculptured in relief' (C. Guichardt, *Funérailles et diverses manières d'enseuelier des Romains, Grecs, et autres nations* [Lyon 1581] 379.

21 For a true or radiating vaulting there is no evidence in Asia Minor before the Macedonian period. The corbel principle, for example, is still used in the somewhat later Lion Tomb of Knidos, but there over a circular chamber. On arches and vaults, see T.D. Boyd, 'The Arch and Vault

in Greek Architecture,' *AJA* 82 (1978) 83–100; M. Andronikos, 'Some Reflections on the Macedonian Tombs,' *BSA* 82 (1987) 1–16.
22 Vitruvius 2.7.13
23 Martial 1.1
24 Guichard (supra n20) 52
25 Pliny *NH* 36.4.30
26 Waywell (supra n17) 56. Waywell's measurements, 6.40 m and 6 m, cannot equal 10 and $9\frac{3}{8}$ ft.
27 Jeppesen (supra n17 1976) 95 suggests that the lower statue base around the podium walls had groups of fighting warriors both on horseback and on foot, while the upper portrayed hunting scenes on the west side, like those of the Alexander Sarcophagus, and a sacrificial procession on the north side.
28 Both friezes are made of the same material with similar tooling on the back of the blocks. However, in contrast to the Amazon frieze, few fragments of the Centauromachy have been discovered. The small number of fragments and the slightly projecting concave foot profile lead Jeppesen to suggest that this frieze ornamented the pedestal of the quadriga base.
29 The exact height of the columns is not known, but they measured more than nine times their lower diameter; they could have been as high as 12 m.
30 K. Jeppesen and J. Zahle, 'Investigations on the Site of the Mausoleum 1970/1973,' *AJA* 79 (1975) 78: 'Axial column spacing is almost 3 m precisely – 15 cm less than the spacing calculated by F. Krischen and seems to shake the theoretical arguments on which he based his interpretation of Pliny's description of the Mausoleum.'
31 Pliny *NH* 36.4.31
32 Pliny's Phythis is probably the same person as Vitruvius's Pytheos, who also worked on the Temple of Athena at Priene; see H. Riemann, 'Pytheos,' *RE* 24 (1963) 371. W. Voigtländer has suggested that this same Pytheos also worked in Egypt (W. Voigtländer, *Der jüngste Apollontempel von Didyma*, IstMitt–BH 14 [Tübingen 1975] 46); see also N. Demandt, 'The Relocation of Priene Reconsidered,' *Phoenix* 40 (1986) 35–44.
33 Jeppesen (supra n17, 1976) 91; the architectural remains would indicate 30 cm as the most likely module. See also Waywell who states: 'If the feet length used was 32 cm then the 30 cm unit or module which manifestly runs through much of sculpture and architecture would be 15 dactyls of a 32 cm foot.'
34 Jeppesen's reason for altering the dimensions given by Pliny has to do with the inconsistencies of Pliny's text (see Jeppesen [supra n17, 1976]). According to Pliny, the height of the structure (on the basis of a 32-cm foot

unit) was 44.80 m or 140 ft, and its circumference approximately 141 m or 440 ft.

35 It has been suggested that at least the sculptural decoration of the Halikarnassos mausoleum was the result of different periods. E. Buschor, *Maussollus and Alexander* (Munich 1950) 101, says that work was resumed after 333 BC and continued till 320 BC; however, it is known from history that Alexander burned down the city because of the fierce resistance of its population against his army. From the historical point of view, the second century could be a favourable period for additional work and/or repairs of the mausoleum. The Treaty of Apamea (188 BC) secured the city's independence until 129 BC, when it became part of the Roman province of Asia. Vermeule suggests that work on the peribolus continued in the imperial age (c.c. Vermeule, *Roman Imperial Art in Greece and Asia Minor* [Cambridge, MA 1968] 223). See also M. Havelock, 'Round Sculptures from the Mausoleum at Halikarnassos in *Studies Presented to G.M.A. Hanfmann* (Mainz 1971) 55.

36 Portraits seem to have become more numerous after 350 BC. A recently discovered tomb at Vergina (Great Tumulus, Tomb no. II) has a kline in the main (burial) chamber. Along one of the longer sides of the kline there were fourteen standing figures of high relief; each of the ivory heads is an individual portrait. The large tomb at Kallithea (see p. 103) near Athens also has well-preserved portraits.

37 F. Krischen, *Weltwunder der Baukunst in Babylonien und Jonien* (Tübingen 1956). Krischen proposes the tower of Babel and the Tomb of Cyrus among the forerunners of the Halikarnassos mausoleum. The pyramid as a crowning element defintely points to Babylon and (or) to Egypt, as does the Egyptian type of brother-sister marriage between Mausolos and Artemisia. The pyramids suggest eternity as tumuli do. Tumuli often crown hilltops as at Belevi or Nemrut Dağ. The tumulus of Antiochos I of Kommagene on Nemrut Dağ, over 2000 m above sea-level, is an extreme example of a ruler being elevated above earthly existence (see F.K. Dörner, *Kommagene* [Regensburg 1981]).

38 Le Bas, published by S. Reinach, *Voyage Archéologique* (Paris 1888) 47, pl. II-9, and A. Westholm, 'The Architecture of the Hieron,' *Labraunda* I² (Lund 1963) 12, 101–5, figs 56–58

39 Westholm (supra n38) 103

40 Le Bas (supra n38) pl. II-9 nVIII

41 J. Crampa, 'The Greek Inscriptions,' *Labraunda* III² (Stockholm 1972) 101

42 Newton, *Discoveries* 480; C.T. Newton, *Travels and Discoveries in the Levant* vol. 2 (London 1865) 214, and idem, *Essays on Art and Archaeology* (London 1880) 82; F. Krischen, 'Löwenmonument und Maussol-

leion,' *RM* 59 (1944) 173; H.H. Büsing, *Die griechische Halbsäule* (Wiesbaden 1970) 21, 77, 83 fig. 29; Lawrence *GrArch* 196, 197, 310 n10, fig. 108

43 I.C. Love, 'A Preliminary Report of the Excavations at Knidos,' *AJA* 76 (1972) 63–4. It has also been suggested that the Portico was designed by Sostratos of Knidos. Pliny (*NH* 36.18.83) actually states in connection with the work of Sostratos: 'The same architect is said to have been the very first to build a promenade supported on piers: this he did at Knidos.' Probably all later examples of widened central spans in Doric derive to some extent from fifth-century Athenian monuments such as the Mnesiklean Propylaia and the Stoa of Zeus in the Agora. However, it should be borne in mind that widening of the central span had been commonplace in Ionic temple façades from archaic times onward; the appearance of this feature in the Doric designs of classical Athens, and subsequently in other regions as well, is simply another example of the influence of Ionic on classical and later Doric.

44 Newton *Discoveries* 487

45 In the reconstruction proposed by the excavators the door on the north side is not indicated.

46 Decorative shields, besides being military emblems, also can be interpreted as symbols of protection from evil spirits. They often appeared on Macedonian-inspired monuments from the later fourth century onward, e.g., Tomb of Alkestas at Termessos.

47 Newton *Discoveries* 502

48 G.E. Bean and J.H. Cook *BSA* 47 [1952] 181 n44) date the lagynos after the mid fourth century. The small container is called a lekythos by the authors.

49 Gebe Kilisse: W. Radth, 'Siedlungen und Bauten auf der Halbinsel von Halikarnassos,' *IstMitt-BH* 3 (1970) 219; Asarlik: Newton *Discoveries* 586; Halikarnassos: Jeppesen (supra n17) 50–1

50 See P.R. Franke and M. Hirmer, *Die griechische Münze* (Munich 1964) pl. 186; H.A. Cahn, *Kleine Schriften zur Münzkunde und Archäologie* (Basel 1975) 17ff.

51 For the possible relocation of the city at the end of the peninsula, see Bean and Cook (supra n48) 202; Love questions the theory, *AJA* 77 (1973) 421.

52 Pliny *NH* 36.4.20

53 See S.G. Miller, 'The Philippeion and Macedonian Hellenistic Architecture, *AM* 88 (1973) 189. Of course, this architectural feature did not originate in Macedonia.

54 O.J. Roger ('Le Monument au Lion d'Amphipolis,' *BCH* [1939] 35) compar-

ing the Lion Tomb at Amphipolis with that of Knidos says: 'Les différences ne sont que dans les details d'organisation et de proportions; le schéma général est identique!'

55 See Le Bas (supra n38) 149. The reconstructed drawing of the monument (pl. II-7, III, and IV) shows no doorway, though its existence is likely. It may be noted that in early drawings of the Knidian Lion Tomb the doorway is also missing, though it still exists today.

56 Texier-Pullan 146; Akurgal *Ruins* 262

57 See G.V. Gentili, 'Resti di un grande mausoleo ellenistico a Siracusa,' *Archivio Storico Siracusano* 13–14 (Syracuse 1967–8) 25.

58 P.M. Fraser and G.E. Bean, *The Rhodian Peraea and Islands* (London 1954) 41. Fraser says that on the lintel of the door was an inscribed epitaph. According to this epitaph the dead man was Diagoras, whose statue crowned the top of the pyramid; furthermore the façade of the tomb was guarded by a pair of lions. Its date falls within the second century.

59 Akurgal *Ruins* 262. Other comparable ideas appeared, for example, on Samothrace: K. Lehmann, *Samothrace: A Guide to the Excavations and the Museum* (New York 1966) fig. 30.

60 J. Keil, 'Vorläufiger Bericht über die Ausgrabungen in Ephesos,' *ÖJhBeibl* 28 (1933) 28–44; Keil, *ÖJhBeibl* (1935) 116–45 and idem, *ÖJhBeibl* 30 (1936–7) 175–95; C. Praschniker, 'Die Datierung des Mausoleums von Belevi,' *AnzWien* 20 (Vienna 1949); Keil, 'Die Gräber des Mauso-leums von Belevi,' *AnzWien* 4 (Vienna 1949); G. Kleiner, *Diadochen*; B. Schmaltz, 'Zum Sarkophag des Mausoleums bei Belevi,' *ÖJh* 49 (1968–71) 63–7; H. Bauer, 'Korinthische Kapitelle des 4. and 3. Jahrhun-derts v. Chr.,' *AM-BH* 3 (Berlin 1973); C. Praschniker and M. Theuer with contributions by W. Alzinger, R. Fleischer, E. Fossel-Peschl, V. Mitsopoulos, E. Reuer, and O. Schottenhaml, *Das Mausoleum von Belevi* (*Forschungen in Ephesos* VI [Vienna 1979]) with extended, detailed bibliography 123–8. See also the review of the publication by W. Martini, *Gymnasium* 88 (February 1982) 72–5.

61 As will be seen below, the so-called Tomb of the Ptolemies on Rhodes has a similar concept as far as the core of the monument is concerned.

62 The column shafts had twenty-four flutes except for one that had, oddly enough, only twenty. According to Keil (supra n59, 1935, 122) their lower diameter measured 0.92 m and the calculated total height was 8.50 m. A. von Gerkan (*Von Antiker Architektur und Topographie – Gesammelte Aufsätze* [Stuttgart 1959] 223) states that if the column diameter was ca 1 m, the height should be ca 10 m. The average height of the capitals is approximately 1.1 m. Each capital has two rows of eight acanthus leaves with an unusually high abacus on top (one-fifth of the total height).

The ratio of width to height of 2:3 recalls the capitals of the Lysikrates
Monument in Athens, while the overall design is perhaps closest to
that of the capitals of the Arsinoeion in Samothrace (289–281 BC).

63 For Langaza, see T. Macridy, 'Un Tumulus Macédonien à Langaza,' *Jdl* 26
(1911) 193. For Telmessos, see below, p. 97. The 1.40-m-wide and
0.27-m-high plinths were made of a very hard, dark-bluish marble originat-
ing from the neighbourhood of Kos Pinar. Eleven plinths still exist, though
some only in fragments.

64 In this arrangement the remarkable feature was the insertion of the cyma
reversa anthemion frieze between the epistyle and the dentils. Only a
few examples of such a design are known from the later fourth and early
third centuries: the Tholos at Epidauros, the Monument of Aristaineta at
Delphi, the Naos at Didyma, and the Kastabos temple. Furthermore, at
Belevi, in the 'S' form of anthemion frieze, the concave upper section
is wider than the convex lower part. Another unusual feature of the Belevi
entablature is the form of the dentils; their upper sections were slightly
recessed or cut back, thus forming a continuous 'ledge.' As far as one can
tell, such a practice became common only in Roman times. Regarding
the lion heads, F. Willemsen, discussing the lion heads from the Naos at
Didyma, says: 'Mit den Löwen vom Belevi gehen sie fraglos eng
Zusammen' (*OlForsch* 4 [1959] 67).

65 Of the located coffer reliefs seven belonged to the north side and seventeen
to the rest of the pteron. The securing of the coffers to their background
was by dowels in a manner employed in the Propylon of the Temenos in
Samothrace.

66 No blocks that could have come from the stepped pyramid were found;
however, the nature of the building, if it ever had been completed, presupposes
its existence. Praschniker (supra n60, 1948, 272–3) suggested an angle of
45° rather than 30° for the pyramidal roof.

67 The arrangement suggested seems to indicate that the designer of the Belevi
Mausoleum was familiar with the plan of the Didyma adyton or vice
versa (see Voigtländer [supra n32] 48). The fragments of (two-thirds free-
standing) Doric columns found on the site have a diameter of 0.80 m
and 24 flutes. The position of these engaged columns in the cella is uncertain; however, they could have been attached to pilasters as on the
façade of the Ionic tomb at Vergina (fig. 130).

68 For the possible date of the Naiskos building at Didyma, see Voigtländer
(supra n32) 67; P. Halleström and T. Thieme, *Labraunda: The Temple
of Zeus* (Swedish Excavations and Researches vol. 1, part 3, Stockholm
1982) 46, where the authors state: 'Another series of important monuments – the temple and the Naiskos at Didyma, the Artemision at Sardis

and the mausoleum at Belevi – dates from the last few years of the
fourth century and early part of the third century.' However, the date of
the Naiskos at Didyma is probably not before 250 BC, which would still not
exclude the possibility that stone carvers familiar with one project also
worked on the other.

69 In connection with the clamp and dowel holes it should be noted that the
ceiling slabs of the peristyle of the Epidauros Tholos also show circular
holes in addition to the impressions of clamps (G. Roux, L'Architecture de
l'Argolide aux IVe et IIIe siècles avant J.C. [Paris 1948] 15 fig. 34). A
similar technical detail is found at Kastabos where blocks no. 19 and 36
'recall the round dowel-holes – or peg-holes – on column drums from
the Belevi Mausoleum' (J.M. Cook and W.H. Plommer, The Sanctuary of
Hemithea at Kastabos [Cambridge 1966] 141); and column drums from
the temple of Apollo at Klaros, ca 300 BC, also show similarities to Belevi
column drums (see S. Dimitriou and G. Klammet, Die türkische Westküste [Munich 1975] 190).

70 See J. Ganzet, 'Zur Entwicklung lesbischer Kymationformen' Jdl 89 (1983)
147. On the basis of the Lesbian cyma decoration the author prefers
an early-third-century date for the Belevi complex.

71 A. Schöber, Der Fries des Hekateions von Lagina (Baden bei Wien 1933)
67. P.W. Lehmann, Samothrace 3: The Hieron (Princeton 1969) 346,
says of the Belevi sculptures: 'Some of Keil's associates favored the second
century date ... In the meantime, the relative merits of a late fourth
or a late second century date for its sculptures, the evaluation of their style
as late classical or classicistic, must remain a difficult and disputed
question.'

72 S. Kasper, 'Der Tumulus von Belevi,' AA (1975) 223. The tumulus was
probably erected for a certain Pixodaros, a local ruler, whose memory
was honoured throughout the fifth and fourth centuries.

73 Halikarnassos came under the control of Lysimachos in the 280s BC. Consequently he must have seen the mausoleum in that city, giving inspiration for his own monumental tomb. The structure, thus, could have been
designed for Lysimachos but because of political circumstances he was
buried elsewhere after 281 BC. Then Antiochos II (Theos) became the ruler
of the region in 248 BC, when building activity was probably resumed.
The sudden death of Antiochos II in 246 BC ended the work; however, it is
conceivable that he was buried in the more or less finished tomb. Some
of the sculptural decoration suggests work in the second century that was
probably done during the regin of Antiochos III, between 197 and 190 BC.
Finally, the monument was restored partially in the first or second century
AC for the burial of an unknown Roman.

74 For all these monuments, see below: Tomba Ildebranda (p. 115ff); Tomb of the Ptolemies (p. 85ff); Ptolemais tower tomb (p. 128ff).

75 Actually the Belevi Mausoleum could be considered as a 'mixed construction' because its core is rock-cut.

76 The most comprehensive study of the monument is by P. Schatzmann, 'Das Charmyleion,' *Jdl* 49 (1934) 110–27, with earlier bibliography. See also S.M. Sherwin-White, 'Inscriptions from Cos,' *ZPE* (1977) 205–17.

77 R.H. Simpson and J.F. Lazenby, in 'Notes from the Dodecanese II,' *BSA* 65 (1970) 61, remark without any further elaboration: 'The elements of the façade appear to be late Hellenistic.' The date of the inscription is discussed in detail by Sherwin-White (supra n76) 207: 'The inscription, variously dated by its early editors between the fifth and third centuries BC, is a fine example of Coan Hellenistic lettering. The letter forms (alpha with straight and not broken cross-bar, omicron sometimes smaller than other letters and generally in the middle of the line, and sometimes a tall oval omicron), the gently apicated strokes and the general regularity of the hand all point to a date in the third century BC, probably within the first half.' Furthermore, the form of the cyma mouldings also supports a date around 300 BC (see Ganzet [supra n70] 145).

78 E. Dyggve, *Lindos: Fouilles et Recherches* II (1952); H. Kähler, *Lindos* (Zurich 1971) 23–4

79 For the recently investigated temenos wall and its proposed reconstruction at Kamiros, see H. Lauter, 'Struktur statt Typus,' *AA* (1982) 703–10 and fig. 6. If the proposed reconstruction is correct, then it is very likely that both monuments were designed by the same person.

80 The tomb at Asgourou near Rhodes is briefly discussed by M. Lauter-Bufe, 'Zur Fassade des Scipionengrabes,' *RM* 89 (1982) 45–46. It is approximately 10-m-wide and 3.2-m-high rock-cut tomb with a façade of four engaged Doric columns. The columns carry a Doric entablature with three triglyphs per intercolumniation. In the centre of the façade is a doorway leading to the tomb chamber; it measures 2.25 × 4.25 m on plan.

81 L. Ross, 'Griechische Baudenkmäler,' *AZ* 19 (1850) 210–14; Newton (supra n42 1865 vol. 1) 179; *Clara Rhodos* I (1928–9) 55 fig. 38. See also M. Lauter, 'Kunst und Landschaft – ein Beitrag zum rhodischen Hellenismus,' *AntK* 15 (1972) 49–59, and P.M. Fraser, *Rhodian Funerary Monuments* (Oxford 1977) 5.

82 The measurements, as in most other rock-cut tombs, differ somewhat from column to column, from step to step, etc. For example, the column diameters may vary as much as 7–8 cm, as may also the height of the steps.

83 According to Lauter (supra n81) 55, the sides of the monument measured

97 ft and 'Das Dach dürfte Zelt oder Pyramiden-form gehabt haben, wovon die Reste der Aufschüttung noch eine Vorstellung vermitteln.' Fraser (supra n81) 5 says that a rock-cut staircase led to an upper storey that was surmounted by a pyramidal structure.

84 The work carried out on the site by Italian archaeologists did not reveal any additional rooms. The restoration of the columns to the left of the doorway is misleading, because the shafts did not reach down to the level of the threshold block of the door but ended above it, as can still be seen on the right side of this entrance.

85 Newton (supra n42) 1865 vol. 1) 180

86 For the history of the period, see H.H. Schmitt, *Rom und Rhodos* (Munich 1957).

87 Fraser (supra n81) says that the design of the tomb has 'some affinity with Carian monuments, and it is possible that the monument was erected for some eminent Carian individual or family of the period of Carian rule in the middle of the fourth century.' However, Lauter's date (supra n81) 57 of the turn of the third/second century seems to be more likely.

88 Stucchi 153. The author also suggests a first-century BC date for this so-called Tomba dei Tolomei.

89 *Jerusalem Revealed: Archaeology in the Holy City 1968–1974* (Jerusalem 1975) 17–18. For the Tomb of Hamrath, see Lawrence *GrArch* 210.

90 From the top of the structure some of the other tombs in the vicinity can be seen; there is a beautiful view over the sea towards the coast of Asia Minor.

91 Unfortunately, today it is hard to make out the badly eroded outlines of the capitals. The general lack of Corinthian capitals in rock-cut architecture speaks against the use of the order, especially in a small tomb.

92 T. Wiegand, 'Zweiter vorläufiger Bericht über die Ausgrabungen der königlichen Museen zu Milet,' *AA* 17 (1902) 149–50

93 The columns were all fluted except for their inner sides tangent to the cella walls. Below the echinus, four annulets decorated the neck of the capitals.

94 There was one triglyph for each intercolumniation, except for the façade where there were three above the doorway, and two between the side bays.

95 J. Keil and A. Wilhelm, 'Denkmäler aus dem rauhen Kilikien,' *MAMA* III (Manchester 1931) 59 fig. 89, pl. 31 n90; E. Will, 'La tour funéraire de la Syrie,' *Syria* 26–27 (1949–1950) 270 fig. 7

96 Keil-Wilhelm (supra n95) 60

97 Will (supra n95) 271

98 Benndorf-Niemann *Gjölbaschi*; F. Eichler, *Die Reliefs des Heroon von*

Gjölbaschi-Trysa (Vienna 1950); for additional bibliography also consult *Enciclopedia dell'Arte Antica* (Rome 1966) 1028, and Borchhardt *Bauskulptur* 141–3; W.A.P. Childs, *The City Reliefs of Lycia* (Princeton 1978) 13f.

99 E. Falkner, *The Museum of Classical Antiquities* I (London 1851) 41. It should not be surprising that an impressive setting was chosen for the heroon; it was a common practice in antiquity to select mountains and hillsides for tombs and temple sanctuaries. The natural contours of the Mediterranean region provided countless opportunities for such locations.

100 Interestingly enough, the often depicted Persio-Lycian theme, the power of the hero-ruler, does not appear hear.

101 Benndorf-Niemann *Gjölbaschi* 42: 'Die Abgrenzung des geweihten Platzes, das Temenos, hat das griechische Heroon mit dem Göttesheiligtum als ein der Idee nach Unerlassliches, den Hain oder die Baumpflanzung als einen bedeutungsvollen Schmuck gemein.'

102 Ibid.: 'Vom Göttesheiligthum unterschieden war das Heroon durch das factische oder symbolische Grab, das den Kern der Anlage bildete, und durch die abweichende Art der Opfer and Culthandlungen, welche dem Dienste der Unterweltsgötter glichen.'

103 W.W. Wurster, 'Stadtdarstellungen auf lykischen Reliefs,' *Architectura* 7–9 (1977–9) 129, dates the complex to the first quarter of the fourth century.

104 Benndorf-Niemann *Gjölbaschi* 43

105 P. Bernard, 'Fouilles d'Ai Khanoum. Etude d'archéologie et d'histoire sur l'héllenisme en Asie centrale,' vol. 1 (Texte et figures) *Mémoires de la* D.A.F.A. 21 (Paris 1973)

106 See, for example, Stucchi fig. 175, Tomb S 185.

107 Perrot-Chipiez *Hist* III 103. See also M. Dunand, 'Le temple d'Amrith dans la Pérée d'Aradus,' *AmIran* Supplement 6 (Berlin 1979) 247–8; N. Saliby, 'Regards sur le Temple d'Amrit,' *AmIran*, ibid. 277–81. Both authors date the complex to the sixth century. P. Wagner, *Der ägyptische Einfluss auf die phönizische Architecktur* (Bonn 1980) 5, indicates that we are dealing with a cult place that was in use till late Hellenistic times.

108 See E. Dyggve, F. Poulsen, and K. Rhomaios, *Das Heroon von Kalydon* (Copenhagen 1934).

109 Benndorf-Niemann *Gjölbaschi* 250: 'Ohne Einwirkung mutterlandischer, insbesondere attischer Kunst freilich ist kein ostgriechisches Denkmal dieser Zeit zu denken. Das Heroon erinnert an den Peribolos mit dem Freiermord in Korinth, an das von Kimon gestiftete Theseusheiligthum in Athen, dessen berühmte Gemälde die Umfassungsmauern des Heroen-

grabes in umlaufenden Hallen verziert haben mögen wie die Friesreliefs in Trysa.'

110 M. Robertson, *History of Greek Art* I (Cambridge 1975) 405

111 C. Nylander *Ionians* 124

112 G. Kleiner, *Die Ruinen von Milet* (Berlin 1968) 12

113 T. Wiegand, 'Vierter vorläufiger Bericht über die Ausgrabungen der königlichen Museen zu Milet,' *AA* 21 (1906) 36–8

114 Pausanias 7.26

115 The arrangement of loculi, of course, differed from place to place.

116 Diod. Sic. 19.75.1–5

117 Kleiner (supra n112) 132

118 K. Tuchelt, 'Bouleuterion und Ara Augusti,' *IstMitt* 25 (1975) 91–140

119 For the description of the terrain, see also Arrian 1.27.6.

120 The two best-preserved ones are published by C. Lanckoronski, *Städte Pamphyliens und Pisidiens* 2 (Vienna 1892) 70.

121 Perrot-Chipiez *Hist* III 615

122 I. Kleemann, *Der Satrapensarkophag aus Sidon* (Berlin 1958)

123 Kleiner (supra n60) 78

124 Diod. Sic. 18.26.6

125 Kleiner (supra n60) 78 n34

126 For another similar arrangement at Termessos, see Lanckoronski (supra n120) fig. 21.

127 C.M. Havelock, *Hellenistic Art* (London 1971) 252 pl. XI

128 See also Kleiner (supra n60) 76.

129 Ceka 210–11

130 Kleiner (supra n60) 79

131 J. Borchhardt and J. Neumann, 'Dynastische Grabanlagen von Kadyanda,' *AA* 83 (1968) 226 fig. 39. Here could be mentioned the so-called Rider Tomb at Cova in the SE necropolis of Rhodes. The badly eroded figure of a horseman in armour is in high relief and set in a deep recess with loculi behind it. Fraser (supra n81) 4 describes the rest of the tomb as follows: 'Facing him [i.e., the horseman] on the left side there are other figures and objects, including a figure pouring libation into a kantharos, below which is a small cavity for offerings, and a circular funerary altar encircled by a wreath or a snake, while on the right wall there is a conspicuous relief of a snake and on the left side there are female figures in movement.' The date of the tomb is Hellenistic.

132 E. Breccia, *La Necropoli di Sciatbi* (Cairo 1912) pl. XXIII

133 Heuzey-Daumet pl. 33 n2

134 Ibid. pl. 26 n1

135 Ibid. pl. 3 n3; and see also P. Collant and P. Ducrey, *Philippes 1, Les Reliefs*

Rupestres, BCH supplement no. II (Paris 1975) 197–201, figs. 10–15.

136 Diod. Sic. 18.46.47

137 Ibid. 18.47.3

138 However, it is of a more complex type, imitating such a free-standing tomb as the Belevi Mausoleum. For the discussion of the Sovana tomb, see p. 115ff. As noted before, the existence of Corinthian capitals at a rock-cut façade-tomb at Rhodini is questionable.

139 Roos *Caunus*

140 H. von Gall, 'Zu den "medischen" Felsgräbern in Nordwestiran und Iraqi Kurdistan,' AA 81 (1966) 37, with further bibliography

141 Steps were not a common feature in these tombs; the usual access to them in antiquity, as today, was doubtless by ropes lowered from above.

142 In this connection note also a capital from Kavalla, Heuzey-Daumet pl. 1 fig. 7.

143 Akurgal *Ruins* 256 dates the tomb to the fourth century because of the Ionic ovolo of the door lintel. Benndorf-Niemann *Reisen* 41 prefers a date in the later fourth century. See also Roos *Caunus* 94.

144 At Telmessos there are two locations with rock-cut burials. The older types of tombs, those of exclusively Lycian design and some of the elevated sarcophagi, are grouped around the old acropolis hill. At some time during the fourth century it seems that a new cliff site was selected for the Ionic tombs, among them the Tomb of Amyntas. The native Lycian types of rock-cut tombs are much less conspicuous in this new cliff cemetery.

145 The name often appears in association with Macedonian military men; see G. Wissowa RE 1 (1894) 2005, and G. Bean *Lycian Turkey* (London 1978) 40.

146 Borchhardt *Myra*. Actually the SW group is in two sections about 200 m apart; 'between' them is the ancient theatre of Myra. Father NW of the second group (river necropolis) there are also some rock-cut tombs, but they are too far away to be called part of the same assembly.

147 Borchhardt *Myra* 129

148 Texier-Pullan pl. 226

149 For Kaunos, see Roos *Caunus*.

150 For rosettes, see above n5. In most fourth-century contexts meanders seem to indicate the never-ending continuity of life; they are like a continuous chain with no beginning and no end. They appear most often in funerary contexts and in connection with mystery cults, again suggesting the mystery of the continuity of life and death. The pattern is also closely connected with labyrinth representations. Naturally their symbolic function changed or even disappeared withthe progess of time; they could have simply become decorative motifs.

151 Haspels 155

152 Haspels 160. To judge from Haspel's photo of the surviving 'flank' of the lion (still in situ a couple of years ago), the closest parallel for the Gerdek Kaya beast is the lion that surmounted the communal Lion Tomb at Knidos. The Knidian lion is analogous to the Phrygian, not only in pose, but also in position and symbolic function.

153 Haspels 159 compares the tomb with the temple of Hera Basileia in Pergamon, dedicated by Attalos II (see P. Schazmann, 'Das Gymnasion,' in *Altertümer von Pergamon* VI [Berlin 1923] 110 pl. 33). The tomb is also comparable to the distyle-in-antis arrangement of the small Doric temple of Isis on Delos (P. Roussel, *Les cultes égyptiens à Délos* [Paris 1916] 59 fig. 10).

154 See N. Thierry, 'La Cappadoce entre Rome, Byzance et les Arabes,' CRAI (Jan–Mars 1977) 106–12. For other Cappadocian tombs not discussed here, consult von Gall *Felsgräber* 109—12.

155 It is not known whether this upper section was part of the original composition or a later addition.

156 Texier-Pullan 84

157 D. Schlumberger, 'Bornes frontières de la Palmyrène,' *Syria* 20 (1939) 43–7

158 Von Gall *Felsgräber* 104

159 H. von Gall, 'Felsgräber der Perserzeit im pontischen Kleinasien,' AA (1967) 585–95

CHAPTER 4 THE DEVELOPMENT OF HELLENISTIC MONUMENTAL TOMBS OUTSIDE ASIA MINOR

1 For these tombs, see Kurtz-Boardman 108; *Kerameikos* 12 (Berlin 1980) 50.

2 See, for example, the tombs at Rhamnous described by Petrakis in *Praktika* (1977) 1–35 and the larger tombs just outside of the Dipylon gate in Athens, *Kerameikos* 12 (Berlin 1980) 75, 95, 111.

3 E. Tsirivakos, 'Kallithea: Ergebnisse der Ausgrabung,' AAA 4 (1971) 108, and B. Häuptli, 'Bedeutendes Grabmonument in Attika entdeckt,' *AntW* 3 (1972) 54

4 Today the site is a built-in area located at the crossing of Cyprus and Archimedes streets.

5 A.K. Orlandos, *H Arkadike Alipheira* (Athens 1967–8) 203–43

6 For further bibliography on the tombs in Macedonia, see Kurtz-Boardman 376–7; S.G. Miller, 'Hellenistic Macedonian Architecture: Its Style and Painted Ornamentation' (PhD diss., Bryn Mawr College 1971); B. Gossel, 'Makedonische Kammergräber' (PhD diss., Munich 1979);

S.G. Miller, 'Macedonian Tombs: Their Architecture and Architectural Decoration,' *Studies in the History of Art* 10 (Washington 1982) 153–71; J.J. Pollitt, *Art in the Hellenistic Age* (Cambridge 1986) 298–9.

7 Vergina: K.A. Rhomaios, *Makedonikos Taphos tes Verginas* (Athens 1951); Langaza: T. Macridy, 'Un tumulus Macedonien a Langaza,' *Jdl* 26 (1911) 193; M. Paraskevaidis, 'Archaeological Research in Greek Macedonia and Thrace, 1912–1962,' *BalkSt* 3 (1962) 449; Lefkadia-Naoussa: K. Rhomiopoulou, 'A New Monumental Chamber Tomb with Paintings of the Hellenistic Period near Lefkadia,' *AAA* (1973) 87–92

8 There are variations in the employment of the orders from tomb to tomb. The half-columns at Vergina were attached to projecting pilasters. At Lefkadia four engaged columns stand free for three-quarters of their circumference; at Langaza quarter-columns are combined with pilasters at the corners.

9 E.A. Gardner and S. Casson, 'Antiquities Found in the British Zone, 1915–1919,' *BSA* 23 (1918–19) 15 fig. 1

10 See Miller (supra n6 1982) 155 fig. 12.

11 G.A. Soteriades, 'Anaskafai Diou Makedonis,' *Praktika* (1930) 36; J. Boardman, 'Travelling Rugs,' *Antiquity* 44 (1970) 143–4, where the author draws attention to a narrow painted frieze in the funeral chamber that has strong affinities with woven textiles preserved in the 'permafrost' tombs at Pazirik in Siberia.

12 However, one tomb near Stavroupolis was built entirely of local marble; the tomb is recorded in *Praktika* (1953) 133–40.

13 However, there are a few exceptions where thrones were placed in the interior. A good example of such an arrangement is found in the Ionic tomb at Vergina (see H. Kyrieleis, 'Throne und Klinen,' *Jdl-EH* [1969] 156.

14 See M. Andronikos, 'The Royal Tombs at Vergina,' *The Search for Alexander* Exh. Cat. (Boston 1980) 26, and idem, *The Royal Graves at Vergina* (Athens 1980) 5. For the earlier tumuli, see idem, *Vergina* (Athens 1969).

15 Andronikos (supra n14 Boston 1980 and Athens 1980) and idem, *Vergina* (Athens 1984)

16 Andronikos (supra n14 Boston 1980) 27; see also S.I. Rotroff, 'Spool Saltcellars in the Athenian Agora,' *Hesperia* 53 (1984) 351.

17 See Andronikos (supra n14 Boston 1980) 30 fig. 13.

18 In the plaster applied to the façade of the tomb, a red figured sherd was found (see Andronikos [supra n14 Athens 1980] 48).

19 Andronikos (supra n14 Boston 1980) 30 notes that the wall painting is unquestionably a first-rate pictorial design: 'In the center of the composition and the tomb [is] a striking young rider with a spear in his right hand and a wreath in his hair; his pose recalls that of Alexander in the well-known mosaic from Pompeii in the Naples Museum.' A leafless tree 'frames' this central

figure. The significance of this tree, which also appears in the Pompeii mosaic, is not known but seems to have a symbolic meaning connected with the figure of Alexander the Great.

20 Andronikos (supra n14 Athens 1980) 21 and 48 notes that 'the taenia was painted (red) with a white meander pattern.' Furthermore, 'the glyphs of the triglyphs have pronounced curves well-hollowed out at the top.'

21 Other finds from the top of the tomb include two iron swords, the point of a sarissa, and fragments of iron horse trappings.

22 See Andronikos (supra n14 Boston 1980) 37–8.

23 For the controversy surrounding the identity of the person(s) buried in Tomb II, see E.A. Fredricksmeyer, 'Once More the Diadem and Barrel-Vault at Vergina,' *AJA* 87 (1983) 99–102, with further bibliography. Fredricksmeyer, in the light of the inconclusive evidence, states: 'The identity of the Tomb's occupant, whether Philip II or Arrchidaius remains uncertain' (p. 102).

24 Some have taken Plato's *Laws* 947 D-E to indicate the existence of the true arch when he says in connection with the funeral of a Scrutineer: 'Their tomb shall be constructed under ground, in the form of an oblong vault of spongy stone, as long-lasting as possible, and fitted with couches of stone set side by side, in this when they have laid him who is gone to his rest, they shall make a mound in a circle round it and plant thereon a grove of trees, save only at one extremity, so that at that point the tomb may for all time admit of enlargement, in case there be need for additional mounds for the buried.'

25 See N.A. Winter, 'News Letter from Greece,' *AJA* 88 (1984) 56.

26 P. Petsas, *O Taphos ton Lefkadion* (Athens 1966)

27 Stylistically the figures are very close to those of Tomb no. III at Vergina, discovered in 1981 (see fig. 137).

28 R. Martin, 'Sculpture et peinture dans les façades monumentales au IVe siecle av. J.-C.,' *RA* (1968–9) 183, says that the nose profile of the triglyphs cannot be earlier than the beginning of the third century. Miller (supra n6 1971) 102 prefers a late fourth-century date for the 'ears' of the same triglyphs, because they are of the Attic type.

29 The third-century tomb I at Mustafa Pasha (see fig. 176) shows a similar treatment of the painted frieze above the central doorway of the south side, but the execution of the shadow lines is much more sketchy.

30 There are four pilasters (without bases) on all sides except the west, which has the doorway. The necks of the pilasters are painted with discs and surmounted by a band of leaf-and-dart. Presumably garlands were hung on all the walls between the pilasters, as shown in the painted examples in the later tomb of Lyson and Kallikles at Lefkadia (fig. 140).

31 P. Petsas calls the arrangement 'a peristyle with stoas around it' ('Macedonian Tombs,' *Atti del settimo Congresso Internazionale di Archeologia
Classica* I [Rome 1961] 404).

32 Cyrene: M.G. Pierini, 'La tomba di Menecrate a Barce in Cirenaica,' *QAL*
6 (Rome 1971) 23–4; Canosa: 'La Magna Grecia nel quadro dell'arte
ellenistica,' *Atti del nono consegno di studi sulla Magna Grecia*, Taranto,
5–10 October 1969 (Naples 1970) pl. 2, tomb no. 3; Kandyba: W.W.
Wurster, 'Antike Siedlungen in Lykien,' *AA* 91 (1976) 48, gives no
description of the two-storeyed tomb, but simply mentions its existence
'insbesondere zwei Gräber mit lykischer Inschrift, ein zweigeschossiges
Fassadengrab ... '

33 See Martin (supra n28) 171. For other examples of two-storeyed structures,
see J.J. Coulton, *The Architectural Development of the Greek Stoa*
(Oxford 1976), esp. 124.

34 If the Philippeion was indeed designed by a Macedonian architect, as S.G.
Miller believes. See her 'The Philippeion and Macedonian Hellenistic
Architecture,' *AM* 88 (1973) 189–218.

35 According to Diodorus Siculus (18.26.8), the Satrap Arrhidaios spent two
years constructing the funeral carriage of Alexander. For a detailed
study, see K.F. Müller, *Der Leichenwagen Alexanders des Grossen* (Leipzig
1905).

36 The others are the following: the so-called Naoussa or Kinch Tomb, F.K.
Kinch, *Le tombeau de Niausta* Kgl. Danske Vidensk. Selsk. Skrifter, 7. Raekke.
Hist. og. Fil. Afd. IV 3 (1920) 283–8; the Lyson and Kallikles tomb by
C.I. Makaronas and S.G. Miller, 'The Tomb of Lyson and Kalliklos:
A Painted Hellenistic Tomb,' *Archaeology* 27 (1974) 248–59; an Ionic tomb
discovered in 1971 and reported by Rhomiopoulou (supra n7); the so-
called Charouli tomb (G. Daux, *BCH* 83 (1959) 701; and the Theodoridi
tomb, Petsas (supra n31) 402.

37 The site of Aigai has not been located with certainty (see M.G. Daux,
'Aigeai site des tombes royales de la Macédonie antique,' *CRAI* [Nov.–Dec. 1977]
620–30). However, in the light of the new discoveries, the identification
of Vergina with the ancient capital of Aigai has gained new importance
(see Andronikos [supra n14 Boston 1980] 26).

38 A late-fourth-century date seems to be the most likely for the Great Tomb
at Lefkadia (see V.J. Bruno, *Form and Colour in Greek Painting*
[London 1977] 23, and L. Zhivkova, *Das Grabmal von Kazanlak* [Reckling-
hausen 1973] 115). The Ionic frieze of fighting Macedonians and Persians on the façade of the tomb would indicate that the person buried inside
was a high-ranking general of Alexander the Great's army.

39 Ceka 167–217, and N. Ceka, 'Les constructions sépulcrales des cités illyrien-

nes,' *Monumentet* 9 (1975) 35–54. N. Ceka, *The Illyrian City of Low Selca* (Tirana 1985). In connection with the tombs at Basse-Selce, the author also mentions the existence of 'Macedonian-like' tombs in southwestern Albania.

40 The numbering follows the order of discovery of these tombs given by Ceka.

41 Ceka 176: rosettes do not appear in the published drawings of this tomb; compare text, 176 with pl. ix.

42 For Thracian helmet types, see B. Schröder, 'Thrakische Helme,' *Jdl* 27 (1912) 317–44.

43 Ceka 181, n13

44 Heuzey-Daumet 261

45 For further bibliography, see Ceka 190.

46 L. Rey, 'Fouilles de la Mission Frâncaise à Apollonie d'Illyrie (1931–33),' *Albania* (1935 no. 5) 47–8

47 Rey (supra n46) 48

48 See Rhomaios (supra n7).

49 For a fuller bibliography, see F.T. Bertocchi, *La pittura funeraria Apula* (Naples 1964) 30 n1 and 16.

50 See H. Nachod, 'Gräber in Canosa,' *RM* 29 (1914) 279, where the author described the site as follows: 'Die Stelle dieser Grabanlage ist jetzt nur noch als eine Mulde in Boden zu erkennen.'

51 See C. Bonucci, 'Viaggi nella terra di Bari,' *Il Poliorama Pittoresco* 15 (1852–4) 188–96 and E. Gerhard, 'Gräber zu Canosa,' *AZ* 15 (1857) 57–8.

52 It would seem that Bonucci in his detailed drawing of the façade represented its actual state of preservation, while Gerhard shows a graphic reconstruction of the tomb.

53 Recent excavations in south Italy have revealed more and more chamber tombs with columns flanking the entrance, but not necessarily with a pedimental top. In Taranto on the Via Polibio a row of chamber tombs came to light, in which the front has columns (see *JHS* [1970] 42 fig. 19). Particularly interesting is the façade of a chamber tomb found in Salapia; here two Ionic half-columns flank the entrance; in the centre of the sagging cushion of the capitals there are rosettes recalling Hellenistic rock-cut examples in Illyria (Albania) (see E.M. De Iuliis, 'Ricerche ad Arpi e Salapia,' *Economia e Societa nella Magna Grecia* [Taranto 1972] 333).

54 For the capitals, see Nachod (supra n50) figs 16–17.

55 See, for instance, Demus-Quatember *EtGrab* pls 13 and 30.

56 Bertocchi (supra n49) 22

57 Diod. Sic. 29.10.1; Livy 9.10.1

58 Rosi (1924–5) 49; Bianchi-Bandinelli *Sovana* 76–86; Boethius-Ward-

Perkins, 36, 45. The tomb was 'named' by Rosi: 'It is my desire that this nameless ruin should perpetuate the memory of the dead city's most illustrious son – the monk Hildebrand who became Pope Gregory vii' (Rosi [1924–5] 49 n1).

59 For other examples of carved heads in capitals, see Bianchi-Bandinelli *Sovana* 89–92.

60 The entire superstructure above the column tops came to a height of 2.15 m, while the colonnaded section measured 4.30 m.

61 For bibliography and further information on these temples, consult F. Castagnoli, 'Peripteros sine postico,' *RM* 62 (1955) 139–43.

62 Bianchi-Bandinelli *Sovana* 80: 'Il tempio ad alae retratte, pseudoperiptero e inaccessibile dalla parte posteriore, rappresentato dalla pianta dell'Ilde-branda e proprio uno dei due tipi di tempio caratteristicamente etruschi descritti da Vitruvio.' Also see Vitruvius, 4.7.

63 M. Bizzarri and C. Curri very aptly observe: 'A differenza del tempio greco, nel quale il naos, cioe la cella, è la reale abitazione del dio, nel tempio etrusco-italico il carattere sacrale dell'edificio è connesso all'alto basamento o podio, concepito come sede dei rapporti fra i'uomo e le divinita celesti o ctonie. In esso forse sopravvive la parte scoperto, al centro di un'area sacra, simile a quelli dell'oriente caldeo, oppure da una terrazza naturale' (*Magica Etruria* [Florence 1968] 161).

64 See G.A Mansuelli, 'Il monumento funerario di Maccaretolo e il problema dei sepolcri a cuspide in Italia,' *ArchCl* 4 (1952) 70, where the author notes the similarity between the two monumental tombs: 'I precedenti tipologici della tomba Ildebranda vanno ricercati nell'ambiente micro-asiatico, ma qui siamo di fronte non ad una materiale trasposizione, ma ad una interpretazi-one conforme alle tendenze locali. Più che con il Mausoleo, termine di raffronto in questo caso generico la tomba Ildebranda à da mettere in rapporto con il sepolcro di Belevi presso Efeso, sia per le fomme che per la tecnica di taglio nella roccia. Forme dei capitelli e decorazioni sono libere rielaborazioni di elementi ellenistici asiatici.'

65 See Bianchi-Bandinelli *Sovana* 84: 'La Tomba Ildebranda ci mostra uno stadio dell'architettura nell'Italia Centrale immediatamente anteriore al periodo Sillano, col quale Roma entrerà nel gran movimento edilizio, adot-tando, oltre che una nuova technica costruttiva, anche le forme nuove dell'architettura ellenistica microasiatica: il che avvienne fra la metà del secondo e l'inizio del primo secolo a. Cr.' Bianchi-Bandinelli praises Delbrueck's work on Hellenistic influence in Latium, but at the same time criticizes him for restricting the eastern influences in Italy to the period from the mid second century onward and to Rome. However, in his analysis of the Tomba Ildebranda, Bianchi-Bandinelli himself seems to have

stumbled into a similar pitfall in refusing to recognize in later Etruscan arhictecture the possibility of direct Anatolian influence strong enough to have affected entire building projects as early as the later third or the beginning of the second century.

66 See J.P. Oleson's article, 'The Source and Mechanics of Non-Italian Influence on Later Etruscan Tomb Design,' *ArchNews* 5 (1976) 115–23, which, through funerary architecture and literary evidence, tries to show direct connections between cities of Asia Minor and Etruria.

67 For the consequences of the Roman victory at Magnesia-on-the-Maeander, see W.W. Tarn, *Hellenistic Civilization* (Cleveland and New York 1968) 28.

68 For the different dates proposed for the Tomba Ildebranda, see E. Colonna di Paolo, *Necropoli Rupestri del Viterbese* (Novara 1978) 48ff.; M. Torelli, *Etruria* (Rome and Bari 1980) 188, where the tomb is dated to the early third century; S. Steingräber, *Etrurien* (Munich 1981) 212. Steingräber notes that in Sovana there are about 100 monumental rock-cut tombs and more than 200 smaller ones. The large tombs, almost without exception, belong to the third or the second century. Although the problem of the so-called Altar of Domitius Ahenobarbus falls beyond the scope of this study, it should be noted that the interpretation of this mounument proposed by G. Hafner, 'Zwei frühe römische Opferbilder,' *Aachener Kunstblätter* 45 (1974) 17–48, again implies the existence in Rome of some architectural influence of commemorative monuments from the eastern Mediterranean; and Asia Minor is an obvious source for the sort of prototype Hafner has in mind.

69 Bianchi-Bandinelli *Sovana* 74–6

70 G. Dennis, *The Cities and Cemeteries of Etruria* 1 (London 1907) 289; see also Rosi (1924–5) 42; and M. Demus-Quatember, 'Die Tomben mit Tempelfassade in der Nekropole von Norchia,' *Öjh* 40–42 (1953–5) 108

71 The same design of cyma leaves appears for instance on a sarcophagus from Clusium (see H.H. Scullard, *The Etruscan Cities and Rome* [London 1967] fig. 74).

72 There were seventeen heads in the west frieze, while the east had only eleven.

73 See Rosi (1924–5) 46 and Demus-Quatember (supra n70) 111.

74 Demus-Quatember (supra n70) 114

75 Torelli (supra n68) 234 dates both tombs to the third century; Steingräber (supra n68) 362 states: 'Auf jeden Fall handelt es sich hier um eine der frühesten Rezeptionen des dorischen Metopen-frieses in Etrurien, der aus der Magna Graecia-wohl durch Vermittlung Roms-nach Norden gelangte.' He basically accepts a two-phase chronology for the tombs suggested by

Colonna di Paolo (supra n68) 48: the first in the late fourth or early
third century for the gables and the second, around 200 BC, for the frieze.

76 Steingräber (supra n68) 362 suggests Magna Graecia for the source of the
designs.

77 Rosi (1924–5) 38–42

78 Rosi's reconstruction (1924–5) fig. 34 seems to be correct in its main
outlines. Also see Oleson (supra n66) 123 n10.

79 See von Gall Felsgräber 82. It may be a mere coincidence; however, there
are other very similar solutions shared by the Paphlagonian and Etruscan tombs (see ibid. pl. 8).

80 Rosi (1924–5) 41

81 Steingräber (supra n68) 359 places the tomb in the third century, before
the Tomba Ildebranda: 'Die Tomba Lattanzi weist manche Parallelen
(man vergleiche etwa den Greifenfries) mit der Tomba Ildebranda in Sovana
auf, doch dürfte sie etwas früher als jene im 3. Jh. entstanden sein.' Colonna
di Paolo (supra n68) 48 notes Asia Minor as a possible source of influence
and dates the 'Tomba Lattanzi' to the late fourth century; Torelli (supra
n68) 234 accepts such an early date for the tomb.

82 Bianchi-Bandinelli Sovana 74

82 See, for example, a late-fourth-century terracotta model of a two-storeyed
stage building (J. Bethe, 'Die hellenistischen Bühnen und ihre Decorati-
onen,' Jdl 15 [1900] 61 fig. 2).

84 See H. Koch, 'Hellenistische Architekturstücke in Capua,' RM 22 (1907)
407.

85 Stucchi 40

86 Other examples of two-storeyed columnar treatment are discussed in connection with the Lefkadia Great Tomb (see p. 107ff).

87 See L. Crema, L'Architettura Romana (Torino 1959) 126–27; E. Nash,
Pictorial Dictionary of Ancient Rome 2 (Tübingen 1962) 352–6;
F. Coarelli, 'Il Sepolcro degli Scipioni,' DialAr 6 (1972) 36–106; A. Boethius, Etruscan and Early Roman Architecture (Harmondsworth 1978)
135, 209; H.B. Lauter-Bufe, 'Zur Fassade der Scipionengrabes,' RM 89
(1982) 35–46.

88 Livy 38.56.4. Presumably one of the tombs was a cenotaph.

89 The podium once carried historical paintings, but these were white-washed
from time to time and consequently they have almost completely
disappeared.

90 Lauter-Bufe (supra n87) 35 proposes a new reconstruction for the exterior
of the tomb. The façade, including the podium, comes to about 9 m in
height. The side openings of the podium were not placed symmetrically as
had been suggested in earlier reconstructions. The six attached Ionic

half-columns (each approximately 5.50 m high) possessed Attic-Ionic bases and there were eleven flutes for each column shaft.

91 V. Saladino, *Der Sarkophag des Lucius Cornelius Scipio Barbatus* (Würzburg 1970); review by W. Hornostel in *Gnomon* 45 (1975) 524–7

92 Lauter-Bufe (supra n87) 39 prefers an earlier date for the façade: 'Das Augenmerk ist dabei auf Felsfassadengräber des Hellenismus (3/2. Jahrhundert v. Chr.) zu richten, wobei auf die Übereinstimmung in der gennanten konstituierenden Elementen (länger Säulenprospekt bei seitlich abgeschlossenem Vorhof) zu achten ist.' Accordingly, the author dates the earliest façade (which can be reconstructed) at the beginning of the second century, to about the same time that the sarcophagus of Scipio Barbatus was executed. Lauter-Bufe notes that the construction of the podium indicates that the first phase of the entire project might date back as early as 300 BC.

93 Crema (supra n87) 126–7; Nash (supra n87) 357–8

94 See M. Verzar, 'Frühaugusteischer Grabbau in Sestino Toscana,' *MélRome* 86 (1974) 385.

95 Consult F. Matz's review of B. Goetze, *Das Rundgrab in Falerii* (Stuttgart 1939) in *Gnomon* 17 (1941) 215–22.

96 R. Delbrueck, *Hellenistische Bauten in Latinum* 2 (Strassburg 1907) 37–41; D. Vaglieri, 'Roma, Anno 1907,' *NSc* 4 (1907) 410–14; Nash (supra n87) 319–20; A. Golfetto, 'Das Grabmal des C. Publicius Bibulus in Rom,' *AntW* 10 (1979) 56–7

97 Vaglieri (supra n96) 413–14; and Golfetto (supra n96) 56: 'Die Inschrift steht auf der Vorderseite und stand nochmals auf der rechten Nebenseite, die jedoch vermauert ist (nur die Zeilenanfänge sind noch sichtbar).'

98 For the various dates, see Delbrueck (supra n96) 41 who prefers a date in the time of Sulla; T. Frank, *Roman Buildings of the Republic* (Rome 1924) 144, and M.E. Blake, *Ancient Roman Construction from the Prehistoric Period to Augustus* (Washington, DC, 1947) 147, date the structure at around 60 BC; F. Coarelli, *Guida Archeologica di Roma* (Rome 1974) 234, suggests an early first century BC date for the tomb.

99 Outside Rome, perhaps the closest in design to the tomb of C.P. Bibulus is the relatively well-preserved funerary monument of Numisius Ligus at Sepino (ancient Saepinum). For more details, see *Sepino* published by the Instituto di Archeologia dell'Universita di Perugia (Campobasso 1979) 110–12. For other less well-preserved or documented Republican tombs in and around Rome, see A.M. Colini, *I Sepolcri Reppublicani di Via Statilia* (Rome 1953) 1–15; F. Coarelli, *Rom-Ein archäologischer Führer* (Freiburg

1975) 64, 187, 226–7; H.A. Stützer, *Das antike Rom* (Cologne 1979) 294ff.

100 Crema (supra n87) 129; P. Marconi, *Agrigento* (Florence 1929) 124; P. Griffo, *Agrigento* (Palermo 1962) 100; F. Coarelli in *Storia della Sicilia* 2 (Naples 1979) 170

101 J. Charbonneaux, R. Martin, and F. Villard, *Das hellenistische Griechenland* (Paris 1971) 53 suggest a third-century date for the monument, while Crema (supra n87) 129 places the tomb in the first half of the first century BC.

102 Nash (supra n87) 329–32; *CIL* I² (VI 1958) 1203–6; P.C. Rossetto, *Il Sepolcro del Fornaio Marco Virgilio Eurisace a Porta Maggiore* (Rome 1973), with further bibliography.

103 In Pompeii there are no securely datable large tombs before 80 BC; the earliest monumental structure is the 'Garland Tomb' (see V. Kockel, *Die Grabbauten vor dem Herkulaner Tor in Pompeii* [Mainz 1983] 32). For tombs at Ostia and on the Via Appia, see H. Schaal, *Ostia der Welthafen Roms* (Bremen 1957) 165ff; L. Quilici, *La Via Appia da Roma a Bovillae* (Rome 1977).

104 Cyrene also had a number of archaic tumuli, but they were earth mounds; the earliest one dates around 600 BC and it is known as the tumulus of Battus.

105 See Stucchi 78–80; A. Rowe (ed.), *Cyrenaican Expedition of the University of Manchester 1952* (Manchester 1956) on round tombs in general 4–18; J. Cassels, 'The Cemeteries of Cyrene,' *BSR* 23 (1955) 11–14. (The numbering of the tombs in Cyrene follows Stucchi's system.)

106 Among the later examples, one of the best preserved is the Tomb of Kleobulos at Lindos on the island of Rhodes (fig. 55). This tomb is datable to the second century (see H. Kähler, *Lindos* [Zurich 1971] 25). Other Hellenistic structures of similar design are to be found at Thebes (see W. Heyden and A. Mallwitz, *Die Bauten in Kabirenheiligtum bei Theben* [Berlin 1978] 30).

107 Stucchi 74–8. Stucchi uses for Zawani the name Suni el-Abiad; and the type of tomb under discussion is called 'tomba a tempietto,' See also Cassels (supra n105) 14–17.

108 Analogous elevated sarcophagi, but on a smaller scale and of much finer execution, are found on the island of Paros. These Parian sarcophagi are generally dated to the second century (see O. Rubensohn, 'Parische Künstler,' *Jdl* 50 [1935] 49–69.

109 See below, p. 130ff.

110 For a general discussion of these tombs, with further detailed bibliography, see Stucchi 149–63 and Cassels (supra n105) 7.

111 J.R. Pacho, *Relation d'un Voyage dans la Marmarique, la Cyrenaique* (Paris 1827) pls 45 and 46. Stucchi 81–2

112 Cassels (supra n105) 17 restores 'above the entablature more steps,' without indicating whether they formed a pyramid or not.

113 Stucchi 95, 139

114 Stucchi dates the monument to the second half of the fourth century, comparing it with the less 'ornate' rock-cut monument at Eski Foça in Ionia (i.e., the Taş Kule tomb); however, there is little if any resemblance between the two. His other comparison, with a small-scale monument (perhaps the crowning element of a pilaster) now in the Syracuse museum (fig. 94), is more appropriate; but this piece has been dated to middle or late Hellenistic times by G.V. Gentili, 'Resti di un grande mausoleo ellenistico a Siracusa,' *Archivio Storico Siracusano* 23–24 (1967–8) 25.

In local Cyrenaican context Tombs N_{57}, N_{58} and S_{185} show a vague resemblance to Tomb N_{180} (see Stucchi 81n4 and 176). However, these tombs are all later than N_{180} and their exterior forms show a strong resemblance to tomb structures in Alexandria.

115 C.H. Kraeling, *Ptolemais* (Chicago 1962) 113; Stucchi 178

116 L. Crema, *L'Architettura Romana* (Torino 1959) 273, considers the decoration to be the forerunner of composite capitals. The site of the monument was explored again in 1980. The results of the new exploration would support the use of the Corinthian order instead of the Ionic for the second storey. (The new reconstruction of the tombs was outlined by S. Stucchi in a public lecture given in early 1981 in Rome, 'L'architettura urbana cirenaica in rapporto a quella della chora viciniore ed a quella Libya ulteriore, con speciale riguardo all'età ellenisitica.')

117 See Stucchi 178; Crema (supra n116) 273.

118 Adriani *Repertorio* 146 notes: 'La località e nota anche col nome di Mafrusa, donche la doppia denominazione con la quale la tomba e citata nella letteratura archeologica, di ipogeo di Suq-el-Wardiyan o di Mafrusa.' However, if one wishes to distinguish the two, Wardian is the western section of the district.

119 A. Adriani, *Lezioni sull'arte Alessandrina* (Naples 1972) 122

120 A detailed account of the hypogeum is given by H. Thiersch, *Zwei antike Grabanlagen bei Alexandria* (Berlin 1904) 6.

121 For the possible location of Alexander's tomb complex, see P. Bernhard, 'Topographie d'Alexandrie: le Tombeaux d'Alexandre et le Mausolée d'Auguste,' *BCH* 80–81 (1956–7) 129–56; full bibliography in P.M. Fraser, *Ptolemaic Alexandria* I (Oxford 1972) 15, with notes. M. Nowicka, 'Les Tombeaux Hellénistiques d'Alexandrie,' *Archeologia War* 17 (1966) 115–42.

122 E. Breccia, *La Necropoli di Sciatbi* (Cairo 1922); I. Noshy, *The Arts in Ptolemaic Egypt* (London 1937) 30; M. Lyttelton, *Baroque Architecture in Classical Antiquity* (London 1974) 41–2

123 Noshy (supra n122) 30 remarks that 'the Doric half columns decorating the vestibule are identical with the columns of Arsinoe's chapel.' See also H.H. Büsing, *Die griechische Halbsäule* (Wiesbaden 1970) 59 and 78.

124 Excavated and recorded in publication by A. Adriani, *Annuaire du Musée Gréco-Romain 1933–35* (Alexandria 1936); see also Adriani (supra n119) 115.

125 Stylistically comparable to the large frieze on the façade of the Lefkadia Great Tomb and to the horseman in the so-called Kinch tomb near Lefkadia.

126 Tholos representations in a similar funeral context appeared on wall paintings in the Graeco-Egyptian cemetery at Hermopolis. For pictures, see S. Gabra, 'New Proof of Greek Influnce in Ptolemaic Egypt,' *ILN* (21 April 1934) 598–9.

127 H. Kähler, *Der grosse Fries von Pergamon* (Berlin 1948) 173n69. The author dates the painted panel to the third quarter of the third century.

128 H. Lauter, 'Ptolemais in Libyen, ein Beitrag zur Baukunst Alexandrias,' *Jdl* 86 (1971) 149. On p. 153, Lauter refers to the anta capitals of the kline chamber (oecus no. 10); 'In der unvegetabilischen Bildung seiner Helices erinnert es noch an Kapitelle des frühen 3. Jahrhunderts.'

129 For Cyprus, see K. Nicolaou, *Ancient Monuments of Cyprus* (Nicosia 1968) 23 pls 22 and 23; for Cyrene, see Stucchi 151–60.

130 There is one small-scale, entirely rock-cut, tomb at Pogredac in Albania, mentioned above (see p. 110), where the simple, undecorated front of the actual burial-place is preceded by a miniature auditorium. In general, however, only the scaenae frons seems to have been reproduced in funerary architecture.

131 Adriani (supra n119) 117

132 See Thiersch (supra n120) 1.

133 For Anfushi, see Adriani *Repertorio* 191–4.

134 These segmental pediments are generally dated late in the Ptolemaic period; see Lyttelton (supra n122) 46–7.

135 For Mafrusa, see Adriani *Repertorio* 146–7.

136 For Wardian, see H. Riad, 'Quatre tombeaux de la necropole ouest d'Alexandrie,' *Société Archéologique d'Alexandrie*, Bullletin 42 (1967) 82–9 (Tomb no. 1).

137 A major study of the Pharos and its related monuments was published by H. Thiersch, *Pharos, Antike, Islam und Occident* (Leipzig and Berlin 1909); see also Fraser (supra n121) 17–20, with further bibliography.

138 See Fraser (supra n121) 17.

139 A. Adriani, *Annuaire du Musée Gréco-Romain* 3 (Alexandria 1940–50) 133. The tower was restored in 1937–9, and is still standing to a height of ca 20 m. See also Fraser (supra n121) 144–6.

140 One of the earliest known combinations of a sailor's landmark (perhaps a lighthouse) with a memorial comes from the late sixth or early fifth century. An epigram from Thasos refers to the twofold purpose of the tower: 'I am the memorial of Akeratos, son of Ph...erides, and I lie at the roadstead's utmost point bringing safety to ships and to sailors: so farewell' (M.N. Tod–J. Baker-Penoyre, 'Thasos,' *JHS* 29 [1909] 96). Knidos, on the Asia Minor coast, had a number of tower-like funerary monuments that could have had a double purpose. Newton *Discoveries* 502 notes that, besides being tombs, 'they may have served as a chain of watchtowers, and for communication signals.' The same might have been the case with the fourth-century heroon at Limyra, as noted above.

141 H.G. Horn and C.B. Rüger (eds), *Die Numider* (Bonn 1979). This exhibition catalogue provides further material on most of the tombs discussed in this section; see especially the entry by F. Rakob, 'Numidische Königsarchitektur in Nordafrika,' 119–71.

142 A. di Vita, 'Il Mausoleo Punico-Ellenistico "B" di Sabratha,' *RM* 86 (1976) 273–85; C. Picard, 'La conception du mausolée chez les Puniques et chez le Numides,' *Rivista di Studi Fenici* 1 (1973) 31–5

143 At Halikarnassos the ration was much 'heavier' (1:1.5) than at Suweida in Syria (1:1.1), while in the Tomb of Absalom in Jerusalem the ratio is slightly more 'slender' (1:2.50) overall; however, the Sabratha monument is much slimmer in appearance than its counterpart in Jerusalem.

144 Picard (supra n142) 34 draws attention to the possible symbolical meaning of the decoration; the kouroi 'ressemblent aux génies funéraires égyptiens chargés de monter la garde auprès des morts;' Beş 'évoque la victoire sur la mort qui procure le repos éternel;' while the idea of a tripod is the evocation of triumph, placed on the scene of (final) victory. Furthermore, the entire structure: 'Ce n'est donc pas un tombeau, "demeure d'éternite" à la mode égyptienne ou un temple funéraire comparable au fameux monument de Mausole, mais un pilier géant en forme d'obélisque, dressé auprès du tombeau, et qui appartient à cette famillle de monuments syro-palestiniens dénommés nephesh, et représentant la personnalité du ou des défunts enterrés au dessous.'

145 C. Poinssot and J.W. Salomonson, 'Un monument Punique inconnue: le mausollé d'Henchir Djaouf,' *OudMed* 44 (1963) 82, suggest that Phoe-

nicio-Cypriot (called by them 'Aeolic') capitals were introduced to Carthage via Cyprus in the fifth or early fourth century.

146 One relief shows Beş with lions, the other Hercules slaying the Nemean lion, while the third has several figures of uncertain meaning.

147 According to di Vita (supra n142) 285, the structure dates from aobut 200 BC; Picard (supra n142) 35 prefers a date around 300 BC.

148 See Rakob (supra n141) 149–56, and Horn and Rüger (supra n141) 28–9.

149 C. Poinssot, Les Ruines de Dougga (Tunis 1958) 58–61. The tomb was restored in 1908–10.

150 Poinssot and Salomonson (supra n145) 70 note that the bilingual inscription was removed from the monument in 1842 and it is not fully preserved; therefore, the association of the tomb with any name is conjectural. Horn and Rüger (supra n141) 27 mentions the possibility that the funerary monument was built for Massinissa himself. Rakob (supra n141) 158 also says that it was perhaps the cenotaph of Massinissa.

151 See Rakob (supra n141) 158–68 and Horn and Rüger (supra n141) 28 and 30.

152 Rakob (supra n141) 167, fig. 105

153 The lower section of the tomb to about a height of 6 m was reassembled between 1930 and 1932. Unfortunately it was another example of superficial workmanship, whereby the original effect of neatly fitted ashlars, seen and recorded in the nineteenth century, was not followed. Instead, a random selection of blocks was assembled, giving an impression of poor masonry.

154 The type persisted in Roman times, but the size of the tower tombs, with a few exceptions, decreased (see P. Romanelli, Topografia e Archeologia dell'Africa Romana in Enciclopedia Classica III [Torino 1970] 264–78.

155 Horn and Rüger (supra n141) 30

156 M.G. Camps, 'Nouvelles observations sur l'architecture et l'âge du Medracen, mausolée royale de Numidie,' CRAI (October 1973) 470–513

157 Ibid. 512

158 If the Medracen is to be dated to the third century, then it must have been the burial-place of one of the kings of the dynasty of Syphax. Horn and Rüger (supra n141) 27 and Rakob (supra n141) 35 date the tumulus to the time of Massinissa.

159 Camps (supra n156) 492 observes that these doors in their design 'inspirées des constructions religieuses puniques de style égyptisant.'

160 M. Christoffle, Le Tombeau de la Chrétienne in Arts et Métiers Graphiques (Paris 1951); Lawrence GrArch 189

161 See Rakob (supra n141) 142.

162 For smaller tumuli with circular interior corridors, see Rakob (supra n141) 142. The burial arrangement at the El Khroub tower tomb is also circular, but in other respects it is hardly comparable to the Kbour-er-Roumia tumulus.

163 Romanelli's suggested date (supra n154) 269 from the fourth to the sixth century AC, for technical reasons, is far too late for the tumulus.

164 See H. Rolland, *Le Mausolée de Glanum* 21st supplement to *Gallia* (Paris 1969) 79–84 with further bibliography.

165 For Ugarit, see J. Margueron, 'Ras Shamra 1975 et 1976. Rapport préliminaire sur les campagnes d'automne,' *Syria* 54 (1977) 175–9.

166 See R. Le Baron Bowen Jr and F.P. Albright, *Archeological Discoveries in South Arabia* (Baltimore 1958) 235–8 figs 182–188.

167 D. Ussishkin, 'The Necropolis from the Time of the Kingdom of Judah at Silwan, Jerusalem,' *BiblArch* 33–35 (1970–2) 34–46

168 L.Y. Rahmani, 'Jason's Tomb,' *IEJ* (1967) 61–100; G. Foerster, 'Architectural Fragments from Jason's Tomb Reconsidered, *IEJ* 28 (1978) 152–6; and for a general discussion of the tombs of Jerusalem, including the Tomb of Jason, and additional bibliography, see *Encyclopedia of Archaeological Excavations in the Holy Land* II (London 1976) 629–41; *Jerusalem Revealed, Archeology in the Holy City 1968–1974* (Jerusalem 1975) 17–20; M. Harel, *This Is Jerusalem* (Jerusalem 1977) 124–59. Earlier literature: R.A.S. MacAlister, 'The Rock-cut Tombs in Wady er-Rababi, Jerusalem,' *PEFQ* (1900) 225–48, (1901) 145–58, 397–402, (1902) 118–21, 237, 244; C. Watzinger, *Denkmäler Palästinas* 2 (Leipzig 1935) esp. 1–79

169 N. Avigad, 'Aramaic Inscription in the Tomb of Jason,' *IEJ* 17 (1967) 101–11. For a two-line cursive inscription in Greek, see P. Benoit, 'L'Inscription grecque du tombeau de Jason,' *IEJ* 17 (1967) 112–13.

170 A single support occurs in the Thrasyllos Monument at Athens and in a few rock-cut tombs in Lycia; for a well-preserved Ionic example at Kyaneai, see Petersen and von Luschan *Reisen* 22 pl. III.

171 The profile of the base is closest to the Attic-Ionic type; however, between the two tori there is a cyma reversa moulding instead of a scotia. A similar profile appears in the later Tomb of Absalom, but without the upper torus (see N. Avigad, *Ancient Monuments in the Kidron Valley* [Jerusalem 1954] 97 fig. 56/1).

172 Foerster (supra n168) 152

173 See, for example, the Sidi Gaber complex (fig. 183) or the layout of Tomb no. 2 at Anfushi (Adriani, *Repertorio* 2 pl. 106 fig. 360/n 141).

174 A comprehensive study of the Marissa necropolis was published by J.P. Peters and H. Thiersch, *Painted Tombs in the Necropolis of Marissa (Marèshah)* (London 1905) 16 fig. 1; 30 fig. 5. For suggested dates, see 77.

175 For further discussion of the possible comparative material see Foerster (supra n168) 155.

176 The Bene Hezir tomb and all the other funerary monuments in the Kidron Valley discussed here are treated in detail by Avigad (supra n171); see also H.E. Stutchbury, 'Excavations in the Kidron Valley,' PEQ 94–95 (1960–1) 191–213.

177 Interestingly enough, S. Munk, Palestine–Description Géographique, Historique et Archéologique (Paris 1845) pl. 36, reconstructed the top of the monument in the form of a stepped pyramid with further architectural ornaments above it.

178 Avigad (supra n171) 44

179 For further bibliography, see especially Stutchbury (supra n176) and Büsing GrHalbs 21.

180 L.H. Vincent, Jérusalem de l'Ancien Testament 1 (Paris 1954) 332–42, dates the tomb far too early, to the third century.

181 See Büsing GrHalbs 22.

182 Fluted column shafts in rock-cut architecture were rare. They seem to have appeared more often in the more expensive tombs where the columns were free-standing. Besides increasing the costs of labour, the execution of flutes could have also presented extra difficulties where the rock was brittle. The few existing examples of fluted rock-cut column shafts include the Tomba Ildebranda at Sovana, the Archokrateion on Rhodes, and Tomb 3 at Basse-Selce in Albania.

183 The superimposition of (mostly cubic) elements of diminishing sizes had been employed in early Semitic shrines (see M.V. Seton Williams, 'Palestinian Temples,' IRAQ 11 [1949] 77–89). In the Tomb of Absalom the concept is somewhat modified to correspond to the fashion of the times.

184 For the monument of the Julii at St Rémy, see Rolland (supra n164) 79–84; for the Rundbau at Ephesos, see H. Alzinger, 'Augusteische Architektur in Ephesos,' Öjh supplement 17 (Baden bei Wien 1974) 37–40.

185 In addition to Avigad (supra n171), see also his previous article on the subject, 'Architectural Observations on Some Rock-cut Tombs,' PEQ 82–83 (1944–7), esp. 115–19.

186 See C.R. Conder and H.H. Kitchener, The Survey of Western Palestine, Memoirs 2 (London 1882) 313–15; M.R. Savignac, 'Chronique,' RBibl 7 (1910) 124–7.

187 The building at Araq el-Emir, long believed to be a mausoleum, has been identified by recent excavations as a temple (see E. Will, 'L'Edifice dit Qsar el Abd à Araq al Amir (Jordanie),' CRAI [1977] 69–85).

188 For comparative material, see Avigad (supra n185) 118.

189 See Conder and Kitchener (supra n186) 313–15 and Savignac (supra n186) 124–7.

190 E.g., at Praeneste; see Delbrueck (supra n96) 148 fig. 86, and cf. v.1 pl. 20 for the decorative rosettes on tombs.

191 The association of the complex with Queen Helena seems to have been borne out by finds from the interior of the tomb, including a sherd with the name 'Helena' and a sarcophagus with an inscription referring to 'Helena the Queen.' See Harel (supra n168) 133.

192 Josephus *Antiquities* 20.95

193 The pyramids could have disappeared as early as the destruction of Jerusalem by Titus, because Pausanias, who mentions Helena's tomb (8.16.5), says nothing of the pyramids.

194 K. Galling, 'Ein Etagen-Pilaster-Grab in Norden von Jerusalem,' *Deutscher Palästina – Verein, Zeitschrift* 59–60 (1936–7) 111–23 pl. 4, and N. Avigad, 'The Rock-carved Façades of the Jerusalem Necropolis,' *IEJ* 1 (1950–1) 95–106

195 Galling (supra n194) 116. Here could also be mentioned the similar 'vestigial' architraves in Roman republican work, such as the Doric temple at Cori.

196 For further bibliography, see *Encyclopedia of Archaeological Excavations* (supra n168) 633.

197 J. Jotham-Rothschild, 'The Tombs of Sanhedria,' *PEQ* 86–87 (1952–3) 23–8; 'Short Guide to the Rock-cut Tombs of Sanhedriyya,' *Atiqot* 1 (1956) 68–81; L.Y. Rahmani, 'Jewish Rock-cut Tombs in Jerusalem,' *Atiqot* 3 (1961) 93–120

198 Rahmani (supra n197) 96 fig. 3, and Avigad (supra n185) 119–22

199 Avigad (supra n194) 100

200 Josephus *Antiquities* 13.211–13

201 B and D 3 (1909) 98–101; Büsing *GrHalbs* 21

202 H.W. Waddington, *Inscriptions Grecques et Latines de la Syrie* (Paris 1870) 532 n2320

203 M. Gawlikowski, *Monuments funéraires de Palmyre* (Warsaw 1970) 23 n66, mentions that according to the local helpers who participated in the excavations, the burial was under the monument.

204 P. Perdrizet, 'Le Monument de Hermel,' *Syria* 19 (1938) 47–41, pls 11–13; D. Krencker and W. Zschietzschmann, *Römische Tempel in Syrien* I (Berlin 1938), discuss both monuments, Hermel: 161–2, figs. 231–234; Kalat Fakra: 50–5, figs 73–80.

205 Krencker and Zschietzschmann (supra n204) 54 doubt the funerary nature of the edifice: 'Das Monument erinnert im Aufbau mit der Kammer im Kern an rechnen, dass es kein Grabturm, sondern ein Kultmal sehr eigentümlicher Art war.'

206 For the inscription, see Krencker and Zschietzschmann (supra n204) 55.
207 For the history of the Nabataeans, see H.P. Roschinski, 'Geschichte der Nabataen,' *BonnJbb* 180 (1980) 129–54.
208 The main sections dealing with the Nabataeans are the following: Diod. Sic. 2.48.1–9, 19.94. 1–10, 97.1–4, 100.1–2; Strabo 16.2.16–34.
209 Diod. Sic. 3.43.4
210 Strabo 16.4.21
211 See B and D 2 137–73.
212 For all the tombs discussed in the following pages, including the Khazneh, see A. Negev, 'The Nabataeans and the Provincia Arabia,' *Aufstieg und Niedergang der römischen Welt* II, Principat 8 (Berlin and New York 1977) 520–682, and idem, 'Die Nabatäer,' *AntW* special ed. (1976) 79–80; G.R.W. Wright, 'The Khazneh at Petra: A Review,' *ADA* 6–7 (1962) 24–52; A. Schmidt-Colinet, 'Nabatäische Felsarchitektur,' *BonnJbb* 180 (1980) 189–230; A. Hadidi, 'Nabatäische Architektur in Petra,' *BonnJbb* ibid. 230–6; F. Zayadine, 'Photogrammetrische Arbeiten in Petra,' *BonnJbb* ibid. 237–52; M. Lindner, 'Deutsche Ausgrabungen in Petra,' *BonnJbb* ibid. 253–64.
213 Athenaeus *Deipn* 5.205
214 Wright (supra n212) 32 points out the sacral significance of the cube for Semites, for example the Kaaba, which is venerated in Mecca.
215 For possible Alexandrian influences in the Khazneh capitals, see K. Ronczewski, 'Kapitelle des El Hasne in Petra,' *AA* 47 (1932) 38–89; D. Schlumberger, 'Les formes anciennes du chapiteau corinthien en Syrie, en Palestine et en Arabie,' *Syria* 14 (1933) 283–317. Negev (supra n212) 596; Lyttelton *BArch* 73
216 The importance in late Hellenistic theory of attention to such details in purely ornamental designs is underscored by Vitruvius's harsh criticism of current developments in wall painting, and by his story of the mathematician Leikymnios and the design for the small theatre at Tralles by Apatourios of Alabanda (Vitruvius 7.5.2–7).
217 See a detailed study of the building by G. Pesche, *Il Palazzo delle Colonne in Tolemaide* (Rome 1960). For a reconstruction of the palace, see his pls 6 and 10.
218 The absence of comparative material may be partly due to the paucity of excavations in the region of Petra; only three buildings have been studied in any detail: the theatre in the necropolis, a monumental gate, and the Qasr Bint Faraun complex not far from the main gate of the city.
219 For the reconstruction of the stuccoed wall, see Lyttelton *BArch* 67 fig. 18.
220 According to Schmidt-Colinet (supra n212) 190, on the basis of the inscrip-

tion both the temple complex and the propylon to the city are to be dated to the late first century BC.

221 The eagle emblems and Isis figures as symbols and protectors of royalty appear on Nabataean coins.

222 See Negev (supra n212) 597. For some of the results of the new excavations at Petra, see P.C. Hammond, 'Cult and Cupboard at Nabataean Petra,' *Archaeology* 34 (1981) 27–34.

223 For the description of the capitals, see Negev (supra n212) 596.

224 The plans of these buildings can be seen in Negev (supra n212) 609 fig. 14 and 169 fig. 16.

225 The sides, however, had to be cut back extensively to attain the desired height of the façade. The sandstone in this region of Petra is much harder than in the eastern necropolis and accounts for the better preservation of the Deir.

226 Among the many accounts by visitors who saw the monument during the last century, it is interesting to note Bartlett's impression, which was shared by a good many others: 'It is a gigantic monument, producing from its vastness and wildness of its situation, an impression almost of awe; but it is very defective in its style, for it is ponderous without grandeur, and elaborate without elegance' (quoted by B and D 2 333).

227 Because of the brittle nature of the rock, some of the ornaments were carved separately and attached. There is also evidence of the use of stucco and painted surfaces, especially in the interior.

228 For the English translation of the inscription, see I. Browning, *Petra* (London 1973) 223.

229 For a short discussion of this Hegra tomb and related monuments, see B and D 2 151.

230 Jaussen and Savignac investigted the site of Hegra. Of the seventy-nine hewn funerary monuments, more than half are dated by inscriptions, all belonging to the first century AC (see A. Jaussen and R. Savignac, *Mission Archéologique en Arabie 1–2* [Paris 1909 and 1914]).

231 A good example is the theatre of Petra, placed amid a large number of rock-cut tombs and, thus, suggesting that the theatre played an important part in local funerary cults.

232 P. Bernard, 'Fouilles d'ai Khanoum,' *CRAI* (April–June 1975) 180–9; H.P. Francfort and J.C. Liger, 'Fouilles d'ai Khanoum: campagne de 1974,' *BIFAO* 63 (1976) 25–39

233 See Francfort and Liger (supra n232) 36n4.

234 The time of the first building period of the 'temple tomb' is strongly supported by the pottery found on the site (see Francfort and Liger [supra n232] 38).

CONCLUSION

1 Akurgal *Ruins* 120 fig. 41a
2 G.M.A. Hanfmann, 'On the Palace of Croesus,' in *Festschrift für Frank Brommer* (Mainz 1977) 151
3 For a further elaboration of the subject, see M. Gothein, 'Der griechische Garten,' *AM* 34 (1909) 34–52;P. Grimal, *Les jardins romains* (Paris 1943); J.J. Hatt, *La tombe gallo-romaine* (Paris 1951) 65.

APPENDIX 1 ROOF CONSTRUCTIONS

1 For such a suggestion, see Kurtz-Boardman 193–4.
2 Rhodes (Pontamo): *Clara Rhodos* II, 118; Aigina: G. Welter, *Aigina* (Berlin 1938) 57; Krannon: V. Milojčič, 'Ausgrabungen in Thessalien, Herbst 1959,' *AA* 75 (1960) 176
3 Few of the extant Macedonian tombs have been recorded in detail in publications. The existence of nearly 100 Macedonian tombs is known; yet many of these tombs have never even been mentioned in the literature. Thus the number of façades without pediments is not known exactly. If there are only a few examples of tomb façades without pediments, we cannot help wondering why these, and only these, lacked a feature that is invariably found in other examples.
4 Cicero *Philippics* 2.43; see also his *Orations* 3.46.
5 Pedimental theatre-façades, e.g., in the terracotta model in Naples (fig. 241) and in the generally accepted restoration of the theatre at Segesta (fig. 242), may be derived from tombs. One might also mention the traditional restoration of the Thersilion at Megalopolis with a pediment. The problem is that we cannot be certain whether the pediment has the same significance for Greeks as for Romans. See also A. Alföldi, 'Die Ausgestaltung des monarchischen Zeremoniells am römischen Kaiserhofe,' *RM* 49–50 (1934–5) 1–118.
6 The use of true vaulting had been established for a long time in the ancient Orient before the Greeks employed the technique. A good example of a vaulted tomb comes from the mid-second-millennium Elamite site at Tepti-Ahar: 'The sophistication of the Elamite builders is best shown in the oval vaulted roofs, well illustrated in the tomb of Tepti-Ahar where its oval vaulted roof, built of baked brick with gypsum mortar, has survived for almost three thousand five hundred years' (E.O. Negahban, 'Architecture of Haft Tepe,' *AMIran-Supp.* 6 [Berlin 1979] 9–29).
7 Unfortunately, little is known of Macedonian architecture. Consequently it cannot be stated whether barrel vaulting existed in Macedonian palatial or domestic buildings.

8 Lawrence *GrArch* 229

9 See T.D. Boyd, 'The Arch and the Vault in Greek Architecture,' *AJA* 82 (1978) 96, fig. 12.

10 The situation with regard to vaulting is comparable with that resulting from the introduction of concrete in ancient architecture. In Italy this material was known for several centuries before its potential in different types of structures was fully appreciated.

11 Hoddinott 28; see also idem, *The Thracians* (London 1981) 119–26.

12 G. Tsanova and L. Getov, *Trakiskata Grobnitsa pri Kazanluk* (Sofia 1970)

13 Hoddinott (supra n11 1981) 126 notes: 'The brief use of high quality fired brickwork solely for tombs was confined to this small area; its appearance has still to be explained.'

14 Hoddinott 98

15 W. Radt, 'Die Leleger auf der Halbinsel von Halikarnassos,' *AntW* 6 (1975/3) 3–16

16 Gajdukevic 256–302

17 For a concise study on the development of arches in Italy, see G. Lugli, 'Considerazioni sull'origine dell'arco a conci radiali,' *Palladio* 2 (1952) 9–31, esp. figs 17–30. For some of the corbel-vaulted tombs in Etruria, see V.S. Tacconi, 'Territorio e Architettura Etrusca a Sesto Fiorentino (Florence 1978) 89–123.

18 M. Gimbutas, 'Timber-Graves in Southern Russia,' *Expedition* 3 (1961/3) 14–22. The construction and interior arrangement of the larger 'timber graves' recall some of the wooden chambers in the Gordion region, but in Anatolia the chambers were much more complex and later in date than those of south Russia.

19 In connection with the 'timber' cultures it may be noted that Scythian nobles employed a type of burial that remained unchanged from about the eighth century on. Minns 194 and some present-day East European archaeologists, believe that the kourgans evolved from rather simple local constructions in wood. However, this theory remains questionable. Among other arguments against it is the fact that in Lycia and elsewhere, the change from wooden to stone architecture regularly left recognizable timber forms 'petrified' in the stone, even when the stone structures were modified and adjusted to the technical requirements of the new medium. In the stone chambers of the kourgans, in contrast, there are no such reminiscences of wooden prototypes; the stone chambers appeared rather suddenly, and in a developed form, without evidence of previous experimentation in the medium.

The dates assigned to the kourgans by Russian archaeologists are generally accepted and used, although we cannot check their accuracy.

20 The earliest comprehensive report on the Gold Kourgan appeared in K. Neumann, *Die Hellenen im Skythenlande* (Berlin 1855) 498. For more up-to-date publications, see V.F. Gajdukevic, *Bosporskije Goroda* (Leningrad 1981) 6–54, with additional bibliography.

21 The Great Tumulus at Vergina (still under excavation by Andronikos and his team) also contained at least three separate burials, of which the largest, noted above (Tomb II), is said to be that of Philip II. The situation is by and large comparable to that found in the gold Kourgan; and as far as we can tell a member of the Macedonian royal house, Antigonos Gonatas, decided to cover all three of the Vergina burials by a common earth mound.

22 Gajdukevic 271 states: 'Die Idee von Komposition und Konstruktion ist ganz offensichtlich von auswärts importiert, vielleicht aus Thrakien, wo runde Grabmäler (Tholoi) seit der ersten Hälfte des 4. Jahrhunderts v.u. Z. weit verbreitet waren.'

23 J. Durm, 'Die Kuppelgräber von Pantikapaion,' *Öjh* 10 (1907) 230–42. See also Gajdukevic 271.

24 Strabo 7.7.4

25 R.C. Bosanquet, 'Excavations at Praesos I,' *BSA* 8 (1901–2) 231–70

26 *Thera* II, 94 and 98

27 W.R. Paton and J.L. Myres, 'Karian Sites and Inscriptions II,' *JHS* (1896) 245

28 Åkerström 154. For a special study dealing mostly with Etruscan tombs that have domes over square ground-plans, see J. Fink, *Die Kuppel über dem Viereck* (Munich 1958).

29 Durm (supra n23) 241, and Gajdukevic 273

30 Lugli (supra n17) 10

31 M.J. Mellink, 'Archaeology in Asia Minor,' *AJA* 71 (1967) 173, calls the technique 'Galatian corbeled roof.'

32 A. von le Coq, *Auf Hellas spuren in Ostturkistan* (Leipzig 1926) 79; M.G. Brambilla, 'Tipi di Case Contadine Armene,' *Palladio* 23–24 (1974–6) 197–212

33 B. Filov, 'The Bee-Hive Tombs of Mezek,' *Antiquity* 11 (1937) 303; see also Hoddinott 344, and A.M. Mansel, 'Trakya Kirklareli, Kubeli Mezarlari (Die Kuppelgräber von Kirklarelei in Thrakien),' *Belleten* 6 (1943) 37.

34 L. Botusarova and V. Kolarova, 'Le tombeau à coupole des environs de Plovdiv,' *Studia in Memoriam K. Skorpil* (Sofia 1961) 279

35 H. Vetters, 'Ephesos,' *ÖstArchaeollnst Grabungen* (1971–2) 41–6

36 Ibid. 117

37 Akurgal *Ruins* 248

38 See A.M. Mansel, 'Gemlik Tümülüs Mezari,' *Belleten* 38 (1974) 181–9, with an extensive bibliography relating to the subject in general.

39 E. Mamboury, 'Das Grabmal von Mudanya,' *Atti del I. Congresso Internazionale di Preistoria e Protoistoria Mediterranea* (1952) 472.

40 Mansel (supra n38) 187

41 D. Tokgöz, 'İğdire Tümülüs Kazisi Raporu,' *TürkArkDerg* 22–23 (1975–6) 151–3

42 E. Schneider Equini, 'La Necropoli di Hierapolis di Frigia,' *MonAnt* (1972) 132

43 M.J. Mellink, 'Archaeology in Asia Minor,' *AJA* 67 (1963) 189

44 R.S. Young, 'The Campaign of 1955 at Gordion: Preliminary Report,' *AJA* 60 (1956) 250–2

45 Lawrence *GrArch* 230

46 Young (supra n44) 251

47 Schneider Equini (supra n42) 127

48 M. Demus-Quatember, 'Zur Konstruktionweise der "Tomba di Pitagora" bei Cortona,' *Palladio* 7–8 (1957–8) 49–51 and 'Zur Tomba di Pitagora (Nachtrag)' 193. See also J.P. Oleson, 'The Galeotti Tomb at Chiusi; The Construction Techniques of the Etruscan Barrel-Vaulted Tombs,' *StEtr* 44 (1976) 69–85.

49 M.M. Chiari, 'La Tomba dell Faggeto in Territorio Perugino. Contributo allo studio dell'architettura funeraria con volta a botte in Etruria,' *Quaderni dell'Istituto di Archeologia dell'Università di Perugia* 3 (1975) 25–37, where examples analogous to the Faggeto tombs are discussed.

50 Chiari (supra n49) 25 states that the type 'rientra nel numero esiguo di tombe monumentali con copertura a volta di conci radiali la cui diffusione in Etruria e limitata alle sole Orvieto, Chiusi, Cortona e Perugia.' According to A. d'Ambrosio, 'Una Tomba Sannitica a S. Prisco di Caserta,' *Accademia di archeologia, lettere e belle arti* 46 (Naples 1971) 205–10, the tomb type with monolithic lunettes also existed in the vicinity of Naples. The design seems to have been introduced to Italy from Greece and Asia Minor and then rapidly spread in Etrusia in the third century. P. Chiarucci, 'Una nuova proposta per l'individuazione del sepolcro di Pompeo Magno,' *Documenta Albana* (Albano 1980) 55–74, suggests that at tomb chamber near Albano – which is typologically similar to the above-described tombs – was the actual burial-place of Pompey the Great. The tomb has a dromos of which the retaining walls are executed in the opus reticulatum technique. The structure is datable to the mid first century BC.

51 Chiari (supra n49) 39

52 Schneider Equini (supra n42) 113 and 129

APPENDIX 2 SARCOPHAGI, THOLOI, AND MONUMENTAL TOMBS

1 G. Rodenwaldt, 'Sarkophagprobleme,' *RM* 58 (1943) 4, states: 'Monumentale Steinsarkophage gab es vor der archaischen Epoche Griechenlands in Ägypten, in Assyrien und in Phönikien.' The author also gives an extended bibliography relating to the subject in general. See also B. Schmidt-Dounas, *Der Lykische Sarkophag aus Sidon, IstMitt BH* 30 (Tübingen 1985); E. Brümmer, 'Griechische Truhenbehälter,' *Jdl* 100 (1985) 1–168.

2 I. Kleemann, 'Der archaische Sarkophag mit Säulendekoration in Samos,' in *Festschrift für Friedrich Matz* (Mainz 1962) 44–55

3 H. Walter, *Das Heraion von Samos* (Munich 1976) 70

4 K.F. Johansen, 'Clazomenian Sarcophagus Studies,' *ActaArch* 12–13 (1941–2) 64, says that the 'Knowledge of the Egyptian mummy coffin caused them [i.e., Klazomenians] to reshape the rectangular θηκη in the direction of the anthropoid idea.'

5 See R.M. Cook, *Greek Painted Pottery* (London 1972) 136 and 345, with further bibliography relating to the subject of Klazomenian sarcophagi.

6 Ibid. 137

7 Akurgal *Phryg Kunst* 129 and 283, fig. 258

8 Ibid. figs 52–53 and 69–72

9 G.V. Gentili, 'Iscrizione arcaica sul coronamento di cippo gelese del Museo di Siracusa,' *Epigraphica* 8 (1946) 11–18

10 Ibid. 18

11 Orsi, see esp. 340, 380, 515–35, 737.

12 See Orsi 368: 'Nel'interno agli angoli quattro svelte colonnine ioniche a nove canellature, sormontate da capitelli angolari, il cui echino ed il tegolino decorati di foglie rosse e bleu.'

13 Orsi pl. 46. They are comparable with a number of the later sarcophagi from Aegina, where there are also interior corner columns without capitals (fig. 265). For a discussion about why there are such architectural features inside the sarcophagus, see A. Wasowicz, 'Tombes de Paestum et Sarcophages Grecs,' *Miscellanea di Studi Classici in Onore di Eugenio Manni* 4 (Rome 1980) 2199–2207.

14 Orsi 529

15 Ibid. 528

16 Boethius and Ward-Perkins 44, 544 n14, and 555 n25 pl. 18. The burial-chamber of this Etruscan tomb is entirely rock-cut; consequently, from the technical point of view, the supports were not needed.

17 P. Marconi, *Agrigento* (Florence (1929) 102 fig. 64

18 See, for example, W. Altmann, *Architektur und Ornamentik der antiken Sarkophage* (Berlin 1902) 35 fig. 11.

19 F. Coarelli, 'Il Sepolcro degli Scipioni,' *DialArch* 6 (1972) 93 n133; V. Saladino, *Der Sarkophag des Lucius Cornelius Scipio Barbatus* (Würzburg 1970). See also the review of Saladino's book by W. Hornbostel, *Gnomon* 45 (1973) 576.

20 P. Bernard, 'Les bas-reliefs Greco-Perses de Dascylion à la lumière de nouvelles découvertes,' *RA* (1969¹) 17–18

21 E. Pfuhl and H. Möbius, *Die ostgriechischen Grabreliefs* 1 (Mainz 1977) 9. See also Bernard (supra n20) 20, where the author suggests a date around 400 BC.

22 O. Hamdy Bey and T. Reinach, *Une Nécropole Royale à Sidon* (Paris 1892); V. von Graeve, *Der Alexandersarkophag und seine Werkstatt* (Berlin 1970) 19, 22, and 165, with further bibliography; H. Gabelmann, 'Die Inhaber des Lykischen und des Satrapensarkophages,' *AA* (1982) 493–5

23 E. Akurgal, C. Mango, and R. Ettinghausen, *Treasures of Turkey* (Geneva 1966) 55

24 Von Graeve (supra n22)

25 Ibid. 21 notes: 'Wie sich der "lykische" Sarkophag in der Steilheit des Kastens seinen Vorbildern annähert, so erinnert der Alexandersarkophag in seiner auffallenden Breitenlagerung an die Massverhältnisse eines griechischen Tempels.'

26 Hamdy Bey and Reinach (supra n22) 262; Minns 332; C. Watzinger, *Griechische Holzsarkophage aus der Zeit Alexanders des Grossen* (Leipzig 1905) 45; A. Wasowicz, 'Objets antiques en bois des collections du musée du Louvre de Paris,' *ArcheologieaWar* 15–17 (1964–6) 177–201; M. Vaulina and A. Wasowicz, *Bois Grecs et Romains de l'Ermitage* (Wroclaw 1974) 103–5 and 115; Wasowicz (supra n13) 2199–2207

27 Minns 333

28 Vaulina and Wasowicz (supra n26) 115 date the sarcophagus to the first or second century AC. The main criterion for dating the sarcophagus to the Roman era is that the use of applied stucco in the above-described context did not appear in the region before the first century AC. The authors indicate that the only 'architectural sarcophagus' that can be securely dated to the mid fourth century comes from the Zmeinyj tumulus (52ff.).

29 Minns 322; Gajdukevic 294 figs 87–89

30 See Gajdukevic 295.

31 T. Papazaphiri, 'Ellenistikos tafos Agrias (An Hellenisitic Cist-grave from the Neighbourhood of Volos),' *Thessalika* (1962) 34

32 Ibid. 34

33 *Roma Medio Repubblicana* (Rome 1973) 274

34 G. Kleiner, 'Hellenistische Sarkophage in Kleinasie,' *IstMitt* 7 (1957) 7.

35 O. Rubensohn, 'Parische Künstler,' *Jdl* 50 (1935) 49–69; see also L. Ross, *Inselreisen* 1 (Stuttgart 1840) 143, who mentions the existence of elevated sarcophagi on the island of Siphnos. Sarcophagi of less pretentious design than the Parian example are also to be found on the island of Cyprus (see V. Karageorghis, 'Chronique des Fouilles à Chypre en 1978,' *BCH* [1979] 677).

36 For a comprehensive study of the funerary monuments on Rheneia, see M.T. Couilloud, 'Les Monuments Funéraires des Rhénée,' *Explorations Archéologiques de Délos* 30 (Athens 1974).

37 See M.T. Couilloud, 'Monuments Funéraires de Rhénée,' *BCH* 94 (1970) 545.

38 G. Roux, *L'Architecture de l'Argolide aux IVᵉ et IIIᵉ siècles avant J.C.* (Paris 1961) 131–200

39 C.A. Di Stefano, 'Scoperta nella necropoli di Lilibeo,' *Kokalos* 20 (1974) 162–71

40 Ibid. 168

41 A.H. Borbein, 'Die griechische Statue des 4. Jahrhunderts v. Chr.,' *Jdl* 88 (1973) 43–212; see esp. 48–55.

42 Dinsmoor 239; Borbein (supra n41) 58 n59

43 For instance the well-preserved Ionic rock-cut tomb with one column in antis at Kyanei (Petersen and von Luschan, *Reisen* pl. III).

44 Şahin 86 states: 'Für seinen [i.e., the mausoleum's] Enfluss auf die Entstehung der Säulenaltäre spricht erstens seine Erbauungszeit kurz vor der Erscheinung der Säulenaltäre und zweitens, dass die ersten Säulenaltäre gerade in Tegea und Ephesos errichtet wurden, also in Orten, wo ein Künstler des Maussolleions, nämlich der Bildhauer-Architekt Skopas, weiter beschäftigt worden war. Eine weitere Unterstützung für diese Behauptung ist die Ähnlichkeit der Bauformen des Maussolleions mit dem Altar der Artemis in Ephesos.'

It is known from ancient literature that some altars were also actual tombs, (e.g., the altar tomb of Aiakos mentioned by Pausanias 2.29.6). For the 'double character' of some of the large altars, see V. Stähler, 'Pergamonaltar,' in *Festschrift für Dörner* (Berlin 1978) 860–963.

SELECTED BIBLIOGRAPHY

Bold-face entries indicate abbreviations used in the notes.

ANCIENT AUTHORS

Arrian. *Anabasis.* Loeb edition, trans. E.I. Robson. 1929–33. [Loeb editions were published in London and Cambridge, MA.]

Athenaeus. *The Deipnosophists.* Trans., C.B. Gulick. London and New York: 1972

Cicero, *De legibus.* Trans., G. de Plinval. Paris 1968

– *Orations.* Loeb edition, trans. E.W. Sutton. 1959–60

– *Philippics.* Loeb edition, trans. W.C.A. Ker. 1938

Diod. Sic.: Diodorus Siculus. *World History.* Loeb edition, trans., C.H. Old-father. 1933–

Herodotus, *History.* OCT, trans., C. Hude. Oxford 1927

Hipponax. *Fragments of his iambic poetry.* Trans., O. Masson. Paris 1962

Homer. *Iliad.* Loeb edition, trans. A.T. Murray. 1954–7

– *Odyssey.* Loeb edition, trans. W.B. Sanford. 1948.

Josephus, F. *The Antiquities of the Jews.* In *The Works of Flavius Josephus.* Trans., W. Whiston. Philadelphia 1860

Ktesias, *Persika.* Trans. J. Gilmore. In *Fragments of the Persika of Ctesias.* London and New York 1888

Martial. *Epigrammaton libri.* Loeb edition, trans. W.C.A. Ker. 1919–20

Nicander. *Theriaca.* Trans., A.S.F. Gow and A.F. Scholfield. 1953. Cambridge, Eng.

Pausanias. *Description of Greece.* Loeb edition, trans., W.H.S. Jones, H.A. Ormerod, and R.E. Wycherley. 1935–55

Plato. *Laws.* Loeb edition, trans. R.G. Burry. 1926

240 Selected Bibliography

Pliny the Elder. *Natural History.* Loeb edition, trans., H. Rackham, W.H.S. Jones, and D.E. Eichholz 1938–63
Strabo. *Geography.* Loeb edition, trans., H.C. Jones and J.R.S. Sterrett 1917–32
Theophrastos. *Historiae Plantarum.* [HistPlant]. Trans., A. Hort. London and New York 1961
Vitruvius. *De Architectura.* Loeb edition, trans. F. Granger. 1931–4

SECONDARY SOURCES

Adriani, A. *La Nécropole de Moustafa Pasha. Annuaire du Musée Gréco-Romain 1933–35.* Alexandria 1936
– *Lezioni sull'arte Alessandrine.* Naples 1972
Adriani Repertorio: Adriani, A. *Repertorio d'Arte dell'Egitto Greco-Romano* series C 1–2. Palermo 1963 and 1966
Åkerström, A. *Studien über die Etruskischen Gräber.* Lund 1934
Akurgal, E. *Bayrakli: die Ausgrabungen in Alty-Smyrna.* Ankara 1950
Akurgal, E.; C. Mango; and R. Ettinghausen. *Treasures of Turkey.* Geneva 1966
Akurgal Anatolien: Akurgal, E. *Die Kunst Anatoliens.* Berlin 1961
Akurgal PhrygKunst: Akurgal, E. *Phrygische Kunst.* Ankara 1955
Akurgal Ruins: Akurgal, E. *Ancient Civilizations and Ruins of Turkey.* Istanbul 1970
Albright, F.P. *Archeological Discoveries in South Arabia.* Baltimore 1958
Alföldi, A. *Early Rome and the Latins.* Ann Arbor 1965
Alföldi-Rosenbaum, E. *Anamur Nekropolü: The Necropolis of Anemurium.* Ankara 1971
Altertümer von Pergamon 6 (Berlin 1923)
Altmann, W. *Architektur und Ornamentik der antiken Sarkophage.* Berlin 1902
Andronikos, M. *The Royal Graves at Vergina.* Athens 1980
– *Vergina.* Athens 1984
Andronikos MacedTomb: Andronikos, M. 'Regal Treasures from a Macedonian Tomb.' *National Geographic Magazine* 154 no. 1 (July 1978)
Archaeological Newsletter. New York 1946–
Archivio Storico Siracusano. Siracusa 1955–
Arts et Métiers Graphiques. Paris 1927–
B and D: Bruennow, R.E., and A. von Domaszewski. *Die Provincia Arabia* 1–3. Strassburg 1904/1905/1909
Badawy, A. *A History of Egyptian Architecture.* Los Angeles 1966
Balkan Studies. Thessalonike 1960–

241 Selected Bibliography

Barnett, R.D. *The Nimrud Ivories*. London 1975
Bean *Aegean:* Bean, G.E. *Aegean Turkey*. London 1967
Bean-Cook: Bean, G.E., and J.H. Cook. 'The Cnidia.' *BSA* 47 (1952) 171–212
Benndorf-Niemann *Gjölbaschi:* Benndorf, O., and G. Niemann. *Das Heroon von Gjölbaschi-Trysa*. Vienna 1889
Benndorf-Niemann *Reisen:* Benndorf, O., and G. Niemann. *Reisen in Lykien und Karien* 1. Gesellschaft für Archaeologische Erforschung Kleinasiens. Vienna 1884
Bertocchi, F.T. *La pittura funeraria Apula*. Naples 1964
Betancourt, P.P. *The Aeolic Style in Architecture*. Princeton 1977
Bianchi-Bandinelli *Sovana:* Bianchi-Bandinelli, R. *Sovana*. Florence 1929
Bizzarri, M., and C. Curri. *Magica Etruria*. Florence 1968
Blake, M.E. *Ancient Roman Construction from Prehistoric Period to Augustus*. Washington 1947
Boethius and Ward-Perkins: Boethius, A., and J.B. Ward-Perkins. *Etruscan Cities*. London 1975
Borchhardt *Bauskulptur:* Borchhardt, J. *Die Bauskulptur des Heroons von Limyra*. IstForsch 32. Berlin 1976
Borchhardt *Myra:* Borchhardt, J. *Myra: eine lykische Metropole in antiker und byzantinischer Zeit*. IstForsch 30. Berlin 1975
Borchhardt, J., G. Neumann, and K. Schulz. 'Das Grabmal des Sohnes des Ta aus Hoiran in Zentrallykien.' *Öjh* 55 (1984) 68–131
Bossert, H.T. *Altanatolien*. Berlin 1942
Breccia, E. *La Necropoli di Sciatbi*. Cairo 1912
Broneer, O. *The Lion Monument at Amphipolis*. Cambridge 1941
Bruennow, R.E., and A. von Domazewski. See **B and D** above.
Bruno, V.J. *Form and Colur in Greek Painting*. London 1977
Bruns-Özgan, C. *Lykische Grabreleifs des 5. und 4. Jahrhunderts v. Chr,* Istmitt-BH 33. Tübingen 1987
Bryce, T.R. *The Lycians in Literary and Epigraphic Sources*. Copenhagen 1986
Burford, A. *The Greek Temple Builders at Epidauros*. Liverpool 1969
Burney, C. *From Village to Empire*. Oxford 1977
Buschor, E. *Maussollus und Alexander*. Munich 1986
Büsing *GrHalbs:* Büsing, H.H. *Die griechische Halbsäule*. Wiesbaden 1970
Butler *Sardis* I: Butler, H.C. *Sardis* 1. Publications of the American Society for the excavation of Sardis. Leyden 1922
Butler *Syria* II A: Butler, H.C. *Ancient Architecture in Syria*. Publications of the Princeton University Archaeological Expedition to Syria in 1904–5, Division II A. Leyden 1907
Cadoux, D.J. *Ancient Smyrna*. Oxford 1938

Cassels: Cassels, J. 'The Cemeteries of Cyrene.' *BSR* 23 (1955) 1–44
Ceka: Ceka, N. 'La ville illyrienne de la Basse-Selce.' *Iliria* 2 (Tirana 1972) 167–216
Charbonneaux, J.; R. Martin; and F. Villard. *Hellenistic Art 330–50 B.C.* London 1973
Childs, W.A.P. *The City-Reliefs of Lycia.* Princeton 1978
Christoffle, M. *Le Tombeau de la Chrétienne.* Paris 1951
Clara Rhodos: Rhodes. Instituto Storico-Archeologico. 1928–
Coarelli, F. *Guida archeologica di Roma.* Rome 1974
Colini, A.M. *I Sepolcri Reppublicani di Via Statilia.* Rome 1953
Cook, J.M., and W.H. Plommer. *The Sanctuary of Hemithea at Kastabos.* Cambridge 1966
Cook, R.M. *Greek Painted Pottery.* London 1972
Coulton, J.J. *The Architectural Development of the Greek Stoa.* Oxford 1976
Crema, L. *L'Architettura Romana.* Torino 1959
Dalman, C. *Petra und seine Felsheiligtümer.* Leipzig 1908
DarSag: Daremberg and Saglio. *Dictionnaire des Antiquités Greques et Romaines.* Paris 1904
Deltour-Levie, C. *Les Piliers Funéraires de Lycie.* Louvain-La Neuve 1982
Demus-Quatember *EtGrab:* Demus-Quatember, M. *Etruskische Grabarchitektur.* Baden-Baden 1958
Dennis, G. *The Cities and Cemeteries of Etruria* 1–2. London 1883
DeVries, K. *From Athens to Gordion.* Philadelphia 1980
Die Nabatäer. Exhibition catalogue. Bonn 1981
Dinsmoor: Dinsmoor, W.B. *The Architecture of Ancient Greece.* London 1950
Dragendorff, H. *Theraeische Graeber.* Berlin 1903
Duhoux, Y. *Le Disque de Phaestos.* Louvain 1977
Dunand, M.. R. Duru. *Oumm el-Amed.* Paris 1967
Dyggve, E. *Lindos: Fouilles et Recherches* II (Berlin 1952) and III–2 (Copenhagen 1960)
Dyggve, E., F. Poulsen, and K. Rhomaios. *Das Heroon von Kalydon.* Copenhagen 1934
Eichler, F. *Die Reliefs des Heroon von Gjölbaschi-Trysa.* Vienna 1950
Explorations Archéologiques de Délos 30. École Française d'Anthènes 1974
Fellows *Discov:* Fellows, C. *An Account of Discoveries in Lycia.* London 1841
Fink, J. *Die Kuppel über dem Viereck.* Munich 1958
Fouilles de Xanthos. See *FX* below.
Frank, T. *Roman Buildings of the Republic.* Rome 1924
Franke, P.R., and M. Hirmer. *Die griechische Münze.* Munich 1964
Fraser, P.M. *Ptolemaic Alexandria* 1–3. Oxford 1972
Fraser, P.M. *Rhodian Funerary Monuments.* Oxford 1977

Fraser, P.M., and G.E. Bean, *The Rhodian Peraea and Islands* (London 1954)
FX: Fouilles de Xanthos 1–5 (Paris 1958–74)
FX I: Demargne, P., P. Coupel, and P.. Prunet. *Les Piliers Funéraires.* Paris 1958
FX II: Metzger H., and P. Coupel. *L'Acropole Lycienne.* Paris 1963
FX III: Coupel P., and P. Demargne. *Le Monument des Néréides.* Paris 1969
FX IV: Metzger, H., L. von Bothmer, and J.N. Coldstream. *Les Céramiques Archaiques et Classiques de l'Acropole Lycienne.* Paris 1972
FX V: Demargne, P., P. Prunet, and P. Coupel. *Tombes-Maison, Tombes Rupestres et Sarcophages.* Paris 1974
Fyfe, T. *Hellenistic Architecture.* Cambridge 1936
Gajdukevic: Gajdukevic, V.F. *Das Bosporanische Reich.* Vienna 1974
von Gall *Felsgäber:* Gall, H. von. *Die paphlagonischen Felsgräber. IstMitt-BH.* Tübingen 1966
Gawlikowski, M. *Monuments Funéraires de Palmyre.* Warsaw 1970
Gerkan, A. von. *Von Antiker Architektur und Topographie – Gesammelte Aufsätze.* Stuttgart 1959
Gökoğlu, A. *Paphlagonia.* Kastamonu 1952
Gossel, B. 'Makedonische Kammergräber,' PhD diss. Munich 1979
Graeve, V. von. *Der Alexandersarkophag und seine Werkstatt. IstForsch* 28. Berlin 1970
Griffo, P. *Agrigento.* Palermo 1962
Gruben, G. *Die Tempel der Griechen.* Munich 1976
Gusmani, R. *Neue epichorische Schriftzeugnisse aus Sardis* Cambridge, MA, 1975
Ham, H.G., and C.B. Rüger, ed. *Die Numider.* Exhibition catalogue. Bonn 1979
Hamdy Bey, O., and T. Reinach. *Une Nécropole Royale à Sidon.* Paris 1892
Hanfmann: *BASOR.* Periodical reports on the campaign at Sardis
Hanfmann, G.M.A. *From Croesus to Constantine.* Ann Arbor 1975
– *Letters from Sardis.* Cambridge, MA, 1972
Harel, M. *This Is Jerusalem.* Jerusalem 1977
Haspels: Haspels, C.H.E. *The Highlands of Phrygia.* Princeton 1971
Havelock, C.M. *Hellenistic Art.* London 1971
Hellström, P., and T. Thieme. *Labraunda: The Zeus Temple.* Stockholm 1892
Herzfeld, E. *Archaeological History of Iran.* London 1935
– *Iran in the Ancient East.* London and New York 1941
Heuzey-Daumet: Heuzey, L., and H. Daumet. *Mission Archéologique de Macédoine.* Paris 1876
Hoddinott: Hoddinott, R.F. *Bulgaria in Antiquity.* London 1975
Hoddinott, R.F. *The Thracians.* London 1981
Hoepfner: Hoepfner, W. 'Das Grabmonument des Pythagoras aus Selymbria.' *AM* 88 (1973) 145–63

Idil, V. *Likya Lahitleri.* Ankara 1985

Jaussen, A., and R. Savignac. *Mission Archéologique en Arabie 1–2.* Paris 1909/ 1914

Jeppesen, K. *Labraunda* I¹. *The Propylaea.* Lund 1955

Jerusalem Revealed: Archaeology in the Holy City 1968–1974. Jerusalem 1975

Kähler, H. *Der grosse Fries von Pergamon.* Berlin 1948

– *Lindos.* Zurich 1971

Karageorghis, V. *Salamis in Cyprus.* London 1969

Kerameikos 12. Berlin 1980

Klammet, G. *Die türkische Westküste.* Munich 1975

Kleeman *Satrapensark:* Kleemann, I. *Der Satrapensarkophag aus Sidon.* Berlin 1958

Kleiner *Diadochen:* Kleiner, G. *Diadochen-Gräber.* Wiesbaden 1963

Kleiner, G. *Die Ruinen von Milet.* Berlin 1968

Kockel, V. *Die Grabbauten vor dem Herkulaner Tor in Pompeii.* Mainz on the Rhine 1984

Koenigs, W. 'Ein archaischer Rundbau in Kerameikos zu Athen.' PhD diss. Munich 1974

König, F.W. *Die Persika des Ktesias von Knidos.* Graz 1972

Kraeling, C.H. *Ptolemais: City of the Libyan Pentapolis.* Chicago 1962

Krencker, D., and W. Zschietzschmann. *Römische Tempel in Syrien 1.* Berlin 1938

Krischen, F. *Weltwunder der Baukunst in Babylonien und Jonien.* Tübingen 1956

Kubinska, J. *Les monuments funéraires dan les inscriptions grecques de l'Asie Mineure.* Warsaw 1968

Kurtz-Boardman: Kurtz, D.C. and J. Boardman. *Greek Burial Customs.* London 1971

Labraunda I¹: A. Westholm. 'The Architecture of the Hieron.' *Labraunda* I². Lund 1963

Lanckoronski, C. *Städte Pamphyliens und Pisidiens 2.* Vienna 1892

Lawrence GrArch:. Lawrence, A.W. *Greek Architecture.* London 1957

Lauer, J.P. *Le Mystère des Pyramides.* Paris 1974

Le Bas. Published by S. Reinach. *Voyage Archéologique en Grèce et en Asie Mineure 1842–1844.* Paris 1888

Le Coq, A. von. *Auf Hellas Spuren in Ostturkistan.* Leipzig 1926

Lehmann, K. *Samothrace: A Guide to the Excavations and the Museum.* New York 1966

Lehmann, P.W. *Samothrace 3: The Hieron.* Princeton 1969

Lindner, L. ed. *Petra und das Königreich der Nabatäer.* Nürnberg 1980

Loeb: The Loeb Classical Library

245 Selected Bibliography

LSJ: Liddell, H.G.; R. Scott; and H. Stuart-Jones. *Greek-English Lexicon.* 9th ed. Oxford 1940

Lyttleton *BArch:* Lyttelton, M. *Baroque Architecture in Classical Antiquity.* London 1974

Machatschek, A. *Die Nekropolen und Grabmäler in Gebiet von Elaiussa-Sebaste. DenkschrWien* 96. Vienna 1967

Mallwitz, A. *Die Bauten in Kabirenheiligtum bei Theben.* Berlin 1978

Marconi, P. *Agrigento.* Florence 1929

Martha, J. *L'Art Étrusque.* Paris 1889

Masson, O. *Les Fragments du Poete Hipponax.* Paris 1962

Mélanges Mansel 1–3. Ankara 1974

Mélanges Maspéro 1. Cairo 1935–8

Miller, S.G. 'Hellenistic Macedonian Architecture: Its Style and Painted Ornamentation.' PhD diss. Bryn Mawr College 1971

Minns: Minns, E.M. *Scythians and Greeks.* Cambridge 1913

Mnemosynon Th. Wiegand. Munich 1938

Möbius, H. *Die ostgriechischen Grabreliefs.* Mainz on the Rhine 1977

Morris, I. *Burial and Ancient Society.* Cambridge 1987

Mostafavi, S.M.T. *The Land of Pars.* Chippenham 1978

Müller, K.F. *Der Leichenwagen Alexanders des Grossen.* Leipzig 1905

Munk, P. *Palestine – Description Géographique, Historique et Archéologique.* Paris 1845

Nash, E. *Pictorial Dictionary of Ancient Athens* 1–2. Tübingen 1962

Naumann, R. *Architektur Kleinasiens.* Tübingen 1971

Negev, A. 'The Nabataeans and the Provincia Arabia.' *Aufstsief und Niedergang der römischen Welt* II. Principat 8. Berlin and New York 1977

Neumann, K. *Die Hellenen in Skythenlande.* Berlin 1855

Newton *Discoveries:* Newton, C.T. *A History of Discoveries at Halicarnassus, Cnidus and Branchidae.* London 1862

Newton, C.T. *Essays on Art and Archaeology.* London 1880

– *Travels and Discoveries in the Levant* 1–2. London 1865

Nicholls: Nicholls, R.V. 'Old Smyrna: The Iron Age Fortifications and Associated Remains on the City Perimeter.' *BSA* 53–54 (1958–9) 35–137

Nicolaou, K. *Ancient Monuments of Cyprus.* Nicosia 1968

Noshy, I. *The Arts in Ptolemaic Egypt.* London 1937

Nylander *Ionians:* Nylander, C. *Ionians at Pasargadae.* Uppsala 1970

OCT: Oxford Classical Texts

Odenthal, J. *Syrien.* Cologne 1982

Öst Archäol Inst Grabungen: Österreichisches Archäologisches Institut (Vienna) Grabungen

OlForsch: Olympische Forschungen. 1944–

Orlandos, A.K. *H Arkadike Alipheira*. Athens 1967–8

Orsi: Orsi, P. 'Gela.' *MonAnt* 17 (1906)

Pacho, J.R. *Relation d'un Voyage dans la Marmarique, la Cyrénaique* 1–2.
Paris 1827

Pagenstecher, R. *Nekropolis*. Leipzig 1919

Parrot, A. *The Arts of Assyria*. New York 1961

Peck, W. *Griechische Versinschriften*. Berlin 1955

Pekridou, A. *Das Alkestas-Grab in Termessos*. *IstMitt-BH* 32 Tübingen 1986

Perrot-Chipiez Hist: Perrot, G., and C. Chipiez. *Histoire de l'Art dans l'Anti-
quité* I-x. Paris 1882–90

Pesche, G. *Il Palazzo delle Colonne in Tolemaide*. Rome 1960

Petersen and von Luschan Reisen: Petersen E., and F. von Luschan. *Reisen
in Lykien, Milyas und Kibyratien* 2. Gesellschaft für Archaeologische
Erforschung Kleinasiens. Vienna 1889

Petsas, P. *O Taphos to Lefkadion*. Athens 1966

Pfuhl, E., and H. Möbius. *Die ostgriechischen Grafreliefs*. Mainz on the Rhine
1977

Poinssot, C. *Les Ruines de Dougga*. Tunis 1958

Pyl, K. T. *Die griechischen Rundbauten*. Griefswald 1861

Quilici, L. *La Via Appia da Roma a Bovillae*. Rome 1977

RE: Pauly-Wissowa, *Real-Encyclopadie der klassischen Altertumswissenschaft*
Recueil Plassart. Paris 1976

Reuer, E., and O. Schottenhalm. *Das Mausoleum von Belevi. Forschungen in
Ephesos* 6, Vienna 1979

Rhodes. See **Clara Rhodos** above.

Rhomaios, K.A. *Makedonikos Taphos tes Verginas*. Athens 1951

Richter, G.M.A. *The Archaic Gravestones of Attica*. London 1961

Robertson, M. *History of Greek Art* 1–2. Cambridge 1975

Rolland, H. *Le Mausoleé de Glanum*. 21st Suppl. to *Gallia*. Paris 1969

Roma Medio Repubblicana. Exhibition catalogue. Rome 1973

Romanelli, P. *Topografia e Archeologia dell'Africa Romana. Enciclopedia Classica* 3. Torino 1970

Roos Caunus: Roos, P. *The Rock-cut Tombs of Caunus* 1–2. Göteborg 1972

Roos, P. *Survey of Rock-cut Chamber-Tombs in Caria*. 1: *South-eastern Caria
and the Lycio-Carian Borderland*. Göteborg 1985

Rosi: Rosi, G. 'Sepulchral Architecture as Illustrated by the Rock Façades
of Central Etruria.' *JRS* I, 15–15 (1924–5) 1–59 and II, 16–17 (1926–7)
59–96

Ross, L. *Inselreisen* 1. Stuttgart 1840

Rossetto, P.C. *Il Sepolcro del Fornaio Marco Virgilio Eurisace a Porta Maggiore*.
Rome 1973

Roussel, P. *Les Cultes Egyptiens à Delos*. Paris 1916

Roux, G. *L'Architecture de l'Argolide aux ive et iiie siècles avant J.C*. Paris 1961

Rowe, A. *Cyrenaeican Expedition of the University of Manchester 1952*. Manchester 1959

Şahin: Şahin, M.C. *Die Entwicklung der griechischen Monumentalaltäre*. Munich 1972

Saladino, V. *Der Sarkophag des Lucius Cornelius Scipio Barbatus*. Würzburg 1970

Sartiaux, F. *De la Nouvelle à l'Ancienne Phocée*. Paris 1914

Schaal, H. *Ostia der Welthafen Roms*. Bremen 1957

Schaefer, H., and W. Andrae. *Die Kunst des alten Orients*. Berlin 1925

Schmidt, E. *Geschichte der Karyatide*. Würzburg 1982

Schmidt Persepolis iii: Schmidt, E.F. *Persepolis iii – The Royal Tombs and Other Monuments*. Chicago 1970

Schmidt-Dounas, B. *Der Lykische Sarkophag aus Sidon, IstMitt-*bh 30. Tübingen 1985

Schmitt, H.H. *Rom und Rhodos*. Munich 1957

Schöber, A. *Der Fries des Hekateions von Lagina*. Baden bei Wien 1922

Scullard, H.H. *The Etuscan Cities and Rome*. London 1967

Seiler, F. *Die griechische Tholos*. Mainz 1986

Shahbazi, A.S. *The Irano-Lycian Monuments*. Teheran 1975

Société Archéologique d'Alexandrie, Bulletin

Steingräber, S., *Etrurien*. Munich 1981

Stucchi: Stucchi, S. *Architettura Cirenaica*. Rome 1974

Studia in Memoriam K. Skorpil. Sofia 1961

Studies in the History of Art 10. Symposium Series i, b. Barr-Shamar and E.N. Borza, eds, *Macedonia and Greece in Late Classical and Early Hellenistic Times*. Washington 1982

Studies Presented to G.M.A. Hanfmann. Mainz 1971

Stutzer, H.A. *Das antike Rom*. Cologne 1979

Tacconi, V.S. *Territorio e Architettura a Sesto Fiorentino*. Florence 1978

Tarn, W.W. *Hellenistic Civilization*. Cleveland and New York 1968

Texier, C. *Asie Mineure*. Paris 1862

Texier-Pullan: Texier, C., and P. Pullan. *Description de l'Asie Mineure* 3. Paris 1849

***Thera** ii:* Hiller von Gaertringen and others. *Thera* ii. Berlin 1902

The Search for Alexander. Exhibition catalogue. Boston 1980

Thiersch, H. *Painted Tombs in the Necropolis of Marissa* (Mareshah). London 1905

– *Pharos, Antike, Islam und Occident*. Leipzig and Berlin 1909

– *Zwei antike Grabanlagen bei Alexandria*. Berlin 1904

Torelli, M. *Etruria*. Rome and Bari 1980

Toynbee, J.M.C. *Death and Burial in the Roman World*. New York 1982

Tsanova, G., and L. Getov. *Trakista Grobnitsa pri Kazanluk*. Sofia 1970

Vanden Berghe, L, *Archéologie de l'Iran Ancien*. Leiden 1959

Vaulina, M., and A. Wasowicz. *Bois Grecs et Romains de l'Ermitage*. Wroclaw 1974

Vermeule, C.C. *Roman Imperial Art in Greece and Asia Minor*. Cambridge, MA, 1968

Vincent, L.H. *Jérusalem de l'Ancien Testament* 1. Paris 1954

Voigtländer, W. *Der jüngste Apollontempel von Didyma. IstMitt-BH* 14. Tübingen 1975

Vollmoeller, K.G. *Griechische Kammergräber mit Totenbetten*. Bonn 1901

Wagner, P. *Der ägyptische Einfluss auf die phönizische Architektur*. Bonn 1980

Walter, H. *Das Heraion von Samos*. Munich 1976

Watzinger, C. *Griechische Holzsarkophage aus der Zeit Alexanders des Grossen*. Leipzig 1905

– *Denkmäler Palästinas* 1–2. Leipzig 1935

Waywell, G.B. *The Free-standing Sculptures of the Mausoleum at Halikarnassos in the British Museum*. London 1978

Welter, G. *Aigina*. Berlin 1938

Wenning, R. *Die Nabatäer – Denkmäler und Geschichte*. Göttingen 1987

Westholm, A. *Labraunda* I². 'The Architecture of the Hieron'. Lund 1963

Young, R.S. *Gordion: A Guide to the Excavations and Museum*. Ankara 1968

– *Three Great Early Tumuli*. Philadelphia 1981

Zahle-Kjeldsen *CentrLycia:* Zahle J., and K. Kjeldsen. 'A Dynastic Tomb in Central Lycia. (New Evidence for the Study of Lycian Architecture in the Classical Period).' *ActaArch* 47 (1976) 29–46

Zhivkova, L. *Das Grabmal von Kazanlak*. Recklinghausen 1973

Zschietzschmann, W. *Wettkampf und Übungstätten in Griechenland*. Stuttgart 1960

ILLUSTRATIONS

1 Tomb types in Lycia. Fellows *Discov* 128–30

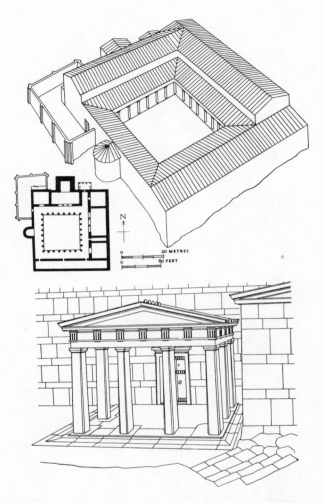

2 Kalydon, Heroon. E. Dyggve, F. Poulsen, and K. Rhomaios, *Das Heroon von Kalydon* (Copenhagen 1934) fig. 100

3 Nea-Paphos (Cyprus), Hellenistic peristyle tomb

a

4 Pasargadai, Tomb of Cyrus: a / general view; b / plan and elevation;
c / elevations and profile of cornice; d / plans and section drawings.
a–b / Nylander *Ionians* (1970) figs 30 and 31; c–d / *Iran* 2 (1964)
23 figs 1 and 2

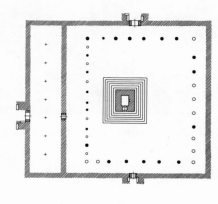

b

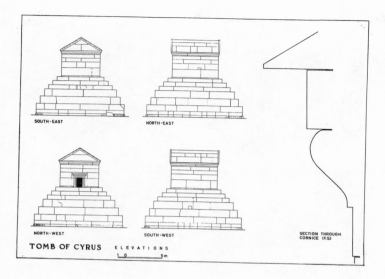

SOUTH-EAST   NORTH-EAST

NORTH-WEST   SOUTH-WEST   SECTION THROUGH CORNICE (F.S.)

TOMB OF CYRUS   ELEVATIONS
1 0   5m

c

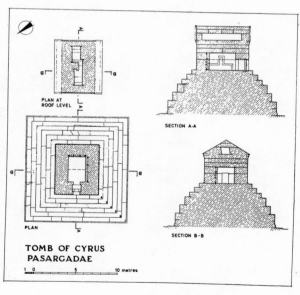

PLAN AT ROOF LEVEL

SECTION A-A

PLAN

SECTION B-B

**TOMB OF CYRUS
PASARGADAE**

1 0   5   10 metres

d

a

5 Buzpar, Persian tomb: a / general views; b / plans and elevations. a–b / *Iran* 2 (1964) pl 3 and fig. 3

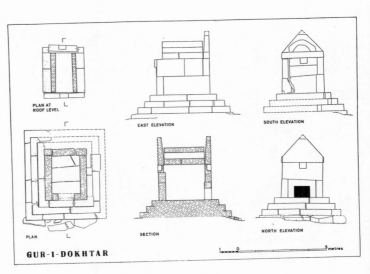

b

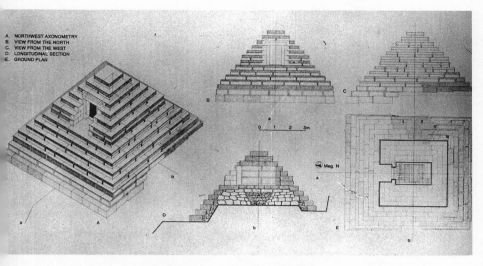

A. NORTHWEST AXONOMETRY
B. VIEW FROM THE NORTH
C. VIEW FROM THE WEST
D. LONGITUDINAL SECTION
E. GROUND PLAN

6 Sardis, stepped Pyramid Tomb. Hanfmann *Letters* (1972) fig. 192

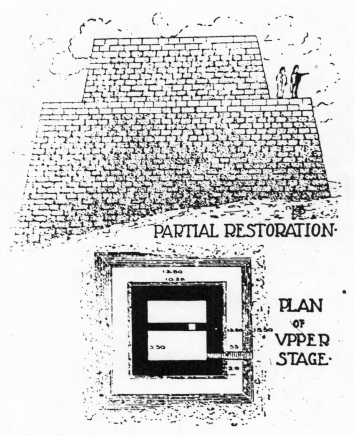

PARTIAL RESTORATION·

PLAN
OF
VPPER
STAGE·

7 Is-Safiyeh (Syria), stepped pyramid. Butler *Syria* II A, 125

8 Midas City, Pyramid Tomb. Haspels fig. 37

9 Amrith, Phoenician funerary monuments. J. Odenthal, *Syrien*
(Cologne 1982) fig. 31

10 Amrith, tomb with a pyramidal top. Perrot-Chipiez *Hist* v fig. 98

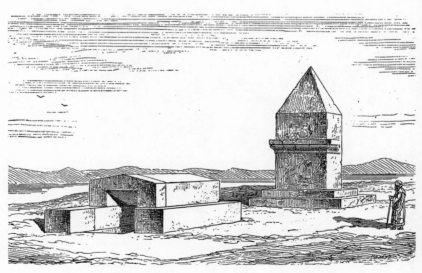

11 Region of Amrith, the so-called Burdj el-Bezzak tomb. Perrot-Chipiez *Hist* v
fig. 99

12 Etruria, stepped circular tomb. *MonInst* 1 (1832) pl. 41

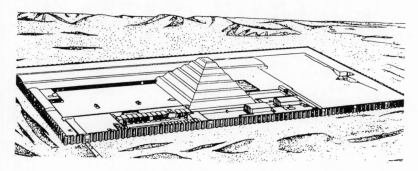

13 Egypt (Saqqara), stepped pyramid of Djoser. W. Wolf, *Die Kunst Aegyptens* (Stuttgart 1957) fig. 64

14 Assyria, obelisk-like victory stele. A. Moortgart, *Die Kunst des alten Mesopotamien* (Cologne 1967) fig. 251

15 Egypt (Deir el-Medineh), smooth-sided pyramids. J.P. Lauer, *Le Mystère des Pyramides* (Paris 1974) fig. 35

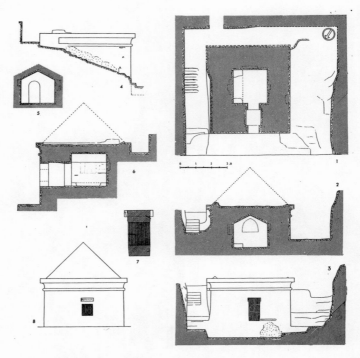

16 Jerusalem, Tomb of the Pharaoh's Daughter. N. Avigad, *Ancient Monuments in the Kidron Valley* (Jerusalem 1954) fig. 14

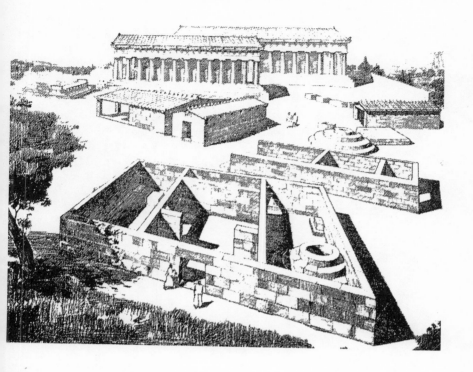

17 Akragas (Agrigento), stepped circular altar. G. Gruben, *Die Tempel der Griechen* (Munich 1976) fig. 244

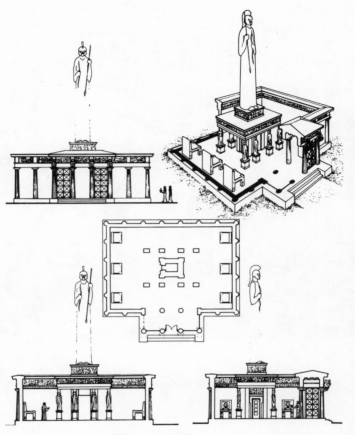

18 Amyklai, Throne of Apollo, proposed reconstruction. *RA* (1976/1) fig. 7

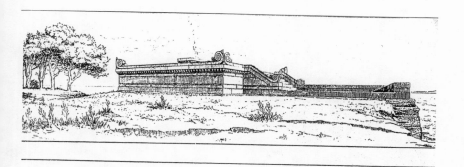

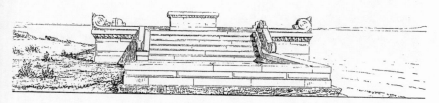

19 Monodendri, monumental altar. F. Krischen, *Weltwunder der Baukunst in Babylonien und Jonien* (Tübingen 1956) 35

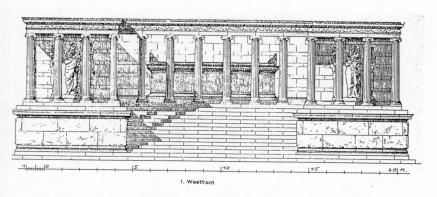

1. Westfront

20 Magnesia-on-the-Maeander, monumental columnar altar. Şahin fig. 23

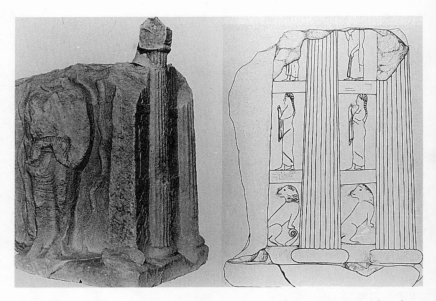

21 Sardis, columnar shrine to Kybele. G.M.A. Hanfmann, 'Greece and Lydia:
The Impact of Hellenic Culture,' *Huitième Cong. Intern. d'Archéologie Classique*
(Paris 1965) 495 figs 1–3

22 Fiechter's reconstruction of the Throne of Apollo at Amyklai. *RA* (1976/1) fig. 3

23 Tomb of Porsenna, reconstruction proposals. F. Messerschmitt, 'Das Grabmal des Porsenna,' *Das Neue Bild der Antike* (1942) 58 figs 4 and 5

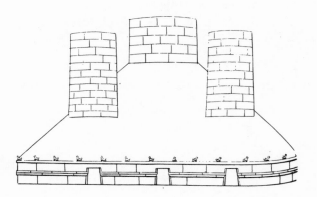

25 The Cucumella at Vulci, proposed reconstruction. E.C. Gray, *Tour to the Sepulchres of Etruria* (London 1841) 300

a

24 Albano: a / view of the monumental tomb on the Via Appia; b / proposed reconstruction of the monumental tomb on the Via Appia. b / J. Durm, *Die Baukunst der Griechen* (Leipzig 1910) 143

b

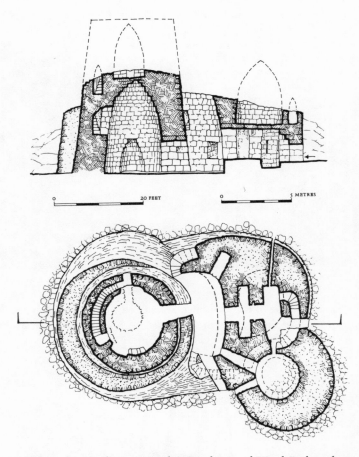

26 Palmavera, Sardinian nuraghe. Boethius and Ward-Perkins fig. 5

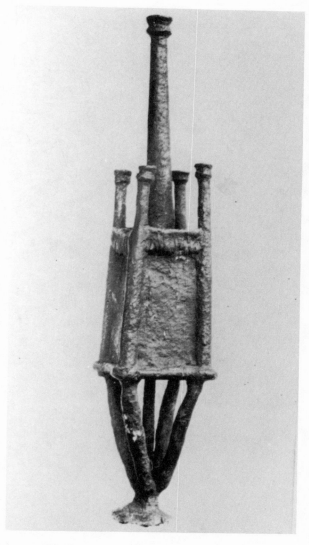

27 Bronze model of a nuraghe type of construction. *BdA* 65 (1984) 68

28 Phaistos Disk. *BCH* 99 (1975) 33

29 Xanthos, Inscribed Pillar. *AA* 85 (1970) 378 fig. 31

30 Antiphellos, elevated sarcophagus

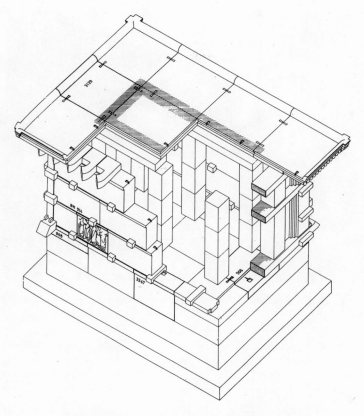

31 Xanthos, heroon 'G'. *RA* (1976/1) 260 fig. 16

32 Apollonia (Lycia), dynastic tomb. *ActaArch* 47 (1976) 30 fig. 1

33 Xanthos, heroon 'F.' *FX* II fig. 27

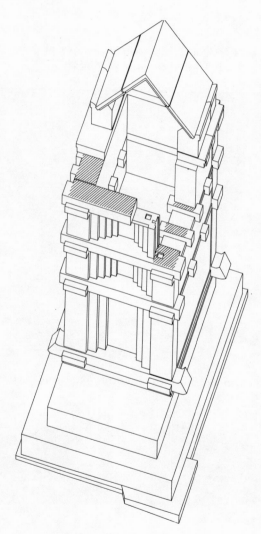

34 Xanthos, heroon 'H.' FX II fig. 24

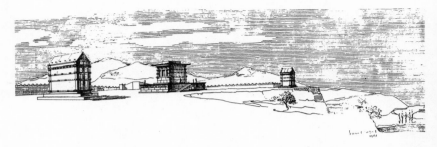

35 Xanthos, heroa 'F,' 'G,' and 'H,' reconstructed view of the site with heroon 'G' in the centre. *FX* II fig 28

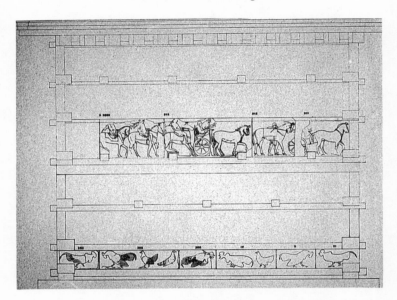

36 Xanthos, heroon 'G', proposed reconstruction. *Syria* 42 (1965) 267 fig. 2

37 Sardis, Pactolus pediment. *BASOR* 245 (Winter 1982) fig. 25

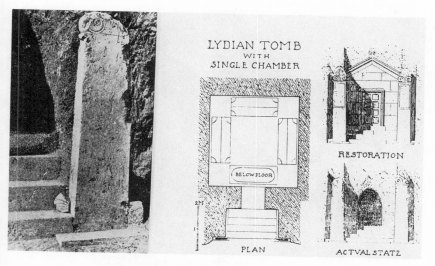

38 Sardis, Lydian chamber tomb. *RA* (1976/1) fig. 4

39 Kaunos, façade of the unfinished tomb B2 (the largest of the group)
on the right

40 Midas City, Midas Monument. Haspels fig. 8

41 Köhnüş (Phrygia), Lion Tomb. Haspels fig. 131

42 Naqsh-i-Rustam, rock-cut Persian royal tomb. Perrot-Chipiez *Hist* v fig. 34

a

43 Eski Foça, Taş Kule: a / general view; b / plan; c / section elevation.
b–c / Perrot-Chipiez *Hist* v figs 40 and 41

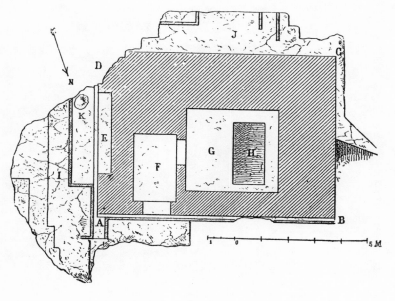

b

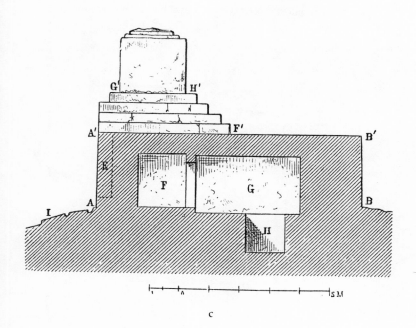

c

a

44 Tomb of St Charalambos near Magnesia ad Sipylum: a / general view;
b / plan. Perrot-Chipiez *Hist* v figs 40 and 41

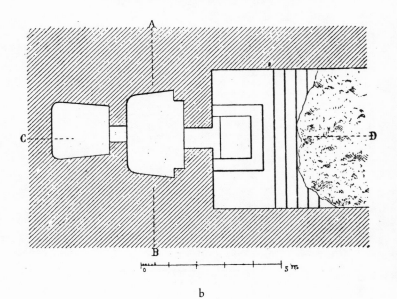

b

45 Paphlagonia, Kalekapi tomb. AA 82 (1967) 586 fig. 1

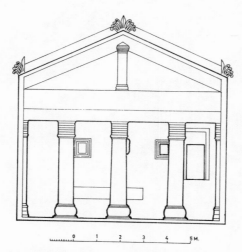

46 Paphlagonia, Gerdek Boğazi tomb at Karakoyunlu. Von Gall *Felsgräber* 74 fig 8

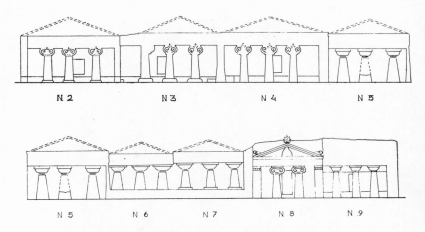

N 2   N 3   N 4   N 5

N 5   N 6   N 7   N 8   N 9

47 Cyrene, rock-cut tombs, N₂–N₉. Stucchi fig. 28

48 Egypt (Beni Hassan), rock-cut tombs. Perrot-Chipiez *Hist* I fig. 167

49 Gordion, Great Tumulus, distant view

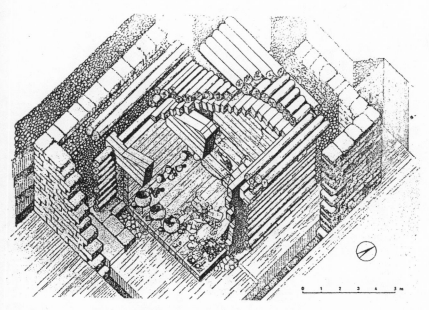

50 Gordion, Great Tumulus, tomb chamber. B. Hronda, *Handbuch der Archäologie* 1 (Munich 1971) fig. 90

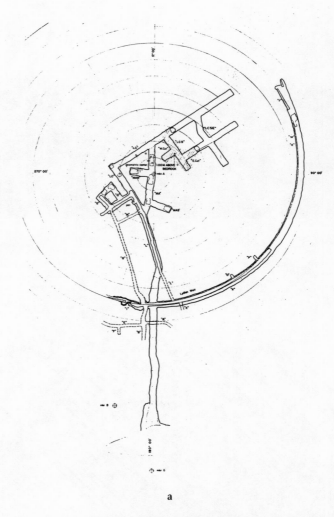

a

51 Sardis, tumulus of Gyges: a / plan; b / inside girdle. Hanfmann *Letters*
(1972) figs 109 and 112

b

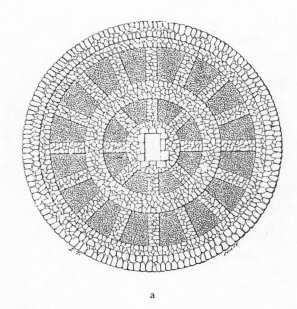

a

52 Bayrakli (ancient Smyrna), Tomb of Tantalos: a / plan; b / reconstruction.
Perrot-Chipiez *Hist* v figs 14 and 15

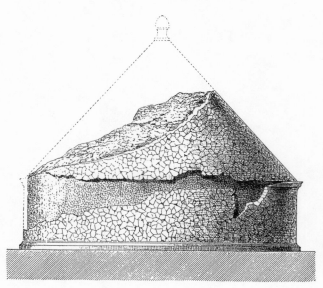

b

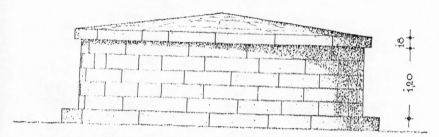

53 Corfu, cenotaph of Menekrates. *Mnemosynon Th. Wiegand* (1938) 52 fig. 6

54 Cyrene, built tumulus. Stucchi fig. 73

55 Lindos, Tomb of Kleoboulos. *Lindos* 3 (1960) 507 fig. 13⁷ and 13⁸

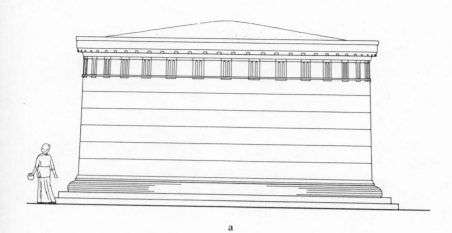

a

56 Kerameikos, 'Rundbau': a / reconstruction according to W. Koenigs;
b / entablature. a–b / *Kerameikos* 12 (Berlin 1980) pls 9 and 10

b

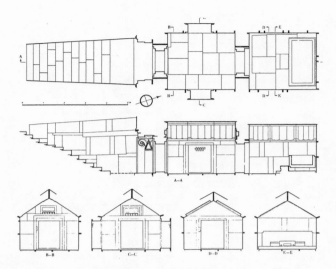

57 Cyprus, Royal Tomb v. *OpArch* 2 (1941) 37 fig. 10

58 Mycenae, Treasury of Atreus. Sir B. Fletcher, *A History of Architecture* (London 1975) 190C

59 Xanthos, Nereid Monument, view today

60 Xanthos, Nereid Monument, southeast corner of the podium

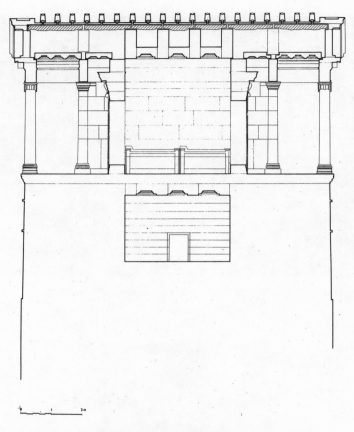

61 Xanthos, Nereid Monument, cross-section. FX III² pl. 42

62 Xanthos, Nereid Monument, restored view. FX III² pl. 100

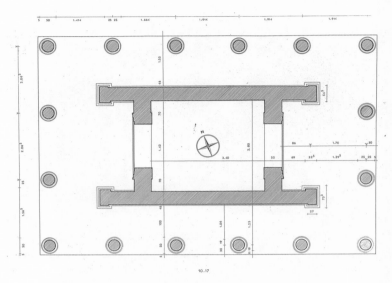

63 Xanthos, Nereid Monument, plan. *FX* III² pl. 43

64 Akragas (Agrigento), temple of Zeus Olympios (model)

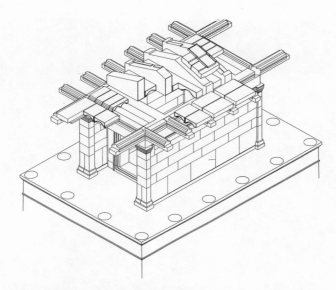

65 Xanthos, Nereid Monument, roof-construction. FX III² pl. 41

66 Xanthos, Nereid Monument, east pediment FX III² pl. 98

67 Xanthos, Nereid Monument, reconstruction in the British Museum

68 Limyra, fourth-century heroon, actual state

69 Limyra, fourth-century heroon, restored view of complex. AA 85 (1970)
357 fig. 2

70 Limyra, fourth-century heroon, west side. Borchhardt *Bauskulptur* fig. 25

71 Athens, Erechtheion, Karyatid Porch

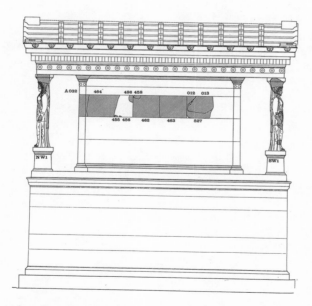

72 Limyra, fourth-century heroon, north side. Borchhardt *Bauskulptur* fig. 23

73 Delphi, Siphnian treasury

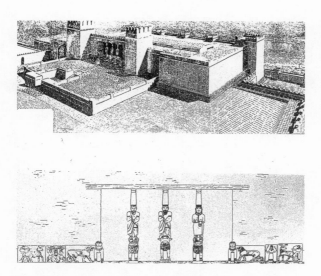

74 Tell Halaf, entrance gate to the temple palace. AA 85 (1970) 368

75 Limyra, fourth-century heroon, acroteria of northern façade.
Antalya Museum

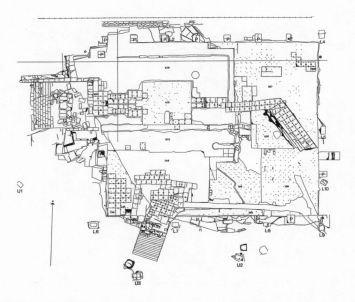

76 The Mausoleum at Halikarnassos, plan. *IstMitt* 26 (1976) suppl. 1

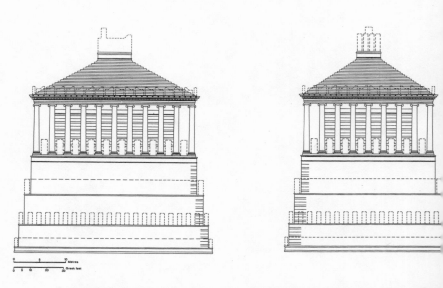

77 The Mausoleum at Halikarnassos, proposed reconstruction. G.B. Waywell, *The Free-standing Sculptures of the Mausoleum at Halikarnassos in the British Museum* (London 1978) figs 8 and 9

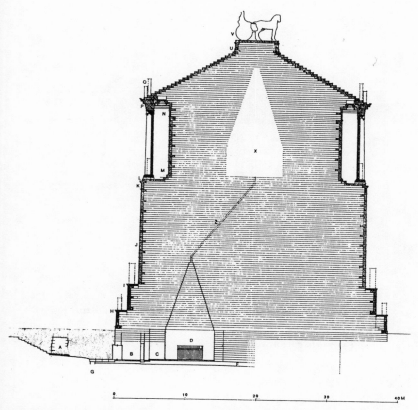

78 The Mausoleum at Halikarnassos, cross-section. *IstMitt* 26 (1976) 55 fig. 4

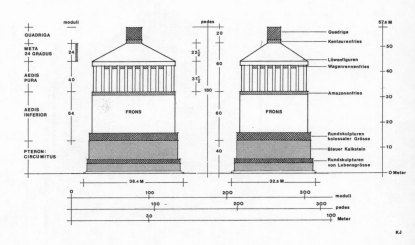

a

79 The Mausoleum at Halikarnassos: a / Jeppesen's reconstruction with measurements; b / Jeppesen's reconstruction of the east side; c / model of the monument with its enclosure. a–c / *IstMitt* 26 (1976) suppl. 2 figs. 13 and 25

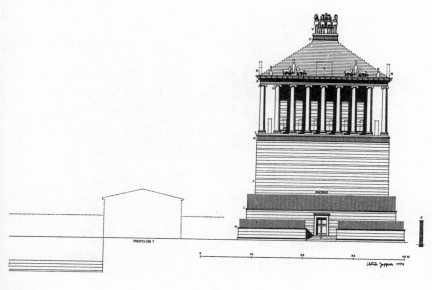

b

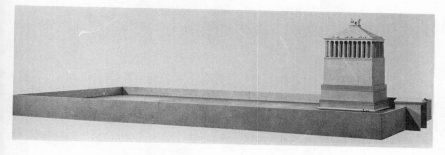

c

80 Labraynda, monumental tomb, drawings of Le Bas. Le Bas (1888) pl. ii-9

81 Labraynda, monumental tomb, general view. *Labraunda* I² (1963) fig. 56

82 Labraynda, monumental tomb, interior. *Labraunda* I² (1963) fig. 58

a

83 Labraynda, monumental tomb, entrance side: a / distant view;
b / close-up view

b

84 Labraynda, monumental tomb, view of gneiss slabs

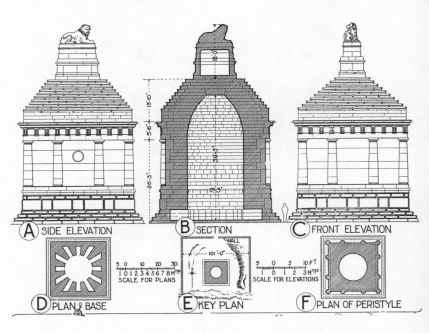

85 The Lion Tomb at Knidos, reconstruction. Sir B. Fletcher, *A History of Architecture* (London 1975) 160 A-F

86 The Lion Tomb at Knidos, core of the structure

87 The Lion Tomb at Knidos, interior

88 The Lion Tomb at Knidos, lion. British Museum

89 The Lion Tomb at Knidos, traces of the temenos wall

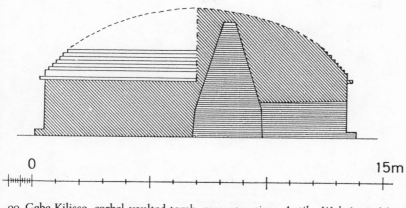

90 Gebe Kilisse, corbel-vaulted tomb, reconstruction. *Antike Welt* (1975/3) 16
fig. 25

91 Amphipolis, Lion Tomb. *BCH* 63–65 (1939–41) 37 fig. 19

92 Alinda, monumental tomb. Drawing after Büsing *GrHalbs* pl. 29

a

93 Kaş, monumental tomb: a / general view; b / entablature.
Photo by F.E. Winter

b

94 Syracuse Museum (Italy), funerary cippus. G.V. Gentili, 'Resti di un grande mausoleo e ellenistico a Siracusa,' *Archivio Storico Siracusano* 13–14 (Syracuse 1967–8) pl 4[1]

95 Turğut (Rhodian Peraea), partly rebuilt tomb. Fraser and Bean (1954) pl. 11

96 Belevi Mausoleum, side view of the rock-cut core

a

97 Belevi Mausoleum: a / view of south side with recess for tomb chamber;
b / reconstructed tomb chamber. b / *Öjh* 29 (1935) fig. 51

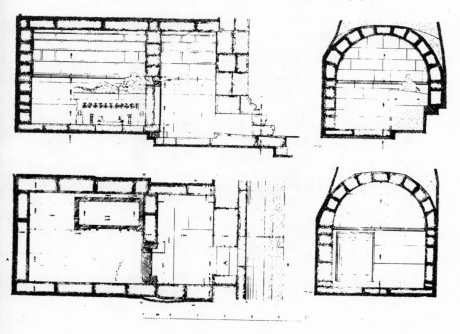

b

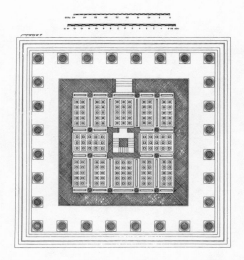

98 Belevi Mausoleum, plan of the upper storey. *Forschungen in Ephesos* 6 (Vienna 1979) fig. 21

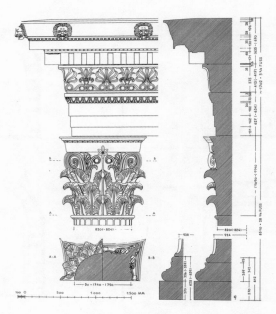

99 Belevi Mausoleum, entablature. *Forschungen in Ephesos* 6 (Vienna 1979) fig. 32

100 Belevi Mausoleum, present state of upper floor

a

101 Belevi Mausoleum: a / reconstructed view of the north side; b / cross-section. a / Praschniker (1948) 273 pl. 1; b / *Forschungen in Ephesos* 6 (Vienna 1979) pl. 10

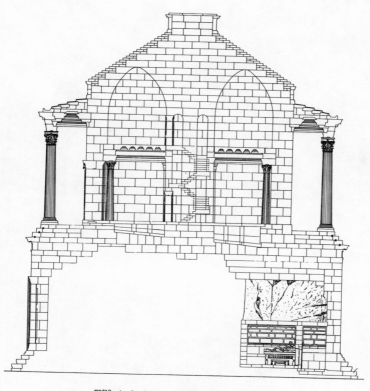

b

102 Belevi Mausoleum, unfinished moulding

103 Island of Kos, Charmyleion, restored elevation of façade. *Jdl* 49 (1934) 117 fig. 5

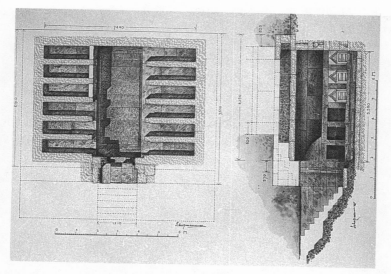

104 Island of Kos, Charmyleion, plan and cross-section of basement. *Jdl* 49 (1934) 114 fig. 2

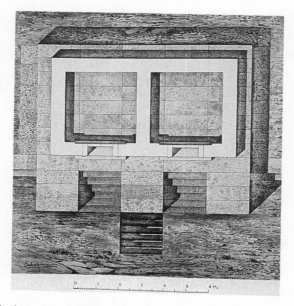

105 Island of Kos, Charmyleion, plan of ground floor. *Jdl* 49 (1934) 112 fig. 1

106 Lindos, Archokrateion, view of the tomb façade today

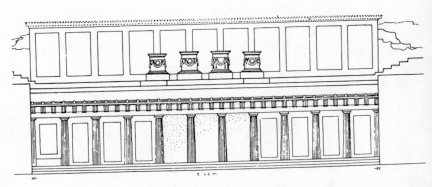

107 Lindos, Archokrateion, reconstructed view of the façade. H. Kähler, *Lindos* (1971) fig. 10

108 Rhodes, monumental tomb at Rhodini, general view

109 Rhodes, rock-cut tomb façade at Rhodini

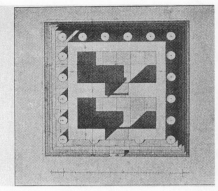

110 The Ta Marmara tomb near Didyma, reconstruction and plan. *AA* 17 (1902) 150 figs. 5 and 6

111 Diocaesarea-Olba, tomb of a priest king, general view today

112 Gölbaşi-Trysa, heroon, reconstructed view. *AntW* (1971/4) fig. 1

113 Gölbaşi-Trysa, heroon, general view of the south wall. Model from
Benndorf-Niemann, *Gjölbaschi* (1889) fig. 2

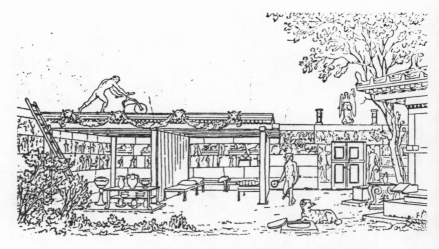

114 Gölbaşi-Trysa, heroon, 'cult corner,' Benndorf-Niemann, *Gjölbaschi* fig. 31

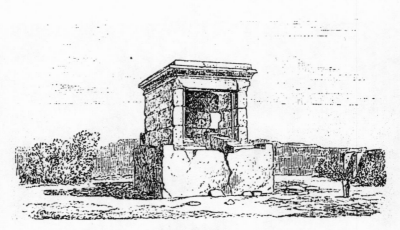

115 El Maabed, Syria, heroon. Perrot-Chipiez *Hist* III (1885) fig. 40

a

116 Miletos, heroon on the theatre hill: a / view today; b / plan of complex.
b / Kurtz-Boardman fig. 71

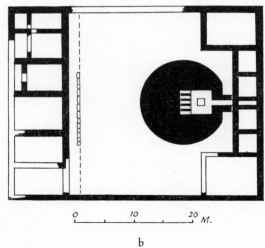

b

117 Termessos, tomb of Alkestas, view today

118 Termessos, tomb of Alkestas, drawings of the interior. Lanckoronski (1892)
fig. 16, 17

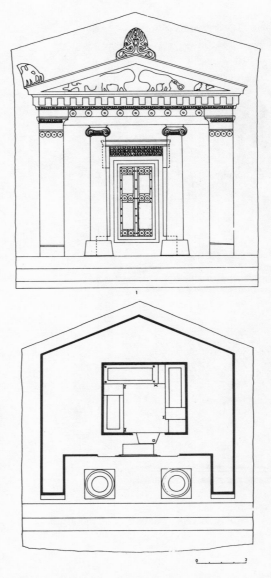

119 Kaunos, Ionic façade-tomb. Roos *Caunus* pl. 36).

120 Telmessos, Tomb of Amyntas

121 Myra, general view of river necropolis

122 Myra, Tomb no. 69. Texier-Pullan pl. 46

a

123 Myra, Tomb no. 69, back wall of the porch: a / actual state; b / drawing.
b / Texier-Pullan pl. 225

b

124 Gerdek Kaya (Phrygia), rock-cut tomb. Haspels pl 85

125 Maziköy (Kappadocia), rock-cut tombs. *CRAI* (January–March 1977) 105
fig. 6

126 Maziköy (Kappadocia), tomb with large 'frieze,' CRAI [January–March 1977]) 107 fig. 7

127 Dikili Taş (Kappadocia), monumental tomb, drawing. Texier-Pullan pl. 92

128 Amaseia, aedicula type of rock-cut tombs. *AA* 82 (1967) 594 fig. 10

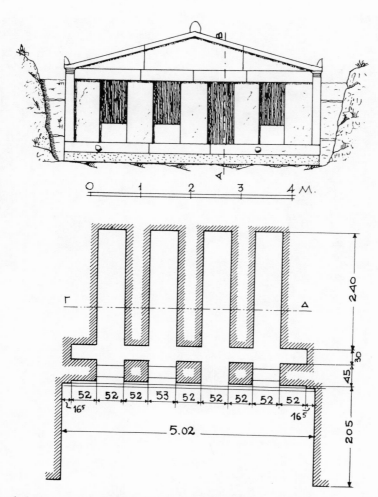

129 Alipheira, monumental tomb, plan, and façade. A.K. Orlandos, *H Arkadike Alipheira* (Athens 1967–8) fig. 142

130 Vergina, Ionic tomb

131 Lefkadia-Naoussa, Ionic tomb. *AAA* 6 (1973) 89 fig. 2

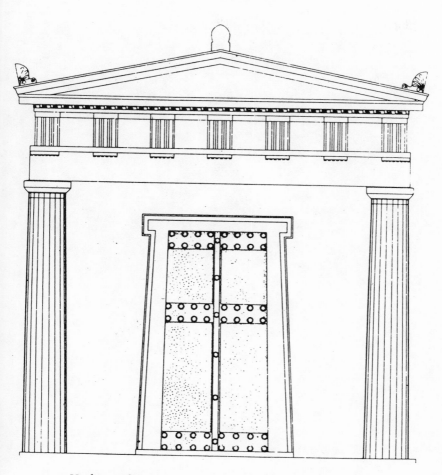

132 Haghios Athanasios, Doric tomb. *Makedonika* 15 (1975) fig. 25

133 Dion, tomb, exterior with Doric frieze

134 Dion, tomb, Ionic column in the interior

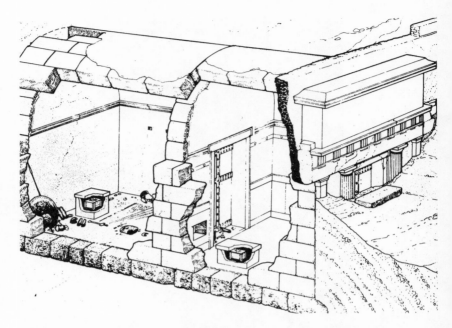

135 Vergina, Great Tumulus, Tomb II. M. Andronikos, *The Royal Graves at Vergina* (Athens 1980) 36 fig. 22

136 Region of Vergina, Tomb no. I. *AJA* 88 (1984) pl. 19 fig. 9

137 Region of Vergina, Tomb no. III. *AJA* 88 (1984) pl. 19 fig. 10

138 Lefkadia, Great Tomb, façade. Kurtz-Boardman fig. 75

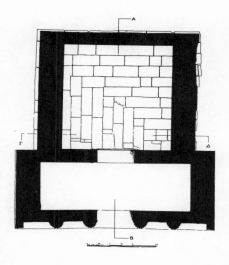

a

139 Lefkadia, Great Tomb: a / plan; b / interior of main chamber. a–b / RA
(1968/1) 178 figs 5 and 6

b

140 Macedonia, the Lyson and Kallikles tomb. *Archaeology* 37 (1974) 255

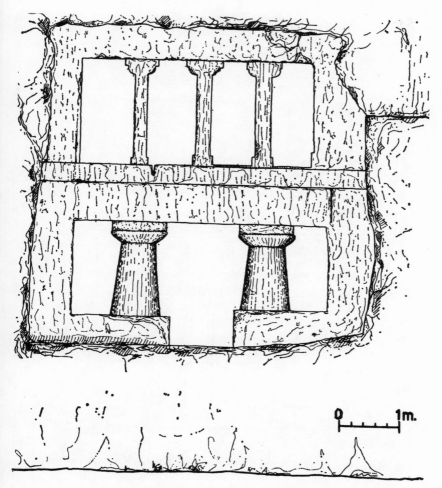

141 Barka (Cyrenaica), tomb façade. Stucchi fig. 30

142 Canosa, Tomb no. 3, façade. After Gerhard on the tombs at Canosa *AZ* (1857) pl. 104

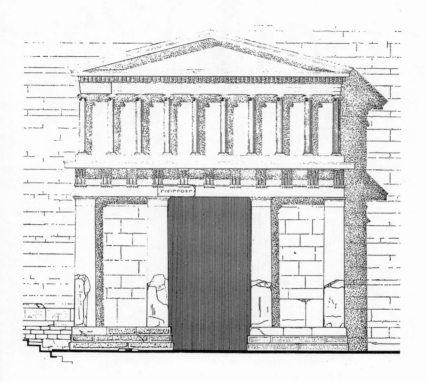

143 Thasos, gate of Zeus and Hera. *RA* (1968–9) 173 fig. 1

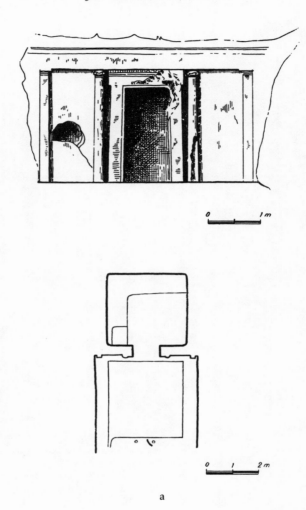

a

144 Basse-Selce (Albania), Tomb 1: a / drawings of façade and plan; b / façade today. a–b / Ceka pl. 9 and fig. 5

b

a

145 Basse-Selce (Albania), Tomb 2: a / drawing of exterior and cross-section;
b / exterior today. a–b / Ceka pl. 10 and fig. 6

b

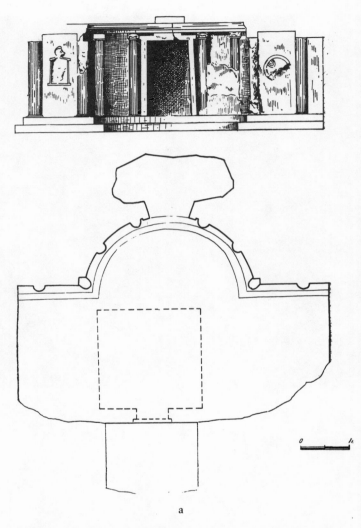

a

146 Basse-Selce (Albania), Tomb 3: a / drawing of exterior and plan; b / exterior today. a–b / Ceka pl. 11 and fig. 7

b

147 Basse-Selce (Albania), Tomb 3, details. Ceka pl. 12

148 Basse-Selce (Albania), Tomb 4. Ceka fig. 12

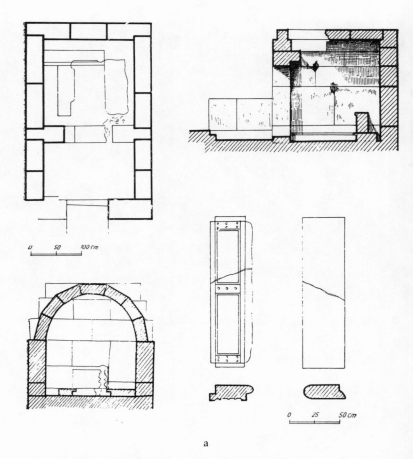

a

149 Basse-Selce (Albania), built vaulted tomb: a / details; b / view today.
a–b / Ceka fig. 15 and pl. 14

b

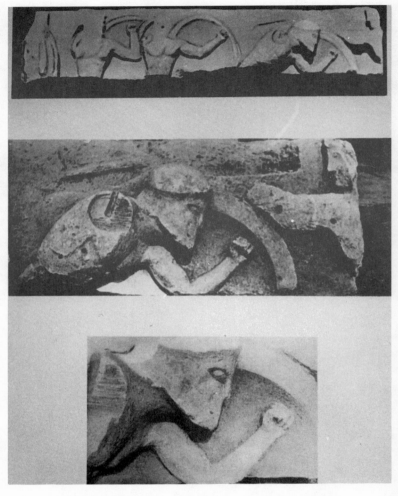

150 Albania, relief from Apollonia. *Albania* 5 (1935) pl. 15

151 Canosa, Tomb no. 3: F.T. Bertocchi, *La pittura funeraria Apula* (Naples 1964) figs 10 and 11. Reconstruction of the façade by Bonucci (on the right)

152 Canosa, Tomb no. 2, interior. F.T. Bertocchi, *La pittura funeraria Apula* (Naples 1964) fig. 9

a

153 Sovana, Tomba Ildebranda: a / view today; b / restored façade and plan.
b / Boethius-Ward-Perkins fig. 18

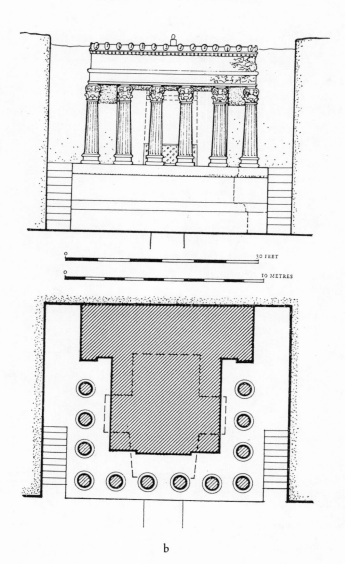

30 FEET

10 METRES

b

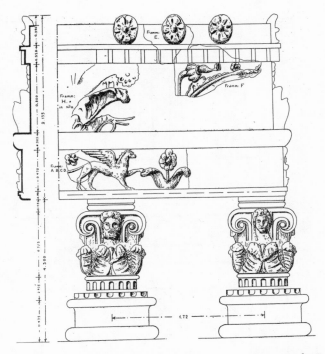

154 Sovana, Tomba Ildebranda, drawing of columnar order. Bianchi-Bandinelli *Sovana* fig. 30

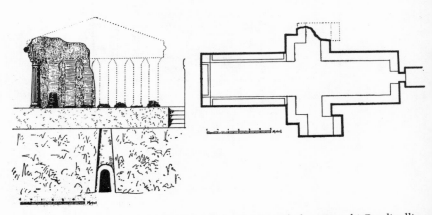

155 Sovana, Grotta Pola, drawing of the façade and plan. Bianchi-Bandinelli *Sovana* fig. 19

156 Norchia, Doric tombs, general view. *Öjh* 40–42 (1953–5) 109 fig 28

157 Norchia, Tomba Lattanzi, restored façade. Rosi (1924–5) fig. 34

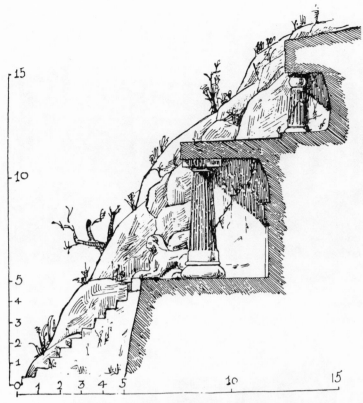

158 Norchia, Tomba Lattanzi, cross-section. Rosi (1925–5) fig. 35

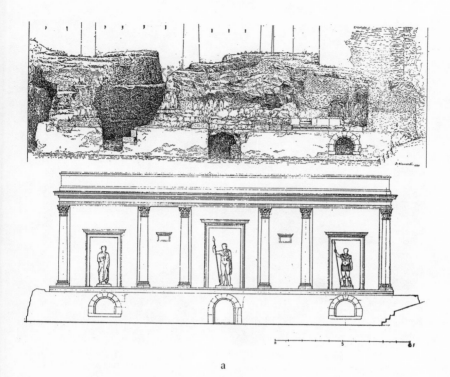

a

159 Rome, tomb of the Scipios: a / traditional reconstruction; b / reconstruction according to Lauter-Bufe. a / *DialAr* 6 (1972) 64 fig. D; b/ RM 89 (1982) 36 fig. 1

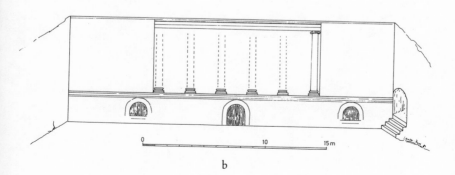

b

160 Rome, tomb of the Sempronii. E. Nash, *Pictorial Dictionary of Ancient Rome* 2 (London 1961) 357 fig. 1133

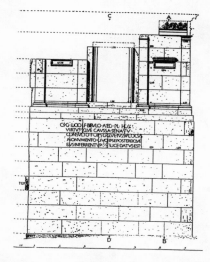

161 Rome, tomb of C.P. Bibulus, view today (above), drawing of façade (below). E. Nash, *Pictorial Dictionary of Ancient Rome* 2 (London 1961) 320 fig. 1086

162 Akragas (Agrigento), Tomb of Theron, general view

163 Rome, tomb of M.V. Eurysaces, general view

164 Zawani (region of Cyrene), built rectangular cella-like 'temple tombs.' *BSR* 23 (1955) pl. 5c

165 Gasr Gebra (region of Cyrene), monumental elevated sarcophagi. Stucchi fig. 74

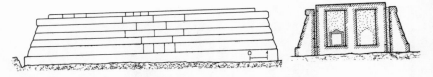

166 Cyrene, mastaba tomb, E19. Stucchi fig. 164

167 Cyrene, courtyard tomb, N₅₅. Stucchi fig. 134

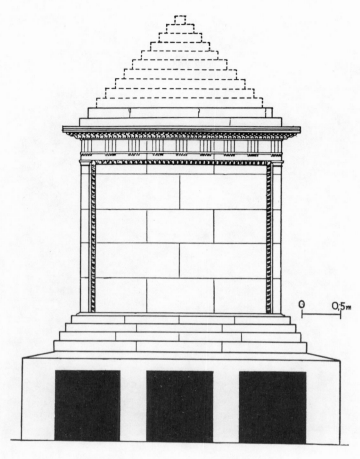

168 Cyrene, tomb N$_{180}$. Stucchi fig. 80

169 Ptolemais, tower tomb, ruins today. Stucchi fig. 200

170 Ptolemais, tower tomb, proposed reconstruction. Stucchi fig. 201

171 Alexandria, Alabaster Tomb, interior (above) and general view of the exterior (below). Adriani *Repertorio* series C (1963) pl. 63

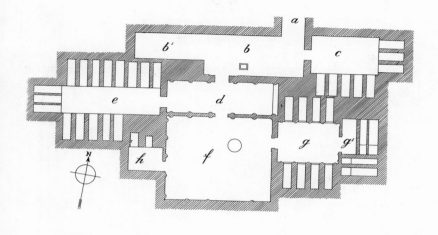

a

172 Alexandria, Shatbi necropolis: a / plan; b / Doric half-columns.
a–b / Adriani *Repertorio* series C (1963) pl. 45 fig. 171 c and d

b

173 Alexandria, Shatbi necropolis, engaged Ionic columns from room g. Adriani *Repertorio* series C (1963) pl. 44 fig. 168

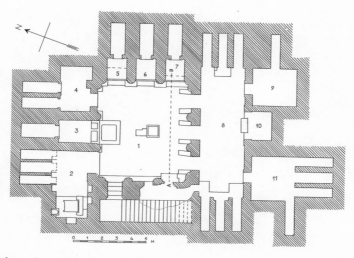

174 Alexandria, Mustafa Pasha Tomb 1, plan. Adriani *Repertorio* series C (1963) pl. 48 fig. 181

175 Alexandria, Mustafa Pasha Tomb 1, general view

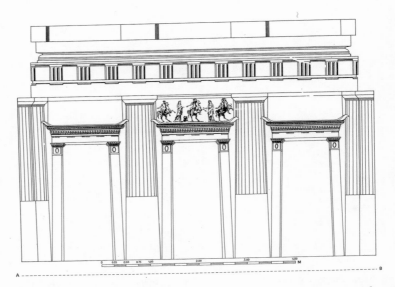

176 Alexandria, Mustafa Pasha Tomb 1, south façade with paintings. Adriani
Repertorio series C (1963) pl. 51 fig. 186

177 Alexandria, Mustafa Pasha Tomb 1, Corinthian pilaster capital

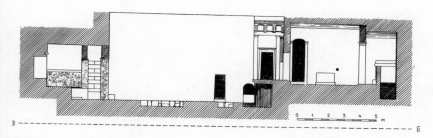

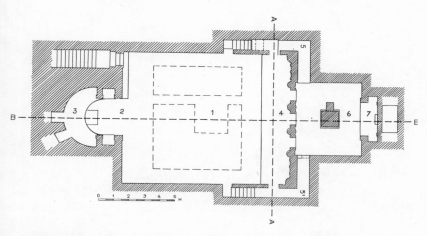

178 Alexandria, Mustafa Pasha Tomb III, cross-section and plan. Adriani
Repertorio series C (1963) pl. 54 figs 191 and 192

a

179 Alexandria, Mustafa Pasha Tomb III: a / restored view of 'stage' side;
b / view today of 'stage' side. a / Adriani *Repertorio* series C (1963) pl. 55
fig. 196

b

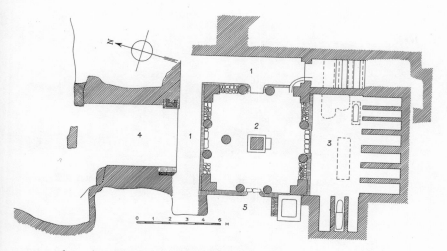

180 Alexandria, Mustafa Pasha Tomb IV, plan. Adriani *Repertorio* series C
(1963) pl. 58 fig. 204

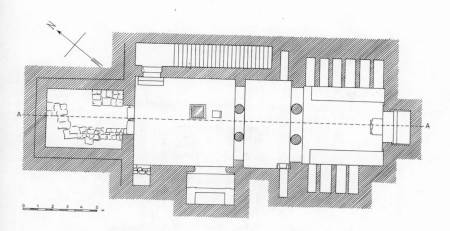

181 Alexandria, Mustafa Pasha Tomb II, plan. Adriani *Repertorio* series C (1963)
pl. 52 figs 187–189

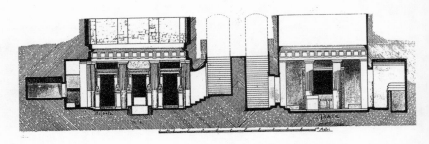

182 Alexandria, Mustafa Pasha Tombs I and II, cross-section. Adriani *Repertorio* series C (1963) pl. 51 fig. 185

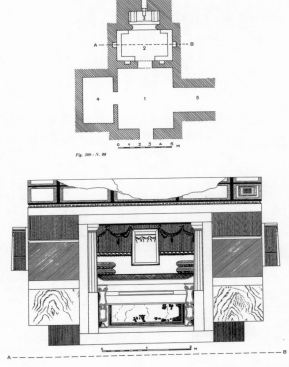

183 Alexandria, tomb at Sidi Gaber, plan and cross-section. Adriani *Repertorio* series C (1963) pl. 60

184 Taposiris Magna (Egypt), general view of lighthouse tomb. A. Adriani,
Lezioni sull'arte Alessandrine (Naples 1972) fig. 18

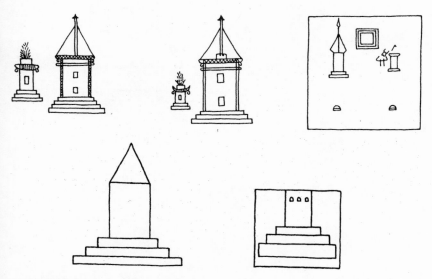

185 Djebel Mlessa (Tunisia), drawings of various funerary monuments. *Die
Numider* exhibition catalogue (Bonn 1979) fig. 68

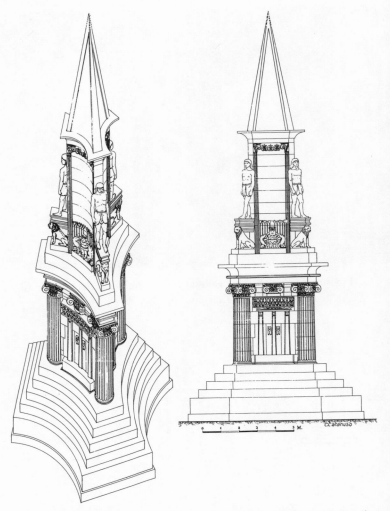

186 Sabratha (Libya), Mausoleum 'B,' restored view. RM 83 (1976) 83 fig. 76

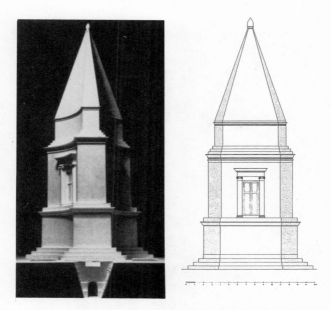

187 Siga (Algeria), tomb of a Massylian king, reconstruction. *Die Numider* exhibition catalogue (Bonn 1979) fig. 71.

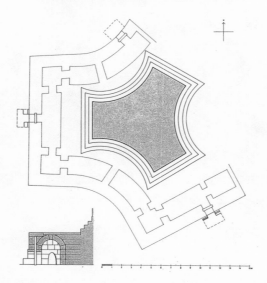

188 Siga (Algeria), tomb of a Massylian king, plan. *Die Numider* exhibition catalogue (Bonn 1979) fig. 73

189 Dugga (Tunisia), Tomb of Ateban. *Jdl* 89 (1974) 237 fig. 26

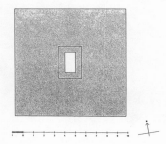

190 El Khroub (Algeria), monumental tomb known as Es Souma, restored view and plan. *Die Numider* exhibition catalogue (Bonn 1979) figs 87 and 88

191 El Khroub (Algeria), monumental tomb known as Es Souma, ruins today.
Die Numider exhibition catalogue (Bonn 1979) fig. 85

a

192 Algeria, Medracen tumulus: a / general view; b / views of engaged Doric
order. a / Lawrence *GrArch* pl. 92; b / A. Lézine, *Architecture Punique*
(Publications de l'université de Tunis 1958) pl. 15

b

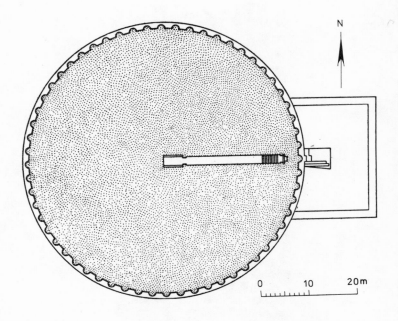

193 Algeria, Medracen tumulus, plan. *Die Numider* exhibition catalogue
(Bonn 1979) fig. 56

a

194 Algeria, Kbour-er-Roumia tumulus: a / general views; b / model. a–b / *Die Numider* exhibition catalogue (Bonn 1979) figs 60–61 and pl. 15

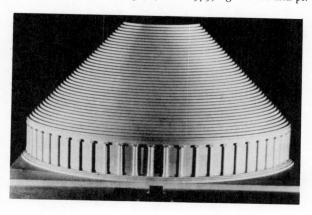

b

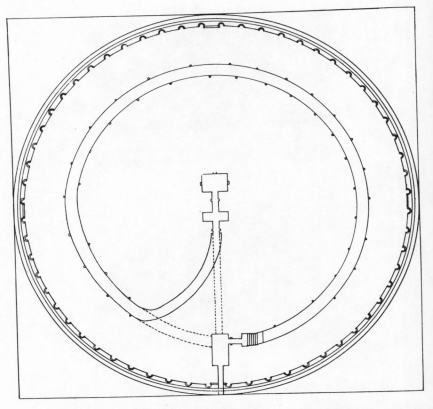

195 Algeria, Kbour-er-Roumia tumulus, plan. *Die Numider* exhibition catalogue
(Bonn 1979) fig. 59

196 St Rémy (France), Monument of the Julii

197 Rome, Mausoleum of Augustus in centre, reconstructed view

198 Ugarit (Ras-Shamra), chamber tomb, interior. *Syria* 54 (1977) figs 1–2

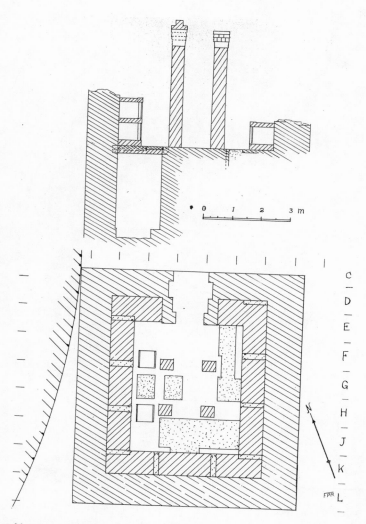

199 Yemen, monumental tomb. R. LeBaron, *Archaeological Discoveries in South Arabia* (Baltimore 1958) fig. 182

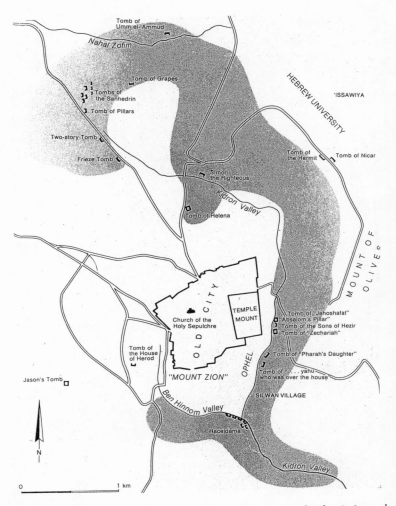

200 Jerusalem, locations of the major necropoleis. M. Harel, *This Is Jerusalem* (Jerusalem 1977) 127

201 Jerusalem, Tomb of Jason, general view. *IEJ* 17 (1967) pl. 13

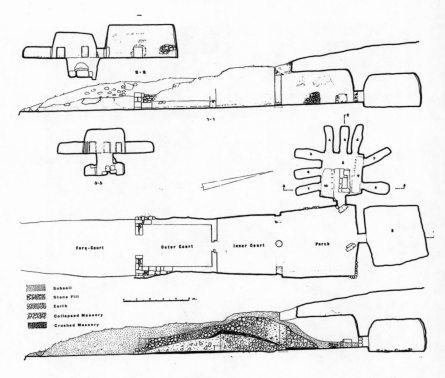

202 Jerusalem, Tomb of Jason, plan and cross-sections. *IEJ* 17 (1967) fig. 3

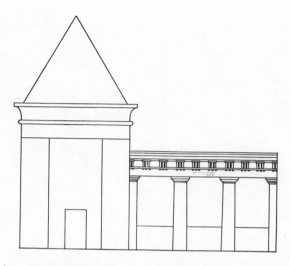

203 Jerusalem, Tomb of Bene Hezir. N. Avigad, *Ancient Monuments in the
Kidron Valley* (Jerusalem 1954) 95 fig. 57/1

204 Jerusalem, the Tomb of Zachariah, general view

a

205 Jerusalem: the Tomb of Absalom on the left, the tombs of Bene Hezir and Zachariah on the right; b / the Tomb of Absalom with the Tomb of Jehoshaphat in the back

b

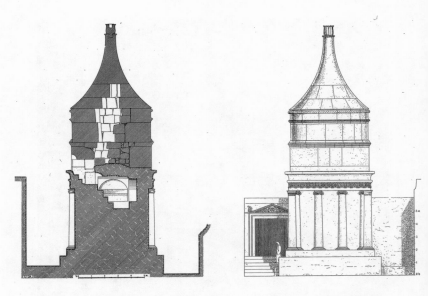

206 Jerusalem, the Tomb of Absalom, cross-section and restored view.
N. Avigad, *Ancient Monuments in the Kidron Valley* (Jerusalem 1954) 54 figs
40–41

207 Ephesos, Rundbau on the slope of Panayirdağ. *Öjh* suppl. 17 (Baden bei Wien 1974) 39

208 Wadi el-Ammed (region of Jerusalem), the Cave of Umm el-Ammed. *PEQ* 83 (1947) 116 fig. 2

209 Wadi el-Ammed (region of Jerusalem), the Cave of Umm el-Ammed, Ionic
capital and entablature. *PEQ* 83 (1947) 117 fig. 3

210 Araq el-Emir (Jordan), Hyrkanos complex. *CRAI* (1977) 70

211 Deir ed-Derb tomb (region of Samaria), façade. *RBibl* 19 (1910) pl. 2

212 Deir ed-Derb tomb (region of Samaria), entablature. *RBibl* 19 (1910) fig. 12

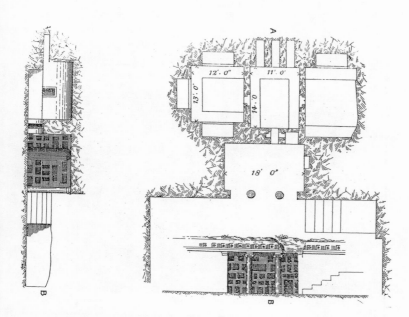

213 Deir ed-Derb tomb (region of Samaria), plan and cross section. C.R. Conder and H.H. Kitchener, *The Survey of Western Palestine* 2 (London 1882) 314

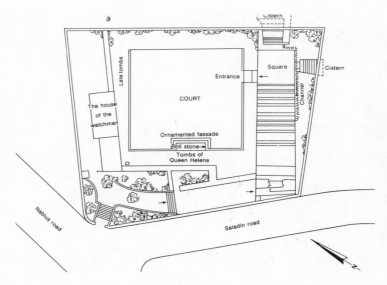

214 Jerusalem, Tomb of Queen Helena, plan. M. Harel, *This Is Jerusalem*
(Jerusalem 1977) 132

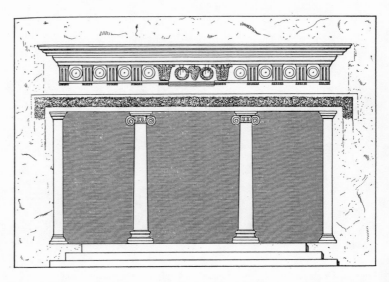

215 Jerusalem, Tomb of Queen Helena, main façade. *IEJ* 1 (1950–1) 104 fig. 8

216 Jerusalem, Two-storied or Pilaster Tomb. *Deutscher Palästina Verein,
Zeitschrift* 59–60 (1936–7) III pl. 4

217 Jerusalem, the tomb of Herod and his family, entrance way with rolling
stone. *The Encyclopedia of Archaeological Excavations in the Holy Land*
2 (London 1976) 636

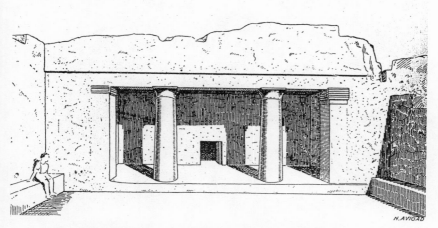

218 Jerusalem, Two-columned tomb (Tomb no. 8). *PEQ* 82 (1947) 120 fig. 5

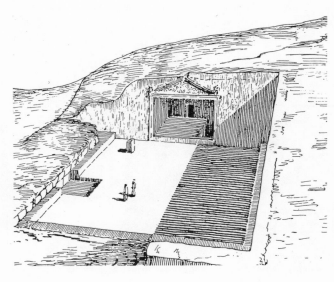

a

219 Jerusalem, Sanhedrin Tombs: a / courtyard; b / façade of main entrance. a–
b / *PEQ* 86–87 (1952-3) 24 fig. 1

b

220 Jerusalem, tomb with Doric entablature. *IEJ* 1 (1950–1) 100 fig. 5

a

221 Suweida (Syria), Tomb of Hamrath: a / in the early twentieth century; b / reconstructed drawings. a–b, B and D 3 (1909) 97 figs 992 and 99, figs 994–995

b

222 Hermel (Lebanon), monumental tomb. D. Krencker and
W. Zschietzschmann, *Römische Tempel in Syrien* I (Berlin 1938) 162
fig. 223

223 Kalat Fakra (Lebanon), commemorative/funerary monument. D. Krencker and W. Zschietzschmann, *Römische Tempel in Syrien* I (Berlin 1938) 54 fig. 79

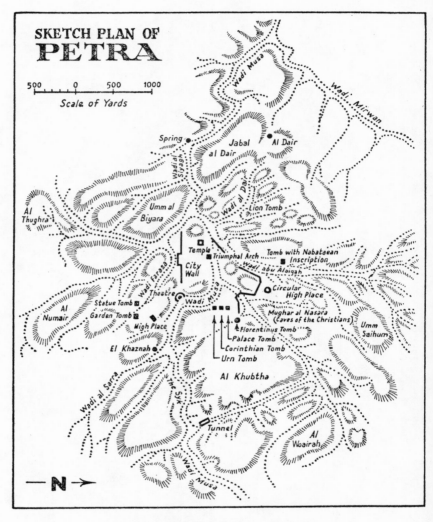

224 Plan of the Nabataean capital at Petra

a

225 Petra, the Khazneh (Treasury): a / view today; b / drawing of the façade.
b / PEF 1 (1911) pl. 16

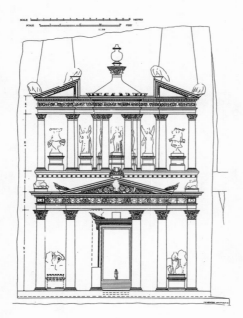

b

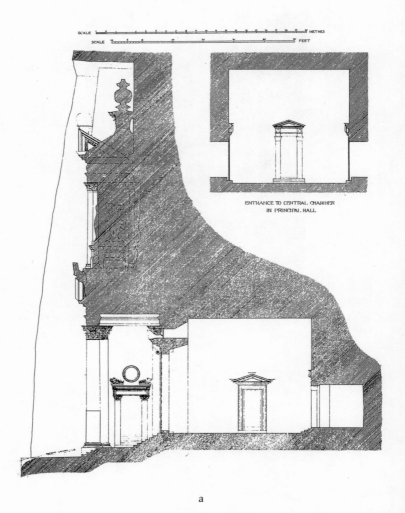

a

226 Petra, the Khazneh (Treasury): a / cross-section looking south to the main chamber; b / vestibule. a / *PEF* 1 (1911) pl. 17

b

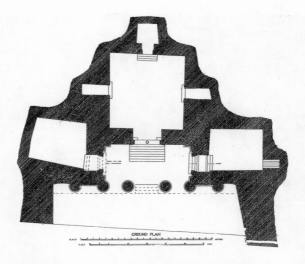

227 Petra, the Khazneh (Treasury): ground plan (*PEF* 1 [1911] pl. 15).

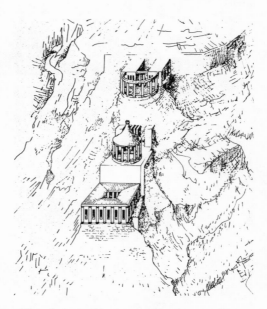

228 Masada, north palace complex, restored view. *AntW* 8 (1911/1) 34 fig. 5

229 Petra, Corinthian Tomb. B and D 2, 168 fig. 192

a

230 Petra, the Deir (the Convent): a / view today; b / drawing of the façade.
B and D 2, 187 fig. 220

b

231 Petra, Nabataean (column/pilaster) capital

a

232 Petra, Palace Tomb: a / view today; b / drawing of the façade. b, B and D
2, 169 fig. 193

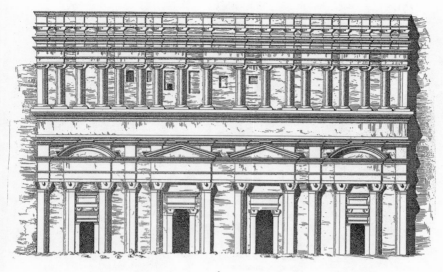

b

a

233 Petra, Tomb of Sextius Florentinus: a / view today; b / drawing of the
façade. b / B and D 2, 170 fig. 194

b

a

234 Petra, Urn Tomb: a / view today; b / drawing of the façade. b / B and D 2, 168 fig. 191

b

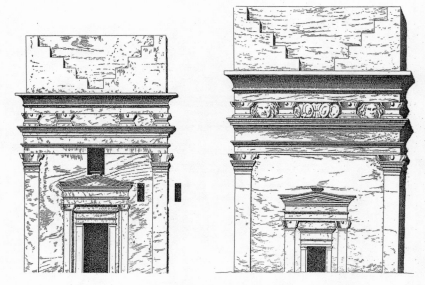

235 Petra, 'Hegra' tombs. B and D 2, 149 fig. 138

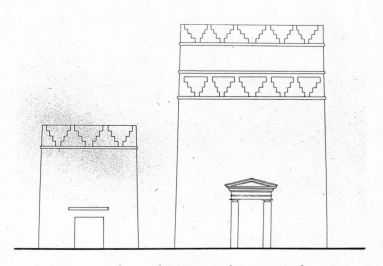

236 Petra, pylon tombs. Negev *Nabataeans* 580 fig. 41

237 Ai-Khanoum (Afghanistan), temple tomb, foundation courses.
CRAI (April–June 1975) 184 fig. 12

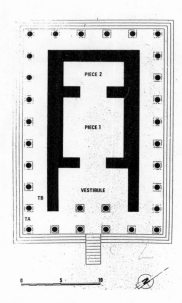

238 Ai-Khanoum (Afghanistan), temple tomb, plan. *CRAI* (April–June 1975) 184
fig. 12

239 Tholos tomb at Krannon

240 The Palatitza Tomb. L. Heuzey and H. Daumet, *Mission archéologique de Macédoine* (Paris 1876) pl. 15

241 Terracotta model of a stage from Naples. A. Levi, *Catalogo delle Terracotte de Napoli* (Naples 1934) fig. 134

242 Reconstructed view of the stage at Segesta. M. Bieber, *The History of the Greek and Roman Theater* (Princeton 1971) fig. 600

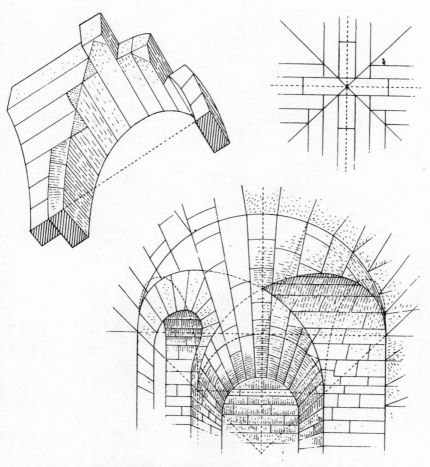

243 Pergamon, intersecting vaults. Lawrence *GrArch* fig. 15

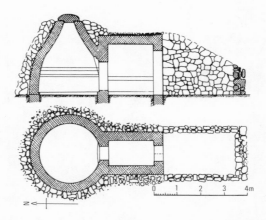

244 Kazanlik, chamber tomb, plan and cross-section. Hoddinott (1975) fig. 15

245 Cortona, Secondo Melone del Sodo tomb. Demus-Quatember *EtGrab* pl. 9

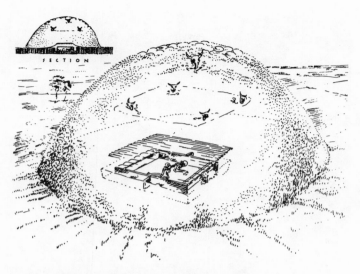

246 South Russian timber grave. *Expedition* 3 (1961/3) fig. 2

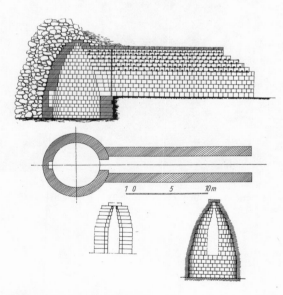

247 Region of Pantikapaion, Gold Kourgan, plan and cross-sections. Gajdukevic pl. 67

248 Region of Pantikapaion, Czarskij or Royal Kourgan, dromos. Gajdukevic
pl. 68b

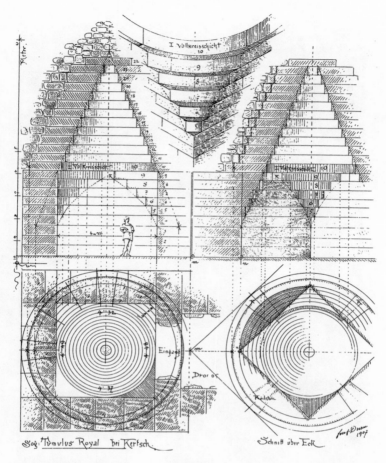

249 Region of Pantikapaion, Czarskij or Royal Kourgan, plans and cross-sections. *Öjh* 10 (1907) 235 fig. 72

250 S. Cerbone (region of Populonia), corbelled corner. Demus-Quatember
EtGrab pl. 2

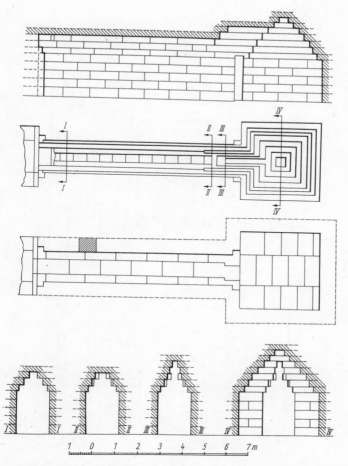

251 Melek-Česme, kourgan, drawings of the tomb chamber and dromos. *Öjh* 10
(1907) 240 fig. 77

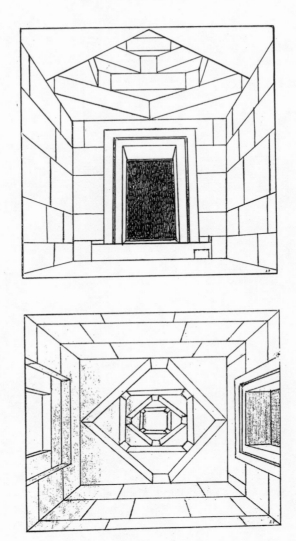

252 Chamber tomb at Kurt-Kale (region of Mezek). *Belleten* 38 (1974) figs 22
and 23

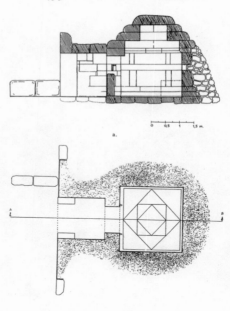

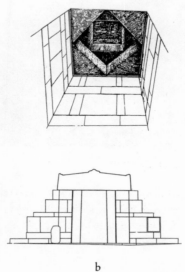

a

253 Filibe tomb (region of Plovdiv): a / plan and cross-section; b / roof and entrance way. *Belleten* 38 (1974) fig. 8

b

a

254 Mylasa, Gümüş Teken: a / view today; b / view of roof construction;
c / drawings from 1909. b–c / J. Durm, *Die Baukunst der Griechen*
(Leipzig 1910) figs 320–321

b

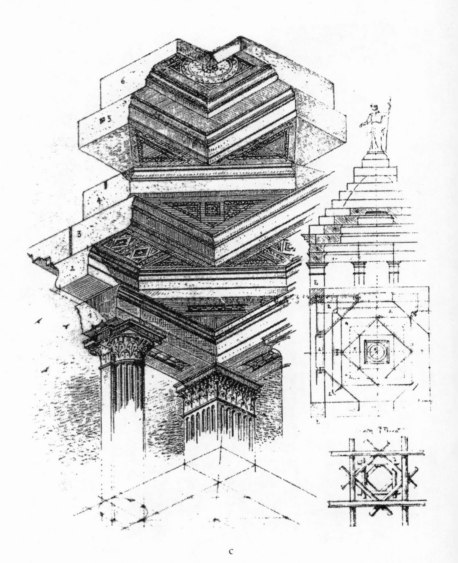

c

a.

255 Gemlik on the Propontis, chamber tomb. *Belleten* 38 (1974) fig. 8

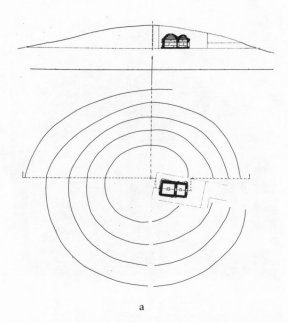

a

256 Gordion, chamber tomb: a / plan and cross-section of tumulus; b / plan and cross-section of tomb chamber. *AJA* 65 (1956) pl. 81

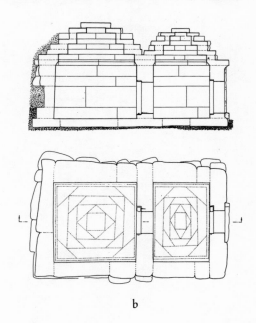

b

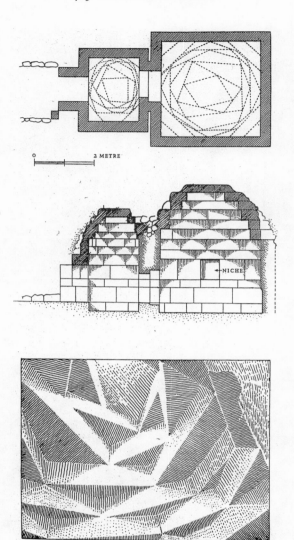

257 Tomb C at Karalar, plan, cross-section, roof construction. Lawrence *GrArch*
fig. 127

a

258 Tumulus at Hierapolis: a / exterior of now-exposed tomb chamber; b / view
of roof construction. b / *MonAnt* 48 (1972) pl. 23b

b

259 Cortona, Tomb of Pitagoras. *Palladio* 7–8 (1957–8) 50 fig. 2

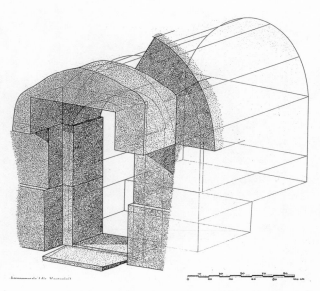

260 Faggeto (region of Perugia), chamber tomb. Chiari (1975) 36

261 Samos, sarcophagus with applied architectural decoration. Kleeman (1962)
pl. 12

262 Izmir, Klazomene sarcophagus, lid. Akurgal *Anatolien* fig. 258

263 Syracuse museum, top of a funerary cippus. Akurgal *Anatolien* fig. 260

264 Gela, sarcophagus with interior columns. Orsi fig. 285

265 Aegina, sarcophagus with interior columns. *AA* 46 (1931) 275

266 Sarcophagus of Scipio Barbatus. R. Lanciani, *The Ruins and Excavations of Ancient Rome* (New York 1897) fig. 124

267 Payava sarcophagus. Dinsmoor fig. 23

268 Daskylion, Stele no. 1, detail. *RA* (1969/1) 18 fig. 2

269 Mourning Women sarcophagus. Kurtz-Boardman fig. 73

270 Alexander Sarcophagus. Kurtz-Boardman fig. 74

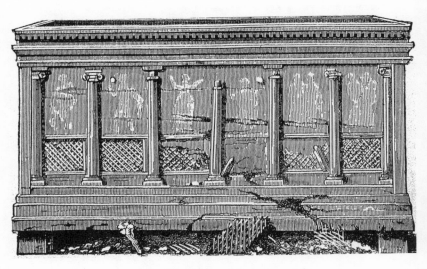

271 Niobid Sarcophagus. Minns (1913) fig. 241

272 South Russian sarcophagus with inlaid panels. Gajdukevic fig. 89

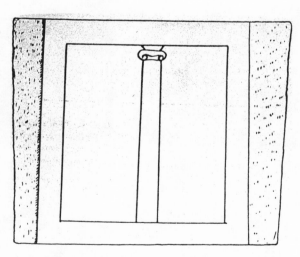

273 Volos, cist grave, panel. *Thessalika* 4 (1962) 31 fig. 3

274 Rome (Museo Barracco), cinerary urn. *Medio Repubblicana* (1973) pl. 82

275 Iznik, sarcophagus. *IstMitt* 7 (1957) pl. 5[1]

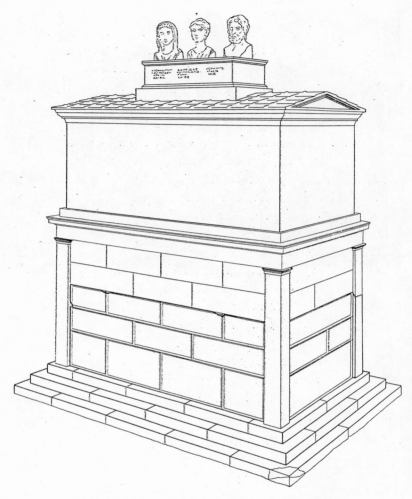

276 Paros, elevated sarcophagus. *Jdl* 50 (1935) 67 fig. 12

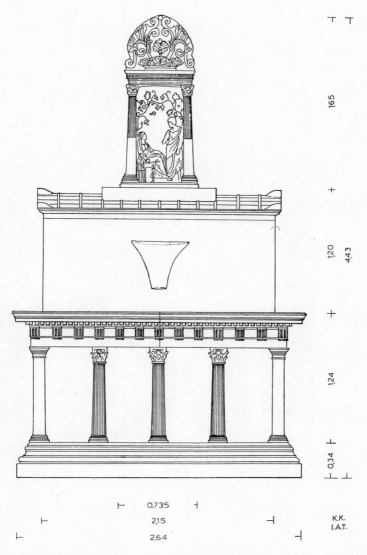

277 Delos (island of Rheneia), elevated sarcophagus. *Delos* 30 (1974) 227 fig. 9

278 Athens, Thrasyllos Monument. *AA* 53 (1938) 66 fig. 39

Photo credits: figures 4a–b / Nylander *Ionians*; 4c–d, 5a–b / *Iran* 2 (1964); 6, 51 / Hanfmann *Letters*; 13 / Wolf, *Die Kunst Aegyptens*; 14 / Moortgart, *Die Kunst des alten Mesopotamien*; 15 / Lauer, *Le Mystère des Pyramides*; 16, 203, 206 / Avigad, *Ancient Monuments in the Kidron Valley*; 40, 41, 124 / Haspels; 9 / Odenthal, *Syrien*; 17 / Gruben, *Die Tempel der Griechen*; 18, 31, 38 / *RA* (1976/1); 139a–b / *RA* (1968/1); 143 / *RA* (1968–9); 168 / *RA* (1969/1); 19 / Kirschen, *Weltwunder der Baukunst in Babylonien und Jonien*; 20 / Şahin; 21 Hanfmann, 'Greece and Lydia'; 23 / Messerschmitt, 'Das Grabmal des Porsenna'; 26, 153 / Boethius and Ward-Perkins; 27 / *BdA* 65 (1984); 28 / *BCH* 99 (1975; 91 / *BCH* 63–65 (1939–41); 29, 69, 74 / *AA* 85 (1970); 45, 128 / *AA* 82 (1967); 32 / ActaA 47 (1976); 33, 34, 35 / *FX* II; 61, 62, 63, 65, 66 / *FX* III; 36 / *Syria* 42 (1965); 198 *Syria* 54 (1977); 37 / *BASOR* 245 (Winter 1982); 46 / Von Gall, *Felsgräber*; 47, 54, 141, 165, 167, 168, 169, 170 / Stucchi; 50 / Hronda, *Handbuch*; 55 / *Lindos* 3 (1960); 56 / *Kerameikos* 12 (1980); 57 / *OpArch* 2 (1941); 58, 85 / Fletcher, *A History of Architecture*; 70, 72 / Borchhardt *Bauskulptur*; 75 / Antalya Museum (author's photo); 76, 78, 79a–c / *IstMitt* 26 (1976); 275 / *IstMitt* 7 (1957); 77 / Waywell, *The Free-standing Sculptures*; 81, 82 / *Labraunda* I² (1963); 88 / British Museum (author's photo); 90 / *Antike Welt* (1975/3); 93 / Winter, private collection; 94 / Gentili, 'Resti di un grande mausoleo'; 95 / Fraser and Bean; 98, 99, 101 / *Forschungen in Ephesos* 6 (1979); 107 / Kähler, *Lindos*; 113 / Benndorf-Niemann, *Gjölbaschi* (1889); 116, 138, 269, 270 / Kurtz-Boardman; 119 / Roos *Caunus*; 125, 126, 210 / *CRAI* (1977); 237, 238 / *CRAI* (1975); 129 / Orlandos, *H Arkadike Alipheira*; 131 / *AAA* 6 (1973); 132 / *Makedonika* 15 (1975); 135 / Andronikos (1980); 136, 137 / *AJA* 88 (1984); 140 / *Archaeology* 37 (1924); 144, 145, 146, 147, 148, 149 / Ceka; 151, 152 / Bertocchi, *La pittura*; 156 / *Öjh* 40–42 (1953–5); 207 / *Öjh* suppl 17 (1974); 159a / *DialAr* 6 (1972); 159b / *RM* 89 (1982); 160, 161 / Nash, *Pictorial Dictionary*; 164 / *BSR* 23 (1955); 171, 172a–b, 173, 174, 176, 178, 179a, 180, 181, 182, 183 / Adriani *Repertorio* (1963); 184 / Adriani, *Lezioni*; 185, 187, 188, 190, 193, 194a–b, 195 / *Die Numider* (1979); 186 / *RM* 83 (1976); 189 / *Jdl* 89 (1973); 192a, 243, 257 / Lawrence *GrArch*; 192b / Lézine, *Architecture Punique*; 197 / model, *BSR* 10 (1927) pl 11; 199 / LeBaron, *Archaeological Discoveries*; 200, 214 / Harel, *This Is Jerusalem*; 201, 101 / *IEJ* 17 (1967); 215, 220 *IEJ* 1 (1950–1); 208, 209 / *PEQ* 83 (1947); 218 *PEQ* 82 (1947); 219a–b / *PEQ* 86–87 (1952–3); 217 / *Encyclopedia of Archaeological Excavations*; 236 / Negev *Nabataeans*; 242 / Bieber, *History of the … Theater*; 244 / Hoddinott; 245, 250 / Demus-Quatember *EtGrab*; 246 / *Expedition* 3 (1961/3); 247, 248, 272 / Gajdukevic; 252, 253a–b, 255 / *Belleten* 38 (1974); 256 / *AJA* 65 (1956); 273 / *Thessalika* 4 (1962); 274 / *Medio Repubblicana* (1973); 277 / *Delos* 30 (1974)

INDEX OF NAMES AND PLACES

Phoenix Supplementary Volumes Series